INTERNATIONAL

MARKETING

6TH EDITION

SUBHASH C. JAIN
THE UNIVERSITY OF CONNECTICUT

SOUTH-WESTERN
™
THOMSON LEARNING

Australia · Canada · Mexico · Singapore · Spain · United Kingdom · United States

International Marketing, Sixth Edition by Subhash C. Jain

Publisher: Dave Shaut
Senior Acquisitions Editor: Pamela Person
Developmental Editor: Mardell Toomey
Senior Marketing Manager: Joseph A. Sabatino
Media Technology Editor: Kevin von Gillern
Media Production Editor: Robin Browning
Production Editor: Amy S. Gabriel
Manufacturing Coordinator: Sandee Milewski
Cover Design: Tinbox Studio Inc., Cincinnati
Cover Image: © PhotoDisc, Inc.
Production House: Pre-Press Company, Inc.
Compositor: Pre-Press Company, Inc.
Printer: West Group

Printed in the United States of America
1 2 3 4 5 03 02 01 00

For more information contact South-Western, 5101 Madison Road, Cincinnati, Ohio, 45227 or find us on the Internet at http://www.swcollege.com

For permission to use material from this text or product, contact us by
• **telephone: 1-800-730-2214**
• **fax: 1-800-730-2215**
• **web: http://www.thomsonrights.com**

Library of Congress Cataloging-in-Publication Data
Jain, Subhash C., 1942–
    International marketing/Subhash C. Jain.—6th ed.
        p. cm.
    ISBN 0-324-06370-9 (alk. paper)—ISBN 0-324-10086-8 (international : alk. paper)—ISBN 0-324-06373-3 (cases v. : alk. paper)—ISBN 0-324-10085-X (cases v. : international : alk. paper)
    1. Export marketing—Management. 2. Export marketing—Management—Case studies.   I. Title.

HF1416 .J35 2001
658.8'48—dc21

00-059565

To Aarti and Amit

CONTENTS

After decades of resting comfortably at the top of the global marketplace, U.S. business has awakened to fierce competition. As more countries become industrial powerhouses and their companies seek larger marketplaces, international marketing as a discipline of study achieves greater significance than ever before. Japan, the most potent of all the new competitors, is pushing into such American strongholds as biotechnology and supercomputers. Western Europe is coming up fast in aeronautics and office equipment. The newly industrialized countries of China, Taiwan, South Korea, Malaysia, Singapore, India, and Brazil are establishing themselves as low-cost producers of everything from steel to television sets. In addition, the U.S. faces new competition in Canada and Mexico as a result of the North American Free Trade Agreement (NAFTA).

At the same time that American supremacy is being challenged, the powerful force of technology is driving the world toward a converging commonality: the emergence of global markets. Millions worldwide want all the things they have heard about, seen, or experienced via new communication technologies. To capitalize on this trend, American companies must learn to operate and compete globally, as if the world were one large market, ignoring superficial regional and national differences.

Global markets offer unlimited opportunities. Corporations geared to this new reality can benefit from enormous economies of scale in production, distribution, marketing, and management. By translating these benefits into reduced world prices, they can dislodge competitors who still operate with the past perspectives. Today, only companies capable of becoming global will achieve long-term success.

As more business battles cross borders, managers must broaden their view of markets and competition. Doing business in a global economy requires a lot of new learning—including how to find the right country in which to build a plant, how to coordinate production schedules across borders, and how to absorb research wherever it occurs. They must learn what sort of people to hire, how to inculcate a global mentality in the ranks, and when to sell standardized products instead of customizing them for local markets.

Only a few managers are capable of handling the competitive rigors of the new global marketplace. Even in companies long accustomed to doing business overseas, managers find it difficult to look beyond their own domain to consider the capabilities and needs of the company as a whole to serve the global marketplace. Business schools across the country face a similar problem in producing global strategists. They must focus on the development of business education programs that explain how to function effectively in today's global business environment.

During the 1980s the American Assembly of Collegiate Schools of Business (AACSB) had offered seminars emphasizing how business schools might internationalize their curriculum. The U.S. Department of Education continues to provide funding for enhancing international business education. These kinds of support have helped many schools in adding international components to their existing courses, and in developing new international courses. Despite these efforts, in most business education programs insufficient attention is paid to the international dimension of business. A study commissioned by AACSB on the future of management education and development summarizes the problem:

> International business is an area of the curriculum where we found a considerable amount of, at worst, lip service, and, at best, serious concern on the part of deans and faculty (but, we should

point out, *not* on the part of most corporate-sector respondents). It was one of the four specific areas most often mentioned in both interviews and on the surveys as needing more emphasis in the curriculum. The problem, as most acknowledged, is how to implement this—whether to do it through adding more specific courses on international business, international finance, international marketing and the like, or by putting more emphasis on international issues in courses already in the curriculum. This whole area has been the object of much discussion within the business school community, and we probably cannot shed much additional light on the curriculum aspects of the matter except to say this: Although there seems to be an increasing awareness among business school deans and faculty that more ought to be done to emphasize this area, this awareness of sensitivity so far does not appear to us to have been translated into a great deal of action. More is being done now than ten years ago, and this seems clearly demonstrable by an examination of curricula and in interviews with knowledgeable observers, but much more needs to be done.*

As business schools globalize their curriculum, various specific international courses are being added to give students a worldwide perspective. Because of the deep impact of local customs and business practices on marketing, marketing requires separate exposure in the international context, more so than any other area of business. Many business schools now have international marketing courses at the undergraduate level, and some even at the graduate level. Many more schools are rapidly adding such courses.

Skills Developed Through Study of the Sixth Edition

The sixth edition of *International Marketing* has been developed based on the methodological and theoretical underpinnings developed in various social sciences. This book also integrates major marketing paradigms and frameworks. In each case, the cultural, legal, political, and institutional implications of international operations are properly analyzed. The text aims to make the reader an "informed observer" of the global marketplace. In addition to covering all important frameworks of marketing, concepts from other disciplines (for example, finance and accounting) are touched upon, since those must be grasped to fully understand the perspective of conducting marketing across national boundaries.

This book is designed to enable readers to develop skills for making marketing decisions in the global context, addressing issues like the following:

- *Finding new markets to replace saturated markets.*
- *Customizing products for the demands of new markets.*
- *Determining which products are in demand by world customers.*
- *Determining how to best reach the customers.*
- *Applying the pricing strategies that are most appropriate.*
- *Determining which distribution channels are adequate to serve the world customers.*
- *Overcoming barriers that hinder implementation of marketing programs.*

Retained Features of the Sixth Edition

Throughout the book, a *variety of examples* are used to illustrate the points made. Important frameworks and theories are explained with quotes from original sources. *Learning objectives* are found at the beginning of each chapter. Included at the end of the text material are *30 cases* that describe unique decision-making situations in international market-

---

*Lyman W. Porter and Lawrence E. McKibbin, *Management Education and Development: Drift or Thrust into the 21st Century?* (New York: McGraw-Hill Book Company, 1988), p. 8.

ing. The cases provide adequate information for an intelligent and lively discussion, and should enhance the learning experience.

New to the Sixth Edition!

The sixth edition has been prepared based on the feedback received from over 100 colleagues who responded to a survey on the content and structure of an international marketing course. Based on their thoughtful feedback substantial changes were made resulting in the following distinguishing features in this edition:

- *New topics* covering recent developments like the European Monetary Union, Asian Currency Crisis, economic liberalization among developing countries and other issues.

- *Expanded discussion* of entry strategies, international trade, U.S. exports, and marketing planning and strategy.

- An in-depth look at the role played by *international agreements and institutions in formulating global marketing strategies*, including discussion of the progress of the European Monetary Union.

- "*International Marketing Highlights*" boxed articles describing interesting ideas, stories, and factual information relevant to marketing decisions; Over 100 of these boxes appear throughout the book, describing real-world episodes in international marketing decision-making.

- *New and interesting examples*, both from industrialized and developing nations, to illustrate underlying concepts.

- Discussion of the latest round of *GATT talks* (i.e., the Uruguay Round) and *NAFTA*.

- *Substantial revision of chapters* on economic analysis of global trade and business, multinational sales management and foreign sales promotion, export management, and marketing planning and strategy for international business.

- *Updated* statistics, illustrations, and references to provide the most current perspectives on the subject.

- *Complete revision of the 15 cases* included from the previous edition, plus *15 new cases*. These 30 short and long cases involve such well-known companies as Colgate-Palmolive, Gillette, FedEx and UPS, Kodak and Fuji, Carvel, Seagram, IKEA, Nestlé, PSA Peugeot Citroën, ABB, Hewlett-Packard, Outback Steak House.

- Positioned at the end of each chapter, *creative questions* challenge the students on their understanding of concepts and theories presented in the text and lead to lively discussion.

- *Improved organization* of the material within the chapters for a better flow of ideas.

- Condensed coverage to keep the text to a *semester length* without compromising thoroughness.

Supplements

Instructor's Resource Kit on CD-ROM (ISBN 0-324-06371-7) includes a variety of pedagogical aids such as answers to end-of-chapter discussion questions, true-false and multiple-choice examination questions, transparency masters, solutions to cases, suggestions for further reading, and a listing of additional cases. Also included is a *PowerPoint Slide Presentation* with over 100 slides to complement classroom lectures. All cases in the back of the book are available as a stand-alone book, *International Marketing Cases* (ISBN 0-324-06373-3) suitable for students with relatively little background in marketing.

Personal Attention by the Author

I am personally available by phone, e-mail, or during conferences to discuss and advise colleagues on the structure of their international marketing course.

Acknowledgements

A project like this cannot be completed without help and advice from different sources. I have been fortunate in having the counsel of many scholars who contributed comments and criticism on previous editions. Although it is impossible to recognize them all here, I would like to thank Sanjeev Agarwal, Iowa State University; Lyn S. Amine, St. Louis University; S. Tamer Cavusgil, Michigan State University; Claude Cellich, International University, Geneva; John R. Darling, Louisiana State University at Shreveport; Roberto Friedman, University of Georgia; Pervez N. Ghauri, University of Groningen; Thomas Greer, University of Maryland; Andrew C. Gross, Cleveland State University; Erdener Kaynak, Pennsylvania State University at Harrisburg; Vinay Kotharis, Stephen Austine State University; James C. Nicholas, Connecticut World Trade Association; C.P. Rao, Kuwait University; Ravi Parameswaran, Oakland University; Ronald J. Patten, DePaul University; John K. Ryans, Jr., Kent State University; Saeed Samiee, University of Tulsa; Albert Stähli, Graduate School of Business Administration, Zurich; and Attila Yaprak, Wayne State University.

I also want to thank the following individuals for their permission to include cases written by them: Jacqueline M. Abbey, Georgetown University; Mohammed Ali Alireza, University of San Diego; Bill Bambara, University of Connecticut; Michel Berthelier, Group EM Lyon; Grady D. Bruce, California State University; Fullerton; Roland Calori, Group EM Lyon; Ellen Cook, University of San Diego; Golpira Eshghi, Bentley College; Madelyn Gangelbad, University of Missouri at Kansas City; Philip Hunsaker, University of San Diego; Michael Lubatkin, University of Connecticut; Gordon H. G. McDougall, Wilfrid Laurier University; Franklyn A. Manu, Morgan State University; Karen L. Newman, Georgetown University; Stanley D. Nollen, Georgetown University; Francese Parés, IESE, University of Navarra; George M. Puia, Indiana State University, Krishnan Ramaya, University of Southern Indiana; Lluis G. Renart, IESE, University of Navarra; José Antonio Segarra, IESE, University of Navarra; Ven Sriram, Morgan State University; Marilyn L. Taylor, University of Missouri at Kansas City; Suzanne Uhlem, Lund University; Philippe Very, Group EM Lyon; and Andrew Zacharakis, Babson College. I am indebted to Stephen M. Walsh, State University of New York College at Oneonta, for contributing 125 objective questions to the *Instructor's Manual.*

A special mention of appreciation must go to my doctoral student, Piotr Chelminski, for library search, for coordinating various revision chores and for computer work. I would like to thank the staff of our International Programs Office, especially Associate Director, Kelly Dunn, Graduate Assistant, Jay Chhatbar, and staff assistants, Amy Hotsko, Will Flynn, and Nicole Terry, for their administrative support. I am thankful to many writers and publishers for granting me the permission to include excerpts from their works.

The talented staff at South-Western deserves praise for their role in shaping the sixth edition. Team director, Dave Shaut, offered excellent advice and direction on the structure of the sixth edition and the acquisitions editor, Pamela Person, took the initiative in getting the project off the ground. Development editor, Mardell Toomey, did a superb job of coordination, and production editor, Amy S. Gabriel, did an excellent job of managing the manuscript to completion. I am indebted to them for their help. Thanks are due to Jennifer Carley of Pre-Press Company, Inc., for the fine job of production.

I want to thank my dean, Thomas G. Gutteridge, for his encouragement and support in this endeavor, and my former professor, Stuart U. Rich of the University of Oregon, who continues to influence my thinking through his writings.

Finally, my thanks go to my wife and our children, Aarti and Amit, who have put up with me through the hectic times of book revision. They provided the time, support, and inspiration so necessary to complete a project of this nature.

Subhash C. Jain

PART I

Framework of International Marketing

CHAPTER 1

Aspects of International Advertising

CHAPTER FOCUS

After studying this chapter, you should be able to

◼ Explain the growing importance of international business.

◼ Describe how international marketing differs from domestic marketing.

◼ Discuss the significant role of multinational corporations in the expansion of business on an international scale.

◼ Compare alternative entry routes into foreign markets.

One of the most significant economic developments since World War II is the increasing internationalization of business. Although business has been conducted across national boundaries for centuries, during the last four decades business dealings have escalated on a global scale. Leading corporations around the world have increasingly turned their attention to international business in order to maintain a competitive edge in today's dynamic economic scene.

This increase of international business affects the world economic order profoundly. It is a change with an impact comparable to that of the Industrial Revolution. In fact, today's global activity has been described as the second Industrial Revolution. Today's market provides not only a multiplicity of goods, but goods from many places. It is not surprising if your shirt comes from China, your jeans from Mexico, and your shoes from Italy. You may drive a Japanese car equipped with tires manufactured in France, nuts and bolts manufactured in India, and paint from a U.S. manufacturer (see International Marketing Highlight 1.1).

Consider McDonald's emerging MacWorld. Big Macs are on sale in 100 countries. By 2005, more than half of all the firm's restaurants are expected to be abroad. Business outside the United States is lucrative. In 1995 the 38 percent of McDonald's restaurants outside the United States accounted for 47 percent of its $29.9 billion in worldwide sales and 54 percent of its $2.6 billion operating profit. In 1995 the average sales at each of the company's restaurants abroad rose from $2.25 million to $2.42 million. Yet in America aaverage sales fell from $1.58 million to $1.54 million. Operating profit margins show a similar trend.[1]

International Marketing Highlight 1.1

Do You Know Where Your Ford Was Made?

The 1992 Ford cars get controllers for their antilock brakes from Germany, engine computers from Spain, shock absorbers from Japan, and key axle parts from England. Windshields, instrument panels, seats, and fuel tanks are made in Mexico.

Source: Fortune, June 17, 1992, p. 53.

Worldwide consumers, particularly those in the developed countries, truly live in a global village. Young Europeans, Americans, and Japanese alike sport Benetton sweaters made in Italy, covet Japanese compact disc players, and haunt similar hangouts.

And America is irrevocably enmeshed in this global business (see International Marketing Highlight 1.2). We export some 20 percent of our industrial production, and we sell two out of five acres of our farm produce abroad.

In 1999 U.S. exports of goods and services supported a total of 14.4 million U.S. jobs. From 1993 to 1999, exports accounted for approximately 80 percent of U.S. real economic growth. The U.S. Department of Commerce estimates that over 38,000 U.S. manufacturing companies export, slightly more than one-third of all U.S. firms.[2] Almost one-third of U.S. corporate profit derives from international trade and foreign investment. The share of trade in the gross national product has more than doubled in the past decade. Considering our potential exposure to import penetration, more than three-fourths of U.S. goods are now effectively in international competition, and more than half the supplies of 24 important raw materials, ranging from petroleum to cobalt, come from foreign sources.

International Marketing Highlight 1.2

Globalization of Dollar Demand

There are now $422 billion of U.S. currency in circulation worldwide. More than two-thirds of this currency circulates abroad. So it is no wonder that when the United States rolled out redesigned, hard-to-counterfeit bills in 1996, the Treasury planned on spending $31 million over five years on brochures in 23 languages to convince people around the world to accept the new bills. The dollar has clout even in Iran, Iraq, and Cuba. It can pay your way even in remote villages.

Source: USA Today, March 15, 1996, p. 1.

Global marketing for U.S. companies makes sense when we realize that about 95 percent of the world's population and two-thirds of its total purchasing power are currently located outside this country. Even for relatively small companies, the global business activity has become irresistible. The U.S. Department of Commerce reports that 60 percent of American firms exporting today have fewer than 100 employees.[3]

A Conference Board study showed that a commitment to the international marketplace is important to sustained growth and superior profitability. Sales for firms with no foreign activities grow at half the average, whereas those for firms with international activities grow faster in every industry and in most size categories. Profitability as well rises for firms with a broad global scope. Companies with foreign plants in all three major global regions (North America, Europe, and the Pacific Rim) significantly outperform companies with more restricted international activities, both in return on assets and return on equity.[4]

Briefly, a worldview based on outmoded concepts of nationality and traditional antagonisms among nations and ethnic groups is not useful in today's global business environment. In fact, the first conceptual leap toward a pragmatic and productive businessperson's worldview would be to dismiss such a view outright and instead consider the inhabitants of different countries as a single race of consumers with shared needs and aspirations. Attaining this concept is critical, because recognition of new opportunities requires an awareness of new realities.

Doing business is a creative enterprise. Doing business outside one's own country is a much more demanding, complicated enterprise. Consider advertising. In the United States television advertising of consumer products is taken for granted. However, in many countries, such as the Netherlands, commercials are not permitted on television. In other countries television advertising is permitted only on a limited scale. In Switzerland, commercials are broadcast between 6:30 AM and 8:00 AM on weekdays. As another example of cultural differences, consider alcohol use in Japan, where drinking is widely considered part of the work ethic. Many businessmen openly talk about getting drunk. Whiskey is advertised abundantly on television. Beer is sold from vending machines on the street. All this would be unthinkable in the United States.

Similarly, the retailing industry structure varies dramatically across nations. In the United Kingdom, France, and Germany, an everincreasing percentage of total retail sales is made through large national retailing chains. In Italy, China, and Brazil, the retail industry is made up essentially of independent "mom and pop" stores. Still other countries have strong cooperative retailing or buying groups.

Just from this limited consideration of marketing perspectives, it is clear that international business necessitates an awareness of the clash of cultural standards among countries. These differences require analytical abilities and business acumen of the international marketers.

Overview of the Book

In this chapter we will examine what international marketing is, how it differs from domestic marketing, and why international marketing must be studied as a separate subject. Chapter 2 analyzes the rationale behind worldwide economic activity.

Chapters 3 and 4 provide the perspectives of the international marketplace. Chapters 5 through 7 in Part Three review the international institutions and agreements that continually create the conditions of the worldwide economic scene in which international marketing is conducted. Part Four, Chapters 8 through 11, explores the economic, cultural, political, and legal environments that affect business decisions. Chapters 12 through 16 are devoted to marketing decisions about products and their price, distribution, and promotion. Chapter 17 examines exporting.

The two final chapters deal with marketing planning and control. Chapter 18 discusses corporate organizational arrangements for international marketing management. Chapter 19 introduces the formulation of marketing strategy within the context of international business and provides a foundation for the advanced study of international marketing.

After establishing an understanding of the state of the art of international business, we will discuss the crucial role of the marketing function in conducting business across national boundaries, present a framework for making international marketing decisions, explore the reasons firms engage in foreign business, and describe the various modes of entry. Finally, we will consider the pivotal importance of the multinational corporation in global business.

International Business

The term *international business* refers to a wide range of activities involved in conducting business transactions across national boundaries. Taking a comprehensive approach to operations of both large and small firms engaged in business overseas, we will consider international marketing as it has developed and as it must, in the author's opinion, change in the future.

Perspectives of U.S. Business Overseas

Although many U.S. firms had long engaged in international business ventures before World War II, greater impetus to overseas expansion came after the war. While the U.S. government was helping to reconstruct war-torn economies through the Marshall Plan, by providing financial assistance to European countries, the postwar American economy emerged as the strongest in the world. America's economic assistance programs, in the absence of competition, stimulated extensive U.S. corporate interest overseas.

In recent years, overseas business has become a matter of necessity from the viewpoint of both U.S. corporations and the U.S. government. Many U.S. industries face increasing foreign competition. Take the shoe industry for example. The share of U.S. producers plunged from 50 percent in 1981 to 28 percent in 1985 to 19 percent in 1997.[5] The bicycle industry provides another example: the import share of bike sales jumped to 62 percent in 1997 from 40 percent in 1993.[6]

Faced with saturated markets at home, U.S. corporations have been forced to look for new markets. The flat growth rate of the beer industry in the early 1980s necessitated Anheuser-Busch's exploration of the huge overseas beer market. The company estimates that by the year 2003, foreign operations will account for almost one-fourth of its earnings.[7]

Other companies have similar stories. In brief, whereas in the 1950s and 1960s international business was a means of capitalizing on new opportunity, today's changing economic environment has made international business dealings vital for survival.

Essentially, there are two aspects of international business: direct investment and trade.

Direct Investment At the end of 1998, according to a U.S. Department of Commerce report, the U.S. direct investment abroad stood at $981 billion, up from $716 billion in 1996.[8] Over 65 percent of U.S. direct investments overseas have traditionally been in developed countries, with Europe accounting for over 47 percent of the total. Canada took a 10 percent share, while Japan, Australia, and New Zealand collectively represented 8 percent of the total. Latin America's share was 22 percent. The rest of Asia accounted for just under12 percent of the total.[9] It is interesting that, although, for cultural, political, and economic reasons, the most viable opportunities were found in Western Europe, Canada, and to a lesser extent Japan, many developing countries provided a better return on direct U.S. investments. According to a U.N. study, for example, in 1998 the profitability of U.S. investment in Africa was 25.5 percent, in Asia and the Pacific 20.4 percent, in Latin America 15.0 percent, in Canada 5.7 percent, and in Europe 9.4 percent.[10]

Direct foreign investment in the United States has come traditionally from Europe and Canada. Almost $652 billion of the $813 billion in book value of direct foreign investment in the United States at the end of 1998 came from the Netherlands, the United Kingdom, Canada, Germany, Japan, and Switzerland. By contrast, about $2.5 billion came from the 13 nations of the Organization of Petroleum Exporting Countries (OPEC).[11]

Foreign investments in the United States have taken the form of both wholly owned subsidiaries and stock ownership. For example, Bic Pen Corporation (a French company), BMW (a German company), Lever Brothers (an English company), Nestlé S.A. (a Swiss company), and Toyota Motor Corporation (a Japanese company) operate U.S. subsidiaries as part of their worldwide operations. Other foreign investments are in the form of stock ownership in U.S. corporations. For example, a Swiss-Swedish company, ASEA Brown Boveri (Holding) Ltd., bought a controlling interest in Combustion Engineering Inc. and Westinghouse Electric Corporation's smaller electrical-transmission equipment unit. Likewise, a Dutch company, Royal Ahold, maintains about two-third's ownership in Stop & Shop, a large food chain.

Trade (Goods and Services) The other aspect of international business is trade. In 1999 the United States exported an estimated $958.5 billion in goods and services. Imports during the same year amounted to $1,229.8 billion, resulting in a balance-of-trade deficit of $271.3 billion. The subject of trade will be explored in detail in Chapter 17, but it is important to note here that the U.S. share of the world exports in 1999 for manufactured goods—measured by value—comes to about 13 percent, slightly higher than it was in the mid1990s.[12]

The traditional view of foreign trade as an exchange of tangible goods is increasingly giving way to the realization that trade encompasses both goods and services. As the economies of more and more countries have become service-oriented, foreign sales of engineering, consulting, banking, transportation, motion pictures, insurance, tourism, franchising, construction, advertising, and computer services are gaining recognition as significant factors in the foreign trade position of many nations. The importance of such exported U.S. services is borne out by the fact that deficits in merchandise trade have been partially balanced by growing services exports. Services exports and their income from overseas U.S. affiliates reached an estimated $275.5 billion in 1999, compared with $225 billion in 1997. Services imports in 1999 were estimated at $199.7 billion, giving a favorable balance of $75.8 billion.[13]

Why Go International?

Traditionally, the major focus of U.S. business has been on its large and expanding domestic market. In recent years, however, new factors have made international business the more desirable alternative for growth. These factors are expected to persist and to have even greater impact in the future.

Whether or not a company conducts international business, its competitors are likely to hail from all over and challenge its position in its own home market. For example, foreign manufacturers, including many from the Third World, have created problems for such established U.S. firms as USX, LTV, and other stay at home steelmakers.

Market Saturation Markets for a variety of goods in the United States, as is true of other industrialized countries, are becoming saturated far faster than new markets are being found. Staple consumer goods such as cars, radios, and TVs already outnumber U.S. households, and other products are fast approaching the same level. The slowing growth of the U.S. population means that the number of households is likely to grow at less than 1.6 percent per year to the year 2005, and demand for consumer goods is unlikely to grow any faster. This point is illustrated by the baby food market, in which Gerber Products Company has 70 percent of the U.S. market yet nonetheless, has trouble growing—it loses 10,000 customers a day as tots start taking grownup's food. The U.S. birth rate is declining, making it harder to replace Gerber consumers. Moreover, infants are eating less baby food on average these days.[14]

Thus, companies in many industries must develop new markets to continue to operate successfully. International markets, especially those where market saturation is a distant threat, provide an attractive alternative. Consider the cigarette industry. Sales have stagnated in the United States, but Third World countries offer rich markets. In Indonesia, per capita cigarette consumption quadrupled in the last 10 years. Kenya's consumption has been rising 10 percent annually. And Third World markets are unburdened by many of the restraints imposed in the United States and other industrialized nations. Firms generally can advertise freely on radio and television, and packages need not carry health warnings.

To transform global challenges into new opportunities, smart companies seek markets across national borders (see International Marketing Highlight 1.3). For example, Disney's theme park in France, following its entry in Japan, shows how important it is for a company to expand overseas in the wake of market saturation at home. Some United States hospitals, facing tighter health care budgets and dwindling occupancy rates, have started seeking foreign patients.[15]

International Marketing Highlight 1.3

Coors Brews Big Plans for Korea

Coors is going where the growth is. With Korean beer sales expanding 15 percent a year, compared with a puny 2 percent in the United States, Coors Brewing Co. has formed a joint venture with Jinro, Korea's largest producer of alcoholic beverages, to build a 1.0 million-barrel Coors brewery in Seoul. Coors expects to capture 20 percent of the Korean market before long.

This is Coors's first plant outside the United States, part of an international expansion program for America's third-largest brewer, which wants to be in 25 markets outside the United States by 2003. Coors beer is now available for sale in nine foreign countries.

Source: Company records of Coors Brewing Co.

U.S. Trade Deficit American industry grew up in a climate of private enterprise—nationwide markets without trade barriers to hamper the full development of economic efficiency. Most decisions could be made without considering how they would affect world market position. But such is no longer the case. U.S. business faces a declining share of world-manufactured exports and a continuing trade deficit. Just as an individual family should not, and cannot in the long run, live beyond its means, neither should a nation.

Therefore, the staggering U.S. trade deficit has to be balanced—That means the United States must make a strong attempt to increase exports.

Foreign Competition In many industries U.S. firms face fierce and intense competition from foreign manufacturers. For example, foreign competitors are invading what was once Xerox Corporation's undisputed turf by offering low-priced, high-quality copying machines. Xerox no longer can take industry leadership for granted. In a crowded field, with some 14 competitors from Japan alone, the battle resembles the one being fought by U.S. automakers against foreign importers.

Another example of intense foreign competition is the $82 billion textile industry. Garment imports increased threefold between 1985 and 1995, to $32 billion a year. Some 300 textile mills have been closed since 1980, and over 200,000 jobs have vanished. Industry experts think that textile apparel imports will continue to grow 15 percent annually. At this pace, imports will have 85 percent of the U.S. market by the year 2003.[16]

For still anohter example, we can return to the auto industry, where Japan is once again offering U.S. markets a new level of competition. In 1999, the Toyota Camry and the Honda Accord emerged as the two best-selling cars in America. (Germany's Volkswagen Passat was the third best-selling car.) Japanese invasion of the U.S. auto market shows how foreign competition can harm the local industry (see International Marketing Highlight 1.4).

The truth of the matter is that the United States' ability to compete in the world market has eroded significantly during the past 25 years. Most of this decline has occurred in such traditional industries as steel, automobiles, consumer electronics, apparel, and machine tools. Recently, even high-tech industries have become susceptible. Competition has forced some companies to shift their consumer electronics manufacturing to the Far East, which explains why the high-tech industry is losing its edge.[17] Even this measure did not succeed for General Electric, which in 1986 sold 80 percent of its consumer electronics business (including the RCA brand acquired in late 1985) to Thomson, France's state-owned leading electronics manufacturer. The last American-owned television maker, Zenith, has lost money on operations since the mid 1980s, and finally sold out to Lucky Goldstar of Korea. Thus in the color television business the United States completely gave up, yielding the market to Japanese, European, and Korean companies.[18]

------------------------------ **International Marketing Highlight 1.4** ------------------------------

How Japanese Automakers Invaded the U.S. Market

During the late 1960s Japanese car manufacturers wanting to enter the U.S. market looked for a niche and found one at the low end of the market: students and other consumers who wanted no-frills transportation. The small-and-cheap car market, as it so happened, was a niche that did not interest the Detroit auto companies. (Even relatively small American-made cars, such as Ford's Falcon and Fairlane, were essentially family cars.) The only formidable presence in this market was Volkswagen. Even so, VW could not fill the wide-open, small-car market fast enough. The Japanese companies responded by following a time-tested military strategy: taking uncontested ground first.

Toyota and Honda first began to introduce their cars into the United States around 1967. U.S. automakers paid little attention to the newcomers; they derided the Japanese cars as cheap models suitable only for a market that did not interest them in the first place. Essentially, the American automakers' attitude was to let Volkswagen fight it out with Datsun and Honda. Meanwhile the Japanese focused on providing low-cost products, built up a following (and, more important still, a low-cost, high-quality manufacturing base), then gradually introduced larger, better, higher-priced models.

Now Toyota, Nissan, Honda, Mitsubishi, and other major Japanese manufacturers have established themselves as a permanent, formidable presence in the U.S. automobile market. These companies have moved beyond their initial niche to satisfy America's demands for a wide variety of high-quality cars. The Detroit automakers have had an increasingly difficult time competing effectively against them.

The declining international position of the United States in the high-tech area is a matter of serious concern. More troubling is the fact that many of these high-tech products derive from technology developed in the United States. Phonographs, color televisions, audiotape recorders, and videotape recorders were all invented here, yet U.S. companies have practically no business left in these products (see International Marketing Highlight 1.5).

One way for U.S. companies to meet the challenge from foreign companies is to enter the home markets of their foreign competitors. Just as Japanese cars gained favor with American consumers in the early 1980s, there may be Japanese car buyers interested in U.S. cars now and in the future—but not if these cars have their steering wheels on the wrong side.

■■■■■■■■■■■■■■■■ **International Marketing Highlight 1.5** ■■■■■■■■■■■■

There Goes Another One

In recent years U.S. companies have conceded one homegrown industry after another to more aggressive and competitive foreign rivals. First came cameras, then televisions, tape recorders, stereo equipment, and semiconductors. Recently, Cincinnati Milacron, the last independent U.S. producer of heavy industrial robots, agreed to sell the business to a subsidiary of Switzerland's Asea Brown Boveri.

Milacron retreated from the $4 billion market after 13 years because its share of the business had dwindled from a commanding 75 percent to just 10 percent, and its losses from robotics had been mounting since the mid 1980s.

Source: Business Week, September 24, 1990, p. 71.

Emergence of New Markets The world is changing fast, resulting in the emergence of new markets. In the 1990s new business opportunities developed from the European Community, enhanced by the reunification of Germany, and the thriving economies in the Pacific Rim countries. In the next century, China, Latin America, and the emerging market-based economies in Eastern Europe promise new opportunities. Elsewhere in developing countries, momentum toward *privatization* (the transfer of business ownership from government to private citizens or institutions) and liberal policies are promising signs as well see International Marketing Highlight 1.6).

For U.S. marketers, despite the recent currency crisis, the Pacific countries hold great promise. A market of more than 2 billion potential consumers is emerging. In the last 25 years, as the Pacific region began its time-bending leap into the twentieth century, millions of Asians began an equally rapid transition from rural to urban, from agrarian to industrial, from feudal to contemporary society. With more of the Pacific region's rural population traveling to the cities to shop every day, the demand for goods and services—from the most basic household commodities to sophisticated technical devices—is soaring. The growing importance of Asia for the United States is supported by the fact that the share of America's exports that goes to Europe has fallen from 31 percent to 20 percent over the past 20 years, while the share going to Asia has risen from 20 percent to 30 percent.[19] Asia is the fastest growing market for most of the West's top brands. Those in the luxury-goods and fashion businesses reckon that roughly a third of their sales are now to Asia (including Japan), and by 2005 this region will make up half of the world's luxury-goods market.[20]

International Marketing Highlight 1.6

Gerber Locates a Niche in India

Gerber Products Company has undertaken extensive market research in India. Despite India's predominantly poor population, the country has a prosperous middle class and a small but wealthy upper class that Gerber considers a promising market.

Until recently, most Indians have been unlikely to show any interest in Western-style baby foods. Lately, though, the convenience of such products, plus their status appeal, has heightened consumers' curiosity and openness. Initial focus groups show that baby foods have high potential for success in certain areas of the subcontinent.

According to PepsiCo, early in the next century China is expected to be the second-largest market after the United States. The Chinese soft-drink market accounted for just 700 million cases last year, or about 13 servings a person, compared with about 8 billion cases, or nearly 800 servings a person, in the United States, showing the huge potential for growth. As another example, each year the average Chinese household shoots a little less than half a roll of film. If only it could be persuaded to snap a full roll, that would be the equivalent of adding an entire American market to the world film business. If Eastman Kodak could coax the Chinese not just to take those extra shots but to take them using Kodak film, the company would double its global sales. [21]

The emerging markets in developing countries can help many U.S. corporations counter the results of demographic changes in the Western nations. In most advanced nations of the world, birth rates are declining, whereas population in the developing countries is growing. Consider the automobile industry. The people-per-car ratio is 725 in India, 680 in China 431 in the Philippines, 270 in Thailand, 114 in Brazil, 89.5 in Mexico, 47 in South Korea, and 36 in Poland. In the United States, Europe, and Japan, the respective figures are 1.7, 2.5, and 3, showing the tremendous potential in the developing countries.[22] Similarly, the number of people per television set is 1.2 in the United States compared with about 30 in developing countries, again showing significant market potential among the latter. Nike reckons that its domestic sales averaging $20 for each American may be nearing a ceiling. By contrast, the per capita Nike sales in Japan are $4, in Germany $3, and in China and India just over two cents. It is the developing countries where Nike looks for growth[23] (see International Marketing Highlight 1.7).

International Marketing Highlight 1.7

DVDs Real Market: China

The most promising market for the digital videodisks is not in the United States, but in China. In 1997 more DVD players were shipped in China than the United States It makes sense: after all, China is a land of 1.2 billion people. There are nearly 300 million TV sets, but broadcast programming is limited, and the average household does not have a VCR. China is a video tabula rasa, ready and willing to go digital with the latest hardware.

Source: Fortune, December 29, 1997, P. 62.

Globalization of Markets Theodore Levitt asserts that technology has homogenized worldwide markets and that, companies should therefore produce globally standardized products and market them in the same way to people everywhere.[24] All the principal barriers to the growth of such markets have weakened in the last decade. Tariffs have been reduced by the world trade agreements. Transportation costs have declined with the use of containerization and larger-capacity ships. Many products have emerged that pack very high value into very small packages. Consumer needs in the industrialized nations have become increasingly similar, and purchasing power in many countries has increased sharply. In consequence, a multitude of distinct national markets is beginning to coalesce into a true world market for a number of products in different industries. This development can be a source of competitive advantage for companies that plan their strategies accordingly.

A few examples will suggest how extensive the global product phenomenon has already become. Kids everywhere play on Nintendo and listen to music on a Sony Walkman. The videocassette recorder (VCR) market took off simultaneously in Japan, Europe, and the United States, but the most extensive use of VCRs today is probably in places like Riyadh and Caracas. Shopping centers from Dusseldorf to Rio sell Gucci shoes, Yves St. Laurent suits, and Gloria Vanderbilt jeans. Siemens and International Telephone & Telegraph (ITT) telephones can be found almost everywhere in the world. Mercedes-Benz and the Toyota Corolla are as much objects of passion in Manila as in California.

Just about every gas turbine sold in the world has some General Electric technology or component in it, and what country doesn't need gas turbines? How many airlines around the world could survive without Boeing or Airbus equipment? Developing country markets for high-voltage transmission equipment and diesel-electric locomotives are bigger than those in the developed countries. Today's new industries—robotics, videodiscs, fiber optics, satellite networks, high-technology plastics, and artificial diamonds—seem to be global at birth.

Opportunities via Foreign Aid Programs Although in recent years U.S. foreign aid programs for developing countries have declined gradually, in the 1950s and 1960s they provided billions of dollars to developing countries to undertake programs of economic buildup. Most of these programs required that aid recipients spend U.S. money on goods and services from U.S. corporations, except in cases where the desired goods were available only from non-U.S. sources. In either circumstance, the aid money created new markets in developing countries. Even more recent aid programs, small as they were ($15.3 billion in 1999—$8.9 billion in economic support and $6.4 billion for military hardware), provided opportunities for some businesses to go abroad.

Other Reasons A variety of other reasons make conducting business across national boundaries profitable and attractive. One is the possibility of achieving economics of scale. In industries where economies of scale are feasible, a large market is essential, so if the home market is not large enough, entering foreign markets may be an attractive alternative. Polaroid Corporation, a dominant force in the U.S. photographic industry, claims to have achieved economies of scale by entering foreign markets.

Another reason for engaging in international business is that it provides a safety net during business downturns. Usually a recession starts in one country and takes several quarters to move into other countries. It is said that European economies are affected by a U.S. recessionary trend after about six months. Thus, firms that do business internationally can shift their emphasis from U.S. to foreign markets during the recession. For example, during the U.S. recession of 1991, multinational companies were able to shift their marketing focus to Europe and Asia, where an economic boom was in progress.[25]

In many industries, labor constitutes a major proportion of costs. Since labor cost in developing countries is much lower than in the United States, it is economically attractive for the companies to expand foreign operations. For example, electronics companies depend on hundreds, sometimes thousands, of young women to do the painstaking job of assembling tiny parts that are shipped to the United States for use in computers and other products. Labor sometimes represents as much as half of the cost of these parts, so the cheaper the labor, the higher the profit. Thus, a number of U.S. companies—Hewlett-Packard, Intel, National Semiconductor, and ITT, among a dozen others—have gone as far as Malaysia to save on labor cost.

Some nations offer tax incentives to attract foreign businesses to their countries. An important motive for extending such tax incentives is to increase scarce foreign exchange and create jobs at home. Typically, a company finding such tax concessions viable will establish a plant in the low-tax country and then sell the manufactured goods locally, as well as exporting from there to its primary markets.

Many companies find it more desirable to develop and/or test new products outside the United States This practice avoids exposure to competitors and, to some extent, keeps new development information secret until the product is ready for full introduction. Ford Motor Company, for example, did much of its world-car development in Germany.

Some international markets are less competitive than the U.S. market; several are still in an embryonic stage. Further, in some instances, governments will give companies a monopoly or quasi-monopoly position if they assemble and produce their products there. Many companies follow their customers at home abroad. Take the case of steelmakers. They are following their customers—automakers and manufacturers of appliances, heavy equipment, and machine tools—all over the world. For example, Whirlpool Corporation decided in the early 1990s to go global. It now manufactures in 13 countries, including China and India. Its steel suppliers are now catching up in these emerging markets.[26]

Finally, international presence provides expanded access to advances in technology, worldwide raw materials, and diverse international economic groups. For example, European auto manufacturers led the way in fuel injection technology. An active U.S. auto company presence in Europe provided earlier insights into this technology.

International Marketing and Its Growing Importance

Stage of International Involvement

The term *international marketing* refers to exchanges across national boundaries for the satisfaction of human needs and wants. The extent of a firm's involvement abroad is a function of its commitment to the pursuit of foreign markets. A firm's overseas involvement may fall into one of several categories:

1. *Domestic*: operating exclusively within a single country.
2. *Regional exporter*: operating within a geographically defined region that crosses national boundaries. Markets served are economically and culturally homogeneous. If activity occurs outside the home region, it is opportunistic.
3. *Exporter*: operating from a central office in the home region and exporting finished goods to a variety of countries. Some marketing, sales, and distribution is outside the home region.
4. *International*: operating regionally in a somewhat autonomous fashion, but with key decisions made and coordinated from the central office in the home region. Manufacturing and assembly, marketing, and sales are decentralized beyond the home region. Both finished goods and intermediate products are exported outside the home region.
5. *International to global*: operating with independent and mainly self-sufficient subsidiaries in a range of countries. While some key functions, such as research and de-

velopment (R&D), sourcing, and financing are decentralized, the home region is still the primary base for many functions.

6. *Global*: operating as a highly decentralized organization across a broad range of countries. No geographic area (including the home region) is assumed a priori to be the primary base for any functional area. Each function (including R&D, sourcing, manufacturing, marketing, and sales) is performed in the location(s) around the world most suitable for that function.

Typically, the journey begins at home. Companies operating exclusively within a single country reach the limits to growth in their home market and face the need to expand to achieve further growth. The time that it takes to reach this outer growth limit depends almost entirely on the size of the home market. North American companies will take longer to reach the outer limit than will companies in Singapore, South Korea, Taiwan, and Japan, whose home markets are substantially smaller and provide less room to grow. Once the domestic barrier is reached, companies evolve into an export modality, either on a limited, regional basis where markets are still economically and culturally homogeneous, or on a broader basis where finished goods are exported to a variety of countries. Regional exporters and export companies continue to run operations from a central office in the home market, though some marketing, sales, and distribution functions begin to crop up elsewhere.

As companies become more successful in their export operations, they reach that critical point where the need to achieve greater proximity to overseas markets becomes paramount. At this point, such companies begin to replicate their business systems in new markets by creating relatively autonomous regional operations. Manufacturing and assembly, marketing, and sales are decentralized, and both finished goods and intermediate products are exported outside the home region, but key decisions are made, or at least coordinated, by a head office in the home region. Companies that have reached this stage of evolution may be characterized as "international" companies. The replication of a company's business system in various locations around the world does not, however, represent a long-term formula for profitable growth, so ultimately international companies face the need to optimize their businesses globally by adopting a global model of operation. For global companies, no one geographic area is assumed to be the primary base for any function—R&D, sourcing, and manufacturing are situated in the most suitable locations worldwide.

Why Study International Marketing?

We have already examined the factors that make international business an important field of endeavor from the viewpoint of a businessperson. How does this importance extend to marketing? Marketing is more significant, both for doing business abroad and for analyzing the impact of international happenings on business at home, than other functions of a business—such as manufacturing, finance, and research and development—because marketing responds to the local culture and to the business's multiple interrelationships with the local environment. Growing internationalization of business brings about changes in the positioning of competitors and the appropriate competitive strategies. "You can't sell what people won't buy" is a truism. Consumers overseas have different needs and expectations than those in America.

The only way to guarantee long-term competitive success is to provide better value to customers. Consider the Japanese market. American companies and U.S. government agencies complained that restrictions, in the form of tariffs and visible (and invisible) nontariff barriers and constraints, excluded much U.S. business from Japanese markets. However, an unbiased analysis showed that American business had not made a great effort to enter the Japanese market. As has been remarked,

Americans still are going to have to practice the marketing methods they preach if they are going to exploit the opportunities that are opening up in Japanese markets. In short, U.S. businesses still must find out what the Japanese consumers want, tailor products to fit the Japanese market, and put these products into suitable distribution channels.[27]

A U.S. Chamber of Commerce report indicated that U.S. business had fallen short of success in Japan because it failed to keep track of changes in Japan's marketing environment. Certain U.S. consumer goods such as automobiles, watches, cigarette lighters, and whiskey had been regarded in Japan as status symbols and were consumed by a limited number of wealthy buyers. Distribution of such products had been organized emphasizing the exclusiveness of the products and brand prestige. This traditional mode of marketing luxury items was inadequate to substantially increase exports to Japan or to develop a mass market. In brief, if imports were to become a part of Japanese daily life, rather than just status symbols, U.S. manufacturers had to reexamine pricing policies and distribution channels and then develop products that better fit Japanese consumers' needs.[28]

In other words, U.S. companies frequently fumble overseas because they fail to respond to the peculiarities of the markets. Apple Computer, Inc., had the market to itself when it became the first company to sell a personal computer in Japan. But the company began to lose ground for failing to do the right things. Apple didn't provide Japanese manuals. The computers arrived with keyboards that didn't work, and the packaging was shoddy.[29] Similarly, American automakers would like the Japanese to buy their cars, but they do not manufacture cars with steering on the right side to accommodate Japanese driving.

Another mistake by U.S. corporations is to pursue the short-term strategy of selling luxury goods to the affluent classes in developing countries instead of securing mass markets that would provide long-term benefits. For example, malnutrition is a common problem in a number of developing countries. Therefore, vitamin pills are important. But U.S. firms sell the same vitamin at about the same price in poor countries as they do in the United States. Only the minority upper class in those countries can afford the pills.

Mass markets are ready for U.S. products, but American businesses have not responded to the opportunities with responsible marketing. To cash in effectively on the opportunities these markets represent, in developing countries and elsewhere, U.S. corporations must become more sophisticated marketers.

Domestic versus International Marketing

The basic nature of marketing does not change when it extends beyond national boundaries, but international marketing, unlike domestic marketing, requires operating simultaneously in more than one kind of environment. Operations in the different environments must be coordinated, and the experience gained in one country used for making decisions in another country. The demands are tough, and the stakes are high. International marketers not only must be sensitive to different marketing environments internationally, but also must be able to balance marketing moves worldwide to seek optimum results for the company.

The impact of environment on international marketing can be illustrated by the watch industry. New technology, falling trade barriers, and changing cost relationships have affected the competitive patterns of the industry worldwide. Only companies with global perspective are operating successfully. A few *world companies* sell *world product*s to increasingly brand-conscious consumers. This multinationalization of the watch industry has resulted in four producers—Switzerland, Japan, Hong Kong, and the United States—dominating the scene by emphasizing brand names. Their manufacturing operations are specialized by country according to costs of specific processes, components, and subassemblies.

To successfully compete globally, rather than simply operate domestically, companies should emphasize: (1) global *configuration* of marketing activities (i.e., where activities such as new product development, advertising, sales promotion, channel selection, marketing research, and other functions should be performed), (2) *global coordination* of marketing activities (i.e., how global marketing activities performed in different countries should be coordinated); and (3) *linkage* of marketing activities (i.e., how marketing activities should be linked with other activities of the firm).[30]

Many marketing activities, unlike those in other functional areas, must be dispersed in each host country to make an adequate response to the local environment. Not all marketing activities need to be performed on a dispersed basis, however. In many cases, competitive advantage is gained in the form of lower cost or enhanced differentiation if selected activities are performed centrally as a result of technological changes, buyer shifts, and evolution of marketing media. These activities include production of promotional materials, sales force and service support organization training, and advertising. Further, international marketing activities dispersed in different countries should be properly coordinated to gain competitive advantage. Such coordination can be achieved by (1) performing marketing activities using similar methods across countries (2) transferring marketing know-how and skills from country to country, (3) sequencing marketing programs across countries, and (4) integrating the efforts of various marketing groups in different countries.

Finally, a global view of international marketing permits marketing to be linked to upstream and support activities of the firm, As a result, marketing can unlock economies of scale and learning in production and R&D by (1) providing the information necessary to develop a physical product design that can be sold worldwide—a universal product; (2) creating demand for more universal products even if historical demand has been for more varied products in different countries; (3) identifying and penetrating segments in many countries that will buy universal products; and (4) providing services or local accessories that effectively tailor the standard universal product to local needs.

Framework of International Marketing

Marketing decisions relative to product, price, promotion, and distribution must be made whether business is conducted in the United States, France, Japan, or Mexico. But the environment within which these decisions are made is unique to each country. This differential of environment distinguishes international marketing from domestic marketing.

Typically, a firm should make domestic marketing decisions only after considering internal and external environments. *Internal environment* factors primarily refers to corporate objectives, corporate organization, and resource availability. *External environment* factors include competition, technological change, the economic climate, political influences, social and cultural changes, pertinent legal requirements, current ethical business standards, and changes among marketing channels.

A U.S. firm will face the same internal and external factors doing business in a foreign market as it faces domestically, but from an entirely different environmental perspective. Consider the following factors: Economic conditions vary from one country to another. The antitrust laws in the United States are much tougher than those in some countries, such as Japan. The United States has a two-party political system; many countries, such as Mexico, do not. Women have an important decision-making role as consumers in the United States and in other Western countries, but this is not the situation among the Islamic nations. As a matter of fact, business environments vary tremendously even among countries that are geographically in the same region or that have the same cultural heritage. For instance, it would be wrong to assume that the United States and England have common marketing environments. There may be some similarities, but overall the two are very different.

Exhibit 1.1 depicts the marketing decisions and environments of international marketing. The nature of decision making in international business is essentially the same as in domestic business. Consideration of environment, however, is more philosophically abstract. The internal and external environmental aspects listed previously combine to

EXHIBIT 1.1   Decisions and Environments of International Marketing

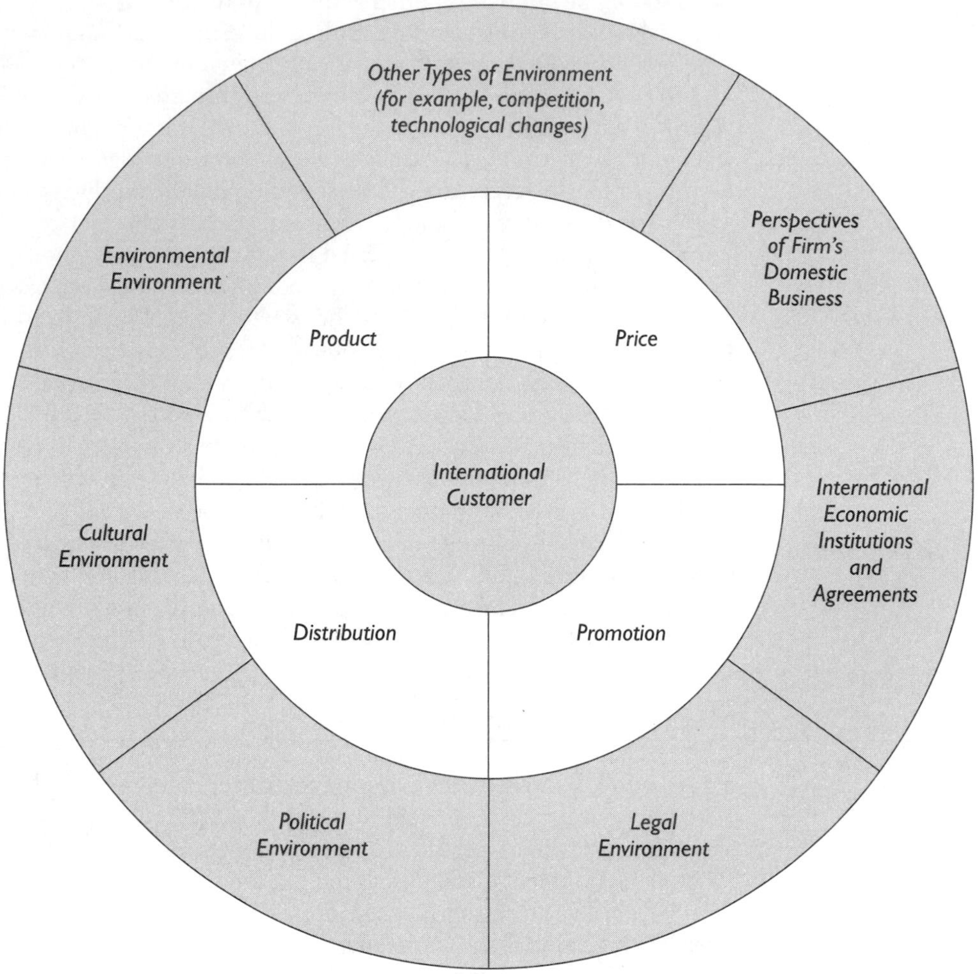

create a unique environmental reality for each individual country that the international marketer must perceive. The economic, cultural, political, and legal aspects of each environment must be understood by the international marketer, along with the effect of international economic institutions such as the International Monetary Fund (IMF) and agreements such as the World Trade Organization (WTO) Accord and the North American Free Trade Agreement (NAFTA).

Also, an international marketer must be sensitive to certain aspects of the domestic environment, such as competition and technological changes, included in Exhibit 1.1 under "Other Types of Environments". Marketing decisions to serve the international customer require consideration of the firm's domestic business as well—its objectives and strategies, commitments and resources, and organization structure.

Multinational Corporations

The *multinational corporation (MNC)* is the principal instrument in the expansion of business on an international scale. In barely four decades, it has become, by all accounts, the most formidable single factor in world trade and investment. The MNC plays a decisive role in the allocation and use of the world's resources by introducing new products and services, creating or stimulating demand for them, and developing new modes of manufacturing and distribution. Current rates of energy consumption, for example, would be unthinkable without the role of MNCs in the development and expansion of the automobile and electrical appliance industries. Indeed, MNCs largely set the patterns and pace of industrialization in today's capitalist economies.

Dimensions of MNCs

The MNC represents the highest level of overseas involvement and is characterized by a global strategy of investment, production, and distribution. According to a U.N. estimate, some 60,000 MNCs were in operation in 1997, controlling more than 500,000 foreign affiliates. Worldwide assets accumulated from past *foreign direct investment* (FDI) stood at $4.2 trillion at the end of 1998. The largest 100 MNCs controlled about 75 percent of the foreign assets of all MNCs and accounted for about 22 percent of their sales.

Most of these large companies were in a handful of industries: 40 percent of their foreign assets were in electronics, followed by petroleum and mining (24 percent), motor vehicles (19 percent), and chemicals and pharmaceuticals (15 percent). Together the largest 200 MNCs control about one third of the world's gross domestic product (GDP).

An important dimension of MNCs is the predominance of large firms. Typically, an MNC's annual sales run into hundreds of millions of dollars. In fact, more than 500 MNCs have annual sales of over $1 billion. The largest 100 MNCs have sales ranging between $10 billion and $178 billion.[31]

Many MNCs derive a substantial portion of their net income and sales from overseas operations. As shown in Exhibit 1.2, the non-U.S. earnings of many large companies exceed 50 percent of the total earnings.

The economic strength of these corporations as compared with other economic entities, including the economies of many nations, suggests an important source of global power. Exhibit 1.3 shows that many MNCs have a higher annual revenue than the gross national product (GNP) of various countries. For example, General Motors generates more revenue annually than the GNP of Denmark or Greece. Similarly, General Electric's annual sales exceed the GNP of New Zealand or Singapore.

EXHIBIT 1.2
Nondomestic Earnings, Sales, and Assets of Selected U.S. Firms: 1998

Company	Percent of Net Earnings	Percent of Sales	Percent of Assets
Avon	65	65	59
Cable & Wireless	83	70	64
Texas Instruments	93	61	44
Coca-Cola	77	67	60
Colgate-Palmolive	78	76	64
Dow Chemical	61	56	58
Gillette	64	63	63
Goodyear	77	47	49
McDonald's	58	58	56
Hewlett-Packard	53	56	53
IBM	66	61	51
Smithkline Beecham	94	78	73
Johnson & Johnson	50	49	41
Xerox	61	50	54

Source: Compiled from various annual reports

Country	Billions of U.S. Dollars
Switzerland	$284.8
Sweden	226.9
Austria	217.2
General Motors	161.3
Denmark	156.4
Ford Motor Company	142.7
Exxon	127.8
Greece	122.9
General Electric	100.5
Colombia	100.1
Singapore	95.1
IBM	81.7
New Zealand	55.8
Mobil	53.5
Sears Roebuck	41.3
Texaco	31.7
Chevron	29.9
Dupont	25.7

*Figures in billions of U.S. dollars.
Source: The World Bank, 1999. Sales figures of corporations taken from the various companies' annual reports for 1999.

Another important feature of MNCs is their predominantly oligopolistic character; that is, they operate in markets that are dominated by a few sellers. Their technological leads, their special skills, and their ability to differentiate their products through advertising are all factors that help to sustain or reinforce their oligopolistic nature. Most MNCs have a sizable number of foreign branches and affiliates: 200 of the largest have affiliates in 25 or more countries.

MNCs are mainly the product of developed countries. However, the relative importance of MNCs from different home countries has changed in the last 15 years—that of Japanese and Western European companies has increased and that of U.S. companies has declined. The available evidence suggests that these shifts are due primarily to changes in the international competitiveness of companies based in different home countries.

MNCs have made significant positive contributions to economic and social progress throughout the world. Through their technological and managerial capabilities, they have helped to develop the material and productive resources of many nations and have worked to meet the world's growing needs for good and services. Their investments have stimulated the diversification of local national economies. Their capital input has helped host governments to fulfill nationally defined economic development goals. They have provided jobs and helped to raise living standards in many areas. Yet MNCs have been strongly criticized in recent years using cheap-labor factories in developing nations[32] (see International Marketing Highlight 1.8).

International Marketing Highlight 1.8

Pangs of Conscience

The marketing pizzazz of Nike Inc.'s "Just Do It" U.S. campaign is nowhere evident in the 12 Indonesian factories run by the company's Taiwanese, South Korean, and Indonesian subcontractors. Although these are some of the most modern factories in the industry, they are drab and utilitarian. Vast sheds house row upon row of mostly young women, who will glue, stitch, press, and box 70 million pairs of Nikes this year. Here a pair of Pegasus running shoes, which retails for $75, costs just $18.25 to put together and ship to the United States Indonesia's military police deal harshly with those workers who rebel, and independent unions are outlawed.

The stark contrast between the tens of millions of dollars that Nike icon Michael Jordan earns and the $2.23 basic daily wage in Indonesia paid by the company's subcontractors has helped make Nike a lightning rod for concern about overseas manufacturing standards. Although Nike claims it is a leader in improving conditions, its Indonesian subcontractors secured an exemption from a minimum-wage increase that would have forced them to pay $8.92 a month extra to each worker at a time when Nike has reported record profits.

Source: Business Week, July 29, 1996, p. 46.

Multinationals from the Third World

The Birla Group of India, United Laboratories from the Philippines, and Autlan of Mexico are among the several hundred MNCs from the Third World whose overseas subsidiaries have increased from dozens in about 1960 to a few thousand today. They are successfully competing for a share of world markets.

These MNCs have gone abroad following the *international product life cycle* concept (see Chapter 2). They began by seeking export markets. When tariffs, quotas, or other barriers threatened overseas markets, they started assembling abroad. Their initial move, and greatest impact so far, has been in neighboring developing countries.

The strength of Third World MNCs comes from their special experience with manufacturing for small home markets. Using low technology and local raw materials, running job-shop kinds of plants, and making effective use of semiskilled labor, they are able to custom-design products best suited to host countries. For example, a Philippines paper company has managed projects in countries ranging from Indonesia to Nigeria. Its managers have drawn on their ability to make paper from inexpensive, locally available materials. In addition, they run a very efficient job-shop operation with printing, folding, and cutting machinery selected or built in-house to make very short runs of a wide range of cigarette, candy, and other packages. These are the types of skills that the Western MNCs have usually forgotten.[33]

Although small-scale manufacturing remains their unique strength, these companies also are moving in other areas that are particularly suited to local conditions. For example, a Thai company uses rice stalks for paper and plantain products for glue. A Brazilian company has developed sunfast dyes and household appliances that resist high humidity and can survive the fluctuating voltages common in the developing world.

The rapid growth of Third World MNCs provides both a threat and an opportunity to the MNCs from the advanced countries. The Third World MNCs can be tough competitors in seeking contract work for building plants that do not require high technology such as steel plants and chemical complexes. But these MNCs also offer profitable opportunities to Western companies for joint operations. Lacking in marketing skills, for example, they may share their special know-how with traditional MNCs in exchange for brand names and skills in promoting new lines.[34] Moreover, as Third World MNCs become visible and viable economic entities, their governments may well become more sympathetic to the needs of MNCs from the developed world.

Entry Strategies

Five different modes of business offer a company entry into foreign markets: exporting, contractual agreement, joint venture, strategic alliance, and wholly-owned subsidiary.

Exporting

A company may minimize the risk of dealing internationally by exporting domestically manufactured products either by minimal response to inquiries or by systematic development of demand in foreign markets. Exporting requires minimal capital and is easy to initiate. Exporting is also a good way to gain international experience. A major part of the overseas involvement of large firms is through export trade.

Contractual Agreement

There are several types of contractual agreements: patent licensing agreement, turnkey operation, coproduction agreement, management contract, and licensing.

Patent Licensing Agreement The *patent licensing agreement* is based on either a fixed-fee or a royalty-based agreement and includes managerial training.

Turnkey Operation The *turnkey operation* is based on a fixed-fee or cost-plus arrangement and includes plant construction, personnel training, and initial production runs.

Coproduction Agreement The *coproduction agreement* was most common in the Soviet-bloc countries, where plants were built and then paid for with part of the output.

Management Contract Currently widely used in the Middle East, the management contract requires that an MNC provide key personnel to operate the foreign enterprise for a fee until local people acquire the ability to manage the business independently. For example, Whittaker Corporation of Los Angeles operates government-owned hospitals in several cities in Saudi Arabia.

Licensing A variety of contractual agreements are encompassed in *licensing*, whereby an MNC marketer makes available intangible assets such as patents, trade secrets, know-how, trademarks, and company name to foreign companies in return for royalties or other forms of payment. Transfer of these assets usually is accompanied by technical services to ensure proper use.[35]

Some of the advantages of licensing are as follows:

1. Licensing requires little capital and serves as a quick and easy entry to foreign markets (see International Marketing Highlight 1.9).
2. In some countries licensing is the only way to tap the market.
3. Licensing provides life extension for products in the maturity stage of their life cycles.
4. Licensing is a good alternative to foreign production and marketing in an environment where there is worldwide inflation, skilled-labor shortages, increasing domestic and foreign governmental regulation and restriction, and tough international competition.
5. Licensing royalties are guaranteed and periodic, whereas shared income from investment fluctuates and is risky.
6. Domestically based firms can benefit from product development abroad without research expense through technical feedback arrangements in a licensing agreement.
7. When exports no longer are profitable because of intense competition, licensing provides an alternative.
8. Licensing can overcome high transportation costs, which make some exports noncompetitive in the target markets.
9. Licensing is immune to expropriation.
10. In some countries, manufacturers of military equipment or any product deemed critical to the national interest (including communication equipment) may be compelled to enter licensing agreements.

■■■■■■■■■ **International Marketing Highlight 1.9** ■■■■■■■■■

Starbucks Steams Ahead in Asia

After Starbucks opened its first Asian store as a joint venture in Japan in 1996, it changed tactics and struck tailor-made licensing deals in seven other countries. Though Starbucks prefers the degree of control joint ventures offer, it had shied away from the capital commitments such a strategy demands. Less than 5 percent of global revenue currently funds international expansion, and the coffee brewer is unwilling to pay for half of every branch it opens in Asia. Franchising would circumvent this problem, but Starbucks is not comfortable having a franchise partner select sub-franchisers, as is typical. Licensing lets the firm maintain control over expansion while limiting financial exposure. The local partner funds the capital costs of expansion—and bears the business risks.

Moreover, secondary benefits accrue from partnering with local outfits, such as instantly gaining valuable regional expertise. For example, Rustan Coffee has operated supermarkets and retail outlets in the Philippines for 45 years, giving Starbucks a head start with distribution and possible supermarket sales. Local partners also help the U.S. company navigate tricky local regulations, such as local content laws in the Philippines or strict quality testing procedures in Japan.

Detailed licensing agreements give the local partners exclusive rights to develop and operate Starbucks retail stores. However, the agreements also stipulate that Starbucks remains involved in every aspect of planning, operations, design and training. Parent-company consultants visit each foreign store at least once a month. Store managers are sent to Seattle for an intensive training course of 12–14 weeks and all menu changes must be discussed with headquarters before being implemented.

Source: Crossborder Monitor, April 26, 1999, p. 12

Some disadvantages of licensing are as follows:

1. To attract licensees, a firm must possess distinctive technology, a trademark, and a company or brand name that is attractive to potential foreign users.
2. The licensor has no control over production and marketing by the licensee.
3. Licensing royalties are negligible compared with equity investment potential. Royalty rates seldom exceed 5 percent of gross sales because of host government restrictions.
4. The licensee may lose interest in renewing the contract unless the licensor holds interest through innovation and new technology.
5. There is a danger of creating competition in third, or even home, markets if the licensee violates territorial agreements. Going to court in these situations is expensive and time consuming and no international adjudicatory body exists.

Joint Venture

Joint venture represents a higher-risk alternative than licensing because it requires various levels of direct investment. A joint venture between a U.S. firm and a native operation abroad involves sharing risks to accomplish mutual enterprise. Joint ventures, incidentally, are the next most common form of entry once a firm moves beyond the exporting stage to a more regular overseas involvement.

One example of a joint venture is General Motors Corporation's partnership with Egypt's state-owned Nasar Car Company to establish a plant to assemble trucks and diesel engines. Another example of a joint venture is between Matsushita of Japan and IBM to manufacture small computers. The alliance between Coca-Cola Co. and Nestlé S.A. to develop and sell ready-to-drink coffees and teas is still another example of a joint venture. Joint ventures normally are designed to take advantage of the strong functions of the partners and supplement their weak functions, be they management, research, or marketing.

Joint ventures provide a mutually beneficial opportunity for domestic and foreign businesses to join forces. For both parties, the ventures are a means to share both capital and risk and make use of each other's technical strength. Japanese companies, for example, prefer entering into joint ventures with U.S. firms because such arrangements help ensure against possible American trade barriers. American firms, on the other hand, like the opportunity to enter a previously forbidden market, to utilize established channels, to link American product innovation with low-cost Japanese manufacturing technology, and to curb a potentially tough competitor.

As a case in point, General Foods Corporation tried for more than a decade to succeed in Japan on its own and watched the market share of its instant coffee (Maxwell House) drop from 20 to 14 percent. Then, in 1975 the firm established a joint venture with Ajinomoto, a food manufacturer, to use the full power of the Japanese partner's product distribution system and personnel and managerial capabilities. Within two years, Maxwell House's share of the Japanese instant coffee market recovered reached close to 25 percent.[36]

Joint ventures, however, are a mixed blessing, with their main problem stemming from one cause: there is more than one partner, and one of the partners must play the key, dominant role to steer the business to success. Obviously, conflicts can arise in the management process.

Joint ventures should be designed to supplement each partner's shortcomings, not to exploit them. It takes as much effort to make a joint venture a success as to start a grass-roots operation and eventually bring it up to a successful level. In both cases, each partner must be fully prepared to expend the effort necessary to understand customers, competitors, and himself or herself. A joint venture is a means of resource appropriation and of easing a foreign business's entry into a new terrain. It should not be viewed as a handy vehicle to reap money without effort, interest, or additional resources.

Joint ventures are a popular mode to seek entry in a foreign country. There is hardly a Fortune 1000 company active overseas that does not have at least one joint venture. Widespread interest in joint ventures is related to

1. *Seeking market opportunities.* Companies in mature industries in the industrialized countries find joint venture a desirable entry mode for new markets overseas.
2. *Dealing with rising economic nationalism.* Often host governments are more receptive to or even require joint ventures.
3. *Preempting raw materials.* Countries with raw materials such as petroleum or extractable material usually do not allow foreign firms to be active there other than through joint venture.
4. *Sharing risk.* Rather than taking the entire risk, a joint venture allows the risk to be shared with a partner, which can be especially important in politically sensitive areas.
5. *Developing an export base.* In areas where economic blocs play a significant role, joint venture with a local firm smoothes the entry into the entire region, such as entry into the European Union (EU) market through a joint venture with a French company.
6. *Selling technology.* Selling technology to developing countries becomes easier through joint ventures.

Although joint venture is an attractive entry mode, it poses a potential for failure. When either partner in a joint venture concludes that the venture is a failure, there are five alternatives to resolve the problem. First, the joint venture may be continued even after it is seen as a failure if the circumstances force the partners to do so—for examples. Both partners may be temporarily dependent on the venture for some critical resource, or one party may have legal basis for forcing continuation. A second option is for one partner to continue the business. A third is for another entity to acquire all or a major portion of the joint venture. A fourth is to create a new organization, independent of the original partners, to run the business. This option is usually relevant for joint ventures that have achieved some measure of success but are no longer useful to the founding partners. Finally, the joint venture may be liquidated.

The choice of which termination strategy to use depends on a number of factors. If either partner is dependent on the joint venture for some critical resource, the preservation of that resource will be a critical consideration in selecting a strategy. Another factor is whether the joint venture could survive as an independent entity. If the joint venture is not dependent specifically on the founding partners, it may be able to shift its association to some other business organization.

If the owners decide not to continue the joint venture, the outcome will depend on whether the venture is worth more as a going concern than its liquidation value. New joint ventures will be less visible and less attractive to potential buyers than old ones. Small joint ventures are unlikely to have the necessary resources to survive as independent organizations. All of these factors suggest that new and small ventures will be liquidated. Larger and longer-established ventures have a greater opportunity for survival.

Strategic Alliance

In recent years, a new type of collaborative strategy in international business has gained popularity. Commonly called strategic alliance, leading firms, particularly in high-tech industries, have used this route for their mutual benefit. Strategic alliances are short of complete merger, but deeper than arm's length market exchanges. They involve mutual dependence and shared decision making between two or more separate firms. Strategic alliances differ from joint ventures in that they encompass select activities and often are formed for a specific period. Strategic goals pursued through strategic alliances are product exchange or supply alliances (aimed to reduce transaction costs by establishing a mutual commitment between the supplying and buying firms); learning alliances (aimed to develop new capabilities through technology transfer or joint research); and market positioning alliances (aimed to develop demand for a product, spread technology, or develop a dominant standard in the market).

Strategic alliances make sense for the following reasons:[37]

1. Their flexibility and informality promote efficiencies.
2. They provide access to new markets and technologies.
3. They all the creation and disbanding of projects with minimum paperwork.
4. Multiple parties share risk and expenses.
5. Partners can retail their independent brand identification.
6. Partners possessing multiple skills can create major synergies.
7. Rivals can often work harmoniously together.
8. Alliances can take multifarious forms, from simple R&D deals to huge projects.
9. Ventures can accommodate dozens of participants.
10. Antitrust laws can shelter cooperative R&D activities.

Strategic alliances are especially useful for seeking entry into emerging markets. MNCs look to emerging markets for growth. Companies in emerging markets look for ways into the burgeoning global economy. Strategic alliances are the obvious solution for both sides. Given this pattern of mutual benefit, it is not surprising that strategic alliances account for at least half of market entries into Latin America, Asia, and Eastern Europe.[38]

Wholly-Owned Subsidiary

MNCs may also establish themselves in overseas markets by direct investment in a manufacturing or assembly subsidiary. Because of the volatility of worldwide economic, social, and political conditions, these *wholly-owned subsidiaries* are the most risky form of overseas involvement. An example of a direct investment situation is Chesebrough-Pond's operation of overseas manufacturing plants in Japan, England, and Monte Carlo. An example of the risk involved in such arrangements is India's Bhopal disaster, in which a poisonous gas leak in a Union Carbide Corporation plant killed over 2,000 people and permanently disabled thousands—in the worst industrial accident that has ever occurred. It has been suggested that MNCs not manufacture overseas where a mishap could jeopardize the survival of the whole company. As a matter of fact, in the wake of the Bhopal accident, many host countries tightened safety and environmental regulations. For example, Brazil, the world's fourth-largest user of agricultural chemicals, restricted the use of the deadly methyl isocyanate.

Conclusion

A firm interested in entering the international market must evaluate the risk and commitment involved with each entry and choose the entry mode that best fits the company's objectives and resources. Entry risk and commitment can be examined by considering the following five factors:

1. Characteristics of the product.
2. The market's external macroenvironment—particularly economic and political factors, and the demand and buying pattern characteristics of potential customers.
3. The firm's competitive position—especially the product's life cycle stage as well as various corporate strengths and weaknesses.
4. Capital budgeting considerations, including resource costs and availabilities.
5. Internal corporate perceptions, which affect corporate selection of information and the psychic distance between a firm's decision makers and its target customers, as well as control and risk-taking preferences.

These five factors combined indicate the risk to be reviewed vis-à-vis a company's resources before determining a mode of entry.[39]

It is useful to remember that a company may use different modes of entry in different countries. For example, McDonald's Corporation deemed it sufficient to license three restaurants on the small Caribbean island of Aruba, but in Japan it has had a joint venture since 1971. The local partner helped McDonald's blanket the Japanese market to such an extent that there are now over 600 outlets across the country, the largest number of McDonald's restaurants in any country outside the United States

Summary

In today's environment even firms that do not seek to do business outside their national boundaries have no choice but to be aware of the international business scene. The U.S. economy, as is true of the economies of other industrialized nations, is so intricately linked to international economics that even strictly domestic business is affected by what takes place in other countries. Thus, all students of business should be thoroughly familiar with the perspectives of international business.

International marketing instruction in particular is required because, of all the functional areas of a business, marketing problems are the most fundamental and the most frequent. Although basic marketing decisions do not change as marketers expand their business from the domestic field to the international field, the environments they must consider while making those decisions can be profoundly different. The major aspects of the international marketing environment include the economic, cultural, and legal and political environments.

International marketing is also affected by international institutions such as the International Monetary Fund and agreements such as NAFTA.

A firm aspiring to enter the international scene may choose from the various entry modes—exporting, contractual agreement, joint venture, strategic alliance, and wholly-owned subsidiary. Each entry mode provides different opportunities and risks.

Today's thrust for growth in international business comes from MNCs. In recent years some of the tactics of the MNCs have become a subject of intense discussion, particularly with reference to their operations in developing countries. The MNC will continue to be an institution of great significance, but leaders of these companies will require an increasing awareness of the needs of host countries in the environment in the future.

Review Questions

1. Why should a business operating entirely in the U.S. domestic market be concerned with happenings in the international business environment?
2. Why should international marketing be considered as a separate field of study even though marketing decisions in both domestic and international markets are basically the same?
3. What are the different modes of entry into the international market? What are the relative advantages and disadvantages of each mode?
4. How can a firm's overseas involvement be categorized?
5. Why do a very large proportion of U.S. firms confine themselves to domestic markets?
6. Why should a firm enter international business? Give examples of each reason.

Creative Questions

1. Usually, MNCs are associated with a particular country—thus, there are U.S. MNCs, Japanese MNCs, etc. Inasmuch as MNCs do business globally, and their stockholders are spread all over the world, is it conceivable that MNCs in the future would be characterized under the authority of an international agency and become stateless? What are the pros and cons of such a move?
2. What is the difference between a joint venture and a strategic alliance? What are the key issues in the successful management of strategic alliances?

Endnotes

1. "Mac World," *The Economist*, June 29, 1996, p.61.

2. See National Trade Data Bank, U.S. Department of Commerce, updated First Quarter 2000.

3. "It's a Small (Business) World," *Business Week*, April 17, 1995, p. 96.

4. *U.S. Manufacturers in the Global Marketplace* (New York: The Conference Board, Inc., 1994, p. 35.

5. U.S. Department of Commerce.

6. Ibid.

7. See Subhash C. Jain, "Global Competitiveness in the Beer Industry: A Case Study," Working Paper (Storrs, CT: Food Policy Center, The University of Connecticut, 1994).

8. The direct investment position is the net book value of U.S. companies and other investors' equity in and outstanding loans to foreign affiliates.

9. Joseph P. Quinlan, "Europe, Not Asia, Is Corporate America's Key Market," *The Wall Street Journal*, January 12, 1998, p. A20.

10. *Transnationals*, October 1995, p. 10.

11. *Statistical Abstract of the United States: 2000* (Washington, D.C.: U.S. Department of Commerce, 2000), p. 682.

12. U.S. Department of Commerce, International Trade Administration.

13. Ibid.

14. Ibid.

15. See "No Smoking Sweeps America," *Business Week*, July 27, 1987, p. 40. Also see James S. Hirsch, "U.S. Liquor Makers Seek Tonic in Foreign Markets," *The Wall Street Journal*, October 24, 1989, p. B1.

16. See Edmund Faltermayer, "Is 'Made in U.S.A.' Fading Away," *Fortune*, September 24, 1990, p. 62.

17. "America's High-Tech Crisis," *Business Week*, March 11, 1985, p. 56. Also see Bernard Wysocki, Jr., "American Firms Send Office Work Abroad to Use Cheaper Labor," *The Wall Street Journal*, August 14, 1991, p. 1.

18. "The Angry Angels at Zenith," *Business Week*, August 12, 1996. P. 32.

19. *The Economist*, February 19, 1994, p. 21.

20. "Asia's Brand Barons Go Shopping," *The Economist*, August 10, 1996, p. 45.

21. "Kodak in China; smile, please," *The Economist*, March 28, 1998, p. 60.

22. *World Almanac*, 2000.

23. Roger Thurow, "In Global Drive, Nike Finds Its Brash Ways Don't Always Pay Off," *The Wall Street Journal*, May 5, 1997, p. A1.

24. Theodore Levitt, "The Globalization of Markets," *Harvard Business Review*, May–June 1983, pp. 92–102.

25. Ibid.

26. Chris Adams, "Steelmakers Scramble in a Race to Become Global Powerhouses," *The Wall Street Journal*, August 1997, p.1.

27. Frank Meissner, "Americans Must Practice the Marketing They Preach to Succeed in Japan's Mass Markets," *Marketing News*, October 17, 1990, p.5.

28. *See* Kenichi Ohmae, *Beyond National Borders* (Homewood, IL: Dow Jones-Irwin, 1987), Chapter 3.

29. Stephen K. Yoder, "Apple, Loser in Japan Computer Market, Tries to Recoup by Redesigning Its Models," *The Wall Street Journal*, June 21, 1985, p. 30.

30. Hirotaka Takeuchi and Michael E. Porter, "Three Roles of International Marketing in Global Strategy," in Michael Porter, ed., *Competition in Global Industries* (Boston: Harvard Business School Press 1986), pp. 111–116.

31. *World Investment Report 1999* (New York: United Nations, 1999).

32. See Rajib N. Sanyal and Turgut Guvenh, "Relations Between Multinational Firms and Host Governments: The Experience of American-owned Firms in China," *International Business Review*, 9 no. 1 (2000): 119–134.

33. See *World Investment Report*.

34. Francis H. Ulgado, Chwo-Ming J. Yu, and Anant R. Negandhi, "Multinational Enterprises from Asian Developing Countries: Management and Organizational Characteristics," *International Business Review* 3, no. 2 (1994): 123–134.

35. See Farok J. Contractor, "Strategic Perspectives for International Licensing Managers: The Complementary Roles of Licensing—Investment and Trade in Global Operations," Working Paper no. 90.002, Rutgers University Center for International Business Education and Research.

36. Kenichi Ohmae, *Triad Power* (New York: The Free Press, 1985), p. 116.

37. "Partness-Partners," *Business Week*, October 25, 1999, p. 106.

38. Ashwin Adarkar, Asif Adil, David Ernst and Paresh Vaish, "Emerging Market Alliances: Must They Be Win-Lose? *The Mckinsey Quarterly*, November 4, 1997, pp. 120–137.

Economic Rationale of Global Trade and Business

CHAPTER FOCUS_____

After studying this chapter, you should be able to

■ Give the rationale for global trade and business.

■ Describe the barriers that nations impose to restrict free trade.

■ Explain the role of the General Agreement on Tariffs and Trade (GATT) in liberalizing world trade.

■ Describe U.S. trade liberalization endeavors.

■ Discuss how a multinational corporation participates in global markets.

Commerce is older than recorded history. Archaeological discoveries provide us with evidence of the antiquity of trade. Thousands of ancient commercial documents indicate that a considerable commercial class existed many centuries before any European or Mediterranean city attained a high degree of civilization. In the ancient world, there had even developed a system of payment of precious objects for traded goods—a forerunner of the modern monetary system.

Trading has evolved through the ages in response to altering needs spurred by changes in technology and philosophy. Growth in trade was particularly stimulated by the discovery and use of metals and by the global horizons provided by advances in transportation and later in communication. As a result of those advances, trade evolved from exchanges among isolated peoples to trade through conquest, then to trade among friendly neighbors, and then to a system of silent barter among both adversaries and friends. In brief, although world trade as we know it today is very different from ancient trading practices, groups of people have always traded.

As civilization progressed around the world, trading became more organized and productive. For example, ancient seaborne commerce was inefficient and, proportionately, insignificant. Piracy and raiding of ships were commonplace. Such hazards discouraged trade expansion and required that harbors be fortified for protection. In modern times, although nations still go to war, piracy and raiding have been virtually eliminated by a variety of treaties, arrangements, and other international laws.

World trade requires that nations be willing to cooperate with each other. Countries naturally trade with those nations with whom they are on friendly terms. Nonetheless, trading often goes on among nations even when political relations are not amicable. For example, the United States and China are on many issues politically opposed, yet the two nations trade with each other. The mutual benefits, or economic advantages, of U.S.–China trade outweigh political differences.

Economic advantage has historically been the most important consideration that trading nations share. This chapter examines and discusses the nature of that advantage and also deals with the political and economic hindrances that produce economic disadvantage and tend to discourage trade, particularly among developed and developing countries.

In the post–World War II period, world trade has multiplied tremendously and has added new dimensions to global economic activity. An example is presented here to depict the emergence of the MNC as the basic institution of present international economic activity. Current international economic activity is much wider in both scope and activity than the traditional importing and exporting trade described by classical economists.

Theory of Comparative Advantage

The classical economists—Adam Smith, David Ricardo, and John Stuart Mill—are credited with providing the theoretical economic justification for international trade. In simple terms, modern trade takes place because a foreign country is able to provide a material or product cheaper than native industry can. For example, if the landed cost of a Japanese-made television set is less than the cost of an American-made one, it makes economic sense to import television sets from Japan. Likewise, if U.S. computers can be sold at cheaper prices in Japan than computers manufactured in Japan, Japanese businesses will find it economically desirable to import U.S. computers.

David Ricardo advanced the concept of *relative or comparative costs* as the basis of international trade. He emphasized labor costs more than other aspects of production. Such aspects as land and capital, in Ricardo's view, either were of no significance or were so evenly distributed overall that they always operated in a fixed proportion, whereas labor did not. In sum, his *theory of comparative advantage* states that even if a country is able to produce all its goods at lower costs than another country can, trade still benefits both countries, based on comparative, not absolute, costs. In other words, countries should concentrate efforts on producing goods that have a *comparative* advantage over other countries, and then export those goods in exchange for goods that command advantage in their native countries.

To illustrate this point, let us assume the following information about the United States and Italy:

Labor Costs per Unit (in Hours)

Country	Hand Calculator	Bottle of Wine
United States	6	8
Italy	30	15

Although these figures show that the production cost of both hand calculators and wine is lower in the United States than in Italy, according to the theory of comparative advantage, the United States is better off specializing in hand calculators and exchanging them for Italian wine. This way, it can obtain from Italy a bottle of wine for only six hours of labor instead of the eight hours that would be required at home. Italy would also gain from the exchange by concentrating on producing wine and exchanging it for hand calculators at the cost of 15 instead of 30 hours of labor. The key to this concept is in the word "comparative"—which implies that each and every country has both definite "advantage" in producing some goods and definite "disadvantage" in producing other goods. But, further, the advantage for some goods may be greater than for others (e.g., hand calculators versus wine for the United States).

The following example quantitatively demonstrates the benefits derived from free trade. Consider two countries, Japonia and Latinia. Japonia has a clear competitive advantage over Latinia in producing both radios and TVS, as follows:

Worker Hours per Unit

	Japonia	Latinia
Radio	1	4
Television Sets	4	8

It follows that 48 worker hours of production will result in 24 radios and 6 television sets in Japonia. The same number of worker hours produces six radios and three television sets in Latinia. Therefore, the two countries can produce a total of 30 radios and 9 television sets with 96 worker hours of effort.

Now suppose Japonia and Latinia choose free trade and tear down the barriers they have erected against each other's products. With the same worker-hour requirement per unit and the same number of worker hours devoted to production, their combined output will change to 32 radios and 10 televison sets.

This is not really a miracle; it simply is *division of labor* based on *comparative advantage*. Under free trade, Latinia is induced to withdraw resources it had devoted to radio production and concentrate entirely on television sets. Consequently, Latinia produces 6 television sets and no radios in 48 hours. Japonia is likewise induced to reallocate some resources and devote 32 worker hours to radios, where its comparative advantage is greatest, leaving the remaining 16 hours for television sets. Thus, 32 radios and 4 television sets are produced with every 48 worker hours of effort.

As a result, the world has more radios and television sets, but are Japonia and Latinia better off individually? To find out, we have to introduce the price system. In doing that, we must realize that price relationships are more important than the prices themselves. Differences in price relationships are what people act upon.

Here is the lineup of prices (we'll use the same prices both before and after free trade):

	Japonia	Latinia
Radios	24,000 yen	600 pesos
Television sets	96,000 yen	1,200 pesos

After free trade, the Japonian retailer can choose a television set at 96,000 yen or 1,200 pesos, corresponding to an exchange ratio of 80:1. The retailer will want to buy pesos whenever they can be obtained for less than 80 yen apiece. The Latinian retailer can choose a radio at 24,000 yen or 600 pesos, corresponding to a ratio of 40:1. This retailer will be in the market for yen whenever more than 40 yen can be exchanged for a peso.

The differential in price relationships between television sets and radios in the two countries has created an entrepreneurial opportunity: buying and selling currencies. Price differentials on many products—and many other factors, including people's expectations concerning the relative economic outlook of the countries involved—play a part in establishing exchange rates. But the Japonian and Latinian marketers in this case should be satisfied if the yen/peso rate falls somewhere between 40:1 and 80:1.

We could choose any number, but let us say that the exchange rate becomes 60:1—right in the middle. Before free trade, a Japonian retailer could buy a shipment of 20 radios and 5 television sets for 960,000 yen. A Latinian retailer could buy the same shipment for 18,000 pesos. After free trade, the Japonian and Latinian retailers, each acting in his or her own self-interest, do their buying. Here is the result:

Japonian Retailer		
20 radios × 24,000 yen		= 480,000 yen
5 TVs × 1,200 pesos × 60 yen		= 360,000 yen
	Shipment	840,000 yen
Savings: 120,000 yen		

Latinian Retailer		
20 radios × 24,000 yen / 60 pesos		= 8,000 pesos
5 TVs × 1,200 pesos		= 6,000 pesos
	Shipment	14,000 pesos
Savings: 4,000 pesos		

In both countries, purchasing power has been increased. Both can afford to buy more of the same things or to buy new things they could not afford before. Both are wealthier.

Possibly you aren't convinced until you can see it "in dollars and cents." So why not create a world price in dollars for radios and television sets, and redo the arithmetic? At a 60:1 yen/peso exchange rate, the dollar price of a TV is $240, since 300 yen equals 5 pesos equals $1. You will find that Japonia will have enough extra radios to sell at $80 each to buy from Latinia the television sets it stopped producing, and it will still have some dollars to spare. Latinia will have dollars left over after selling extra television sets to buy all of the radios it no longer makes.

Rationale for Seeking Comparative Advantage

Every nation seeks to increase the material standard of living of its people, and that living standard increases as a function of *productivity*. With greater productivity, the same amount of labor yields more goods and services. As productivity increases, greater material wealth results. Thus, the rationale for seeking comparative advantage is increased productivity.

Different countries enjoy productivity gains in different ways. Sweden has made a choice of longer vacations; the United States prefers increased material possessions. In both cases, increased productivity yields the desired benefits.

Productivity is enhanced—and the living standard raised—by the *specialization* of production, whereby countries do not try to produce all the goods they require but only those they can produce efficiently. The rest are imported. *Sheltered* businesses—the ones chosen to provide certain goods and services nationally—include health care, government administration, goods distribution, and manufacturers of special goods such as pharmaceuticals and essential military goods.

Businesses included in the sheltered category are influenced by consideration of economic feasibility, national security, and self-sufficiency. Sheltered manufacturing businesses include those in which increased production scale is not great enough to offset the costs of distributing the product to a larger geographic area. This category includes products that, for one reason or another, are expensive to transport, such as milk or sulfuric acid.

For a nation to have a high standard of living, it must export enough goods to balance the import of the goods it cannot efficiently produce itself. Exports are especially important for maintaining the living standard in a country whose resources are limited and whose imports, in balance, are relatively high. Consider Japan, which built a viable export market and in return developed an invulnerable position in many industries. South Korea, Taiwan, and Brazil appear to be following Japan's example by developing export markets.[1]

Exhibit 2.1 presents a hypothetical comparison of two countries whose only export is oil. If the market absorbs the production of both countries, the price is usually set according to the cost of the labor hours required by the least efficient producer, in this case Country B. Country A may set a price slightly lower in order to guarantee the sale of all its output. Regardless, Country A's per-hour income will be much higher than that of Country B. This greater income can be used for higher wages, for reinvestment to support a free health care system for everyone in the country, or for whatever the country desires. In brief, specialization profits Country A and leads it to a higher standard of living.

EXHIBIT 2.1
Relative Productivity: A Hypothetical Example

	Labor Hours per Barrel	
	Country A	Country B
Operating	1	3
Capital cost amortization	1	2
Total	2	5
World price (in labor-hour equivalents)	5.0	5.5
Income (per labor hour)	2.5	1.1

Business Specialization and Trade

The *economic law of comparative advantage* states that every nation benefits when specialization and trade take place. Even when one nation cannot produce any good more efficiently than another can, it is still in the economic interest of both nations for each to specialize. Regardless of its productivity relative to other suppliers, every nation has comparative advantage in producing certain goods rather than others. The specialization and the advantage are achieved on the basis of one or more production factors—natural resources, technology, capital, managerial know-how, and labor.[2]

Classical economists considered labor the chief delineating factor of comparative advantage between two trading nations. In modern days, however, other factors besides labor may be more important in equipping a country for specialization. As a matter of fact, wage levels for blue-collar workers are becoming increasingly irrelevant in world competition. This is because blue-collar labor no longer accounts for enough of total costs to give low wages much competitive advantage. For example, blue-collar costs in U.S. manufacturing account for 18 percent of total costs, but they are down from 23 percent only a few years ago, and they are dropping fast.[3]

In addition to being influenced by the preceding production factors, a country's leverage may change with time and with changes in the political, social, cultural, and economic environment. For example, Japan has a comparative advantage relative to the United States in producing steel. Japan's leverage in steel is based on managerial ability and technology. Even though Japan must import the raw material of iron ore, other factors provide enough leeway to ensure comparative advantage. This does not mean that its current comparative advantage in steel is everlasting. The supplier of Japan's iron ore could stop supplying for political reasons, or another country could develop a technology superior to Japan's and supersede its advantage. Thus, leverage must be not only developed but also maintained for long-term gains.

Natural Resources Nature randomly endowed different regions of the world with natural resources. The natural riches of a place bestow upon it unique economic advantages. But nations are groups of communities arbitrarily organized, usually without regard to such economic considerations as the abundance or lack of natural resources.

The most outstanding example of the possession of a resource providing economic leverage is the abundance of oil in the Middle East. In raw-material exchanges based on natural resources, even if both nations have the same natural resource, one country may be better off than the other because of various physical characteristics of the resource. For example, certain economic considerations—such as seam thickness, depth, and purity of ore bodies or the number of hours required to pump a barrel of oil—come into play. Saudi Arabian oil from a shallow well is a richer resource than Iranian oil from a deep well.

Mineral trade is based on the natural availability of minerals in different countries. The aircraft industry is crucially dependent on cobalt, which is used in jet engine blades. Zambia and Zaire produce two-thirds of the world's cobalt and thus have a natural advantage in this area. Since the metal is important for an essential industry, the random distribution of the natural resource leads to world trade. In brief, the natural resources of a country can permit it to engage in international trade from an advantageous position.

Technology Manufacturers in different countries have different production costs as a result of the unevenness of technological advances. Differences in production scale, run lengths, distribution structure, product mix, and technological development capability, among other things, often determine productivity differences among producers. For example, some Japanese companies can assemble a television set in one-third the time required by their European or American competitors. This advantage is derived from product designs that use fewer components, machines that automate some of the board assembly, and equipment that reduces labor in the handling of materials.

As another example, Japan's technological advantage in manufacturing steel leads it to surpass India in the world markets. This happens despite the facts that (1) Japan must import iron ore from India and (2) Indian labor is much less expensive than Japanese labor.

Managerial Know-How People who bring capital, labor, and resources together to fashion them into a productive organization—one that faces the risks of an uncertain world—occupy strategic positions. Thus, given the same inputs, a country with superior management will likely do better than one with weak management. The importance of managerial know-how can be illustrated by the airlines industry. Most airlines of the free world use the same planes and offer essentially the same services while charging common prices. Yet some carriers outperform others. The difference must be management. Singapore Airlines does better than any other airline, partly because of its lower labor costs, but mainly because of superior management.[4]

Obviously, an explanation of world business involves many elements. However, with a basic understanding of the elements covered so far—comparative advantage and specialization—we can now consider other reasons for nations to engage in international business.

Product Life Cycle and International Trade

The theory of comparative advantage is a classic explanation of world trade. In the late 1960s researchers at the Harvard Business School provided a new explanation of international trade and investment patterns.[5] The new approach uses the *product life cycle model,* which gives significant insight into how MNCs evolve. The product life cycle model states that U.S. products go through four stages:[6]

Phase I, in which U.S. export strength for a product builds.
Phase II, in which foreign production of the same product starts.
Phase III, in which foreign production becomes competitive in export markets.
Phase IV, in which import competition begins in domestic U.S. markets.

During Phase I the product is manufactured in the United States for a high-income market and afterward introduced into foreign markets through exports. At that point, the United States usually holds a monopoly position as the only country able to supply the product. The product continues to be manufactured only in the United States, since business acumen dictates that operations be located close to markets where the demand exists. Overseas customers, however, import the U.S. product in response to their own market demands and thus create a program of export of the U.S. product.

During Phase II, as the product becomes popular, entrepreneurs in other advanced countries, perhaps in Western Europe, venture into producing the same product. The technology involved is by then fairly routine and easily transferred from the United States. Subsequently, the overseas-manufactured product begins to outsell the U.S. export in selected markets because the overseas product benefits from lower labor costs and savings in transportation. The stage where overseas manufacturers are able to compete effectively against U.S. exports has been reached.

In the third phase, the foreign producers begin to compete against the U.S. exports in developing countries. Consequently, the market for the U.S. exports declines further. Between Phases I and II, the U.S. firms begin to consider making direct investments abroad to sustain or regain their original market position.

Phase IV occurs when the foreign firms, strong in their home and export markets, achieve economics of scale and then begin to invade the U.S. home market. Presumably, the foreign firms have lower costs so that, despite ocean freight and U.S. customs costs, they are able to compete effectively against the domestically produced U.S. products.

These four phases complete the product life cycle and describe how American firms that once commanded a monopoly position in a product find themselves being pushed out of their home market.

The product life cycle theory applied to world trade holds that advanced countries like the United States play the innovative role in product development, and then, later on, other relatively advanced countries such as Japan or Western European countries take over the market position held by the innovative country. The second-stage countries go through the same cycle as did the innovative country and in turn lose their markets to the next group of countries, say, emerging countries. In other words, a product initially produced in the United States might eventually be produced only in developing countries, with the result that the United States, Western Europe, and Japan would meet their needs for that product through import from the developing countries.

The product life cycle model has been helpful in explaining the history of a number of products, particularly textiles, shoes, bicycles, radios, television sets, industrial fasteners, and standardized components for different uses. These products, first available only in the United States, Western Europe, and Japan, are now being imported from Korea, Taiwan, Hong Kong, Brazil, Mexico, Malaysia, India, and other emerging countries. South Korea in particular has made enormous strides out-competing Japan in a number of consumer products. Abandoning years of prejudice, Japanese are snatching up low-priced goods from newly industrialized countries. For example, in 1998 an imported 20-inch color television set was available for $475 while a similar Japanese-made set was priced at $730.[7]

Despite its apparent validity in the manufacturing field, the product life cycle model does not provide a complete answer to the growth activities of MNCs.[8] We now turn to some concepts that apply there.

Production Sharing

In the late 1970s Peter Drucker introduced a new concept of international business and trade, *production sharing*, which he described as

> the newest world economic trend. Although production sharing is neither "export" nor "import" in the traditional sense, this is how it is still shown in our trade figures and treated in economic and political discussions. Yet it is actually economic integration by stages of the productive process.[9]

Production sharing arose as a solution to an economic problem in developed countries posed by the fact that higher levels of education there create higher levels of personal expectation, leading to a gradual disappearance of the semiskilled and unskilled labor so necessary to labor-intensive manufacturing. As a result, developed countries turn to developing countries where the availability of labor is a major asset, in order to "share" production of products requiring such labor. This concept also covers the U.S. tariff-schedule advantage of U.S. companies whereby American components made by American labor can be further processed or assembled abroad and then returned to the U.S. market for further work or sale, with duty paid only on the value added.

Drucker describes the process as follows:

> Men's shoes sold in the United States usually start out as the hide on the American cow. As a rule the hide is not tanned, however, in the United States, but shipped to a place like Brazil for tanning—highly labor-intensive work. The leather is then shipped—perhaps through the intermediary of a Japanese trading company—to the Caribbean. Part of it may be worked up into uppers in the British Virgin Islands, part into soles in Haiti. And then uppers and soles are shipped to islands like Barbados or Jamaica, the products of which have access to Britain, to the European Common Market (now European Union), and to Puerto Rico, where they are worked up into shoes that enter the United States under the American tariff umbrella.

Surely these are truly transnational shoes. The hide, though it's the largest single-cost element, still constitutes no more than one quarter of the manufacturer's cost of the shoe. By labor content these are "imported shoes." By skill content they are "American-made." Raising the cow, which is capital-intensive, heavily automated, and requires the greatest skill and advanced management, is done in a developed country, which has the skill, the knowledge, and the equipment. The management of the entire process, the design of the shoes, their quality control and their marketing are also done entirely in developed countries where the manpower and the skills needed for these tasks are available.[10]

Currently, production sharing seems to be quite prevalent, and growing at a rapid pace. It is a new phenomenon for which there are no classic or neoclassic explanatory theories. Strictly speaking, production sharing is different from the traditional idea of international trade. It is a transnational business integration—a new relationship made possible by technological and business forces.[11] Production sharing offers both the developed and developing countries of the world a chance to share their resources and strengths for mutual benefit.

Internalization Theory

A multinational firm can serve a market across national boundaries either by (1) exporting from a production facility located in the country of the parent company or from a third country subsidiary or (2) by setting up production facilities in the market itself. The sourcing policy of the firm is the result of the firm's decisions as to which of its production facilities will service its various final markets. Thus, the firm establishes an international network linking production to markets. Such a network enables the firm to grow by eliminating external markets in intermediate goods and subsequently by *internalizing* those markets within the firm. When international markets are internalized, the internal transfers of goods and services occur. The incentives to internalize intermediate-goods markets are strongest in areas where research inputs and proprietary technology are an important part of the manufacturing process.

Many intermediate-product markets, particularly for types of knowledge and expertise embodied in patents and human capital, are difficult to organize and costly to use. In such cases, the firm has an incentive to create internal markets whenever transactions can be carried out at a lower cost within the firm than they can through external markets. This internalization involves extending the direct operations of the firm and bringing under common ownership and control the activities of the market.

The creation of an internal market permits the firm to transform an intangible piece of research into a valuable property specific to the firm. The firm can exploit its advantage in all available markets and still keep the use of the information internal to the firm in order to recoup its initial expenditures on research and knowledge generation.[12]

The internalization theory assumes that the firm has a global horizon, and it recognizes that the enterprise needs a competitive advantage or a unique asset to expand. However, the underlying thesis of internalization is the firm's desire to extend its own direct operations rather than use external markets. The internalization approach rests on two general axioms: (1) firms choose the least-cost location for each activity they perform; and (2) firms grow by internalizing markets up to the point where the benefits of further internalization are outweighed by the costs.

The internalization theory provides an economic rationale for the existence of MNCs. The sourcing decision rests on the costs and benefits to the firm, taking into consideration industry-specific factors (e.g., nature of the product), region-specific factors (e.g., geographic location), nation-specific factors (e.g., political climate), and firm-specific factors (e.g., managerial ability to internalize).

The internalization theory primarily focuses on the motives and decision processes within the MNC but pays little attention to the host country's policies or other external factors that may affect internalization cost/benefit ratio.

Trade Barriers and Trade Liberation

No matter how we look at it, the internationalization of business and trade appears to perpetuate worldwide prosperity.[13] Despite that fact, not a single country permits international business dealings at will. All impose some sort of barriers to restrict trade and business across national boundaries. But there are reasons for trade barriers as well as for the efforts that have been made internationally to liberate trade. The U.S. effort to promote free trade is particularly interesting.

Trade Barriers

There are two types of barriers that governments impose to restrict foreign trade: tariff and nontariff.

Tariff Barriers *Tariffs* refer to taxes levied on goods moved between nations. The most important of these is the tax usually called the *customs duty* that is levied by the importing nation. But a tax may also be imposed by the exporting nation, and that is called an *export tax*. In addition, a country through which goods pass on the way to their destination may impose a *transit tariff*. The real purpose behind trade barriers is to protect national interest. Exhibit 2.2 lists the major reasons that countries advance for such protection.

Different nations handle tariff barriers differently. A country may have a single tariff system for all goods from all sources. This is called a *unilinear* or *single-column tariff*. Another type of tariff is the *general-conventional tariff*, which applies to all nations except those that

EXHIBIT 2.2
Arguments for Protection

- *Keep-money-at-home argument:* To prevent national wealth from being transferred in exchange with another nation for goods.
- *Home-market argument:* To encourage home industry to perpetuate.
- *Equalization-of-costs-of-production argument:* To make local goods compete fairly against imports that might otherwise be cheaper because of technological advantages or other similar reasons.
- *Low-wage argument:* To protect home industry against competition from imports from low-wage countries.
- *Prevention-of-injury argument:* To safeguard against potential trade concessions that may have to be made in response to multinational trade agreements.
- *Employment argument:* To preserve level of home employment.
- *Antidumping argument:* To prevent dumping of foreign products.
- *Bargaining-and-retaliation argument:* To seek reduction of tariffs by other countries or to retaliate against another country.
- *National security argument:* To be on one's own for national security reasons such as war or natural calamities.
- *Infant-industry argument:* To encourage new industry in the country.
- *Diversification argument:* To promote a broad spectrum of industries in the country.
- *Terms-of-trade argument and the optimum tariff:* To compensate the country for loss in revenue when price elasticity of import demand is greater than zero.
- *The theory of the second-best:* This argument is based on the fact that free trade, while the best alternative, cannot be pursued optimally because of a variety of distortions. As an alternative, new distortions of tariffs may be utilized to neutralize the existing distortions.

Source: Modified from Franklin R. Root, *International Trade & Investment*, 3rd ed. (Cincinnati, OH: SouthWestern Publishing Co., 1983), pp. 306–322.

have tariff treaties (or a convention to that effect) with a particular country. A tariff may be worked out on the basis of a tax permit, called *specific duty*, or as a percentage of the value of the item, referred as *ad valorem* duty. Sometimes both specific and ad valorem duty may be levied on the same item as a combined duty.

Nontariff Barriers *Nontariff barriers* include quotas, import equalization taxes, road taxes, laws giving preferential treatment to domestic suppliers, administration of antidumping measures, exchange controls, and a variety of "invisible" tariffs that impede trade. A. D. Cao has summarized the principal nontariff barriers in the following categories:[14]

1. *Specific limitation on trade.* This category includes the measures that limit the allowable amount of imports, such as *quotas*, referring to quantity or value allowed for specific imported products during a specific period; *licensing requirements*, which obligate exporters and importers of specific products to obtain licenses before trading; *proportion restrictions of foreign to domestic goods*, which limit the quantity of imports to a specified proportion of domestic production; *minimum import price limits*, which require adjustment of import prices to equal or surpass domestic prices; and *embargoes*, which prohibit import of specific products from specific origins.

2. *Customs and administrative entry* **procedures.** This category includes procedural requirements comprising *valuation of imports* (i.e., enforcing a varying valuation process on imported goods that is often left at the discretion of customs officials and is highly arbitrary and discriminatory); *antidumping practices* (i.e., measures against imported goods sold at prices below those in the home market of the exporting country to injure the importing country industry); *tariff classifications* (i.e., arbitrary classification of imported products into a high-tariff category); *documentation requirements* (i.e., enforcing unnecessary and time-consuming bureaucratic requirements); and *fees* (i.e., imposing fees for different services to boost the price of imported goods).

3. *Standards.* This category includes unduly discriminatory health, safety, and quality standards such as *standard disparities* (i.e., imposing higher standards on imported goods than on domestic products); *intergovernmental acceptance of testing methods* (i.e., using tougher testing methods than those used for domestic products to determine the wholesomeness of products); and applying *packaging, labeling, and marketing standards* of the country to imported goods in an unduly stringent and discriminatory way (see International Marketing Highlight 2.1).

4. *Government participation in trade.* This category includes government involvement in trade through *procurement policies* favoring domestic products over the imported ones; *export subsidies* (i.e., providing tax incentives, export credit terms, or direct subsidies to domestic firms); *countervailing duties* (i.e., taxes levied to protect domestic products from the imported products that had been given export subsidy by the exporting country's government); and *domestic assistance programs* (i.e., other forms of assistance given to domestic products to strengthen their position against the imports).

5. *Charges on imports.* This category consists of various types of charges levied on imports to make them less competitive against the domestic goods, including *prior import deposit requirements* (i.e., requiring domestic importers to deposit a percentage of import value with the government before importing); *border tax adjustment* (i.e., levying various taxes on imported products that have been charged to domestic products); *administrative fees* (i.e., making an extra charge for processing import-related requirements); *special supplementary duties* (i.e., unusual charges levied on imports); *import credit discriminations* (i.e., providing credit accommodation to domestic producers); and *variable levies* (i.e., taxing imports at a higher rate than domestic goods). (see International Marketing Highlight 2.2).

6. *Other categories.* These categories include recent measures employed by importing countries to discourage imports such as *voluntary export restraints*, whereby an exporting country, often at the request of the importing country, agrees to limit its exports of a specific product to a particular level, and *orderly marketing agreements*, which refer to explicit and formal agreements negotiated between exporting and importing countries to restrict imports.

████████████   **International Marketing Highlight 2.1**   ████████████

Nontariff Barriers in Japan

Japanese standards are said to be written in a way that often excludes foreign products from the Japanese market. The Japanese standardsetting process is not easily understood, making participation—and even access to information—by foreigners difficult. Other problems include nonacceptance of foreign test data, lack of approval for product ingredients generally recognized as safe worldwide, and the nontransferability of product approval.

America's food processing industry, for example, maintains that these standards are deliberately discriminatory. Unlike the United States and most other countries, whose governments issue lists of additives generally safe for human consumption and a comparable list of substances banned, the Japanese have only one list. A specific additive can be used only for a specific purpose and only in a prescribed amount. Foods containing additives not on the so-called "positive" list may not be imported into Japan, even if those additives are not considered unsafe. The explicit policy of the Ministry of Health and Welfare is against adding ingredients to the positive list.

Regarded as an even more exasperating problem is the fact that Japan does not accept the results of certain testing and certification procedures conducted outside Japan for certain products such as drugs. The United States, on the other hand, generally accepts foreign data from testing done in accordance with appropriate U.S. standards and test procedures.

Furthermore, foreign manufacturers cannot apply directly to Japanese ministries for product approval. Only an approved Japanese entity can hold approval rights. Until recently, if foreign exporters wanted to change agents, their new agents had to reapply for product approval unless their formerly "approved" agents were willing to give up their rights. Of course, American firms could circumvent this constraint by establishing a subsidiary in Japan, but this option is not necessarily open to all manufacturers.

Subsidies, quotas, and monetary barriers are the most common nontariff barriers. Many nations provide *subsidies,* direct payments to select industries to enable them to compete effectively against the imports. For example, since 1980 the U.S. government has been providing a kind of subsidy for the sugar industry to strengthen its position against imports.[15]

Quotas impose a limit on the quantity of one kind of good that a country permits to be imported. A quota may be applied on a specific country basis or on a global basis without reference to exporting countries.[16] The United States, for example, has established quotas for textile imports from particular countries.

Monetary barriers are exchange controls of which there are three widespread types: blocked currency, differential exchange rate, and government approval to secure foreign exchange. *Blockage of currency* totally cuts importing by completely restricting the availability of foreign exchange. This barrier is often used politically against one or more nations. The *differential exchange-rate barrier* refers to the setting of different rates for converting local currencies into the foreign currency needed to import goods from overseas. A government can set higher conversion rates for items whose import it wishes to restrict, and lower rates for imports it does not wish to restrict. Finally, a country may require specific *government approval* before allowing the import of any goods. Most developing countries working toward maintaining a secure foreign exchange position strictly enforce the requirement of obtaining government approval for imports and grudgingly grant it only accompanied by a variety of hindrances and bureaucratic headaches.

━━━━━ **International Marketing Highlight 2.2** ━━━━━

Old Russian Customs

One of the earliest and most educational experiences western managers have in Moscow comes when their possessions pass through Russian customs. Unlike almost any other country, Russia levies import duties—sometimes to the tune of several thousand dollars—on ordinary household removals.

But the latest move by the Russian customs service is making even hardened expatriates blench. In the past, foreign business offices were allowed to import cars, computers, and so forth duty-free, on the understanding that they would eventually reexport them. As of April 1, 1999, this has been cancelled—in a way which leaves foreign companies with potential costs of tens of millions of dollars.

Nor does the customs regime make any allowance for depreciation. In other words, a foreign representative office which has already imported a 1995 Land Rover will now have to pay duty on it—and at its original price ($29,000), rather than its current value (about $12,000). The tariff on new cars is a cool 100 percent. In addition, if any item on a customs declaration is missing, then the whole document becomes invalid. Woe betide the company that has imported, say, an old fax machine and subsequently thrown it away—it risks having to pay additional penalty duties on every other piece of office equipment imported with it. Those who clear their goods late will pay double or treble the usual duties (plus interest, at sky-high Russian rates, from the moment the shipment entered Russia). Even the slightest past infringement leads to the highest category of penalty. Fines of $100,000 and more are, in principle, quite possible on just one car.

Rather than pay the duties, you decide to destroy your imported car? You still pay duty. You arrange to have it stolen? Same result. Even reexporting them may not be possible. Simply removing temporary imports physically from Russia is not enough; the paperwork must be done too.

But for those who know the ropes, theory and practice in Russia are of course different. One western bank has used the services of a security agency run by a well-connected ex-KGB general. For the unfastidious, a corrupt customs officer will charge a few thousand dollars for setting—you hope—everything straight.

Despite squawks of protest, the Russian government—which claims to like foreign investors—has refused to bend. The best offer so far is that, maybe, western companies will be allowed to avoid duties if they donate the goods in question to charities (including those favored by the government, of course).

Source: The Economist, May 8, 1999, p. 68.

Tariff Reduction Programs

Internationally, systematic tariff reduction programs started after World War II. In 1947 the United States and 22 other major trading countries got together in Geneva to find ways to reduce tariffs and remove trade barriers. The **General Agreement on Tariffs and Trade (GATT)** resulted.[17] Since then, eight major efforts to reduce trade barriers have been undertaken under GATT's auspices (see Exhibit 2.3).

The first two rounds, Geneva 1947 and Annecy (France) 1949, are considered significant, both for tariff reduction and for structuring GATT's organization. The Torquay (England) 1951 and Geneva 1956 rounds are regarded as less significant. Insurmountable differences arose among nations over the issue of tariff disparities—that is, the difference between the high tariff of one country and low tariff of another. Next, the Dillon Round in 1962 resulted in further reduction of average world tariff rates. But it fell short of its goals: an across-the-board 20 percent reduction of tariffs and the settlement of problems unresolved since the 1956 meeting, especially those involving trade agreements with less-developed countries.

The Kennedy Round, sixth in the negotiation series, was the most comprehensive round of negotiations in terms of the number of participating countries, the value of the world trade involved, and the size of tariff reductions. The negotiations were concluded in 1972, with tariffs reduced on some 60,000 commodities valued at $40 billion in world trade. Despite its success, the Kennedy Round did not quite meet all the ambitious goals set for it. A major goal was a 50 percent across-the-board reduction in tariffs on industrial products. Overriding national interests forced exceptions to that reduction for such commodities as chemicals, steel, aluminum, pulp, and paper.

The question of tariff disparities, linked with the 50 percent goal, also yielded to exceptions because many Western European countries raised objections. Overall, the Kennedy Round negotiators agreed to tariff cuts on industrial products that averaged about 35 percent. The round was also meant to resolve the problem of nontariff barriers, but the results were rather modest except for the adoption of an antidumping code.

The principal objective of the Tokyo Round in 1973, seventh in the negotiation series, was the expansion and greater liberalization of world trade. The Tokyo Round recognized that the scope of exceptions should be limited and supported the general feeling that the special interests of the developing countries should be borne in mind during the tariff negotiations. This Tokyo Round, concluding in 1978, was the most complex and comprehensive trade negotiating effort attempted to that point. It tried to develop a substantially freer world trading system with balanced opportunities for countries with different economic and political systems and needs. Although the actual achievements fell short of the goals, the overall results of the Tokyo Round were very encouraging.

In the almost 40 years of its existence, GATT can claim some successes: Average tariffs in industrial countries in the mid 1980s tumbled to around 5 percent from an average of 40 percent in 1947. The volume of trade in manufactured goods multiplied twentyfold. GATT's membership increased fivefold. In the 1980s, however, the growing protectionism fostered by the economic difficulties that beset the world in the 1970s served to un-

EXHIBIT 2.3
Dimensions of Agreements under GATT

Major Agreements	Number of Contracting Parties	Value of World Trade Involved (Billions of Dollars)	Percent of Average Tariff Reduction
1947 Geneva	23	$10.0	n.a.*
1949 Annecy, France	33	n.a.*	n.a.*
1951 Torquay, England	37	n.a.*	n.a.*
1956 Geneva	35	2.5	4
1962 Geneva (Dillon Round)	40	4.9	7
1967 Geneva (Kennedy Round)	70	40.0	35
1973 Tokyo (Tokyo Round)	85	115.0	50
1986 Punta del Este (Uruguay Round)	117	530.0	55

*n.a. = not available

dermine the credibility of GATT and threatened the open trading system it upheld. Cars, steel, videos, semiconductors, and shoes followed textiles and clothing into "managed trade." In agriculture, where the United States, the European Union, and Japan were spending a total of $70 billion a year on subsidies, GATT rules proved unworkable. GATT did not cover services (nearly 30 percent of all world trade) or investment abroad or intellectual property (patents, copyrights, and so on), which have been of growing importance to the rich countries as the centers of manufacturing increasingly shift to the developing countries.

It was under such circumstances that in November 1985, 90 countries unanimously agreed to a U.S. proposal to launch a new round of global trade talks, eighth in the negotiation series, in September 1986 in Punta del Este, Uruguay, named the *Uruguay Round*. The focus of this round was on agricultural exports, services, intellectual properties, and voluntary trade limits.

The timing for another round of trade talks could not have been more appropriate. Protectionist forces had been gaining momentum, particularly in the United States. In Europe, where half of all economic activity relates to trade, America's protectionist sentiments had created uneasiness. The Europeans had warned that they would retaliate if the United States adopted protective measures. The developing economies did not know what to do, since the Western nations constituted a big market for their limited exportable products. Individual efforts of different nations to meet the protectionist threat did not succeed. One of the achievements of 40 years of trade liberalization had been the expansion of world trade, which was being challenged in the 1980s. What countries could not accomplish unilaterally, however, they might, it was hoped, be able to accomplish under the GATT umbrella.

The Uruguay Round had generally been acknowledged to be a make-or-break affair for GATT. The intention was to strengthen GATT rules in its traditional areas, especially in agriculture, where the rules were ambiguous; improve its enforcement powers; and extend its scope of neglected areas such as services. But after four years of talks, the Uruguay Round was suspended in December 1990 without an agreement. The talks stumbled over the refusal of various nations to make concessions demanded by various others.

Finally, in December 1993, after tortuous negotiations, trade officials from 117 nations wrapped up a trade pact that slashed tariffs and reduced subsidies globally. It was intended to reduce barriers to trade in goods, including tariffs and such nontariff barriers as quotas, export subsidies, and anti-import regulations. It also was intended to extend the 47-year-old GATT, which functioned as a rule book for international trade, to agriculture, financial, and other services, as well as serving to protect intellectual property such as patents. The Uruguay Round agreement met some of these goals, but negotiators jettisoned several controversial issues at the last minute. Following are its key results.[18]

Tariffs The United States, Europe, and other major industrial powers agreed to eliminate tariffs altogether on pharmaceuticals, construction equipment, medical equipment, paper, and steel. In all, the share of goods imported by developed countries without tariffs should more than double, to 43 percent from 20 percent; for developing countries it should rise to 45 percent from 22 percent. Tariffs also are to be cut substantially on chemicals, wood, and aluminum. Most tariffs on microprocessors would remain at zero, but those on memory chips and others would drop to 7 percent from 14 percent. Industrial tariffs, which now average 4.7 percent of the value of the products traded, would be reduced to an average of 3 percent.

Dumping The agreement provided for tougher and quicker GATT actions to resolve disputes over use of antidumping laws, invoked by the United States and Europe to impose penalties on foreign producers that sell goods abroad below cost. Developing nations, often the subject of such antidumping laws, sought to curtail their use. Nonetheless, the final compromise is closer to the U.S. and European position.

Textiles and Apparel Textiles and clothing are the most important export for many developing countries, accounting for nearly a quarter of their industrial exports. A system of quotas that limited imports of textiles and apparel to the United States and other developed countries, the Multi-Fiber Arrangement, will be phased out over 10 years. Most U.S. textile tariffs would be reduced by about 25 percent.

Intellectual Property The pact provides for 20-year protection of patents, trademarks, and copyrights. However, it allows developing countries at least 10 years to phase in patent protection for pharmaceuticals.

Agriculture Countries that export farm goods will reduce the volume of subsidized exports by 21 percent over 6 years. Bans on rice imports in Japan and South Korea will be lifted. Quotas for imports of sugar, dairy, and peanuts to the United States will be phased out and replaced by tariffs. Initial access to previously closed markets would equal at least 3 percent of domestic consumption; Japan agreed to allow the share of imported rice to increase to 4 percent in 1995 and 8 percent over six years. The largest tariff cuts are for cut flowers; the smallest, for dairy products.

Service Trade in services among GATT members amounts to more than $900 billion a year but has not previously been covered by GATT rules. Developing countries agreed to open their markets in legal services, accounting, and software. However, U.S. negotiators failed to secure access to foreign markets that are largely closed to U.S. banks and securities firms such as Japan, several Southeast Asian nations, and many developing countries. The United States agreed to open its doors to foreign financial-services firms but asserted the right to limit access to firms from nations that fail to reciprocate.

Audiovisual Services Among the very last remaining issues was a dispute between the United States and the European Union, France especially, over European limits on foreign programming shown on European television and the use of taxes on movie tickets and blank videocassettes to subsidize the French film industry. Unable to resolve this thorny issue, negotiators agreed to drop it altogether.

Subsidies The agreement limited government subsidies for research in such goods as computer chips to 50 percent of applied research (that which leads to the first prototype) and 75 percent of basic research, and allowed governments to average the limits for research that was a combination of the two.

Multilateral Trade Organization The agreement created a *World Trade Organization (WTO)* to replace the GATT secretariat. The WTO has more authority to oversee trade in services and agriculture than GATT did.[19]

Estimates by the World Bank and the Organization for Economic Cooperation and Development (OECD) suggest that the Uruguay Round agreement could eventually be worth some $213–$274 billion each year to the world economy.[20] Such numbers, at best sophisticated conjecture, are almost certainly conservative because they do not take into account benefits from strengthening GATT's rules and from liberalizing investment and trade in services. The gains are likely to accrue as follows: European Union, $82 billion, China $38 billion, Japan $29 billion, United States $25 billion, EFTA $15 billion, Latin America $9 billion, other Asian nations $6 billion, and other nations $8 billion (see International Marketing Highlight 2.3).

With the Uruguay Round behind them, at the behest of the United States the WTO members met in Seattle in December 1999 to launch another round of trade talks. The Seattle talks agenda included setting a timetable for global negotiations to lower tariffs, eliminate export subsidies, consider the link between trade rules and labor standards, and initiate talks on trade in agriculture and services. Unfortunately, the talks collapsed, but the delegates from 135 nations agreed to assemble in Geneva for further haggling in a year or two.[21] The main reason for the breakdown of the talks even before getting underway were the protests by more than 35,000 activists who aggressively demonstrated against further globalization. Included among them were the members of the U.S. trade unions and companies who had lost their jobs or businesses to developing countries, as well as those concerned about protection of the environment. But the breakdown of these talks should not be viewed as the end of trade liberalization. Rather, it shows the need for a greater sensitivity to the victims of globalization, wherever they may be (see International Marketing Highlight 2.3).

Despite the problem in Seattle, trade cooperation among nations continues to progress. A noteworthy event has been China's entry into the WTO. In May 2000, the U.S. Congress approved the Chinese deal leading China to joint the WTO as a member. Most of the opposition to China was based on the notion that bringing China into the WTO would make it impossible to get labor and environmental standards incorporated into global trade rules, since China is too big a country to be pushed around.[22] But, under heavy pressure from corporate America, Congress voted for letting China in.

International Marketing Highlight 2.3

Trade and Development: Rich Countries versus Poor Countries

In 1993, when the Uruguay Round, was completed, it was said that poor countries would benefit most. Six years on, that claim sounds rather hollow.

Developing countries have three big complaints. First, they are being forced to open their markets too far, too fast. Second, rich countries are conspiring to keep their markets closed. And third, they lack the resources and information to negotiate effectively, to implement trade agreements, and to exploit world trade rules to their advantage.

The first complaint is wide of the mark. Although developing countries agreed to make deep tariff cuts in the Uruguay Round, that is a gain not a loss. Poor countries benefit from opening their markets, even unilaterally, since consumers can buy cheaper imports, and foreign competition spurs domestic producers to greater efficiency.

But there is a good deal of truth in their other two charges. Rich countries cut their tariffs by less in the Uruguay Round than poor ones did. Since then, they have found new ways to close their markets, notably by imposing antidumping duties on imports they deem "unfairly cheap." Rich countries are particularly protectionist in many of the sectors where developing countries are best able to compete, such as agriculture, textiles, and clothing. As a result, rich countries' average tariffs on manufacturing imports from poor countries are four times higher than those on imports from other rich countries. This imposes a big burden on poor countries. It has been estimated that they could export $700 billion more a year by 2005 if rich countries did more to open their markets.

Poor countries are also hobbled by a lack of know-how. Many had little understanding of what they had signed up to in the Uruguay Round. That ignorance is now costing them dear. A study had indicated that implementing commitments to improve trade procedures and establish technical and intellectual property standards can cost more than a year's development budget for the poorest countries.

Moreover, in those areas where poor countries could benefit from world trade rules, they are often unable to do so. On the whole, poor countries are justified in feeling they get a raw deal.

Source: The Economist, September 25, 1999, p. 89.

U.S. Trade Liberalization

Liberalization of U.S. foreign trade began with the enactment of the Reciprocal Trade Agreement Act of 1934. With that act, Congress authorized the president to reduce then-existing tariff duties by 50 percent. A noteworthy aspect of the act was the inclusion of the *most-favored-nation clause*, which limited discrimination in trade by extending to third parties the same terms provided to contracting parties. This clause has become a fundamental principle of U.S. trade policy.

The Reciprocal Trade Agreement Act of 1934 encouraged bilateral agreements that would increase U.S. exports as long as the exports did not adversely affect domestic industry. In effect, the injury to domestic industry could not take place because of highly protective tariff rates and an item-by-item approach to negotiations that would allow certain commodities to be excluded if a decrease in rates would result in an increase in imports.

The Reciprocal Trade Agreement Act was extended every three years, and by 1945 the United States had concluded negotiations with 29 countries. Overall, the act helped in reducing the average rate of tariffs on taxable imports into the United States from 47 percent in 1934 to 28 percent in 1945. In 1945 Congress authorized the president to cut rates by an additional 50 percent. While the act has been successful in reducing tariff barriers, it did little to reduce such nontariff barriers as quotas and internal taxes.

The second phase in U.S. trade liberalization efforts came in 1947. At that time the United States and 22 other major trading nations negotiated simultaneously for both reduction of tariffs and removal of trade barriers. These efforts, as previously discussed, resulted in the establishment of GATT. GATT institutionalized multilateral tariff negotiations by promoting the unconditional most-favored-nation principle—that is, a tariff reduction given to one trading nation had to apply to all other trading nations that were signatures to the GATT.

The Trade Expansion Act of 1962 marked another phase in U.S. foreign trade policy. This act authorized the president to (1) reduce tariffs up to 50 percent of the rates existing as of July 1, 1962, (2) eliminate tariffs on products in which the United States and Common Market (now European Union) countries together accounted for at least 50 percent of world trade, and (3) eliminate rates that did not exceed 5 percent.[23]

The Trade Expansion Act empowered the president to negotiate across-the-board tariff reductions (rather than item-by-item reductions) and modify the safeguard provisions of the old trade agreements program. As a matter of fact, this act was designed to stimulate not only U.S. exports, but also world trade in general, so that benefits would accrue to all nations as a result of international specialization and trade. When the United States entered trade negotiations for the Kennedy Round, the authority of the Trade Expansion Act of 1962 was in effect.

In the 1970s, despite the urgency for a new international trade perspective, no effective trade legislation was passed by Congress. As a matter of fact, in the 1970s a variety of U.S. government measures hindered rather than helped trade. The Trade Act of 1974 barred export-import credit via the Export-Import Bank, which was established to finance "big-ticket" item exports like aircraft or nuclear power technology. The Foreign Corrupt Practices Act of 1977 imposed jail terms and fines for overseas payoffs by U.S. companies. The Carter administration's human rights legislation denied export-import credit to rights violators. Loans were withheld from South Africa, Uruguay, and Chile. U.S. trade embargoes banned exports to Cuba, Vietnam, Rhodesia, and other countries.

In the 1980s the Reagan administration took a variety of ad hoc measures to deal with emerging crises. In 1982 President Reagan signed the Export Trading Company Act, which was designed to attract manufacturers, export-management companies, banks, freight forwarders, and other export services into joint efforts to gain foreign markets (see Chapter 17). In the fall of 1985, to avert a possible trade war stemming from mounting protectionist pressures in Congress and elsewhere in the nation, the Reagan administration committed itself to join England, France, Germany, and Japan in pressuring the world's financial markets to lower the dollar's value. This action was planned to help the United States reduce its trade deficit. The U.S. government also unveiled a "fair trade" program built around the threat of retaliation against nations that refused to drop barriers to U.S. goods.

A hallmark of the Reagan era was the passage of the Omnibus Trade and Competitiveness Act of 1988 as a long-term solution to the problem of the U.S. trade deficit. This act was the product of a three-year effort involving Congress, the administration, and the business community. It maintained the U.S. commitment to free trade but also provided better trade-remedy tools for judicious use in opening foreign markets.

During the Bush administration, the major emphasis had been on extending the United States–Canada Free Trade Agreement into a truly North American free trade agreement, and on helping Eastern Europe, the former Soviet States, and Latin America toward greater reliance on market forces. Progress continued to be made in implementing the United States–Canada Free Trade Agreement that went into force in 1989, and Congress authorized the president to pursue a similar agreement with Mexico, with the North American Free Trade Agreement (NAFTA) resulting during the Clinton administration.

Early in his administration, President Clinton announced a new export strategy to massively upgrade the U.S. government's trade promotion efforts, in line with the direction set out by Congress in the Export Enhancement Act of 1992. The strategy comprised creating one-stop shops for consolidating federal programs traditionally handled by 19 different agencies, developing a strategic plan for each major country, providing higher-level U.S. government support for foreign government procurement (for example, wooing Saudi Arabia into buying $6 billion worth of Boeing and McDonnell civilian aircraft); increasing the Overseas Private Investment Corporation (OPIC) project limit from $50 million to $200 million (for providing insurance coverage for U.S. companies in developing countries), liberalizing high-tech exports (previously restricted in many nations), and tying foreign aid to American exports.[24] A Trade Promotion Coordinating Committee (TPCC) was established to oversee the implementation of the new export strategy.

In putting together the National Export Strategy, the administration had several assumptions in mind. First, predictions for the American economy, made it clear that no national priority, with the exception of military security, would rank higher than the creation of more and better jobs. To realize this goal, the United States would have to sell more into the marketplace beyond its shores. Second, competition for markets abroad was increasingly brutal. The United States needed to be aggressive and strategic. Traditional competitors such as Japan, France, and Germany, as well as newcomers such as South Korea and Taiwan, had been actively and skillfully seeding new markets and cementing their role as the main supplier of goods and services to countries around the globe. This activity would have to be competed against. Third, many dramatic new opportunities were opening in the world marketplace. In Asia and Latin America, economic growth was healthy, and everywhere governments were turning to open markets, making them significant for U.S.

sales. Fourth, the United States was performing far below its potential. Some 50 firms accounted for nearly half of all exports of goods. Ten states accounted for 64 percent of merchandise exports. There seemed to be tremendous room for export expansion merely if more firms began to think globally.

MNCs and World Markets

Within the last 30 years MNCs have become the most formidable single factor in world trade and investment. They play a decisive role in the allocation and use of the world's resources. They conceive new products and services, create and stimulate demand for them, and develop new modes of manufacture and distribution (see International Marketing Highlight 2.4). Consider the example of Gillette and how it participates in world markets as an MNC.

The Gillette Company

Gillette is the leading manufacturer of blades and safety razors in the world. Its products are sold in more than 200 countries and territories. Although the company's market position varies from country to country, Gillette plays an important role in most blade/razor markets.

The company so dominates shaving worldwide that its name has come to mean a razor blade in some countries. It is the leader in Europe, with a 73 percent market share, and in Latin America, with 91 percent. (In the United States, the company holds a 68 percent share of the net shaving market compared with 13 percent for closest rival Shick.[25]) Indeed, for every blade it sells at home, Gillette sells five abroad, a figure likely to grow as recent joint ventures in China, Russia, and India expand.

The company holds a dominant position in many markets, and in select markets, this dominance extends to its other product lines, such as grooming aids, toiletries, and writing instruments. According to company management, its success in international markets is based on continual efforts at product innovation and improvement, strict quality control, aggressive marketing, and able management worldwide.

In addition to U.S. and Canadian plants, Gillette has manufacturing plants in a number of countries abroad. Shaving products plants are located in Isleworth (United Kingdom), Berlin, Annecy (France), Rio de Janeiro, Buenos Aires, Cali (Colombia), Mexico City, Melbourne, and Seville. These plants serve the host country as well as other countries in the region.

■■■■■■■   **International Marketing Highlight 2.4**   ■■■■■■■

How to Become a Global Company

There is no handy formula for going global, but any company serious about joining the race will have do most or all of the following:

- Make yourself at home in all three of the world's most important markets—North America, Europe, and Asia.
- Develop new products for the whole world.
- Replace profit centers based on countries or regions with ones based on product lines.
- "Glocalize," as the Japanese call it: Make global decisions on strategic questions about products, capital, and research, but let local units decide tactical questions about packaging, marketing, and advertising.
- Overcome parochial attitudes such as the "not invented here" syndrome. Train people to think internationally, send them off on frequent trips, and give them the latest communications technology such as teleconferencing.

- Open the senior ranks to foreign employees.
- Do whatever seems best wherever it seems best, even if people at home lose jobs or responsibilities.
- In markets that you cannot penetrate on your own, find allies.

Source: Jeremy Main, "How to Go Global and Why," *Fortune,* August 28, 1989, p. 76.

During 1999 Gillette derived over 70 percent of its sales and 74 percent of its income from markets outside the United States (excluding Canada)! The company concentrates on three main product areas: shaving, stationery, and small electrical appliances. Razors and blades account for one-third of its sales, but two-thirds of its operating profits.[26]

Organization Traditionally, Gillette International, a division of Gillette Company, was responsible for overseas manufacturing and marketing, which affects almost all of Gillette products including blades and razors, toiletries and grooming aids, and writing instruments. A few years ago, the company restructured its international operations into two groups: Gillette North Atlantic and Gillette International. Gillette North Atlantic integrates the U.S., Canadian, and most of the European operations. Gillette International is responsible for the rest of the world.

Gillette North Atlantic's organization structure integrates European and U.S. operations according to different product groups: blade and razor group, personal care group, and stationery products group. Each group has a North American Division and a European Division, the latter organized into five areas each under the leadership of a general manager as follows: Northern Europe, Western Europe, Southeast Europe, Central Europe, and Iberia.

The integration of European operations within the U.S. organization indicates Gillette's move toward becoming a truly global company. This helps the company take advantage of the European Market integration program.

Gillette International, located at company headquarters in Boston, is organized into three groups: (1) Latin American, (2) Asian-Pacific, and (3) African, Middle Eastern, and Eastern European. Each of the three groups is headed by a group general manager. In addition, there is a staff group called the Gillette International Marketing Department (GIMD), located in Boston and led by a marketing director assisted by individual specialists in each product field and by international coordinators in market research and advertising. These specialists give advice to marketing personnel worldwide.

The organization in each country revolves around a general manager to whom heads of manufacturing, marketing, personnel, and accounting report. Marketing people are employed in sales, market research, sales promotion, and brand management. The Gillette salesforce in each country handles a wide range of Gillette products, including shaving products, toiletries, and writing instruments. The salesforce is organized along the same line in each country and follows essentially the same selling technique.

Decision Making Gillette's global decision-making system is mostly centralized. The recommendations of executives based overseas are sought and considered, but major marketing decisions, including those that concern strategic goals, the price structure, and global advertising, are made in Boston. However, both Gillette International and Gillette North Atlantic are responsible for operational decision making in their own regions.

Within Gillette International, key marketing decisions are generally made at the headquarters level in Boston, where management of the three component regions is also based. Implementation decisions, such as advertising placement and local distribution, are made at the country level.

Subsidiary executives have the authority to set their own prices as long as they stay within the centrally planned positioning strategy. Distribution strategy is similarly planned centrally and adjusted, when necessary, by the subsidiaries.

Advertising campaigns are sometimes fine-tuned at the local level. Promotion campaigns, although developed locally, must also support marketing goals established by headquarters.

Desired price relationships vis-à-vis competing brands and products are defined by product executives at headquarters. Within these parameters, subsidiary executives are responsible for setting prices in their own markets.

As part of its preparation for the post-1992 European Community, Gillette North Atlantic switched to a pan-European packaging strategy that relied less on words and more on symbols to make the same packaging usable in many countries.

Advertising Gillette International's advertising strategy is formulated at the regional level and Gillette North Atlantic's at the product group level. Each uses a single, though different advertising agency to create and coordinate its global campaigns. International retains McCann Erickson whereas North Atlantic primarily uses BBDO Worldwide Advertising Agency.

The decision not to use one agency throughout the world follows logically from the two-region organizational structure Gillette has adopted. Moreover, the company's senior management believes it is unwise to put all its international advertising eggs in one basket. These two agencies were chosen because they were deemed to be particularly strong in the operating region of the respective Gillette entity each is to serve.

Both North Atlantic and International centralize virtually all aspects of advertising. Ads are created at headquarters with only music on the basic soundtrack. Then the various messages to be used in the different countries are dubbed in with voice-overs. Consequently, ads are easily transferable from one market to the next.

In rare instances, when mandated by official regulation, overseas subsidiaries use local actors in locally shot commercials. Even then, however, the creative aspects, including the dialogue, theme, and slogan, are developed in Boston. The Gillette Sensor campaign, "Gillette, the best a man can get," is a good example of the company's global approach.

Foreign Staffing Gillette is firmly committed to staffing foreign subsidiaries with local citizens and third-country nationals. It attributes much of its international success to the strength of its overseas companies and management organizations. The company strives to be perceived as a local company in foreign markets rather than a locally established global company. For this reason, Gillette avoids filling executive openings at its subsidiaries, including those in marketing, with American expatriates.

Within Gillette International, no Americans hold group vice president positions. Latin America is headed by an Argentinean, the Africa/Middle East/Eastern Europe region by a Spaniard, and Asia/Pacific by a Briton. Most general managers are also local nationals or third-country nationals. Within Latin America, six of the seven key general managers are local nationals. Moreover, none of the eight general managers in the Asia/Pacific region is an American.

Gillette North Atlantic is similarly ethnically diverse: The general managers of the company's subsidiaries in Italy, Spain/Portugal, and Northern Europe are Italian, South African, and British, respectively.

Growth Strategy Tailoring its marketing to Third World budgets and tastes—from packaging blades so they can be sold one at a time, to educating the unshaven about the joys of a smooth face—has become an important part of Gillette's growth strategy. The company also tailors its marketing for pens, toiletries, toothbrushes, and other products in developing countries this way. Population trends favor its focus on Third World markets. The market for blades in developed countries is stagnant. Yet the Third World has a very high proportion of people under 15 years old who will be in the shaving population in a very short time. Gillette is in an excellent position to capitalize on this demographic.

Few U.S. consumer-products companies that compete in the Third World have expended as much energy or made as many inroads as Gillette. Since the company targeted the developing world in 1969, the proportion of its sales that come from Latin America, Asia, Africa, and the Middle East has doubled to 25 percent, and the dollar volume has risen eightfold.

In Latin America it began building plants in the 1940s, and Fidel Castro once told television interviewer Barbara Walters that he grew a beard during the Cuban revolution because he could not get Gillette blades while fighting in the mountains. The company's push into Asia, Africa, and the Middle East dates to 1969, when it dropped a policy of investing only where it could have wholly owned subsidiaries. That year, it formed a joint venture in Malaysia, which was threatening to bar imports of Gillette products. Since then it has added one foreign plant nearly every year in countries such as China, Egypt, Thailand, and India.

Gillette always starts with a factory that makes double-edged blades— still popular in the developing countries—and if all goes well, expands later into the production of pens, deodorants, shampoo, or toothbrushes. Only a few ventures have failed: A Yugoslav project never got off the ground, and Gillette had to sell its interests in Iran to its local partners.

Gillette sells familiar products in standardized form all over the world. But in some markets it customizes packaging. For instance, because many Latin American consumers cannot afford a seven-ounce bottle of Silkience shampoo, Gillette sells it in half-ounce plastic bubbles there. In Brazil, Gillette sells Right Guard deodorant in plastic squeeze bottles instead of metal cans (see International Marketing Highlight 2.5). In a few markets, Gillette has developed products exclusively for Third World buyers. The low-cost shaving cream is one. Another is Black Silk, a hair relaxer developed for sale to blacks in South Africa and now being sold in Kenya, Nigeria, and other African countries.

The Gillette case shows how MNCs can capitalize on opportunities far and wide the world over. Having won the loyalty of more than 700 million shavers around the world, from Kashmir to Tierra del Fuego, the company can amortize hefty development costs over fast-growing worldwide markets. Its technique is to establish shaving goods in a new market, then pour a steady stream of other Gillette products through the same retail pipelines. This is the classic approach of a successful MNC. In strictly theoretical terms, MNCs acquire raw materials and capital where they are most abundant, manufacture products where wages and other costs are lowest, and sell in the most profitable markets. In other words, MNCs seek to follow the economic law of comparative advantage—everyone benefits if each does its best work, *no matter where the work is performed.*

Summary

The classic explanation of world trade is provided by the theory of comparative advantage: when one country has an advantage over another in the production of more than one product, then it will enjoy a comparative advantage by producing only the product that provides its greatest advantage and importing the other products in exchange.

■■■■■■■■ **International Marketing Highlight 2.5** ■■■■■■■■

How to Convince People to Shave

The hardest task for Gillette is convincing Third World men to shave. The company recently began dispatching portable theaters to remote villages to show movies and commercials that tout daily shaving. In South African and Indonesian versions, a bewildered bearded man enters a locker room where clean-shaven friends show him how to shave. In the Mexican version, a handsome sheriff, tracking bandits who have kidnapped a woman, pauses on the trail to shave every morning. The camera lingers as he snaps a double-edged blade into his razor. In the end, of course, the smooth-faced sheriff gets the woman.

In other places, Gillette agents with an oversized shaving brush and a mug of shaving cream lather up and shave a villager while others watch. Plastic razors are then distributed free and blades—which, of course, must be bought—are left with the local storekeeper. Such campaigns have a lasting impact.

Source: David Wessel, "Gillette Keys Sales to Third World Tastes," *The Wall Street Journal*, January 23, 1986, p. 35.

Significant world trade and investment patterns in recent years have been examined in various other ways than comparative advantage. Using the concept of product life cycle, Harvard researchers Raymond Vernon and Louis Wells observed that most products are first manufactured in the most developed countries like the United States, then exported to other advanced countries like Japan and those of Western Europe, which soon adapt the product and begin to manufacture it in their own countries. Subsequently, the first manufacturer faces tough competition from the advanced countries not only in its home market but also in the developing countries as well, where cheaper labor is available. This leads the first country to make direct investments in manufacturing in the second countries and thus counter their advantage. Despite this defensive measure, however, the first country may find it difficult to compete. This cycle continues with the result that the developing countries may eventually command the market everywhere.

In response to the limitations of the product life cycle theory, Peter Drucker advanced the concept of production sharing, which postulates splitting manufacturing into stages undertaken in different countries.

Still another theory, internalization, proposes that a firm establishes an international network linking production to its various markets and that this network enables the firm to grow by eliminating external markets in intermediate goods and thus internalizing those markets within the firm.

Two types of trade barriers, tariff and nontariff, have been erected to protect national economies and employment. Efforts at liberalizing international trade in a systematic fashion began after World War II with the establishment of GATT. In all, eight rounds of multilateral negotiations have been held under GATT toward this end. United States legislative efforts have both encouraged and hindered liberal trade with other nations.

Unquestionably, the MNC is the agent of modern day international business. The global business practices of the Gillette Company are illustrative of multinational trade and business in the next century.

Review Questions

1. Differentiate between absolute and relative advantage. Illustrate, with the help of an example, how comparative (relative) advantage encourages trade.
2. Despite the comparative advantage argument, nations continue to opt for self-sufficiency. How would you explain this behavior?

3. What are the limitations of the product life cycle theory of international trade?
4. Use an example to explain the concept of production sharing.
5. What factors lead countries to seek protection against imports?
6. What are the major types of tariffs that nations use against imports?
7. Discuss the major types of nontariff barriers.
8. What role have GATT agreements played in reducing trade barriers?
9. What is the World Trade Organization? What relationship does it have with GATT?

Creative Questions

1. Nontariff barriers continue to be a major deterrent to world trade. Could the forerunner of GATT, the WTO, be entrusted the task of enforcing the implementation of agreed upon rules to eliminate nontariff barriers? Will nations agree to specific rules relative to nontariff barriers? Will they let the WTO punish countries that break the rules?
2. What is the function of the U.S. Trade Representative's Office? How does it differ from that of the U.S. International Trade Commission? For more effective trade policy, should these two organizations be merged?

Endnotes

1. Value can sometimes be uncoupled from production hours, but typically only in cases of long-term scarcity (as with some precious metals) or when the quality of one producer's manufactured products is not matched by other suppliers. In these circumstances, virtual monopolies can develop.

2. See William W. Lewis, Hans Gersbach, Tom Jansen, and Koji Sakate, "The Secret to Competitiveness—Competition," *The McKinsey Quarterly*, November 4, 1993, pp. 29–44.

3. Peter F. Drucker, "Low Wages No Longer Give Competitive Edge," *The Wall Street Journal*, March 16, 1988, p. 23. Also see "Asia's Costly Labor Problems," *The Economist*, September 21, 1996, p. 62.

4. G. Todd Russell, "Business Travelers Rate Asia's Airlines as the World's Best," *The Asian Wall Street Journal Weekly*, November 18, 1985, p. 1.

5. Raymond Vernon, "International Investment and International Trade in the Product Cycle," *Quarterly Journal of Economics*, May 1966, pp. 190–207. Also see Raymond Vernon, *Sovereignty at Bay* (New York: Basic Books, 1971), pp. 65–112; Louis T. Wells, Jr., "Test of a Product Cycle Model of International Trade," *Quarterly Journal of Economics*, February 1969, pp. 152–162.

6. Louis T. Wells, Jr., "A Product Life Cycle for International Trade?" *Journal of Marketing*, July 1968, pp. 1–6. Also see J. F. Hennart, *A Theory of Multinational Enterprise* (Ann Arbor: University of Michigan Press, 1982).

7. James M. Lutz and Robert T. Green. "The Product Life Cycle and the Export Position of the United States," *Journal of International Business Studies*, Winter 1983, pp. 77–94. Also see Sak Onkvisit and John J. Shaw, "An Examination of the International Product Life Cycle and Its Application within Marketing," *Columbia Journal of World Business*, Fall 1983, pp. 73–78.

8. Alicia Mullor-Sebastian, "The Product Life Cycle Theory: Empirical Evidence," *Journal of International Business Studies*, Winter 1983, pp. 95–106.

9. Peter F. Drucker, "The Rise of Production Sharing," *The Wall Street Journal*, March 15, 1977, p. 24. Also see Martin K. Starr, "Global Production and Operations Strategy," *Columbia Journal of World Business*, Winter 1984, pp. 17–22.

10. Peter F. Drucker, "Economics Erases National Boundaries," excerpt ad from *Managing in Turbulent Times* by Peter F. Drucker (New York: Harper & Row, 1979), in *Industry Week*, April 28, 1980, pp. 63–64.

11. Joan Magretta, "An Interview with Victor Fung," *Harvard Business Review*, September–October 1998, pp. 102–117.

12. Peter J. Buckley, *Multinational Enterprises and Economic Analysis* (Cambridge, England: Cambridge University Press, 1982).

13. "The Never-Ending Question," *The Economist*, July 3, 1999, p. 68.

14. A. D. Cao, "Non-tariff Barriers to U.S. Manufactured Exports," *Columbia Journal of World Business*, Summer 1980, pp. 93–102. Also see Alan Bauerschmidt, Daniel Sullivan, and Kate Gillespie, "Common Factors Underlying Barriers to Export: Studies in the U.S. Paper Industry," *Journal of International Business Studies*, Fall 1985, pp. 111–124.

15. "Big Sugar May Be About to Take Its Lumps," *Business Week*, May 15, 1996, p. 45.

16. See: Tacho Bark and Jaime de Melo, "Export Quota Allocations, Export Earnings, and Market Diversification," *The World Bank Economic Review*, 2 (no. 3): 341–348, 1998.

17. At the time of the GATT negotiations, nations were also working toward setting up an international trade organization

(ITO), but the matter was dropped since the participating nations failed to come to an agreement.

18. "The Final Act of the Uruguay Round: A Summary," *International Trade Forum*, No. 1, 1994, pp. 4–21. Also see "Business Aspects of the Uruguay Round Agreements," *International Trade Forum*, No. 2, 1996, pp. 6–10.

19. Helene Cooper and Bhushan Bahrel, "World's Best Hope for Global Trade Topples Few Barriers," *The Wall Street Journal*, December 3, 1996, p. 1.

20. "The Eleventh Hour," *The Economist*, December 4, 1993, p. 23.

21. Helene Cooper et al., "WTO's Failure in Bid To Launch Trade Talks Emboldens Protesters," *The Wall Street Journal*, December 6, 1999, p. A1.

22. "Welcome To The Club," *Business Week*, November 29, 1999, p.34. Also see "China and the WTO: Prepare for Fireworks," *The Economist*, January 22, 2000, p.31.

23. *Future United States Foreign Trade Policy*, report to the president, submitted by the Special Representative for Trade Negotiations (Washington, DC: U.S. Government Printing Office, 1969). Also see Gordon O. Weil, *Trade Policy in the 70s* (New York: The Twentieth Century Fund, 1969).

24. The National Export Strategy," *Business America*, April 1994, pp. 5–10. Also see *Business America*, November 1997, pp. 6–14.

25. Mark Maremont, "Gillette Finally Reveals Its Vision of the Future...," *The Wall Street Journal*, April 14, 1998, p. A1.

26. See Gillette Company's annual report, 1999.

PART 2

Perspectives of International Markets

Global Marketing

After studying this chapter, you should be able to

- Compare market opportunities in different parts of the world.

- Discuss the dimensions of global markets.

- Describe the forces behind market globalization.

- Explain the rationale for segmenting the international market.

- Evaluate different criteria for grouping countries.

There are over 200 countries in the world. It is difficult to imagine that a marketer would be interested in serving the entire global market. Granted, some companies such as Kodak and Coca-Cola are active in over 100 countries. However, such a vast coverage of market develops gradually. Initially, a company may enter just one country or a few countries. From there, the scope may broaden as the company brings other countries within its fold.

Obviously, the company must choose among the countries of the world in order to identify its target markets. Worldwide there is great contrast economically, culturally, and politically among nations. These contrasts mean that an overseas marketer cannot select target countries randomly, but must employ workable criteria to analyze the world market and choose those countries where the company's product or service has the best opportunity for success. While individual countries have peculiarities, they also have similarities that they share with other countries, and such bases render some grouping device feasible.

What are the characteristics of that global marketplace, the international market? What is the rationale for grouping countries into segments? What procedure would a company employ to segment the international market? How can in-country segmentation be achieved?

Global Market

The most basic information needed to appraise global markets concerns population, because the people, of course, constitute the market. The population of the world reached an estimated 6 billion in 1999. According to the latest estimates from the Population Division of the United Nations, this total is expected to increase to 7.2 billion by 2025. Current world population is growing at about 1.3 percent per year. This is a slight decline from the peak rate of 1.9 percent, but the absolute number of people being added to the world's population each year is still increasing. The figure is expected to peak by 2010, at about 75 million additional people per year.[1]

Population growth rates vary significantly by region. Europe has the lowest rate of population growth, at only about 0.3 percent per year. Several European countries are experiencing declining populations, including Austria, Denmark, Germany, Luxembourg, and Sweden. Growth rates are also below 1 percent per year in North America.

The regions with the highest population growth rates are Africa (3 percent per year), Latin America (2 percent per year), and South Asia (1.9 percent per year). China, the world's most populous country, is growing at only about 1.2 percent per year. Even so, that rate means that China's population increases by over 12 million each year. The world's second largest country, India, is growing at over 1.7 percent per year. It reached 998 million in 1999, and is expected to grow to 1.1 billion by about 2010 (see International marketing Highlight 3.1).

One striking aspect of population growth in the developing countries is the rapid rate of urbanization. The urban population is growing at less than 1 percent in Europe and North America, but it is growing at almost 3.5 percent in the developing world. Today 15 of the 20 largest urban agglomerations are in the developing world. By the year 2005, 17 of the 20 largest cities will be in the developing world. The only developed-country cities in the top 20 will be Tokyo, New York, and Los Angeles. The world's largest cities will be Mexico City (26 million), Sao Paulo (24 million), and Calcutta and Mumbai (both over 16 million).[2] These statistics show that the total markets in Europe and North America will not be increasing, because population will not add much to total market size. Of course, these populations are growing older, so that certain segments will have increasing numbers. For example, the total population of Europe increased only 1.6 percent from 1995 to 2000, but the over-65 population increased by 12 percent during the same period.

■■■■■■■■■■   **International Marketing Highlight 3.1**   ■■■■■■■■■■

Babies Are Our Only Customers Worldwide

Gerber Products Co. is going global with a host of child-care products in an effort to break out of its mild-mannered, domestic baby-food niche.

The company has been fine-tuning its "superbranding" campaign for years. It feels it has developed a real following among mothers, and it is going to utilize its brand name to market products in three different categories: food and formula, baby-care products, and clothing.

Market research shows that moms around the globe recognize and trust the Gerber logo. The company's baby food already is sold in Mexico, Puerto Rico, Europe, and the Far East. Sales have expanded into Poland, Egypt, Russia, and Eastern Europe.

However, internationally, the company is an infant. About 95 percent of the babies born in the world are born outside the United States. Yet right now, international sales account for only about 5 percent of the company's total sales.

Gerber will introduce the baby-food lines in new international markets first, then follow with baby-care products and apparel.

Source: Marketing News, September 26, 1991, p. 22.

The population variable provides a snapshot of market opportunity in a country, but a variety of other factors must be considered to identify viable markets. For example, in the developing world, the increase in numbers does not necessarily mean increased market opportunity. The fastest growing region, Africa, is also experiencing low or negative rates of economic growth per capita. Much of Latin America is hampered by huge external debts that force those countries to try to limit imports while using their resources to generate foreign exchange for debt service. In most of these cases, the problem of foreign debt will have to be solved before the growing populations will translate into large markets, despite their economic liberalization programs.

Taking into account factors such as urbanization, consumption patterns, infrastructure, and overall industrialization, let us examine different parts of the global market.

Triad Market

The *triad market* refers to the United States and Canada, Japan, and Western European countries. They account for approximately 14 percent of the world's population, yet they represent over 70 percent of world gross product. As such, these countries absorb the major proportion of capital and consumer products and thus are the most advanced consuming societies in the world. Not only do most product innovations take place in these countries, but they also serve as the opinion leaders and mold the purchasing and consumption behavior of the remaining 86 percent of the world's population.

For example, over 90 percent of the computers worldwide are used by triad countries. In the case of numerically controlled machine tools, almost 100 percent are distributed in the triad market. The same pattern follows in consumer products. Triad accounts for 90 percent of the demand for electronic consumer goods. What these statistics point to is that a company that ignores the market potential of the triad does so at its own peril.[3]

An interesting characteristic of the triad market is the universalization of needs. For example, not too long ago manufacturers of capital equipment produced machinery that reflected strong cultural distinctions. West German machines reflected that nation's penchant for craftsmanship while American equipment was often extravagant in its use of raw materials. But these distinctions have disappeared. The best-selling factory machines have lost the "art" element that distinguished them and have become much more similar, both in appearance and in the level of skills they require to produce. The current revolution in production engineering has brought about ever-increasing global standards of perform-ance. In an era when productivity improvements can quickly determine their life or death on a global scale, companies cannot afford to indulge themselves in a metallic piece of art that will last 30 years (see International Marketing Highlight 3.2).

At the same time, consumer markets have become fairly homogeneous. Ohmae notes,

> The Triad consumption pattern, which is both a cause and an effect of cultural patterns, has its roots to a large extent in the educational system. As educational systems enable more people to use technology, they tend to become more similar to each other. It follows, therefore, that educa-tion leading to higher levels of technological achievement also tends to eradicate differences in lifestyles. Penetration of television, which enables everyone possessing a television set to share so-phisticated behavioral information instantaneously throughout the world, has also accelerated this trend. There are, for example, 750 million consumers in all three parts of the Triad (Japan, the United States and Canada, and the nations of Western Europe), with strikingly similar needs and preferences. . . . A new generation worships the universal "now" gods   ABBA, Levi's and Arpege. . . .Youngsters in Denmark, West Germany, Japan, and California are all growing up with ketchup, jeans, guitars. Their lifestyles, aspirations, and desires are so similar that you might call them "OECDites" or Triadians, rather than by names denoting their national identity.[4]

There are many reasons for the similarities and commonalities in the triad's consumer demand and lifestyle patterns. First, the purchasing power of triad residents, as expressed in discretionary income per individual, is more than 10 times greater than that of residents of developing countries. For example, television penetration in triad countries is greater than 94 percent, whereas in newly industrialized countries it is 25 percent, and for the de-veloping countries less than 10 percent. Second, the technological infrastructure of triad countries is more advanced. Over 70 percent of households there have a telephone, mak-ing it feasible to use such products as facsimile, telex, and digital data transmission/pro-cessing equipment. Such is not the case outside the triad. Third, the educational level is much higher in triad nations than in other parts of the world. Fourth, the number of physicians per 10,000 in triad countries exceeds 30, which creates demand for pharma-ceuticals and medical electronics. Fifth, better transportation infrastructure in the triad leads to opportunities not feasible in less-developed markets. For example, paved roads make rapid adoption of radial tires and sports cars possible.

International Marketing Highlight 3.2

Who Sells What, Where?

There may be "global markets" out there, but "global brands" have not captured them yet. This was the finding of a survey of United States-based manufacturers of consumer non-durable goods. Of the 85 brands included in the survey, 29, or 34 percent, were not mar-keted outside the United States at all. Others were marketed only marginally abroad.

Companies surveyed showed a clear preference for selling their goods in markets cul-turally similar to the United States: Canada and the United Kingdom. While one might argue that Canada was targeted so frequently because of its geographical proximity to the United States, the choice of the United Kingdom cannot be so easily explained. It is as far away as many other foreign countries, and its population and economy are smaller than several other foreign markets.

Among the survey's other key findings:

• *Canada is the star.* Canada was the largest foreign market by far for U.S. brands (33 of the 56 sold abroad). In fact, for 13 brands, Canada is the only foreign market. The United Kingdom was a distant second, being the largest foreign market for five brands. Mexico was next, with four brands, followed by [the former] West Germany with three.

- *Few mega-brands exist.* There were only 14 "mega-brands," ones that could be termed truly global in that they were marketed in more than 50 countries. Those most internationalized were mainly soft drinks, cleaning products, and over-the-counter drugs. Food products rely less on standard branding worldwide.

- *Older products are more international.* An interesting finding was that a majority (57 percent) of the brands sold abroad were launched before 1960. This challenges the notion that new brands are more likely than older brands to be designed for global markets.

- *No name changes.* One might expect the limited distribution of U.S. brands overseas to be offset somewhat by foreign production of exports under different brand names, but this is not the case. Few survey respondents indicated that they sell similar items abroad under different brand names.

Source: International Marketing Review, 6 (1989): 7–19; and *Journal of Advertising,* 17 (1988): 14–22.

Pacific Rim

Despite the recent currency problems of South Korea, Indonesia, and Thailand, the Pacific Rim's growing power is the corporate challenge of the next century.[5] The long-anticipated emergence of the countries in the region (South Korea, Singapore, Taiwan, Hong Kong, Malaysia, Thailand, Indonesia, and the Philippines) as economic powerhouses is shaping up. Steel consumption in the region (including Japan) is higher than in the United States and in Europe. Similarly, demand in the Pacific Rim (again, including Japan) for semiconductors exceeds that of the European Union.

Some view Pacific Rim nations as a better business bet than Eastern Europe. According to them, Eastern Europe's embrace of free enterprise is just a shaky first step toward prosperity, and the hard part will be catching up with the work habits and entrepreneurship of an entrenched capitalistic system. These countries will find it difficult to shed the effects of 45 years of Marxism-Leninism to become "gung-ho" like the Japanese and citizens of the newly industrializing economies.

The Pacific Rim offers a variety of opportunities for American companies, from cars to telecommunications equipment, airline seats and banking services, and a host of other products. However, it is a very competitive market. Not only are potent Japanese companies active in this market, but so are aggressive, growing conglomerates from other countries in the region. Asian producers outside Japan have already gained 25 percent of the global market for personal computers.

Without the fanfare of a common market, the Pacific Rim is becoming an economically cohesive region. A new division of labor is taking place in manufacturing. Japan and the "four dragons"—Singapore, Hong Kong, Taiwan, and South Korea—provide most of the capital and expertise for the region's other nations, which have an abundance of natural resources and labor.

Unlike Japan, other countries in the region are more amenable to buying western products and forming manufacturing alliances with western companies. The point may be illustrated with reference to General Motors Corporation. The company owns a 30 percent stake in a $100 million plant in China that produces up to 60,000 light trucks annually. It has boosted distribution and marketing of Opels in Hong Kong and Singapore. In addition, it exports 14,000 U.S.–made cars to Taiwan annually and plans to assemble 20,000 Opels a year there. Further, it has set up auto assembly operations in Indonesia, Malaysia, and Thailand.[6]

Singapore in particular is promoting what it calls a "growth triangle," in which MNCs can offset the cost of high wages for Singapore's skilled workers by also using lower-paid, less-skilled workers in nearby Indonesia and Malaysia. With the lifting of the

19-year-old trade embargo on Vietnam, another potentially lucrative market has opened in Southeast Asia.

American investments in the region generally pay off handsomely. A U.S. Department of Commerce study showed average annual returns of 31.2 percent in Singapore, 28.8 percent in Malaysia, 17.9 percent in South Korea, 23.6 percent in Hong Kong, 22.2 percent in Taiwan, and 14.1 percent in Japan versus 15.2 percent for U.S. investments in all foreign countries.[7]

For all its burgeoning strength, however, the Pacific Rim faces risks. The region's economic and political stability in the long run could be shaken here and there as strong leaders hand over power, or as they economically overextend. The 1997–1998 currency crisis in the region is a case in point.

The risks of not tapping the region's potential are global. If U.S. companies do not establish a firm position in the region, competitors from Japan, Taiwan, and Korea will gain more strength at home and be prepared to make even bigger assaults on markets in America and Europe.

Postcommunist Countries

The pace of the political transformations that have swept Eastern Europe and the former Soviet Union is unprecedented. As the people of these communist countries toppled their governments, new markets took shape in those regions. The tattered nations are lurching toward a Western economic orbit, and when they reach it, Western Europe's focus will shift eastward. Europe's accent will become more Germanic and Slavic, and its potential economic might will grow to a staggering size—one nearly as large as the United States and Japan combined. As a result, the West stands to gain new markets as well as a labor supply that is well-trained and socially stable. It is a tantalizing prospect that Europe may produce the world's next economic miracle, harnessing the rich dynamism of the West to the untapped talent and energy of the East.[8]

Yet the immediate task of rescuing the backward economies of Eastern Europe is an enormous challenge. Unwinding the command economies without heaping too much pain on the populace is a herculean job. Privatizing industrial units, keeping inflation down, and coping with massive layoffs are some of the difficulties that await. So far, the biggest economies—Czechoslovakia, Hungary, and Poland—are making the most progress. Yugoslavia, racked by ethnic conflict, split into different, warring nations. Less developed Romania and Bulgaria are barely out from under their former rulers.

The challenges are huge, but if the East can forge new links with the West without inflaming the continent's old nationalistic passions, the world may well be headed for a "Pax Europa," with prosperity helping to ensure the peace.

At this time, Eastern Europe is more of a market for foreign investment and aid than for manufactured goods. Since communism crumbled in 1989, foreign investors have been looking hard at Eastern European countries. By the end of 1993 almost 15,000 foreign joint ventures had been established in Poland, Hungary, and former Czechoslovakia.[9] Once the changeover to the market economy is complete, these countries should offer attractive markets, but it is impossible to predict how long the process will take.

Experts claim that Eastern Europe's progress depends on two factors: its ability to attract adequate capital and the ability of the people to tolerate hardships during the changeover. According to one estimate, the cost of modernizing industry and infrastructure in Eastern Europe would be $500 billion over the next 15 to 20 years.[10] Considering the enormity of the task, it may be safe to say that Eastern Europe markets cannot evolve into mass markets on Western lines for another 20 years. In the interim, there will be an ad hoc opportunity for selling capital equipment, telecommunications, and, from time

EXHIBIT 3.1
Household-
Equipment
Ownership: Percent
of Households, in
Selected Countries

	Czech Republic	Hungary	Romania	Ukraine
CD players	27	18	8	3
Color television sets	94	89	70	84
Deep freezers	66	60	24	2
Microwaves	42	40	2	3
Mobile phones	12	18	4	1
Personal computers	15	16	6	1
Telephones (regular)	64	73	39	35
VCRs	40	46	15	16

Source: *The Central and Eastern European Consumer,* OECD, 1999.

to time, limited amounts of consumer goods. As Exhibit 3.1 shows, the household-equipment ownership in Eastern Europe is small except for color television sets. People are still making only modest changes in this respect.

The Commonwealth of Independent States poses similar problems. Russia is taking drastic steps to liberalize its economy quickly. The country is adopting a high-risk austerity program to stabilize its collapsed economy and integrate it with the rest of the world's. Russian leaders are convinced that only a radical reform program can save the country from a return to dangerous central control. However, many wonder if too much is being done too soon. Although prices have begun to increase at a slower pace, and more food is available in stores, enterprises around the country are hurting badly, and unemployment is increasing sharply. At the same time corruption is rampant.

Time is clearly of the essence. With economic pain stirring, Russia could become explosive. On the other hand, Russia could emerge as a healthy economy in the early years of the new century.

To westerners, Russia offers both a challenge and an opportunity. By and large, companies are optimistic about the country, and they are carefully watching its progress. If the economic measures succeed, Russia will offer all sorts of attractive opportunities.

Among other members of the commonwealth, the Baltics (Estonia, Latvia, and Lithuania) are expected to switch to market economies sooner than others. With a total population of less than 8 million, these countries are mere blips on the map of Europe, but they have a highly motivated, well-trained, and low-paid work force. Baltic workers are more productive than Russian workers, and the Baltic countries could emerge as a viable market if their goods could be sold for hard currency in Western Europe. But it is highly uncertain whether those goods could compete in today's European market, even at lower prices, considering the fact that those nations have been isolated from the West for more than 50 years, Even so, there are plenty of companies willing to wait several years until they can establish a manufacturing or service operation in the Baltics to take advantage of the emerging Russian market.

Opportunities in other former Soviet republics are hard to pinpoint at this time. Five of them (Azerbaijan, Uzbekistan, Turkmenistan, Kyrgyzstan, and Tajikistan) have joined Iran, Turkey, and Pakistan to become part of an Islamic common market. Presumably, their economic perspectives would be determined by the policies pursued by their Muslim brethren. Largely Christian Georgia and Armenia will stay closer to Russia in their endeavor to revamp their economies. The direction that Moldavia, Ukraine, and Byelorussia may adopt is uncertain. For example, Moldavia might link up with Romania, while Ukraine and Byelorussia may follow an independent course. In any event, considering their smaller populations, they are unlikely to offer any substantial market opportunity.

Latin America

As governments cut tariffs, welcome foreign companies, and unshackle their economies, market opportunities in Latin America abound. The severe miseries of the 1980s shocked the Latin countries into abandoning the statism, populism, and protectionism that had crippled their economies since colonial times. One after another in the late 1980s, governments in Latin America thrust their businesspeople into the free market, cutting tariffs, welcoming foreign investment, and unloading hopelessly unprofitable state enterprises. Debt is becoming manageable now, and incomes are growing.

The United States has a better opportunity in the region than other nations, since it has the inside track. Western European nations are largely occupied with Eastern Europe, and the Japanese remain focused mainly on developed countries.

Latin America is more attractive, especially to U.S. firms, than Eastern Europe. It can feed itself and has a business infrastructure, albeit rickety. U.S. trade with the region is already 15 times greater than with Eastern Europe. Indeed, Latin America holds the key to the U.S. trade deficit. Per capita consumption of basic foods and beverages in Latin America should continue to grow over the long term. The region's appealing demographics—notably, an expanding population segment of 15- to 50-year-olds and rising household incomes—bode well for U.S. companies in these sectors (see International marketing Highlight 3.3). But new entrants face two distinct challenges: brand loyalty and complex distribution demands. Well-established names and operations have a strong edge in Latin America, and some could endure for years despite growing competition. Foreign brands meet with greater acceptance where there are no home-grown equivalents. For instance, most countries have no local colas and few domestic snack-food brands. This fact accounts for the regionwide success of Coca-Cola and Sabritas, PepsiCo's snack unit.[11]

Latin America's distribution channels are fragmented, particularly in Mexico, where a large proportion of sales occur at mom-and-pop stores, in which shelf space is limited. The rise of supermarkets and hypermarkets, however, which carry many more brands, is facilitating distribution for new players.

International Marketing Highlight 3.3

Segmenting the Latin American Market

Gallup came up with four major categories of Latin American consumers and eight segments within those categories.

The "traditional elite" is 9 percent of the total population and 11 percent of the effective market base, the percentage of the total population excluding the 17 percent extreme poverty population. This segment's monthly income is equivalent to at least U.S. $1,800.

The "emerging professional elite" comprise 12 percent of the total population and 14 percent of the market base, with a monthly income of at least $1,800.

The middle class makes up 27 percent of the population and 33 percent of the market base with a monthly income of $800 to $1,800. The "progressive upper middle class" is 11 percent of the population and 13 percent of the market base. The "self-made middle class" is 9 percent and 11 percent respectively, and the "skilled middle class" is 7 percent and 9 percent, respectively.

The working class, which is 35 percent of the population and 42 percent of the effective market base has a monthly income of less than $800 and contains the "self-skilled working class" (11 percent, 13 percent), the "industrial working class"(12 percent, 14 percent), and the "struggling working class"(12 percent, 15 percent).

Gallup estimates there are 5.5 million traditional elites and 7 million emerging professional elites. Other segments and their estimated populations: progressive upper middle class, 6.5 million; self-made middle class, 5.5 million; skilled middle class, 4.5 million;

self-skilled working class, 6.5 million; industrial working class, 7 million; and struggling working class, 7.5 million.

Sixty-one percent of the self-made middle class and 54 percent of the industrial working class engaged in activities with children. The lowest participation was among traditional elites (34 percent) and emerging professional elites (35 percent).

Buying toys ranked highest among the industrial working class (43 percent bought them), self-made middle class (37 percent), and traditional elite (35 percent). The lowest interest was shown by the self-skilled working class (23 percent), the struggling working class (24 percent), and the emerging professional elite (27 percent).

Movie-going ranked highest among the emerging professional elite (63 percent attended movies), traditional elite (58 percent), and progressive upper middle class (55 percent). Only 29 percent of the self-skilled working class goes to the movies.

Fifty-three percent of the traditional elite, 49 percent of the progressive upper middle class, and 49 percent of the industrial working class buy perfume.

Buying records is most popular among the traditional elite (52 percent), emerging professional elite (48 percent), progressive upper middle class (48 percent), and industrial working class (40 percent).

Source: Marketing News, August 14, 1998. p.5.

Although opportunities beckon, Latin America still suffers from acute economic problems. For example, inflation continues to be high, and the debt problem still looms large. Slow or disappointing progress could turn the poor against free markets and back to a populist, anti-Yankee leader. Nonetheless, the rewards could outweigh the risks. Latin American consumers prefer U.S. products. Capital goods companies (e.g., telecommunications, transportation systems, mining and manufacturing equipment) have a special opportunity as these countries make investments to globalize their businesses.

China and India

China and India are by far the two most populous developing countries on earth. Notwithstanding the large differences in history, politics, and culture that separate them, the size of their populations and the vastness of their lands have stimulated similar responses to the changing global business environment. Both countries seek self-sufficiency, and at the same time are liberalizing their economies to link themselves to the global network.

Since the Tiananmen Square killings in 1989, China has become suspect in western capitals. Yet business opportunities in the country continue to grow. For example, Procter & Gamble launched its China efforts in the Guangzhou region in 1988, focusing on two products, Head & Shoulders shampoo and Oil of Olay skin cream. Both were quick hits. Avon started in 1990 and sold six months' worth of inventory in the first 30 days. Capital goods companies—for instance, Lockheed and Westinghouse—had similar experiences.

Despite communism, capitalistic values are slowly permeating certain parts of the country, particularly the delta area closer to Hong Kong. After the accession of Hong Kong to China, the level of business activity in the country, and hence the market opportunity, has accelerated. If a firm has the patience to endure endless negotiations and maddening bureaucratic tangles, China may provide it with a growing market.

It would be a mistake, however, to assume that the Chinese market will soon emerge on western lines. Only a few Chinese families have annual incomes approaching western standards. Chinese citizens who bring home more than Rm 40,000 ($4,800) constitute less than 0.2 percent of the total population. The average urban household headed by a state-sector employee sees just Rm 4,185 ($505) in disposable income annually; in wealthy cities like Beijing and Nanjing, this sum rises by about 45 percent. In economically robust Guangzhou, the average family makes about $1,250 annually.

Though the average person's cost of living is much lower in China, even urban residents continue to spend a large proportion of their income on food—about 46 percent in 1997. This leaves 12 percent for clothing, 10.7 percent for entertainment and education, 7.6 percent for household goods, and just 4.6 percent for the other purchases. Just 6 percent of families own a car[12] (see International Marketing Highlight 3.4).

■■■■■■■■■■ **International Marketing Highlight 3.4** ■■■■■■■■■■

Not Quite a Billion

It is easy to overestimate the buying power of China's elite consumers. Together they represent no more than 30 million people in cities such as Beijing, Shanghai, Guangzhou and Shenzhen. And for the most part, they are not rich by world standards: according to the latest official government survey, the top 10 percent of city dwellers have an average annual disposable income of just $1,240 a person.

On the other hand, if GDP per head is adjusted for purchasing power, the incomes of the top 10 percent of city dwellers is probably closer to $10,000 a year. The prevalence of wide-screen televisions, fancy stereos, and home-karaoke machines in Shanghai apartments suggests that this new upper-middle class has more money than it admits to. Supposing that the real wealth of affluent Chinese lies somewhere between the two estimates, China's potential market must be somewhere between those of Belgium and Australia.

Put like that, China looks hefty, but not gigantic. But compare China today with China in 1985 (the first year the country conducted comprehensive consumer surveys), and it is clear that China's growth has been rapid.

Among urban households, fewer than one in five households had a color television in 1985; today the average such home has more than one. Then 7 percent had a refrigerator; now 73 percent do. Cameras are four times more common. Among richer urban households, more than half now have a VCR or video CD machine, a pager, air-conditioner and shower, and nearly a third of homes also own a mobile telephone. Every year, millions more Chinese join the ranks of this high-spending elite.

Source: The Economist, January 2, 1999, p.56

India's economic growth has occurred in a political culture that places a high value on national self-reliance and social equity. Thus, despite the fact that India is the world's largest democracy, in the realm of business it has pursued socialist policies. In recent years, however, dismayed by discouraging economic performance, India has started liberalizing the economy. In the early 1990s the government took drastic measures to encourage foreign investment and promote capital markets and exports. The current government aims to establish a worldwide economy through a large-scale liberalization by freeing foreign investment conditions, cutting down protection for Indian industry, and streamlining bureaucratic procedures, but the process is slow and uncertain.

Further, India is in the throes of a middle-class revolution that could transform its attitude toward business. The middle class accounts for some 200 million people and is growing rapidly. The rise of the middle class has sparked a boom in a variety of consumer products, durable and nondurable, a market once confined to a wealthy few. More and more foreign companies are taking advantage of the changing business conditions in India. Recently, such well-known corporations as Timex, Kellogg, and McDonald's have entered the Indian market, something that would have been impossible in the 1980s.

By and large, most Chinese and Indians have low incomes and thus lead spartan lives, as illustrated in Exhibit 3.2, showing standard of living comparisons between China, India, and the United States As incomes in the two giants go up, slowly market opportunities

EXHIBIT 3.2
Standard of Living
Comparisons for
China, India, and
United States: In
Percentages

Standard of Living Indicators	China	India	U.S.
Own an automobile	3	2	90
Have running hot water	1	4	98
Have access to sanitation	24	29	99
Have electricity	95	58	99
Have a telephone	9	7	97
Own a color television set	40	12	97
Own a refrigerator	25	12	97
Own a cat	6	6	31
Own a VCR	6	12	83

Source: Gallup India Pvt. Ltd.

will emerge. But which products to introduce, in what form, and when are the challenges that MNCs face in these frugal markets.[13]

Developing Countries

A basic management reality in today's economic world is that businesses operate in a highly interdependent global economy, and the 100-plus developing countries are very significant factors in the international business arena. They are the buyers, suppliers, competitors, and capital users. In order to determine market opportunity in developing countries, it is important to recognize the magnitude and significance of these roles.

Traditionally, developing countries (including India and China, some Pacific Rim nations, and most Latin American countries) have provided a market for about one-third of all U.S. exports. The largest U.S. exports to developing countries are machinery and transport equipment, agricultural products, and chemicals, but all major product categories share in these markets (see International Marketing Highlight 3.5).

International Marketing Highlight 3.5

"Hmmm. Could Use A Little More Snake"

On any weekday morning, a dozen or so consumers take the elevator to the 19th floor of Cornwall House, a nondescript office building that's home to Campbell Soup Co.'s Hong Kong taste kitchen. There they split off into carrels and take their seats before bowls of soup and eager food scientists. Chosen carefully to get the right demographic mix, such groups are assembled to taste the offerings that Campbell hopes will ignite consumer interest in China and other parts of Asia.

The menu might include cabbage soup, scallop broth, or a local delicacy, such as pork, fig, and date soup. After up to an hour of tasting and observing, the technicians get their answers. Too much pork? Enough scallops?

Such insights are crucial to Campbell as it tries to create new products to whet regional appetites. Diet is a function of local culture, and Asia in particular puts huge demands on a western food company seeking to crack its exotic markets. Campbell opened the Hong Kong kitchen in 1991 to reach 2 billion Asian consumers.

Cooking up regional specialties isn't easy. Fewer than 1 in 20 varieties tested may hit the stores. Nonetheless, Campbell can score big if it gets the formula right. At an average of one bowl a day, the Chinese are among the highest per capita soup eaters in the world.

Campbell enters new markets gingerly. It typically launches a basic meat or chicken broth, which consumers can doctor with meats, vegetables, and spices. Then it brings out more sophisticated soups. The Hong Kong kitchen already has a couple of hits to its credit—new scallop and ham soups came out of the lab. Campbell has also discovered a few surprises. Among the company's biggest sellers across Asia are such U.S. standbys as cream of mushroom and cream of chicken, which researchers believe attract westernized Chinese. One Campbell breakthrough in China, watercress and duck-gizzard soup, was developed in the United States

Local ingredients may count, but Campbell draws the line on some Asian favorites. Dog soup is out, as is shark's fin, since most species are endangered. However, the kitchen staff keeps an open mind when it comes to other fare.

Source: Business Week, March 15, 1993. p. 53.

U.S. business with the developing countries follows closely the economic growth trends recorded in those countries. For example, U.S. exports declined sharply in the early and mid 1980s as purchasing power in those countries was reduced by debt-service problems, declining commodity prices, and the global recession. By 1987, however, these markets recovered more rapidly. U.S. exports to those countries showed a 16 percent gain over the preceding year, compared with increases of only 9 percent in sales to developed countries.[14]

Developing countries are likely to become more important in the global economy in the new century. Market opportunity in these countries rests on their ability to develop economically. That development will depend on two factors:[15] (1) their governments' willingness to encourage growth through liberal monetary and fiscal policies, and (2) the capacity of their managers to operate the productive apparatus in an efficient, effective, and equitable manner.

Traditionally, the U.S. trade focus has been on Europe and Japan. Whereas the industrial nations will continue to be our largest markets for decades to come, another category of country holds far more promise for large incremental gains in exports. These nations, the *"Big Emerging Markets" (BEMs),* comprise the Chinese Economic Area (China, Hong Kong, Taiwan), Indonesia, South Korea, India, Turkey, South Africa, Poland, Argentina, Brazil, and Mexico. The U.S. Department of Commerce estimates that nearly three-fourths of the growth in world trade in the next two decades is likely to take place in the developing countries. Most of this expansion will occur in the BEMs. The BEMs are likely to double their share of world GDP in that time, from today's 10 percent up to 20 percent. By the year 2010, their share of world imports is likely to exceed that of Japan and the European Union combined.

The BEMs will also be the competitive battleground of the future. Japan, Europe, and several developing countries can be expected to be fierce rivals in these markets.

Pursuing U.S. interests in these countries will require deft balancing of commercial and foreign policy considerations. It is in the BEMs that commercial opportunities coexist so closely with the complications of human rights, worker rights, nuclear nonproliferation, and violations of intellectual-property laws. The BEMs, moreover, have enough political influence and aspiration to often effectively challenge U.S. policies in multilateral organizations such as the International Monetary Fund (IMF), the WTO, and the United Nations.

Dimensions of the Global Market

Socioeconomic statistics can help international marketers segment the international market and thus formulate marketing strategy. This macro information is conveniently available from such international organizations as the United Nations, the World Bank, the IMF, and the Organization for Economic Cooperation and Development (OECD). The information relates to such economic aspects as population, income, trade, private consumption expenditures, total stock of durable goods (e.g., passenger cars, trucks, and buses), service facilities (e.g., telephone access lines), consumption of basic materials (e.g., cement, steel), average hourly wage rates, and other.

An example of useful macro information is the fact that per capita GDP of most Western European countries is over $15,000, while that of most Asian countries (except Japan, Hong Kong, South Korea, Taiwan, and Singapore) is less than $1,000. Per capita GDP of the two largest countries (China and India) is $750 and $430, respectively (1998 dollars). Moreover, in most developed countries, the average hourly wage is more than $5, while in most developing countries it is less than $1. In some countries (Sri Lanka, for example), it is as low as $0.19 an hour.

As can be expected, total private consumption expenditures are much higher in industrialized countries than those in the middle- and low-income brackets. By the same token, ownership of passenger cars and other durable goods, as well as consumption of energy and basic materials, is skewed in favor of advanced countries. As a matter of fact, it is the low level of energy consumption and meager use of such materials as steel and cement that characterize less developed countries.

Based on this kind of information, *Crossborder Monitor* has identified the 12 largest markets in the world (see Exhibit 3.3). Interestingly, 5 of these 12 markets are the developing countries of Russia, Mexico, China, Brazil, and India. Obviously, it would be foolhardy for a company to treat all developing countries alike. Some developing countries offer a better market opportunity than the industrialized countries.

EXHIBIT 3.3
Size, Growth, and Intensity of World's 12 Largest Markets

Major Markets	Market Size (% of World Market)		Market Intensity (World = 0)		Cumulative Five-Year Market Growth (%)
	1991	1996	1991	1996	1996
United States	19.55	20.46	5.13	5.60	7.61
Japan	9.85	10.09	4.98	5.82	8.33
China	9.38	8.80	0.23	0.23	36.29
Germany	4.62	5.66	4.65	4.96	15.65
India	4.87	5.04	0.13	0.12	33.39
France	3.50	3.73	4.05	4.60	2.77
Italy	3.57	3.60	4.15	4.38	2.59
United Kingdom	3.11	3.42	3.64	4.13	0.48
Russia	—	2.75	0.96	0.95	−25.08
Brazil	2.53	2.58	0.85	0.98	31.07
South Korea	1.53	2.10	—	2.66	55.45
Canada	1.96	1.95	4.66	4.32	9.04

Market intensity measures the richness of the market, or the degree of concentrated purchasing power it represents. Taking the world's market intensity as 1, the EIU has calculated the intensity of each country or region as it relates to this base. The intensity figure is derived from an average of per capita ownership, production, and consumption indicators. Specifically, it is calculated by averaging per capita figures for automobiles in use (double weighted), telephones in use, TVs in use, steel consumption, electricity production, private consumption expenditure (double weighted) and the percentage of population that is urban (double weighted).
Market size shows the relative dimensions of each national or regional market as a percentage of the total world market. The percentages for each market are derived by averaging the corresponding data on total population (double weighted), urban population, private consumption expenditure, steel consumption, electricity production and ownership of telephones, passenger automobiles and televisions.
Market growth is an average of cumulative growth in several key economic market indicators: population; steel consumption; electricity production; and ownership of passenger automobiles, lorries, buses, and TVs.
Source: *Crossborder Monitor*, November 4, 1998, p. 12.

An interesting characteristic of global markets is their emerging universality. In other words, a one-world market exists for products ranging from cars to consumer electronics to carbonated drinks. Firms today are engaged in world competition to serve consumers globally (see International Marketing Highlight 3.6). It must be cautioned, however, that each nation still has its own cultural peculiarities. Thus, a firm cannot assume that in each case what is good for the home country is good for the world.

A number of broad forces have led to growing globalization of markets:

1. *Growing similarity of countries.* Because of growing commonality of infrastructure, distribution channels, and marketing approaches, more and more products and brands are available everywhere. This fact proves that similar buyer needs exist in different countries. Large retail chains, television advertising, and credit cards are just a few examples of once isolated phenomena that are rapidly becoming universal.

2. *Falling tariff barriers.* Successive rounds of bilateral and multilateral agreements have lowered tariffs markedly since World War II. At the same time, regional economic agreements such as the European Union have facilitated trade relations among member countries.

3. *Strategic role of technology.* Technology is not only reshaping industries, but contributing to market homogenization. For example, electronic innovations permit the development of more compact, lighter products that are less costly to ship. Transportation costs themselves have fallen with the use of containerization and larger-capacity ships. Increasing ease of communication and data transfer make it feasible to link operations in different countries. At the same time, technology leads to an easy flow of information among buyers, making them aware of new and quality products and thus creating demand.

Global markets offer unlimited opportunities. However, competition in these markets is intense. To be globally successful, companies must learn to operate and compete as if the world were one large market, ignoring superficial regional and national differences. Corporations geared to this new reality can benefit from enormous economies of scale in production, distribution, marketing, and management. By translating these benefits into reduced world prices, they can dislodge competitors who still operate with the perspectives of the past. Thus, companies willing to change their perspectives and become global can attain sustainable competitive advantage (see International Marketing Highlight 3.7).

Segmenting the Global Market

A *market segment* refers to a group of countries that are alike in respect to their responsiveness to some aspect of marketing strategy. *Market segmentation* may be defined as a technique of dividing different countries into homogeneous groups. The concept of segmentation is based on the fact that a business cannot serve the entire world with a single set of policies, because there are disparities among countries—both economic and cultural. An international marketer, therefore, should pick out one or more countries as the target market. A company may not find it feasible to do business immediately with the entire spectrum of countries forming a segment. In that case, the firm may design its marketing programs and strategies for those countries it does enter and draw upon its experience with these countries in dealing with new markets.

■■■■■■■■■■   International Marketing Highlight 3.6   ■■■■■■■■■■

Global Disorientation

She arrives on her British Airways flight, rents a Toyota at the Hertz desk in the terminal, and drives to the downtown Hilton hotel. She drops into a chair, flips on the Sony television, and gazes glassily at this week's scandal on "Dallas." Room service delivers dinner along with the bottle of Perrier and the pack of Marlboro cigarettes she ordered. While eating dinner she catches herself nodding off, but is brought back to consciousness by a sudden feeling of disorientation. Is she in Sydney, Singapore, Stockholm, or Seattle? Her surroundings and points of reference over the past few hours have provided few clues.

With the expansion of the international economy and the growth of international business in the post–World War II era, the marketplace has taken on a recognizably similar face in countries around the globe. No longer is the overseas traveler surprised to see a familiar logo flashing from a neon sign or to find a favorite brand from home on sale in a foreign location. The most interesting phenomenon is not just that MNCs have entered the foreign markets. Increasingly, it has become evident that the same few companies compete against each other for leadership positions in numerous national markets worldwide. In automobiles, construction equipment, consumer electronics, cameras, office copiers, airframes, computers, and a variety of other industries, not more than half a dozen MNCs dominate the major markets worldwide.

Source: From a note entitled "Global Competition and MNC Managers," by Christopher A. Bartlett, Harvard Business School, 1985.

International Marketing Highlight 3.7

Why Go Global?

The rules for survival have changed since the beginning of the 1980s. Domestic markets have become too small. Even the biggest companies in the biggest countries cannot survive on their domestic markets if they are in global industries. They have to be in all major markets. That means North America, Western Europe, and the Pacific Rim countries.

Take, for example, the pharmaceuticals business. In the 1970s, developing a new drug cost about $16 million and took four to five years. The drug could be produced in Britain or the United States and eventually exported. Now, developing a drug costs about $250 million and takes as long as 12 years. Only a global product for a global market can support that much risk. No major pharmaceuticals company is in the game for anything other than global products. That helps explain a series of mergers of major drug companies, most recently the marriage of Bristol-Myers and Squibb.

Source: Fortune, August 1989, p. 70.

The importance of segmentation can be illustrated by reference to Massy-Ferguson Ltd., a Toronto-based farm equipment producer. As far back as 1959, this company decided to concentrate on sales outside North America and thus avoid competing head-on with Ford Motor Company, Deere & Company, and International Harvester Company. It took the company years to implement successfully its segmentation strategy before reaching a point where it derives almost 70 percent of its sales outside North America. As a matter of fact, as the market matured in North America, Massey continued to grow and earn substantial income, since demand overseas accelerated while it slowed down in North America. Whereas Ford, Deere, and International Harvester struggled hard to maintain profitability, Massey-Ferguson, because of its decision to avoid the North American segment, showed a fine performance.

To survive and prosper in the increasingly competitive global marketplace many companies are learning to find and dominate "niche markets." For companies of all kinds and sizes, nichemanship is rapidly becoming the new business imperative.

Simply defined, a *niche* is a relatively small segment of a market that the major competitors or producers may overlook, ignore, or have difficulty serving. The niche may be a narrowly defined geographic area, or it may relate to the unique needs of a small and specific group of customers, or it may target some, highly specialized aspect of a very broad group of customers. In some cases, the niche market may actually be very large in numbers of customers even though it is a small percentage of a company's total customer base, particularly if the company operates globally.

The possibilities for niche marketing are virtually endless. So too are the opportunities, as effective niche strategies can be extremely profitable. By focusing on a niche market, companies often develop an excellent understanding of their customers' operations—and how those customers make money. This understanding, in turn, provides an edge when it comes to identifying opportunities for new products and marketing programs. Emphasis on a niche provides a very clear focus for the development of business strategies and action plans.

The importance of niche strategy may be illustrated by the experience of Linear Technology, a Canadian firm.[16] It successfully carved out a niche in the world integrated circuit ("chip") business. Although this market, as a whole, is dominated by major Japanese and American firms, Linear Technology dominates the global market for one narrow segment—audio amplifier chips for hearing aids. Even in Japan, it has achieved more than a 50 percent market share in competition with companies like NEC. By having a broad product line within its specialized area and by focusing on the needs of one set of customers, it has managed to beat all competitors.

A basic problem in market segmentation is choosing the right criteria. Traditionally, geography has been employed to divide the world. However, segmentation based on geography is often less useful than that based on economic and cultural differences among countries.

For example, the countries of the Middle East in no way constitute a homogeneous market. Iran, Iraq, Kuwait, the United Arab Emirates (UAE), Saudi Arabia, Egypt, and Lebanon are all very different. Lebanon has had special problems, while all the others have different legal and political systems. The UAE has no formal business laws at all, Saudi Arabia has fairly new and sophisticated statutes; Egyptian law has a long history and is based on French law. Lately, the Middle Eastern countries have attempted to present a common economic posture through tariff regulations, duties, and the like. But a foreign company cannot take full advantage of these measures because the natural fragmentation of Middle Eastern markets is reinforced by the inherent nationalist tendencies. Therefore, it is not possible for a company simply to go into the cheapest or most liberal country and expect to maximize its profit by trading into the whole area from that base.

The Middle East situation illustrates the point that world markets need to be grouped judiciously for effective market segmentation, and this requires evaluation of culture, law, and politics in order to identify the dimension(s) to be employed in classifying the countries.

Segmentation Process

Five procedural steps should be followed to determine the segmentation criteria for world markets:

1. Develop a market taxonomy for classifying the world markets.
2. Segment all countries into homogeneous groups—that is, groups having common characteristics with reference to the dimensions of the market taxonomy.
3. Determine theoretically the most efficient method of serving each group.
4. Choose the group in which the marketer's own perspective (its product or service and its strengths) is in line with the requirements of the group.
5. Adjust this ideal classification to the constraints of the real world (existing commitments, legal and political restrictions, practicality, and so forth).

A company interested in expanding business overseas can utilize this procedure by first deciding on a criterion for classifying the countries for its product. Not all countries should be analyzed, but only those that appear to offer real potential.

For example, a machine tool manufacturer might segment countries based on need: those requiring simple machines (first-generation machine tools), those requiring medium-size machine tools (say, second-generation machines), and those requiring large, sophisticated machines. The company may find it is well placed to serve the second segment, where medium-size machine tools are needed. Let us assume the following countries fall into this segment: Malaysia, Brazil, Thailand, Indonesia, Philippines, Mexico, and Turkey. To serve this targeted segment, the company might establish three assembly plants, one in Turkey, one in Brazil, and one in Malaysia (assuming other countries in the geographic area would be served through exports from these three countries). However, because the machine tool industry often encounters a lack of scientific personnel in such foreign countries, the company might choose to establish an assembly plant in India (instead of Malaysia), which has a large pool of scientific talent, to serve the Asian part of its segment. It might do so even though the Indian market is highly competitive. This is what is meant by adjustment of the ideal system to the real world.

Criteria for Grouping Countries

As is true in domestic market segmentation, countries of the world can be grouped using a variety of criteria. For example, a company could group world markets (countries) based on a single variable such as per capita GNP or geography. Similarly, religion or political system might serve as a criterion. Alternatively, a combination of a few selected variables could be used—such as political system, geography, and economic status (GNP per capita)—or a large number of variables could be used, similar to what is done in establishing lifestyle or psychographic segments in domestic marketing.

Following is a discussion of economic status grouping, geographic grouping, political system grouping, grouping by religion, cultural grouping, multiple-variable grouping, and intermarket grouping. The discussion ends with a recommended scheme for country classification called the *portfolio approach.*

The choice of an appropriate grouping method depends on the nature of the product. For example, a defense equipment manufacturer would classify countries based on their political systems, whereas an appliance company would look at their economic status.

Economic Status Grouping The simplest way to form economic groups is to classify countries on the basis on GNP per capita. For example, countries with GNP per capita of more than $12,000 might be classified as high-income countries, those with GNP of $1,000 to $7,500 as middle-income, and those with GNP of less than $1,000 as low-income. If we follow this scheme, about 55 countries will fall in the low-income category, 50 in the middle-income category, and 23 will be considered high-income.[17] (Economic status groupings should be differentiated from regional market agreements, discussed in Chapter 7, which are formed using more than strictly economic considerations.)

There is no empirical study showing the economic status classification of countries by GNP per capita to be a viable system. Furthermore, based on domestic marketing experience, it is questionable if a single variable should be used to group countries into homogeneous categories. For example, GNP per capita of Kuwait, UAE, and Hong Kong would put them in the category of industrialized countries, but these countries by no means constitute the same market as industrial countries such as the United States, Germany, Italy, and so on. Additionally, emphasis on economic status alone in classifying countries misses the crucial impact of cultural differences among nations.

The grouping of countries based on GNP per capita assumes, like other economic criteria for segmentation, that market behavior is directly related to income. In domestic marketing, a number of studies have questioned the relevance of income as a discerning variable. In the international arena as well, sole reliance on GNP per capita for international comparisons is considered inadequate. For example, in 1998 Pakistan had a per capita GNP of $480 versus India's $430. However, if the purchasing power of a dollar in the two countries is considered, the per capita GNP for Pakistan comes out to $1,560 in U.S. dollars while that for India is $1,700.[18]

Geographic Grouping One popular way of grouping nations is to classify them along regional lines. Many MNCs organize their worldwide operations into such regions as Western Europe, Latin America, Far East (including Australia and New Zealand), Middle East, and Africa. Geographic grouping of countries has several advantages. First, geographic proximity makes it easier to manage countries blocked together. For example, all countries in Latin America can be managed, say, from a regional headquarters in Brazil. Both transportation and communication are easier to handle on a regional basis. Consider the difficulties of ignoring geographic proximity: Suppose Argentina is grouped with Italy, Spain, and New Zealand, while Brazil is grouped with South Korea, Taiwan, and India (assuming some viable basis). One can see the challenges in managing these far-flung countries as one market.

Moreover, nations in the same geographic region often share cultural traits. And another factor that supports regional classification of countries is the post–World War II organization of countries into trading groups, such as the European Union (EU), MERCOSUR and NAFTA. These organizations are regional in character; that is, countries in the same geographic region decided to join with each other to become large economic entities. Typically, members of a group agree to trade freely with each other without any barriers. In fact, the EU countries go even further and levy common external tariffs. From the point of view of an international marketer, the existence of common economic arrangements among nations by means of groups means that entry into one country will automatically smooth entry into another country belonging to the same group; the same marketing strategy perspective can be applied to one or all. Thus, geographic division of countries appears sound.

Despite these reasons, geographic lumping of countries to form market segments is not always sound. Geographic proximity of countries does not automatically guarantee the same market opportunity for international business. For example, the Philippines and Thailand do not provide as viable markets as Singapore, Malaysia, South Korea, Taiwan, and Hong Kong, even though all these countries are in the same geographic region. Similarly, Mexico is geographically part of the same continent as the United States and Canada, but Mexico obviously differs culturally and economically from the other two.

Political System Grouping Another way of grouping countries is to classify them by their political perspective—For example, democratic republic, dictatorship, communist dictatorship, or monarchy. These categories are used simply to facilitate discussion. As appropriate to a marketer's purposes, they may be refined further. For example, the two-party system of the United States, the multiparty systems of Italy, Israel, and Germany; and the single-party system of Mexico could be used. Dictatorships could be classified as either military or civilian.

Once a suitable set of political categories has been worked out, countries in each group can be considered as homogeneous for purposes of developing marketing strategy. In other words, one marketing strategy would be relevant for the firm's international business with all the countries in a particular political group.

Using politics as the segmentation criterion for grouping countries, Nigeria, Bangladesh, and Argentina would have belonged in the same category in 1988. All then had military dictators, with inclinations toward holding free elections to establish democratic governments. However, from the vantage point of the multinational marketer, their political closeness did not render them potentially similar markets. Argentina was economically much closer to the Western European countries. Nigeria's economic potential is linked with oil prices. And highly populated Bangladesh, ranked among the low-income countries of the world. The differing economic perspectives of the three countries would obviously negate the validity of their grouping according to political environment for marketing purposes.

Grouping by Religion Religion constitutes an important element of society in most cultures. It greatly influences lifestyle, which in turn affects marketing. Following this logic, religion could work out to be a viable criterion for marketing segmentation. What has been said of Latin America, for example, applies to many other parts of the world in regard to different religions.

> The life of the family and of the individual is greatly and continuously involved with the Church. One must not exaggerate the implications of this relationship of the individual, the family, and the community to the Church. But one should also be careful not to underestimate it. It gives the life a certain quality and adds something to the meaning of daily activities which is lacking in the United States.[19]

Religion can be defined as the quest for the values of the ideal life and as involving three components: the ideal itself, the practices for attaining the ideal, and the theology or worldview relating the quest for the ideal to the surrounding universe. This definition relates religion to virtually all aspects of a country's life—its aesthetics, its material culture, its social organization, its language, and even its politics and economics.

Animism, Buddhism, Christianity, Hinduism, Islam, and Judaism are the major religions of the world. Religion as an aspect of cultural environment is discussed in Chapter 9. Briefly, however, animism is a prehistoric form of religion—ancient religion without religious texts. Animism today is found all over the world but is practiced most obviously in African countries. Some Latin American religious practices have animistic tendencies as well.

Hinduism, defined more as a way of life than a religion, is practiced mostly in India. Considered to be 4,000 years old, it reflects a complex set of tenets and beliefs but lacks a common creed or dogma.

Buddhism sprang from Hinduism in India in the sixth century B.C. Buddhists are found mainly in Southeast Asia and Japan. In Burma, Sri Lanka, Thailand, Laos, and Kampuchea it is the dominant religion. There are some Buddhists in western countries, and, presumably, in the People's Republic of China as well.

Judaism is the monotheistic religion of the Jewish people, tracing its origin to Abraham, having its spiritual and ethical principles embodied chiefly in the Bible and the Talmud. Jews do not belong to one race of people. The term *Jew* applies correctly to anyone who is a member of the Jewish faith. Nationally speaking, Jews are Germans, Arabians, Americans, and almost everything else.

Islam is practiced by over 500 million people, living in about 30 countries. The Islamic countries are located mainly in the Middle East, Northern Africa, and South Asia. Islam defines a total way of life. It includes legislation that organizes all human relationships.

Christianity, sometimes referred to as the religion of the Western World, is found all over the globe. With the Protestant Reformation, Christianity increased its emphasis on individuality. Although marked differences exist between the two major divisions of Christianity, Roman Catholicism and Protestantism, both stress similar values such as achievement and thrift. Interestingly, the Protestant countries in particular rank economically among the highest in the world in terms of GNP per capita.

The effect of religion on lifestyle makes it a relevant criterion for grouping countries. Yet the formulation of a common marketing strategy for a group of countries following Islam, or any one religion, may not suffice. Both Pakistan and Saudi Arabia are strong adherents of Islam. However, the economic differences between the two countries would invalidate lumping them together for marketing decision making. Saudi Arabia, with a per capita GNP of $7,740 (1998 estimate), is a customer for a variety of consumer and industrial products. On the other hand, Pakistan, with its per capita GNP of $480 (1998 estimate), offers a very low potential for international marketers. Similarly, France and the Philippines, both primarily Catholic countries, cannot be served by following the same marketing perspective. In brief, while religion via culture plays an important role in determining lifestyle, by itself it may not serve as a viable criterion for grouping countries.

Cultural Grouping Presumably, countries of similar cultures should be amenable to the same marketing strategy. To an extent, cultural groupings make sense, since lifestyle is affected strongly by culture. The problem lies in determining what constitutes a cultural category. Unless we use a variable like religion to serve as a surrogate for culture, it will not be easy to establish cultural categories.

One way to divide countries into homogeneous country groups is to use Geert Hofstede's approach. According to him, the way people in different countries perceive and interpret their world varies along four dimensions: power distance, uncertainty avoidance, individualism, and masculinity.[20]

Power distance refers to the degree of inequality that the population of a country considers acceptable (i.e., from relatively equal to extremely unequal). In some societies, power is concentrated among a few people at the top who make all the decisions. People at the other end simply carry these decisions out. Such societies are associated with high power-distance levels. In other societies, on the other hand, power is widely dispersed, and relations among people are more egalitarian. These are cultures of low power distance.

Uncertainty avoidance concerns the degree to which people in a country prefer structured over unstructured situations. At the organizational level, uncertainty avoidance is related to such factors as rituals, rules orientation, and employment stability. As a consequence, organization personnel in less structured societies tend to face the future as it takes shape without experiencing undue stress. Risk-avoidance behavior is less common in these societies. Their managers abstain from creating bureaucratic strictures that would make it difficult to respond to unfolding events. In contrast, managers in cultures of high uncertainty avoidance engage in activities like long-range planning to establish protective barriers to minimize the anxiety associated with future events.

Individualism denotes the degree to which people in a country are encouraged to act as individuals rather than as members of cohesive groups (i.e., from collectivist to individualist). In individualistic societies, people are self-centered and independent. They seek the fulfillment of their own goals over the group's goals.

Managers belonging to individualistic societies are competitive by nature and show little loyalty to the organizations they work for. In collectivistic societies, members have a group mentality. They subordinate their individual goals to work toward the group goals. They are interdependent and seek mutual accommodation to maintain group harmony. Collectivistic managers have high loyalty to their organizations and subscribe to joint decision making.

Masculinity refers to the degree to which "masculine" values emphasizing assertiveness, performance, success, and competition prevail over "feminine" values emphasizing the quality of life, personal relationships, service, care for the weak, and solidarity. Masculine cultures exhibit different roles for men and women, and tend to perceive "big" as "important." People in such societies are more likely to have a need to be ostentatious than those in feminine societies. Feminine cultures value "small as beautiful," and stress quality of life and environment over purely materialistic gains.

Although the four variables identified by Hofstede for discerning cultural categories appear reasonable, they would require dividing countries into 12 groups—an enormous task of questionable value.

Multiple-Variable Grouping A number of studies in marketing literature have used a large number of variables to form country clusters (cluster analysis).[21] The argument behind the use of multiple variables has been that countries relate to each other in accordance with their cultural, religious, socioeconomic, and political characteristics. Therefore, all of these characteristics should be considered in forming international segments, not just geographic proximity or economic status.

An important grouping study by S. Prakash Sethi used 29 variables to cluster 91 countries.[22] First, a large number of variables were collapsed into smaller, more meaningful groups, or clusters, called *variable clusters* or *V-clusters.* These were discriminatory variables such as GNP, cars, and single-family homes per capita. Second, countries were scored on the basis of each V-cluster. *O-analysis,* meaning *object analysis,* was used, with each country considered an "object" and a large number of countries classified into subgroups called *O-clusters* or *O-types.* The scores were used to identify O-types with similar characteristics.

The multiple-variable approach attempts to combine countries with similar social-economic-political perspectives into segments, but it falsely assumes that countries are indivisible, heterogeneous units.

Intermarket Grouping In recent years, a refined approach for segmenting the market has been suggested in which groups of customers who are alike in different countries form homogeneous segments. In other words, each country's market consists of different segments, and each segment consists of customers from different countries.[23] These segments are called *intermarket segments* (see International Marketing Highlight 11.6).

Assume a U.S. chemical manufacturing company is interested in foreign expansion. The company manufactures different types of chemicals such as pharmaceuticals, fine chemicals, and fertilizers. In its attempts to segment the world market, the company may find small farmers in developing countries a segment worth serving. These customers, whether from Pakistan, Indonesia, Kenya, or Mexico, appear to represent common needs and behavior patterns. Most of them till the land using bullock carts and have very little cash to buy agricultural inputs. They lack the education and exposure to appreciate fully the value of using fertilizer, and they depend on government help for such things as seeds, pesticides, and fertilizer. They acquire their farming needs from local suppliers and count on word-of-mouth to learn and accept new things and ideas. Thus, even though these farmers are in different countries continents apart, and even though they speak different languages and have different cultural backgrounds, they may represent a homogeneous market segment.

Take the case of Mercedes-Benz. It has a worldwide market niche among the well-to-do. Even in Japan, Mercedes is considered the most popular foreign luxury car. Similarly, a designer of men's clothing may find that elites of different countries compose a single market segment. For another company, the teenagers of different countries may work out to be a viable segment (see International Marketing Highlight 3.8). In Exhibit 3.4 the behavioral traits of two intermarket segments: global elite and global teenagers, illustrating the significance of forming segments across nations.[24]

A recent study showed that the following four major types of consumers dominate the world, and their purchase decisions are heavily influenced by the wealth of their nations.[25]

EXHIBIT 3.4   Behavioral Aspects Related to the Identification of Global Consumer Segments

	Global Elites	Global Teenagers
Shared Values	Wealth; success; status	Growth; change; future; learning; play
Key Product Benefits Sought	Universally recognizable products with prestige image; high-quality products	Novelty; trendy image; fashion statement; name brands/novelty
Demographics	Very high income; social status, and class; well-traveled and well-educated	Age 12–19; well-traveled; high media exposure
Media/Communications	Upscale magazines; social-selective channels (i.e., cliques); direct marketing; global telemarketing	Teen magazines; MTV; radio; video; peers; role models
Distribution Channels	Selective (i.e., upscale; retailers)	General retailers with name brands
Price Range	Premium	Affordable
Targeted by Global Firms	Mercedes Benz, Perrier, American Express, and Ralph Lauren's Polo, etc.	Coca-Cola Co., Benetton, Swatch International, Sony, PepsiCo, Inc., etc.
Related Microsegments/Clusters	Affluent women; top executives; highly educated professionals; professional athletes	Preadolescents; female teens; male teens
Factors Influencing Emergence of Segment	Increased wealth, widespread travel	Television media; international education

Source: Salah S. Hassan and Lea Prevel Katsanis, "Identification of Global Consumer Segments," *Journal of International Consumer Marketing*, 3 (2): p. 24. 1994

---

1. "Deal makers": 29 percent of 37,743 respondents from 40 countries concentrate on the process of buying. This is a well-educated group, median age 32, with average affluence and employment.
2. "Price seekers": 27 percent place primary value on the product. This group has the highest proportion of retirees, the lowest education level, mostly female, and has an average level of affluence.
3. "Brand loyalists": 23 percent of the respondents and the least affluent are brand loyalists. The group is mostly male, median age 36, who hold average education and employment.
4. "Luxury innovators": 21 percent seek new, prestigious brands and are the most educated and affluent shoppers, with the highest proportion of executives and other professionals. The group is mostly male with a median age of 32.

In the United States, 37 percent are deal makers, 36 percent price seekers, 17 percent luxury innovators, and 11 percent brand loyalists. Deal makers predominate in Asia, Latin America, and the Middle East. Price seekers dominate in Europe and Japan.

Price seekers exist mainly in competitive, developed markets like Europe and Japan where shoppers generally cannot haggle or negotiate. Deal makers are more often in developing markets that have less brand competition and a tradition of bazaars and open-air markets, where the process of buying is half the fun. The United States straddles the two styles because of its heterogeneous culture and also because shoppers can bargain at many retail outlets and even large category-killer stores.

The concept of intermarket segmenting is relevant not only on a worldwide basis, but especially within a region. For example, it would be a mistake to suppose that women all over the world have similar cosmetic-usage behavior patterns. Like other lifestyle behavior, cosmetic use is deeply affected by culture. Muslim women are supposed to veil in public so cosmetic use among them is likely to be very low. Some Latin women consider excessive cosmetic usage as self-indulgence. Others do not —depending on the specific region. Thus, from the viewpoint of a cosmetic company, stereotyping people globally could prove unproductive. Instead, grouping people in a region where culture and economic conditions do not vary substantially from country to country may represent a viable segment.

Applying the concept of intermarket segmentation in Europe, many companies are pursuing the idea of a *Eurobrand,* that is, a product or brand designed for a market consisting of niches in different Western European countries. The development of satellite communication makes it feasible to simultaneously reach customers in different countries, which would not have been possible through the traditional television channel.

International Marketing Highlight 3.8

The Global Teen Segment

In the world divided by trade wars and tribalism, teenagers, of all people, are the new unifying force. From the steamy playgrounds of Los Angeles to the stately boulevards of Singapore, kids show amazing similarities in taste, language, and attitude. African Americans, Asians, Latinos, and Europeans are zipping up Levi's, dancing to the Red Hot Chili Peppers, and punching the keyboards of their IBM PCs. Propelled by mighty couriers like MTV, trends spread with sorcerous speed. Kids hear drumbeats a continent away, absorb the rhythm, and add their own licks. For the Coca-Colas and the Nikes, no marketing challenge is more basic than capturing that beat. There are billions to be earned.

Teens almost everywhere buy a common gallery of products: Reebok sports shoes, Procter & Gamble Cover Girl makeup, Sega and Nintendo videogames, PepsiCo's new Pepsi Max. They're also helping pick the hits in electronics, from Kodak cameras to Motorola beepers. Teen choices are big business. Last year America's 28 million teenagers spent $57 billion of their own money. In Europe, Latin America, and the Pacific Rim, a swath of over 200 million teens are converging with their American soul mates in a vast, free-spending market that circles the globe.

Source: Shawn Tully, "Teens—The Most Global Market of All," *Fortune,* May 16, 1994, p. 9. ©1994 Time Inc. All rights reserved.

Portfolio Approach The *portfolio approach,* as shown in Exhibit 3.5, proposes dividing countries on a three-dimensional basis according to country potential, competitive strength, and risk. Following this method, 18 country segments are obtained.

Country potential in the portfolio approach refers to the market potential for a firm's product or service in a given country and is based on such factors as population size, rate of economic growth, real GNP, per capita national income, distribution of population, industrial production and consumption patterns, and the like. Both internal and external factors determine *competitive strength.* In a given country, the *internal factors* include the firm's market share; its resources; and facilities, including knowledge of the unique features of that country and the skills and facilities it owns to match these features. *External factors* include strength of competitors in the same industry, competition from industries of substitute products, and the structure of the industry locally and internationally. *Risk*—that is, political risk, financial risk, and business risk (like change in consumer preferences)—is any factor that causes variation in profit, cash flow, or other outcomes generated by involvement in a country.

This approach has the following advantages:

- It is three-dimensional, which implies greater representativeness of the multinational environment.
- Its dimensions are relevant to marketing.

EXHIBIT 3.5   International Market Taxonomy Matrix for Classifying Countries

Competitive Strength

	Strong	Average	Weak	
High				High
				Medium
Risk				Low — **Country Potential**
Low				High
				Medium
				Low

- It treats risk as a separate dimension, which makes it close to the real-world situation, since many countries of the world could have high potential and be attractive if not for a high degree of risk.
- Each of the dimensions is a composite measure of a variety of subfactors. For example, neither GNP nor income level, by itself, is adequate as a descriptor of overall country potential.
- It uses an 18-cell matrix with three levels each of the country-potential and competitive strength dimensions, and two levels of risk. This feature is important, because the world contains not only highs and lows, but middle positions as well.

The portfolio approach requires an abundance of information, both internal and external to the firm, which may not be easy to collect and analyze. Additionally, this approach is more relevant for use at a product or market level than at a headquarters level. Thus, a company involved in marketing a number of products or services abroad would have to work out a number of segmentation schemes. The scheme, however, makes strategic sense and provides an important framework for analyzing opportunities for chosen products in select markets that appear to be potentially viable.

In-Country Segmentation

So far the discussion has dealt with grouping the countries of the world, but the concept of segmentation also is relevant *within* a particular country. Just as markets are segmented in the United States, so can they be segmented in other countries, using simple demographic and socioeconomic variables, personality and lifestyle variables, or situation-specific events (such as use intensity, brand loyalty, attitudes).

For example, a U.S. food company segmented the French market into modern and traditional segments, defining the modern French consumer as liking processed foods while the traditional type looks upon them with disfavor. A leading industrial manufacturer discovered that the critical variable for segmenting the Japanese market was the amount of annual usage per item, not per order or per any other variable. A toiletries manufacturer used geographic criteria—urban versus rural markets in South Africa. Exhibit 3.6 provides an inventory of different bases for market segmentation. Most of these bases are covered in any principles of marketing text.

Besides products and customers, a market can also be segmented by level of customer service, stage of production, price-performance characteristics, credit arrangements with customers, location of plants, characteristics of manufacturing equipment, channels of distribution, and financial policies.

The key is to choose a variable or variables that will divide the market into segments of customers who have similar responsiveness to some aspect of the marketer's strategy. The variable (or variables) should be measurable; it should represent an objective value such as income, rate of consumption, or frequency of buying, not simply a qualitative viewpoint such as the degree of customer happiness. Also, the variable should create segments that could be responsive to promotion. Even if it were possible to measure happiness, for instance, segments based on a happiness variable cannot be reached by a specific medium. Thus, happiness cannot serve as an appropriate criterion because it is not easily manipulated.

Once segments have been formed, the next strategic issue is deciding which ones should be targeted. Criteria are as follows:

1. The segment should be one in which the maximum differential in competitive strategy can be developed.

EXHIBIT 3.6
Bases for Segmentation

1. Demographic factors (age, income, sex, etc.)
2. Socioeconomic factors (social class, stages in the family life cycle)
3. Geographic factors
4. Psychological factors (lifestyle, personality traits)
5. Consumption patterns (heavy, moderate, and light users)
6. Perceptual factors (benefit segmentation, perceptual mapping)
7. Brand and loyalty patterns
8. Product attributes

2. The segment must be capable of being isolated so that competitive advantage can be preserved.
3. The segment must be valid, even though imitated.

Summary

Worldwide there are over 6 billion people living in about 200 countries. Not all people, however, are potential consumers. The global market may be divided into different regions, affording different market opportunities, such as the triad market, Pacific Rim market, postcommunist countries, Latin America, China and India, and developing countries. The richest and most advanced among these is the triad market.

An interesting aspect of today's international business is the globalization of markets. World markets are slowly becoming homogeneous, requiring companies to develop marketing programs to serve consumers across national boundaries. A company interested in marketing abroad needs to decide which countries to enter and how those countries could be grouped together in homogeneous categories. The use of categories limits the need for developing marketing programs for each country separately and permits countries in each group to be served through a common marketing program.

Countries may be classified by such criteria as their economic status, geographic location, cultural traits, religious perspective, political system, socioeconomic-political characteristics, or common intermarket characteristics. In addition, a new approach for grouping countries, the portfolio method, recommends grouping countries based on three factors: competitive strength, risk, and country potential.

The concept of segmentation in the context of international marketing can be carried to another level, that is, segmentation of the in-country market. Just as the U.S. market is segmented in different ways, it may be desirable to segment the market within each country and choose one or more segments to be served. The process of accomplishing in-country segmentation is essentially the same in international marketing as in domestic marketing.

Review Questions

1. What factors make the triad market most attractive?
2. What forces account for the growing globalization of markets?
3. Does the Pacific Rim market (excluding Japan) or the Eastern European market appear to offer better market opportunities?
4. What is the rationale for grouping countries for marketing strategy?
5. Even countries that appear to be the same in so many ways—the United Kingdom and Canada, for example—can nevertheless be very different. Thus, does grouping of countries really help in making sound marketing decisions?
6. Discuss the following: "Philosophical imposition of political boundaries as the starting point in the matter of segmenting the world market is superfluous and dysfunctional. Why should we segment countries? We should rather segment the customers of the world. After all, it may be hypothesized that high-income people, whether living in the United States, France, Brazil, India, Nigeria, Egypt, Sweden, or Mexico, provide a similar potential for a product. If this is true, then it is customer segmentation on a worldwide basis that should be sought and not country classification. Income, education, geography, political views, age, and a host of other demographic and socioeconomic criteria may be used to segment the world market."
7. What are the variables used in the portfolio approach to classify countries? What problems do you anticipate in adapting the portfolio approach in practice?

Creative Questions

1. According to the U.S. government, the most growth in the next century will be in 10 nations called the Big Emerging Markets (comprising China, Indonesia, South Korea, India, Turkey, South Africa, Poland, Argentina, Brazil, and Mexico). Should this list be refined? Which countries should be added to this list? Why? Which countries should be dropped?

2. Often a case is made for making investments in developing countries on the basis that their long-run business potential is high. However, the term "long run" usually is not defined. Should the MNCs invest money in developing countries on the assumption that long-run benefits are assured? If not, should these countries be ignored until they present sustainable business opportunity?

Endnotes

1. *Time,* November 2, 1999, p. 86.

2. *The Futures Group Reports,* March 1989.

3. Kenichi Ohmae, *Triad Power* (New York: The Free Press, 1985).

4. Ibid., p. 23.

5. Rob Norton, "Why Asia's Collapse Won't Kill The Economy," *Fortune,* February 2, 1998, p. 26.

6. See "U.S. Automakers in Asia," in Subhash C. Jain, *International Marketing Management,* 6th ed. (Storrs, CT: Digital Publishing Co., 1999), pp. 824–831.

7. Louis Kraar, "The Rising Power of the Pacific," *Fortune,* Pacific Rim Issue, 1990, p. 80.

8. "Ready to Shop Until They Drop," *Business Week,* June 22, 1998, p. 104.

9. Paul Hofheinz, "Yes, You Can Win in Eastern Europe," *Fortune,* May 16, 1994, p. 110. Also see "Partners-Partness," *Business Week,* October 25, 1999, p. 106.

10. Shawn Tully, "What Eastern Europe Offers," *Fortune,* March 2, 1990, p. 51.

11. Malt Moffett and Helene Cooper, "In Backyard of the U.S., Europe Gains Ground in Trade, Diplomacy," *The Wall Street Journal,* September 18, 1997, p. 1.

12. *Country Monitor,* September 29, 1999, p. 8.

13. "How Not to Sell 1.2 Billion Tubes of Toothpaste," *The Economist,* December 3, 1994, p. 79.

14. *The Global Century: A Source Book on U.S. Business and the Third World* (Washington, D.C.: National Cooperative Business Association, 1989).

15. "Africa: A Flicker of Light," *The Economist,* March 5, 1994, p. 21.

16. Federal Industries (a Canadian firm) Annual Report, 1986.

17. *World Development Report:* 1999 (New York: Oxford University Press, 1999).

18. Ibid.

19. Lane Kelley and Reginald Worthley, "The Role of Culture in Comparative Management: A Cross-Cultural Perspective," *Academy of Management Journal* 1 (1981): pp. 164–173.

20. Geert Hofstede, *Cultural Consequences: International Differences in Work-Related Values* (London: Sage Publications, 1980).

21. See Ellen Day, Richard J. Fox, and Sandra M. Huszagh, "Segmenting the Global Market for Industrial Goods: Issues and Implications," *International Marketing Review,* Autumn 1988, pp. 14–27.

22. S. Prakash Sethi, "Comparative Cluster Analysis for World Markets," *Journal of Marketing Research,* August 1971, pp. 348–354. *Also see* Kenneth Matsuura, *A Classification of Countries for International Marketing,* Master's thesis, University of California, Berkeley, 1968.

23. "Citibank in Indonesia: Targeting the Affluent," *Crossborder Monitor,* July 13, 1994, p. 8.

24. Salah S. Hassan and Lea Prevel Katsanis, "Identification of Global Consumer Segments," *Journal of International Consumer Marketing* 1994 3 (no. 2): p. 24.

25. Kelley Shermach, "Portrait of the World," *Marketing News,* August 28, 1995, p. 20. Also see: Tom Miller, "Global Segments from 'Strivers' to 'Creatives,'" *Marketing News,* July 1998, p. 11.

Appendix

International Consumer Markets

Provided here is statistical information on markets for different kinds of goods and services in select countries. Although consumers around the world are driven by similar needs and desires, their behavior in the marketplace is distinctly influenced by their culture. Cultural differences lead to different tastes, habits, and customs, preventing people from universally preferring the same product attributes, advertising messages, packaging, or presentation.

Culture has a profound impact on how individuals perceive who they are, and what their role is as a member of society. These perceptions are often so thoroughly internalized that they are difficult to express explicitly, but they are revealed through behavior such as consumption. Thus, business success requires aligning the marketing activities to the cultural traits of the society. This approach may be less efficient in terms of standardization but more efficient in terms of creating value for the consumers and thereby resulting in higher returns.

Gross Domestic Product

As noted in Exhibit 3A.1, China's GDP, measured at purchasing power parity (PPP), was $3.8 trillion. This makes it the second-biggest economy in the world, ahead of Japan's GDP of $3.1 trillion, but only roughly half of America's GDP of $7.8 trillion. Most emerging-market economies look relatively larger when measured on a PPP basis, because their exchange rates tend to be undervalued relative to the U.S. dollar. Indeed, 7 of the world's 15 biggest economies are in the emerging world.

Overall Consumption

As Exhibit 3A.2 shows, America's private consumption spending was $5.5 trillion, more than that of any other country. As a percentage of GDP, however, spending by households and firms in Argentina, Egypt, the Philippines, Greece and Turkey was greater than in the United States. For instance, 82 percent of Argentina's GDP was devoted to private consumption in 1997, compared with 68 percent of GDP in America. Consumption by companies and households in Scandinavia was generally lower than in the rest of Europe: in Sweden, for example, it accounted for only 53 percent of GDP. But Sweden looks positively spendthrift compared with Singapore, where private consumption was only 41 percent of GDP. This is partly thanks to the city-state's mandatory savings schemes that discourage private spending. Private consumption is usually the

EXHIBIT 3A.1   GDP / World GDP at PPP

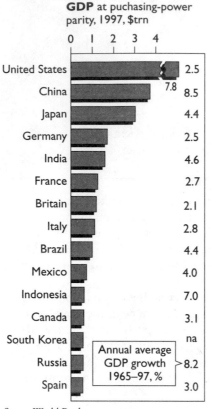

GDP at puchasing-power parity, 1997, $trn

Country	Annual average GDP growth 1965–97, %
United States	2.5
China	8.5
Japan	4.4
Germany	2.5
India	4.6
France	2.7
Britain	2.1
Italy	2.8
Brazil	4.4
Mexico	4.0
Indonesia	7.0
Canada	3.1
South Korea	na
Russia	8.2
Spain	3.0

(United States bar labeled 7.8)

Source: World Bank

World GDP at PPP*
by region, 1997, as % of total

North America 23
Euro-11 16
Other EU 5
Other East Asia 15
Japan 8
South Asia 6
Latin America 9
Africa/Middle East 6
Other 12

Total: $36.4trn

*At purchasing-power parity

Source: World Bank
* At purchasing-power parity

largest single component of a country's GDP. Investment, government spending and net exports make up the rest.

Breakdown of Consumer Spending

As is well known, poor countries spend a greater proportion of their income on food, beverages, and tobacco. Thus, in both China and India expenditure on this category exceeds 50 percent, whereas it is less than 20 percent in the United States, European Union, and Japan (see Exhibit 3A.3).

Hot Drinks

World hot-drink sales reached $53 billion in 1997, 23 percent more than in 1993. Patterns of coffee and tea consumption vary greatly. Most nations, though, drink more coffee than tea. The biggest coffee drinkers are the Swiss, who consume 8.7 kg of coffee each a year (see Exhibit 3A.4). The Irish are by far the biggest tea drinkers: they brew 3.6 kg each a year, far more than the second-place British. Tea is also popular in Turkey, Egypt, Hong Kong, and Russia. Coffee is becoming more popular in many tea-drinking countries, such as Britain. Nevertheless, health concerns are encouraging people to switch to decaffeinated coffee and herbal tea.

EXHIBIT 3A.2   Private Consumption, as % of GDP

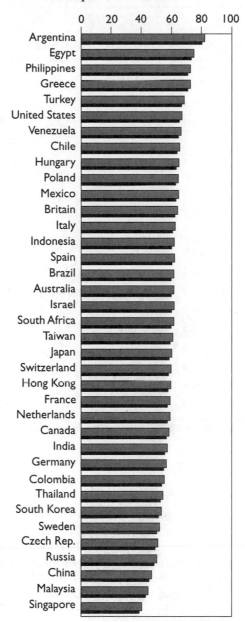

Source: Merrill Lynch

Coca-Cola's Penetration

In the United States, the per capita consumption of Coca-Cola products is 376 eight-ounce servings compared to 6 servings in China and 3 in India. Assuming there are no economic and cultural barriers to drinking Coke, eventually China and India should emerge into large markets (see Exhibit 3A.5).

━━━━━━━━━━━━━ **EXHIBIT 3A.3**   Consumer Spending by Category, as Percent of Total: 1994

	Food, Beverages, Tobacco	Clothing, Footwear, Textiles	Household Fuels	Household Goods	Housing	Health	Leisure and Education	Transport and Communications	Other
Argentina	30.3	11.8	5.4	9.1	11.7	8.8	9.4	13.5	0.0
Australia	21.2	5.4	2.2	6.6	18.2	7.8	10.4	14.8	13.4
Brazil	36.4	4.4	5.4	4.5	25.0	4.6	4.4	8.0	7.4
Canada	18.7	5.1	3.4	8.6	20.5	4.5	11.0	14.0	14.2
China	56.2	8.2	0.0	5.3	10.7	2.9	6.7	3.2	6.9
Colombia	33.5	9.6	2.2	5.7	7.8	4.7	7.8	18.5	10.2
Eastern Europe	36.5	9.4	4.8	6.2	6.2	5.1	8.7	7.3	15.7
European Union	19.1	7.1	3.7	7.9	16.0	6.6	9.2	11.5	18.9
India	51.4	9.7	4.1	2.7	5.6	2.3	3.5	13.7	7.1
Indonesia	40.3	3.9	3.0	9.9	11.7	0.0	1.4	3.7	26.0
Israel	23.7	6.5	3.7	9.8	21.3	8.9	8.5	13.0	4.8
Japan	19.5	5.5	0.0	5.8	21.1	11.3	10.8	9.4	16.6
Mexico	32.4	6.3	0.0	9.6	13.9	4.5	5.8	12.7	14.8
Nigeria	46.1	5.5	0.0	3.4	13.1	0.0	0.0	2.2	29.7
Singapore	19.8	7.0	0.0	9.5	16.5	5.2	15.4	17.3	9.3
South Korea	27.5	3.9	4.0	6.7	12.0	6.2	12.3	13.0	14.4
Thailand	26.7	10.1	1.3	8.4	4.5	8.0	17.1	12.6	11.3
United States	17.2	5.3	2.7	5.0	14.3	15.7	11.3	11.6	16.8

Source: International Marketing Data and Statistics 1996 (London: Euromonitor, 1996), table 2515.

Beer Consumption

The Czechs drink more beer than any other nation. Retail sales there topped 179.5 liters in 1996—almost half a liter a day. Elsewhere sales are stagnant or falling in most beer-drinking countries. In second-place Ireland, sales per head were 136 liters in 1997, only 1.6 percent more than five years earlier. Sales per person fell in 11 of the top 20 beer-drinking countries between 1992 and 1997. Only two notched up double-digit percentage gains: Poland (26 percent) and Slovakia (15 percent). Outside the top 20, sales per head also rose sharply in Colombia (up by 25 percent), Britain (24 percent), Chile (16 percent) and Argentina (10 percent). Sales per head fell most, by 25 percent, in Romania (see Exhibit 3A.6).

Alcohol Consumption

Germans drank an average of 100 liters of alcoholic drinks each in 1998 (Exhibit 3A.7). But that was down from 104 liters per person in 1994. Australians drink almost as much alcohol as the Germans. Egypt, which is mostly Moslem, is the driest country in the chart. Egyptians sipped a mere half-liter of alcoholic drink each in 1998. And that was two and a half times what they drank in 1994.

EXHIBIT 3A.4   Coffee and Tea Consumption, kg per Person, 1997

Source: Euromonitor

EXHIBIT 3A.5   Per Capita Consumption and Market Populations for Coca-Cola

Market	Population in Millions	Per Capita*
China	1,244	6
India	960	3
United States	272	376
Indonesia	203	10
Brazil	163	134
Russia	148	21
Japan	126	150
Mexico	94	371
Germany	82	203
Philippines	71	130
Egypt	64	28
France	59	88
Thailand	59	69
Great Britain	57	118
Italy	57	95
Korea	46	71
South Africa	43	155
Spain	40	201
Colombia	37	116
Argentina	36	207
Benelux/Denmark	32	196
Canada	30	196
Morocco	28	61
Romania	23	57
Venezuela	23	219
Australia	18	276
Chile	15	325
Zimbabwe	12	69
Hungary	10	153
Israel	6	267
Norway	4	272

* Eight-ounce servings of company beverages per person per year (excludes products distributed by The Minute Maid Company).
Source: Coca-Cola Company.

Chocolate Consumption

Britain is the most chocaholic nation in the G7. In 1998 Britons consumed an average of 9.5 kg of chocolate each, nearly a third more than German consumers, and two-thirds more than Americans. Chocolate accounted for two-thirds of the average British's total consumption of confectionery—which, at 14 kg per head, means that the British lead the world in "sweet teeth" as well as "stiff upper lips". British chocolate consumption grew steadily in 1993–98, in contrast to Germany, where consumption has leveled off, and in America, where it has actually fallen (see Exhibit 3A.8).

EXHIBIT 3A.6   Beer Sales, 1997

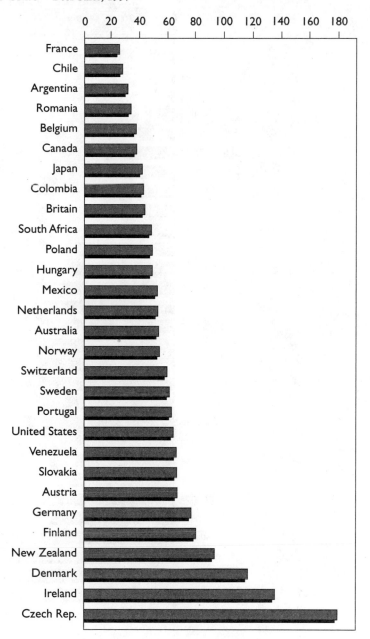

Source: Euromonitor

EXHIBIT 3A.7   Alcoholic-Drinks Consumption, Litres per Person, 1998

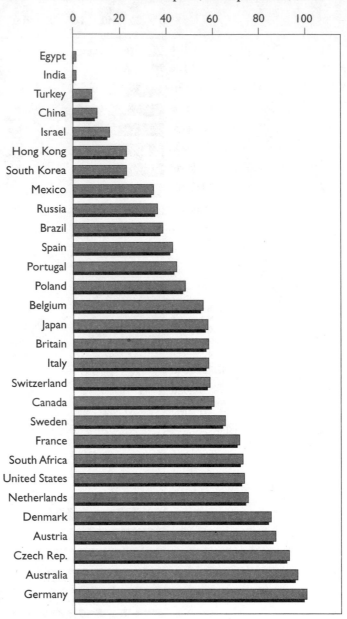

Source: Euromonitor

Health-Care Expenditures

Worldwide sales of over-the-counter health-care products were worth $75 billion in 1998 (see Exhibit 3A.9). Vitamins and dietary supplements make up one-third of the total; cold and allergy remedies account for just under a fifth. Although they still represent only a small share of the overall market, sleeping aids and products to help people give up smoking are the two fastest-growing segments of the market. Richer countries tend to spend

EXHIBIT 3A.8   Chocolate Consumption: Average Sales, 1998, kg per Head

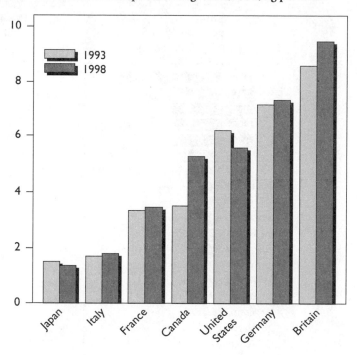

Source: Euromonitor

more on over-the-counter health care than poorer ones. But there are wide disparities, even so. At an average of $135 per person per year, the Japanese spend the most on over-the-counter health care. Americans are second, at $76 per head. At the other extreme, Indians spend an average of only 55 cents.

Videocassette Recorders Ownership

Almost 25 percent of the world's 317 million households with a videocassette recorder (VCR) are in the United States, where an astonishing 82.9 percent of homes now owns one (Exhibit 3A.10). Of the world's television-owning homes, 37.1 percent own a VCR. The popularity of VCRs, a technology now in its 20th year, may be some guide to the prospects for other new media hardware. From market inception, VCRs took between 7 and 11 years to achieve 20 percent penetration of households with television sets in European countries. Other media technologies are unlikely to be taken up much faster. A VCR has an average retail value of $200 in the United States but around $430 elsewhere.

Telephone Use

As a rule, the wealthier a country, the more telephone lines it tends to have. In 1995 rich countries averaged more than one main telephone line for every two people. Poor regions still have relatively underdeveloped telephone networks. South Asia, for example, has only 13 main lines for every 1,000 people, while sub-Saharan Africa has only 11. Hong Kong,

EXHIBIT 3A.9   Health-Care Products*

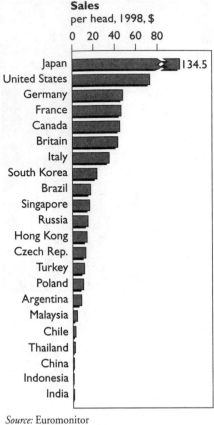

Sales
per head, 1998, $

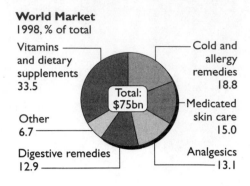

World Market
1998, % of total

Vitamins and dietary supplements 33.5

Other 6.7

Digestive remedies 12.9

Total: $75bn

Cold and allergy remedies 18.8

Medicated skin care 15.0

Analgesics 13.1

Source: Euromonitor
* Over-the-counter

on of the richest emerging markets, has 530 main telephone lines for every 1,000 people. This is more than in Britain or Germany, but fewer than America's 627 lines per 1,000. Greece is not far behind, with 493 per 1,000 people. At the other extreme, India, the poorest country in the chart, has only 13 lines for every 1,000 people (see Exhibit 3A.11).

Recorded Music Sales

Global recorded-music sales rose by 3 percent in 1998, to $38.7 billion. But unit sales fell by 1 percent, to $4.1 billion units. A rise in CD sales of 6 percent was offset by a 10 percent fall in cassette purchases and an 11 percent decline in singles. Sales in America, which made up 34 percent of the world market in 1998, jumped by 11 percent to $13.2 billion (Exhibit 3A.12) Sales in the European Union were up by 3 percent, to $11.6 billion. But Japanese sales fell by 4 percent, to $6.5 billion. Sales in crisis-hit Asia plunged: in Indonesia they were down by 56 percent.

Gold Purchases

Demand for gold has steadied, after slumping in early 1998 in the wake of the Asian crisis. Demand in the 25 main markets totaled 1,712 tonnes in the first nine months of

EXHIBIT 3A.10   VCR Penetration, % of TV Households with a Video Recorder

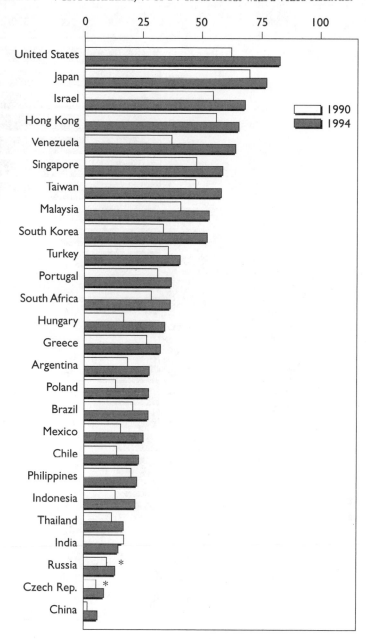

Source: Screen Digest
* 1993

1998, 20 percent down on the same period in 1997 (see Exhibit 3A.13). But whereas gold consumption in the first quarter was 46 percent below the 1997 level, gold use in the three months to September was only 1 percent lower than in the same period in 1997. The world's two biggest gold markets are leading the recovery. Gold consumption in the first nine months of 1999 was up by 19 percent in India and by 17 percent in the United States compared with the same period in 1997. Gold use has risen by 8 percent in Saudi Arabia

EXHIBIT 3A.11   Main Telephone Lines, per 1,000 Persons, 1995

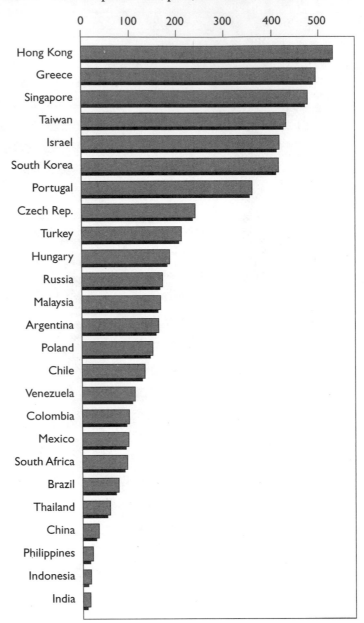

Sources: World Bank, ITU

and by 5 percent in the Gulf states, mainly the United Arab Emirates. But despite the pickup in demand, the price of gold continues to fall. An ounce of gold cost over $400 in early 1996. It cost less than $300 in 1998.

EXHIBIT 3A.12   World Music

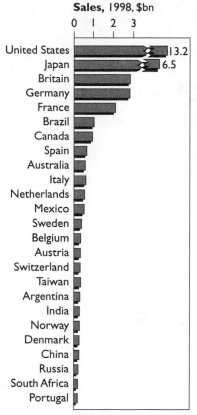

Sales, 1998, $bn

United States	13.2
Japan	6.5

% of Total Sales 1998

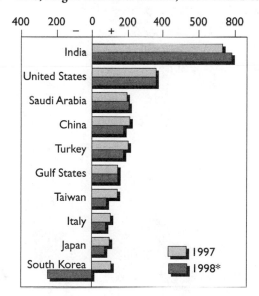

North America 36.6

Europe 33.2

Total: $38.7bn

Others 7.2

Latin America 6.1

Japan 16.9

Source: International Federation of the Phonographic Industry

EXHIBIT 3A.13   **Gold, Largest Consumer Markets, Net Demand Tonnes**

India
United States
Saudi Arabia
China
Turkey
Gulf States
Taiwan
Italy
Japan
South Korea

1997
1998*

Source: World Gold Council
* First nine months at annual rate

International Marketing Research

CHAPTER FOCUS

After studying this chapter, you should be able to

- Explain the importance of marketing research in the context of international business.

- Discuss the procedure for undertaking marketing research across national boundaries.

- Identify sources of secondary data both in the United States and abroad.

- Describe the problems of conducting primary research overseas.

- Discuss the perspectives of an international marketing information system.

The prime function of marketing research is to determine what buyers *want* so that companies can produce and sell those items rather than simply selling whatever can be most easily made. This role of marketing research is the same in domestic and international marketing.

The worldwide marketing research industry had a value of about $10.5 billion in 1999. Of this, the largest single market was the United States, accounting for some $4.9 billion or about 47 percent of the total. Europe accounted for $3.7 billion, 35 percent of the total global marketing research expenditures. Japan, Australia, and New Zealand added another 8 percent. Canada accounted for 5 percent.

The remaining $525 million, about 5 percent of the world total, came from developing countries. Half of that amount was spent in Latin and South America, mainly Mexico, Brazil, Argentina, and Venezuela. The Far East, excluding Japan, accounted for $185 million. The African total would have been very small if not for the $27 million of the $30 million total spent by South Africa. The Middle East, with Saudi Arabia the main market, contributed about $13 million and is a growth area, but one that has slowed in recent years. India, Pakistan, and Sri Lanka added a further $35 million.[1]

The top 25 firms account for almost 70 percent of the industry's worldwide revenue. Global market research is a booming industry, growing at more than 15 percent a year. With competition among retailers and manufacturers intensifying, speedy, accurate research can be crucial to the success of products, particularly new ones. The top 10 marketing researchers are ACNielsen Corp.(U.S.), IMS Health Inc.(U.S.), The Kantar Group Ltd.(U.K.), Taylor Nelson Sofres plc.(U.K.), Information Resources Inc.(U.S.), NFO Worldwide Inc.(U.S.), Nielsen Media Research(U.S.), GfK Group AG(Germany), IPSOS Group S.A.(France), Westat Inc.(U.S.).[2]

The differences in international environments make marketing research more difficult there than in a domestic environment. Consider the research information needed by these potential international marketers:

- A manufacturer of a specialized industrial product, iron fitting, believes that there is potentially a good market for export and wants to begin to develop it. Neither the company's management nor any of its salesforce, however, has knowledge of possible markets or of the nature of the competition.

- A large U.S. corporation is contemplating building a factory in Western Europe. Management wonders if its product should be changed to suit the new market.

- A pharmaceutical company has to decide how to price a prescription drug item manufactured in its factory in Brazil for the Latin American market. Should the same pricing schedule used in the United States be followed? If not, what criteria should be used to set the price?

- A soft drink company must determine how effective its U.S. advertising strategy will be in promoting its product in Southeast Asia.

Such situations are examples of international marketing problems that require marketing research. In each case, the firm's past experience cannot provide an adequate basis for decision. In fact, the information necessary to support management action is more likely to be found outside the organization. Specialized trade journals or government studies or discussions with professional-level personnel who have special industry expertise are likely to be helpful. If all these fail, it may finally become necessary to conduct a customer survey.

This chapter examines the meaning of marketing research and provides a framework for conducting such research. The two types of research, primary and secondary, are differentiated and their procedures discussed. Alternative ways of organizing international marketing research are presented, and the need for establishing an international marketing information system is explained.

Meaning of Marketing Research

The term *marketing research* refers to gathering, analyzing, and presenting information related to a well-defined, specific problem or a project with a beginning and an end. In contrast, *marketing intelligence* is information gathered and analyzed on a continual basis. Unlike marketing research, marketing intelligence is evaluated information whose credibility, meaning, and importance have been established.

Often the term *marketing research* is used interchangeably with the term *market research*, but the latter is conceptually narrower in scope, focusing on current and potential customers—who they are; why they buy a product or service; and where, when, and how they buy it. Both marketing research and market research deal with *marketing mix variables*—product, price, distribution, and promotion—as well as marketing organizational matters and the marketing environment. A *marketing information system* consists of market research, marketing research, and marketing intelligence.

The procedures and methods of conducting marketing research are conceptually the same for both domestic marketing and international marketing. For example, in both cases, before collecting data the researcher must have a clear idea of the research problem or focus. Likewise, only an appropriate sample will yield valuable results in either domestic or international research. But international marketing research differs from domestic marketing in three major ways:

1. The effects of the international environment on the whole company as a profit-oriented unit are considered. For example, the marketing research project concerned with the ramifications of a substantial price hike in a particular foreign country must consider questions that do not apply to the domestic market, such as whether the company's subsidiary will be nationalized if prices are increased beyond a certain level (see International Marketing Highlight 4.1).
2. Many concepts and frameworks (e.g., market segmentation), which constitute the core of marketing decision making in the domestic arena, may be unusable in international marketing, not because the concept cannot be transferred, but because the information necessary to make such a transfer is not available. For example, if there is a lack of current income distribution data on a country, any analysis of the demand for a product will assume incorrect income categories and therefore be invalid.
3. Finally, the ethnocentric nature of marketing makes cultural differences among nations a significant factor. Whereas the culture in a domestic market is already understood, in international marketing the culture must be fully investigated.[3]

To illustrate this last point, consider a recent study that explored the effect of a monetary incentive on the questionnaire response rate. Receipt of one U.S. dollar increased the response rate from Japanese business people but decreased the response from Hong Kong business people. The author of that study noted,

> In this study, Japanese business executives were more compliant than Hong Kongese in general, and the monetary incentive was successful in more than doubling the response from Japan but decreased the response from Hong Kong. These findings may be biased because of the small sample, the sampling frame, or the questionnaire content. However, the results may imply a cultural difference either toward responding to questionnaires, or toward monetary incentives. The cross-cultural researcher should be aware of such problems, and explore the effect of monetary incentives prior to the mass mailing of surveys. Theoretically, monetary incentives may increase response rates in any culture or country; however, the type (local or foreign currency) and amount may be important factors.[4]

Such factors raise a variety of conceptual, methodological, and organizational issues in international marketing research relating to[5]

1. The complexity of research design, caused by operation in a multicountry, multicultural, and multilinguistic environment.
2. The lack of secondary data for many countries and product markets.
3. The high costs of collecting primary data, particularly in developing countries.
4. The problems associated with coordinating research and data collection in different countries.
5. The difficulties of establishing the comparability and equivalence of data and research conducted in different contexts.
6. The intrafunctional character of many international marketing decisions.
7. The economics of many international investment and marketing decisions.

███████████████   **International Marketing Highlight 4.1**   ███████████████

Local Culture and Market Potential

The chairman of a large American soft drink company decided that the firm should target Indonesia for sales of its most popular beverage. @TX2:With a population of nearly 180 million people, Indonesia is the fifth most populous country in the world. Management considered this huge potential market irresistible and worked out a bottling and distribution arrangement to serve the country. The company sold the soft drink syrup to a bottler, who then bottled the drink and distributed it.

Unfortunately, sales were terrible. The drink simply didn't sell. The marketing campaign flopped despite predominantly good initial research, including research into the local competition and government attitudes, because the chairman and his project directors forgot to consider two major factors. First, Indonesia does have 180 million inhabitants, but most of them live in rural areas, still functioning within a preindustrial economy. Most Indonesians simply don't have much money. Second, many of them prefer sweet coconut-based drinks; they are unaccustomed to American-style carbonated beverages. A market for American drinks does exist, but almost exclusively in the major cities. That market—consumers with western tastes and sufficient disposable income to purchase foreign-style beverages—totals only about 8 million people.

Framework for International Marketing Research

Most marketing research studies proceed through a common series of major tasks:

- Define the problem and specify the information needed for support of management's decision-making process.
- Identify alternative sources of information.
- Plan and execute data collection.
- Analyze the data and prepare a report.

Defining the Problem

The first task, defining the problem, sounds deceptively simple but, may be the pivotal task in the entire study. In defining the problem, two important considerations are market structure and product concept. *Market structure* refers to the size of the market, its stage of development, the number of competitors and their market shares, and the channels through which the market is approached.

The importance of market structure in problem definition is shown by a 1963 *Reader's Digest* study, which reported that French and German consumers ate significantly more spaghetti than Italians.[6] This finding was wrong. The study had concerned itself with only packaged, branded spaghetti, and not *total* spaghetti consumption. Because much of the spaghetti sold in Italy is unpackaged and unbranded, the results of the study were totally invalid. The *Reader's Digest* researchers should have clearly defined the kind of spaghetti consumption to be studied in each of the different countries (see International Marketing Highlight 4.2).

■■■■■■■■■■■■■ **International Marketing Highlight 4.2** ■■■■■■■■■■■■■

Health Clubs in Singapore

A widely franchised health club opened a facility in Singapore. With its young, urban population and a widespread appreciation of western culture, Singapore seemed a site destined for success. Moreover, the club's physical appearance and stock of equipment equaled or surpassed that of comparable facilities in the U.S.

Yet the club couldn't sign up enough members. Despite the Singaporeans' interest in sports, the club attracted few of them and ended up catering to the relatively small expatriate community instead. Citizens of Singapore felt little enthusiasm for the American-style health club; they were more attracted either to western competitive sports or to Chinese calisthenics and other traditional Asian forms of exercise.

Source: Charles F. Valentine, *The Arthur Young International Business Guide* (New York: John Wiley & Sons, 1988), p. 74.

In addition, a product may be viewed differently in different cultures. Thus, even before attempting to define the marketing research problem for study, exploratory research may be necessary to understand the ***product concept***, that is, the meaning of the product in a particular environment.

Berent points out that milk-based products are viewed very differently in the United Kingdom and Thailand.[7] In England, they are usually consumed at meals and bedtime for their sleep-inducing, soothing, relaxing properties. In Thailand, the same products are consumed on the way to work and often away from home, for they are considered invigorating, energizing, and stimulating.

Let us assume a multinational marketer is interested in finding out the potential market for a brand of yogurt in England and Thailand. The problem definition in the two countries will have to be stated differently. In the United Kingdom, the yogurt might be primarily perceived by the consumers as a healthful and relaxing product to be used prior to retiring. In Thailand, the research problem would determine if yogurt would be considered mainly an energy food used to start the day.

Identifying Alternative Information Sources

After the problem has been defined, where the necessary information may be found and how to obtain it must be determined. In some cases, the study may be confined to *secondary data*, that is, published information that has been collected elsewhere. Such data may be available free (for example, government statistics), for a price (for example, syndicated research findings), or through restricted distribution sources (for example, trade association statistics).

Let us assume that Ford Motor Company is interested in assembling its new world car in India in collaboration with an Indian company. Before committing itself to the joint venture, Ford would like to study the car's market potential in India over a 10-year period. Fortunately, the Indian government collects a variety of socioeconomic-demographic information on a regular basis. This information is conveniently available. Ford, therefore, can use with confidence such secondary information as population projections, income data, consumer expenditure patterns, and rural-urban population shifts to assess the market potential.

Sometimes internal data are also useful. Existing files, in fact, can often provide important insights into the question at hand. In the preceding example, Ford might have found that it already had sufficient information on population trends in India gathered when the company had earlier negotiated for the assembly of tractors there. Thus, there would be no need for another source of information.

In cases where no amount of investigation of secondary sources or of internal data provides the required information, *primary data* must be compiled through interviews and other direct collection of information. Primary data may be gathered in various ways (to be discussed later), from trade association representatives, governmental experts, managerial personnel, or the buying public.

For example, a company may be interested in introducing its prefabricated houses in Latin America. The company would have to study house-buying behavior in the target countries, information that may not be conveniently available from secondary sources. Consequently, primary data gathering may be necessary. The importance of such information for decision making is revealed in a study on the subject done in the United Kingdom.

> Home ownership in different countries could also have completely different implications. The proverb that "a man's home is his castle" is far more applicable in the United Kingdom (where castles can in fact be found) than in the United States, where the geographic and social mobility of the population means that the regular exchange of homes is a commonplace experience during the life cycle of most families. Therefore, the decision-making patterns of husband and wife, and the amount of effort spent in making a home-buying decision, should be quite different between these two countries.[8]

Thus, before entering the market with prefabricated houses in Latin America, the company has to learn through primary research in which ways houses might mean "home" in various locales.

Data Collection

The actual collection of data, which will be discussed at length in later sections of this chapter, must be planned and executed carefully. Tracking down reliable, usable data sources can be time-consuming. This is particularly so when a variety of sources are pursued concurrently. In fact, the search can go on with decreasing returns unless a person with knowledge of the country appraises the progress being made.

Interview questions must be tested for their appropriateness so that they produce the desired results. A sound approach is to conduct professional-level interviews in two phases: (1) collect basic data and (2) explore interview questions not anticipated at the start of the project.

Once basic data have been collected, the process of cross-checking can begin. This step requires that all information be examined critically for its relevance. Cross-checking establishes the reliability of data by comparing one source with another. It is important to document the criteria used by the project team to determine the reliability of collected data.

Analysis, Interpretation, and Report Preparation

For the final step, the preparation of the report, the data must be analyzed and interpreted. Here also, attention should be paid to a country's cultural traits. For example, in an examination of the beer market it was found that beer was perceived as an alcoholic drink in Northern European countries but as a soft drink in Mediterranean countries. Thus, other products listed with beer as alternative drinks would influence the research findings. Similarly, in Japan noncarbonated fruit juices are often substituted for bottled soft drinks, a practice rare in the United States. In brief, *the significance of different concepts of the product in various countries must be taken into account.*

Reports must be complete, factual, and objective. It is particularly important to communicate the reliability as well as the limitations of the facts presented. Particular attention should be given to the following aspects of a report:

1. Data sources must be identified. Different sources of data warrant varying degrees of confidence. For example, information on a developing country obtained from the

United States Agency for International Development is probably more reliable than the information available from the government of that country.

2. Data projection must be explained and the statistical computations simplified as much as possible.

3. The identity of all those interviewed should be included as well as their titles or qualifications. (This rule does not apply to consumer research.) This requirement may have to be relaxed when anonymity has been guaranteed.

4. The alternative courses of action developed from analysis and interpretation of the data must be labeled as such, clearly reserving to management the responsibility for selecting the appropriate course of action.

Information Requirements of International Marketers

The nature of marketing decisions does not vary from country to country, but the environment differs from country to country. For this reason, the sort of information required to complete a marketing study may vary from one country to another. For example, in a situation where a marketer is free to set prices based on competition, a detailed analysis of competition should be made. However, in a country where the price is set by government, information on governmental cost analysis would be of greater importance. The fact that environment determines what kind of information is needed makes international marketing research efforts quite different from domestic marketing research work.

Exhibit 4.1 shows the types of marketing studies a company may want to conduct in the different areas of promotion, distribution, price, product, or market. Each of these area studies requires a different form of information, as the following discussion makes clear.

Market Information

Market research is required for testing, entering, or leaving a market and deals with market performance, market shares, and sales analysis and forecasting. *Marketing performance research* involves market measurements, either to compare a company's performance against specified standards or to project a possible future outcome. *Market potential* refers to the total market demand under optimal conditions, whereas *market forecast* shows the expected level of market demand under the given conditions. To illustrate, when Pizza Hut decided to expand its business into certain Middle Eastern countries like Saudi Arabia, it conducted beforehand market-potential research for five years in each country.

Market share refers to a company's proportion of total sales in an industry during a set time, usually a year. The market shares held by competitors shape marketing strategy for a company. The competitor with a respectable market share will have a cost advantage over its rivals. This cost advantage can be passed on to the customers through lower prices, which in turn strengthen the company's hold on the market. Because of the strategic importance of market share, business corporations keep constant watch on its fluctuations. Data supplied by industry associations, if properly analyzed, usually show respective market shares.

Past *sales information* can be analyzed in different ways: by amount of profit from different products, by productivity of sales territory (for example, Latin America or Western Europe), or by customer type. Sales analysis can pinpoint problems.

Sales forecasts refer to estimates of future sales of a product during a specific period. The sales forecast is the single most important basis for preparing budgets.

Product Information

Product research means both product-line research and individual product research. This kind of research bears on when to add, delete, or change the product.

A company operating overseas must often decide which product lines it should add, drop, or rejuvenate. These decisions require a variety of information. Consider this exam-

FIGURE 4.1   Types of Marketing Studies Required for Doing Business Abroad

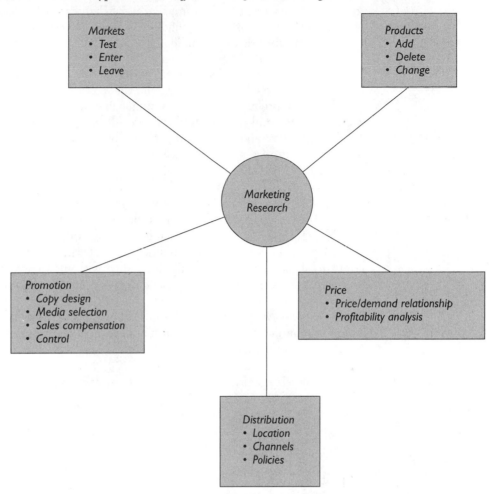

ple. A large paper products company manufactured an expensive line of writing paper, as well as other kinds of paper products. The company had about a 30 percent market share in Latin America, but the demand had been constant for a number of years. As part of a program for simplification of product lines, the company conducted marketing research to see if there had been changes in the office environment in Latin countries that made the use of expensive paper obsolete. and thus warranted dropping that product line.

A manager may also seek marketing research on an individual product as it passes through its life cycle, since different marketing programs must be developed for every stage. It is important to identify the stage a product is in so as to choose the appropriate marketing program. Marketing research can be of real value in plotting a product's life cycle in different countries.

Promotion Information

Promotion research is designed specifically for application in advertising and personal selling. Companies consult this research in order to select appropriate advertising copy and make the best media selection. A trading stamp company operating in Europe, for example, redeemed stamps saved by consumers in two ways, either in merchandise or in travel. Over the years, it was found that more and more customers preferred overseas travel to merchandise. For the company, however, merchandise was more profitable; so the company considered starting an ad campaign to entice consumers into redeeming their stamps in merchandise. As a part of this campaign, a merchandise catalog emphasizing the virtue of material acquisitions as status symbols would be marketed in Europe. The production of the catalog would cost about 2 million dollars. Obviously, the catalog's market effectiveness had to be tested beforehand.

As applied to personal selling, promotion research is designed to solve problems such as that expressed by the sales manager of a U.S. pharmaceutical company: "My salespeople in Italy are not productive enough, even though we pay them a lot more than the industry average there." Marketing research can provide insights into this kind of problem by answering questions about how many salespeople to hire, how much to pay them, how to form sales territories, and how much time to spend on retaining old customers versus developing new accounts.

Distribution Information

Distribution research consists of channel research and location research. As its name implies, *channel research* provides information on the availability of channels and their relative desirability. A water systems manufacturer, for instance, traditionally used manufacturer's representatives for the distribution of its water pumps in the Canadian market. The company, however, was becoming dissatisfied with manufacturer's representatives and wanted to use its own salesforce. A marketing research firm was asked for a study of the effect on sales of making such a change.

Location research concerns decisions about warehousing, inventory, and transportation. For example, the decision to own a warehouse in Germany or to use a public warehouse there requires marketing research.

Price Information

A company sets the prices of its products to meet both short-term and long-term objectives. To set prices, information about the ability of consumers to pay, about dealer reaction, and about the effect of price on demand is necessary. Studies that measure the public perception of a product's quality in relation to price also help in making pricing decisions.

Environment Information

No matter which sort of international marketing study is planned, the researchers must take into account the foreign country's environment in all its aspects: legal, political, social, cultural, and attitudinal, as shown by both the buying habits of its consumers and the business practices of its enterprises. Naturally, familiarity with the environment is equally important in domestic marketing, but in that case most of the necessary knowledge has already been obtained from personal experience. For example, if a U.S. company is interested in doing business in China, it must learn about the political system there, whereas little or no money or effort need be expended on investigating the U.S. political system.

General Research Information

In addition to the specific categories of marketing research discussed thus far, general research information is necessary on the following:

1. *Community-type conditions* (for example, political happenings such as campaigns and elections; cultural events such as county fairs and special annual ethnic or religious celebrations; and national events such as sports, championships, and holidays).
2. *Business conditions* (for example, business ethics and traditional associations).
3. *Lifestyles and living conditions,* that is, social and cultural customs and taboos (for example, marriageable age for men and women and the role of women in society)[9] (see International Marketing Highlight 4.3).
4. General economic conditions (for example, the standards of living of various groups of people and the economic infrastructure—transportation, power supply, and communication).

Also required is

1. Industry information about government decisions affecting the industry.
2. Resource availability (for example, labor and land).
3. Current or potential competitors (that is, general information about their markets and their problems).
4. Competition from U.S. companies, local companies, and third-country companies.
5. Industry policy, concerted actions in the industry, and so forth.

In addition, study-related information is desirable on specific subjects. For example, a study concerned with market potential needs information on supply and demand in market areas of current and potential interest (capacity, consumption, imports, exports). A study concerned with the introduction of a new product requires information about existing products, the technical know-how available in the country, sources of raw material, and leads for joint ventures.

■■■■■■■■■   International Marketing Highlight 4.3   ■■■■■■■■■

Hands-on Market Research

When Sony researched the market for a lightweight portable cassette player, results showed that consumers wouldn't buy a tape player that didn't record. Company chairman Akio Morita decided to introduce the Walkman anyway, and the rest is history. Today it is one of Sony's most successful products.

Morita's disdain for large-scale consumer surveys and other scientific research tools isn't unique in Japan. Matsushita, Toyota, and other well-known Japanese consumer goods companies are just as skeptical about the western style of market research. Occasionally, the Japanese do conduct consumer attitude surveys, but most executives don't base their marketing decisions on them or on other popular techniques.

Of course, Japanese corporations want accurate and useful information about their markets as much as U.S. and European companies do. They just go about it differently. Japanese executives put much more faith in information they get directly from wholesalers and retailers in the distribution channels. Moreover, they track what's happening among channel members on a monthly, weekly, and sometimes even daily basis.

Japanese-style market research relies heavily on two kinds of information: "soft data" obtained from visits to dealers and other channel members, and "hard data" about shipments, inventory levels, and retail sales. Japanese managers believe that these data better reflect the behavior and intentions of flesh-and-blood consumers.

Source: Reprinted by permission of *Harvard Business Review*. An excerpt from "Market Research the Japanese Way" by Johny K. Johansson and Ikujiro Nonaka, May–June 1987, p. 16. Copyright (c) 1987 by the President and Fellows of Harvard College; all rights reserved.

The amount of information to be gathered in a given case depends on the cost/benefit relationship of such information. For example, let us assume a company has an opportunity to export machinery to Kenya. Although normally the company checks on the credit rating of an importer before making a shipment, such a delay might ruin a particular transaction. The company figures out that if the importer does not make the payment as stipulated, it stands to lose $2,000 after accounting for the advance from the importer. On the other hand, the company could have a market research firm do a study on the creditworthiness of the importer for $3,000 in a very short time. So the cost exceeds the benefit, making the study not worth its expense. This example, though oversimplified, illustrates the importance of relating the cost to benefit in terms of time and money before undertaking a marketing research project.

Finally, the nature of information required will vary based on the objective of research. To illustrate this point, Exhibit 4.2 lists the types of information a firm needs to determine export potential. The firm must examine different types of environments as well as undertake market and product research.

EXHIBIT 4.2   Information Needs for Determining Export Potential

Stage One: Preliminary Screening

Preliminary screening involves defining the physical, political, economic, and cultural environment.

Demographic/Physical Environment

- Population size, growth, density
- Urban and rural distribution
- Climate and weather variations
- Shipping distance
- Product-significant demographics
- Physical distribution and communications network
- Natural resources

Political Environment

- System of government
- Political stability and continuity
- Ideological orientation
- Government involvement in business
- Government involvement in communications
- Attitudes toward foreign business (trade restrictions, tariffs, nontariff barriers, bilateral trade agreement)
- National economic and developmental priorities

Economic Environment

- Overall level of development
- Economic growth: GNP, industrial sector
- Role of foreign trade in the economy
- Currency, inflation rate, availability, controls, stability of exchange rate
- Balance of payments
- Per capita income and distribution
- Disposable income and expenditure patterns

Social/Cultural Environment

- Literacy rate, educational level
- Existence of middle class
- Similarities and differences in relation to home market
- Language and other cultural considerations

The export marketer will eliminate some foreign markets from further consideration on the basis of this preliminary screening. An example would be the absence of comparable or linking products and services, a deficiency that would hinder the potential for marketing products.

Stage Two: Analysis of Industry Market Potential

Market Access

- Limitations on trade: tariff levels, quotas
- Documentation and import regulations
- Local standards, practices, and other nontariff barriers
- Patents and trademarks
- Preferential treaties
- Legal considerations; investment, taxation, repatriation, employment, code of laws

Product Potential

- Customer needs and desires
- Local production, imports, consumption
- Exposure to and acceptance of products
- Availability of linking products
- Industry-specific key indicators of demand
- Attitudes toward products of foreign origin
- Competitive offerings
- Availability of intermediaries
- Regional and local transportation facilities
- Availability of manpower
- Conditions for local manufacture

Stage Three: Analysis of Company Sales Potential

The third stage of the screening process involves assessing company sales potential in those countries that prove promising based upon the earlier analyses.

Sales Volume Forecasting

- Size and concentration of customer segments
- Projected consumption statistics
- Competitive pressures
- Expectations of local distributors/agents

Landed Cost

- Costing method for exports
- Domestic distribution costs
- International freight and insurance
- Cost of product modification

Cost of Internal Distribution

- Tariffs and duties
- Value-added tax
- Local packaging and assembly
- Margins/commission allowed for the trade
- Local distribution and inventory costs
- Promotional expenditures

Other Determinants of Profitability

- Going price levels
- Competitive strengths and weaknesses
- Credit practices
- Current and projected exchange rates

Source: S. Tamer Cavusgil, "Guidelines for Export Market Research," *Business Horizons*, November–December 1985, pp. 30–31.

Gathering Secondary Data at Home

There are two kinds of data—primary and secondary. *Primary data* are gathered by the researcher. *Secondary data* are data that have been collected by someone else, either an individual or an organization. Exhibit 4.3 characterizes the two kinds of data. Research based on secondary data may be conducted either at home or abroad. This section discusses secondary research in the United States

U.S. Sources of Data

There are five sources of information in the United States: international agencies, U.S. government, consulting firms, foreign government offices, and banks.

International Agencies The United Nations (UN), the World Bank, and the International Monetary Fund (IMF) gather a variety of economic and social information on different countries of the world. This information is available to the public. For example, the

EXHIBIT 4.3   Characteristics of Primary and Secondary Data

Primary Data

- From knowledgeable individuals
- May be costly in time and travel
- May tend to be subjective
- Must be pilot-tested
- Can be very specific to problems
- Cannot require disclosure of proprietary information

Secondary Data

- From published sources or at the professional level collected by others
- Usually free or low cost
- Can be collected quickly
- May be biased or incomplete
- May be out of date at hand
- Requires careful analysis of limitations

UN Yearbook provides information on worldwide demographics. Also, the World Bank's *The World Development Report* summarizes information on living patterns comprising such indicators as daily calorie supply, life expectancy at birth, and school enrollment. The IMF provides historical information on national economic indicators (GNP, industrial production, inflation rate, money supply) of its member countries. This information is available on computer tapes.

The information available from these international organizations, however, has two drawbacks. First, the information is based on data supplied by each member country, and is difficult to determine what criteria and means have been used. In some cases, the reliability of the data should be questioned because various bureaucrats may have slanted it for their own purposes. Second, the information is dated. It takes time for an international organization to gather information from all over the world, analyze it, and make it available to the public in summary form.

Most university libraries and public libraries in major cities carry the UN and the World Bank publications. The IMF information may be available only in more specialized libraries.

U.S. Government The U.S. Department of Commerce is the single most important source of secondary information. Forty-eight international trade administration district offices and 19 branch offices of the U.S. Department of Commerce in cities throughout the United States and in Puerto Rico provide information and professional export counseling to business people. Each office is headed by a director, supported by trade specialists and other staff. These professionals can help a company's decision makers gain a basic understanding of profitable opportunities in exporting and assist them in evaluating the company's market potential overseas.

Each district office can give information about

- Trade and investment opportunities abroad.
- Foreign markets for U.S. products and services.
- Services to locate and evaluate overseas buyers and representatives.
- Financing aid for exporters.
- International trade exhibitions.
- Export documentation requirements.
- Foreign economic statistics.
- U.S. export licensing and foreign national import requirements.
- Export seminars and conferences.

Most district offices maintain an extensive business library containing the department's latest reports.

The U.S. Department of Commerce information is obtained in two ways: on a regular basis from periodicals such as *Export America* (formerly *Business America*) and on an ad hoc basis from special reports prepared on opportunities for American companies, for example, in Saudi Arabia.

The U.S. Department of Commerce informs businesses not only about international business conditions abroad, but also about events and happenings in Washington and their impact on international business. Information is available on all phases of marketing.

Useful information may also be available from other departments or agencies of the federal government such as the U.S. State Department's Agency for International Development (USAID) or the U.S. Department of Agriculture. Most of these organizations issue newsletters and other publications. An international marketer could subscribe to those pertinent to particular products or markets. Currently, all U.S. government information, entitled *National Trade Data Bank* (NTDB), is available on CD rom, updated every three months. The NTDB information can also be accessed on the internet.

U.S. Consulting Firms Many management consulting firms (including accounting firms) specialize in services for U.S. business abroad. Some of these firms conduct original research. Their findings are available to the international marketer. One such firm is Business International Corporation, a division of *The Economist*. It puts out a number of publications (newsletters issued periodically, studies issued on a regular basis, and ad hoc studies). Another firm that specializes in providing secondary data is Predicasts of Cleveland, Ohio. Similarly, major accounting firms and major banks issue a variety of finance- and accounting-related information on different countries of the world. For example, Price Waterhouse regularly publishes booklets on select countries, providing perspectives on doing business there. Bank of America offers a service entitled World Information Services, which tracks, analyzes, and forecasts economic and business conditions in 100 countries.

U.S. Foreign Government Offices Almost all countries maintain embassies in Washington, D.C. In addition, these countries have consulates and UN mission offices in New York City. A country may have more than one consulate office in the U.S. For example, the government of Brazil maintains consulate offices in New York, Chicago, Dallas, and Los Angeles, in addition to their embassy in Washington, D.C. Usually, an embassy has a commercial attaché who may be a good source of secondary information on the country. The consulate and the UN mission usually have basic information on their country to offer the researcher. For example, let us assume research is being done to prepare a market-potential study in order to decide whether a company should assemble television sets in Nigeria. Import data on this product in Nigeria for the past five years are needed. The Nigerian consulate in New York might have a government publication that quickly and easily provides such information.

. Other units of a foreign government in the United States can serve as important sources of data. For example, a hotel chain interested in constructing a hotel on the Caribbean island of St. Lucia may find the St. Lucian government tourist office in New York City an important source of information on tourist trade there.

Many governments maintain special offices in the United States for the purpose of promoting trade and business with U.S. companies. For example, the Indian government's India Investment Center in New York City offers all sorts of business-related information. If the center does not have the information, it can guide the researcher to the proper source.

U.S. Multinational Banks Both U.S. banks active worldwide (e.g., Citicorp, BankAmerica Corp., Chase Manhattan Bank), and branches of foreign banks in the U.S. are additional sources of secondary information. Many of these banks maintain libraries. They usually offer free access to customers, present and prospective. In some instances, however, a bank may have information a researcher seeks in one of its reports, but the data may not be made available. It is worthwhile, nevertheless, to contact a multinational bank for secondary data.

Advantages of Secondary Research at Home

Secondary research conducted in the United States is less expensive and less time-consuming than research abroad. The research at home keeps the financial commitment to projects at a low level: no contacts have to be made overseas, and no high-level decisions have to be made on exploring markets outside the United States. Research in the home environment affords easy communication with sources of information. In addition, requests for certain kinds of information are often more favorably received by foreign sources located in the United States where political pressure and business customers do not inhibit response. Furthermore, research undertaken in the United States about a foreign environment gains objectivity. The researcher is not constrained by overseas customs or mores and can apply the same standards of quality and analysis as would be used for a project related to domestic business.

Disadvantages of Secondary Research at Home

Secondary research undertaken in the United States has various limitations. First, current information may be scarce in the United States. After all, there is a time lag between data gathering in a foreign country and its transmission here. Further, certain things may be uncovered in the foreign environment that ultimately will bear on the project. For example, a company may be exploring the feasibility of establishing a plant in Saudi Arabia to manufacture air conditioners. Research done in the United States is likely to reveal good potential there for air conditioners based on secondary data such as high per capita income, hot climate, low rate of air conditioners per 100 households, and encouragement by the Saudi government. However, these data omit an important fact about Saudi living: a large proportion of the people live in mud houses. Additionally, there are regions without electricity. Such facts would become immediately obvious to a researcher on the spot.

Secondary Research Abroad

An alternative to doing secondary research in the United States is undertaking secondary research abroad. It should be recognized that the abundance of information available in the United States from both government and private sources is not found in most countries of the world, including the developed ones. Since World War II, however, interest in collecting socioeconomic information has greatly increased throughout the world. As countries have progressed economically, it has become more important to collect and publish statistical information on commercial matters on a regular basis. Indeed, the availability of reliable secondary data appears directly related to the level of economic development of a country. Even among developing countries, data-gathering activity has greatly improved since the 1970s. This trend may be attributed partly to the UN's efforts to impress upon countries the desirability of keeping national statistical information accurate and current.

Foreign Sources of Information

Following are the major sources of secondary information for an international marketer:

Government Sources The single most important source of secondary information in a country is the national government. The quality and quantity of information will vary from country to country, but in most cases information on population statistics, consumption standards, industrial production, imports and exports, price levels, employment, and more is conveniently available from its government. (Data on retail and wholesale trade, however, may be found only in certain countries.) The government data are usually available through a government agency or major publishers in the country. In many countries, marketing-related information gathered by the government is not separated from other sorts of information. Thus, the researcher must go through a plethora of information to choose what is relevant.

Private Sources In many countries there are private consulting firms (like Gallup Research, Business International Corporation of New York City; and Predicasts of Cleveland, Ohio) that gather and sell commercial information (see International Marketing Highlight 4.4). Information from private sources may, in fact, have been collected by the government originally, but the consulting firms analyze and organize it in such a manner that business executives can more easily make sense of it.

The commercial attaché at the U.S. embassy should be able to provide the names and addresses of local consulting firms. For example, International Information Services Ltd. (IIS), a global product pickup service located in Sussex, United Kingdom, provides answers to such specific issues as the most popular pizza flavors in France and retail pricing structure for shampoos in Venezuela compared with its neighbors Colombia and Brazil. Each day over 400 IIS shoppers visit supermarkets in 120 countries searching for information requested by clients such as Coca-Cola, General Foods, Procter & Gamble, Nestlé, and Unilever. The information gathered by IIS shoppers is stored, along with data from the company's comprehensive library of foreign trade publications, in a computerized database, enabling IIS to offer clients continuous updates on new food, household, and pharmaceutical products introduced worldwide. IIS uses these data to compile bimonthly indexes of the new products.[9]

Research Institutes, Trade Associations, Universities, and Similar Sources Although not every country in the world has trade associations or research institutes, in both developed and developing countries (like India, Brazil, South Korea, Egypt) such organizations could be important sources of secondary data. In some countries, they are set up with the help of international agencies or the government. Information on these sources should be sought from the appropriate U.S. embassy.

Local Businesses A U.S. company may be in contact with one or more businesses in a foreign country. These contacts can serve as important sources of secondary data. Even if these businesses have collected no data on their own, they could gather and communicate data available through other local sources such as those mentioned earlier.

■■■■■   **International Marketing Highlight 4.4**   ■■■■■

Direct Mail Responders Love to Shop

The 1990 Target Group Index (TGI) survey by the British Market Research Bureau found that people who respond to direct-response advertising are less brand-loyal and more likely to experiment in their purchasing behavior.

The TGI is a national product and media survey. It measures the use of over 3,000 brands in more than 200 product areas and the use of 450 other services. The survey can be used to link responsiveness data with geographic and demographic information to more accurately target cold mailings.

Although the traditional image of the direct mail respondent is someone who doesn't like to shop, the response to the TGI survey contradicts this notion.

People who respond to direct mail enjoy their shopping more than anyone else, even though they are also the busiest people. They also hunt for bargains more enthusiastically, and are more likely to try new brands.

The TGI also found that in the past 12 months, at least 62 percent of the adult population (over age 15) in the U.K. purchased goods through a mail order catalog or responded to a direct-response advertisement, or did both.

Seventeen million adults (39 percent) responded to direct-response ads, and 19.5 million (43 percent) made purchases through mail order companies.

Source: Direct Mail Information Service, 14 Floral Street, Covent Garden, London WC2E 9RR, United Kingdom.

U.S. Embassies The U.S. embassy (including the resources of other U.S. government agencies abroad such as the Agency for International Development) may also provide secondary data on the country. Sometimes embassy personnel have gathered information on a particular industry in a country in order to understand its impact on U.S. business at home (for example, the impact of the Japanese auto industry on U.S. automobile companies might be better understood with information from the U.S. embassy in Japan). Embassy appointees can be requested to be mindful of U.S. trade prospects for particular raw materials (for example, the U.S. embassy in Colombia would be aware of Colombian coffee bean trade). In addition, the embassy may be able to lead the marketing researcher to other sources of secondary data in the country such as trade associations or research institutes.

Problems with Foreign Secondary Data

Researchers should be aware of the problems and deficiencies that exist in interpreting foreign secondary data.

The Underlying Purpose of Data Collection As mentioned earlier, the single most important source of marketing-related secondary data in a country is the government, and the government as a political institution may not approach data collection with the same objectivity as a business researcher. This problem is particularly severe in developing countries where governments may enhance the information content in order to paint a rosy picture of economic life in the country. Political considerations may well compromise the reliability of the data.

It is worth noting that the United States as a society is more open than other countries. No matter how embarrassing data may appear to be for the government or the nation, the free flow of information is considered desirable. Such, however, is not the case elsewhere. It is not surprising, therefore, that the plight of the poor in the United States seems exaggerated when measured by standards of poverty in developing countries. The researcher should ascertain that the data available from such countries are not distorted in this manner.

Currency of Information Information gathering is an expensive activity, so in governments where it is assigned a lower priority, it is not conducted as frequently as desirable. Consequently, information from overseas is often outdated to the point of being useless. For example, a sensible decision about a housing project in Indonesia could not be made on the basis of 1960s' house prices.

Reliability of Data As mentioned, political considerations may affect the reliability of data. In addition, the reliability of data may be affected by data collection procedures. For example, the sample may not be random, in which case the results cannot be assumed to reflect the behavior of the total population. Even when a good sampling plan has been laid out, it may not be properly adhered to (e.g., the interviewers might substitute subjects when those required by the sampling plan cannot be reached). Numerous other factors may affect the reliability of foreign data.[10]

Researchers should judge for themselves how far to accept such data on the basis of inputs from different contacts in the country about their own experiences with secondary data there. Possibly researchers would be better off undertaking primary data gathering.

Data Classification Another problem has to do with the classification scheme of the available data. In many countries, data are too broadly classified for use at the micro level. For example, in Malaysia the category "construction equipment, machinery, and tools" includes large bulldozers as well as hand-operated drills. Thus, a company interested in manufacturing heavy construction machinery in Malaysia cannot get a clear idea about the current availability of such equipment in the country from the information given under such a category.

Fortunately, the problem of data classification is in the process of being solved. The international trading community has for years been frustrated by the lack of a standardized goods classification system for products. The use of diverse systems has complicated the preparation of documents and the analysis of trade data. Uncertainty in the negotiation and interpretation of trade agreements has slowed the movement of traded goods. However, as countries adopt the Harmonized Commodity Description and Coding System, an international goods classification system designed to standardize commodity classification, information across countries will be similarly classified, eliminating many of the problems that arise from the use of a nonstandardized system. In the United States, the Harmonized System (HS) was adopted on January 1, 1988, requiring all U.S. exporters and importers to conform to the revised classification.

The HS assigns all products a six-digit code to be used by all countries for both imported and exported goods. It is more detailed and contains many new subdivisions to reflect changes in technology, trade patterns, and user requirements.

The HS replaces the Tariff Schedules of the United States Annotated (TSUSA) and Schedule B. The U.S. import and export schedules under the HS will be nearly identical and completely compatible. The only differences will occur with regard to level of detail; in some areas such as textiles, the import schedule will need to be subdivided in much finer detail than is necessary for exports. In addition, both the U.S. import and export schedules will be identical through the first six digits with those of trading partners adopting the HS. Under the current system, a product may be given one code when it is imported, a separate code when it is exported, and various other codes in foreign countries. If the HS is applied on a worldwide basis, any single product will bear the same six-digit base code anywhere in the world. National subdivisions beyond the six-digit level are possible for tariff and statistical purposes.

This system will also provide U.S. exporters with information concerning the tariff classification of their goods in other countries as well as a procedure for bringing goods classification disputes before an international customs council.

Use of a common system would accelerate the movement of goods and associated paperwork. International traders would no longer have to redescribe and recode goods as they move through the international marketplace. Elimination of such obstacles would save both time and money.

The HS consists of 5,019 six-digit headings and subheadings. Developing countries will be able, under certain circumstances, to adopt the system at the four-digit level; developed countries, however, will have to use all six digits. The first two digits represent the chapter in which the goods are found, the next two digits represent the place within the chapter where the goods are described, and the final two digits represent the international subdivisions within the heading.

The United States will further subdivide the 5,019 six-digit international headings and subheadings into approximately 8,800 eight-digit rate lines, or classification lines, and into approximately 12,000 ten-digit statistical reporting numbers. This represents an increase in rate lines of about 1,500 and a decrease of about 2,000 in the statistical reporting numbers from the present system.

Another noteworthy development in making international economic information more useful is a new framework for national-income accounting, the new System of National Accounts (SNA).[11] The new SNA takes into account changes in both the world's economy and in accounting practices in the past 25 years. Its guidelines on accounting for inflation have been beefed up, and the way it measures trade flows has been improved. The new SNA will account for trade in the same way as the IMF's balance-of-payments statistics. Imports of goods will now be valued "free on board" (FOB), that is, at the point of export. (The old system incorrectly lumped in cost, insurance, and freight.) The system will also adopt the IMF's approach to the return on foreign direct investment, treating retained profits of foreign-owned businesses as though they had been repatriated. The new SNA is a joint effort by the UN, the IMF, the World Bank, the OECD, and Eurostat, the Statistical Office of the European Union.

Comparability of Data Multinational corporate executives often like to compare information on their host countries about such matters as review of market performance, strategy effectiveness in different environments, and so on. Unfortunately, the secondary data obtainable from different countries are not readily comparable. Keegan reports, for example, that in Germany television purchases are considered expenditures for recreation and entertainment, while in the United States they are in the category of furniture, furnishing, and household equipment.[12] These discrepancies make brand-share comparison nearly impossible.

Availability of Data Finally, in many developing nations, secondary data are very scarce. Information on retail and wholesale trade is especially difficult to obtain. In such cases, primary data collection becomes vital.

Primary Data Collection

An alternative to secondary data is primary data collection. Primary data presumably provide more relevant information because they are collected specifically for the purpose in mind. However, the collection of primary data is an expensive proposition in terms of both money and time. Thus, the underlying purpose must justify the effort. For example, when a company has to make a decision about appointing a dealer for the occasional sale of its product in a developing country, it is not necessary to have primary data on the long-term market potential. On the other hand, if the company is considering the establishment of a manufacturing plant in the country, it may be important to undertake a market-potential study.

Problems of Primary Data Collection

Primary data collection in a foreign environment poses a variety of problems not encountered in the United States. These problems are related to social and cultural factors and the level of economic development. They can be grouped under three headings: (1) sampling problems, (2) questionnaire problems, and (3) the problem of nonresponse.

Sampling Problems A good piece of research should reflect the perspectives of the entire population. This is feasible, however, only when the sample is randomly drawn (see International Marketing Highlight 4.5). Unfortunately, in many countries it is difficult to get completely representative information on the socioeconomic characteristics of the population. Such information is so incomplete that most samples in the end are biased. Cateora adds,

> In many countries, telephone directories, cross-index street directories, census tract and block data, and detailed social and economic characteristics of the universe are not available on a current basis, if at all. The researcher then has to estimate characteristics and population parameters, sometimes with little basic data on which to build an accurate estimate. To add to the confusion, in some cities in South America, Mexico, and Asia, street maps are unavailable; and in some large metropolitan areas of the Near East and Asia, streets are not identified nor houses numbered.[13]

Limitations aside, directories are available to help the international marketing researcher draw an adequate sample, especially in the industrial marketing area. *Boltin International*, for example, provides names and addresses of more than 300,000 firms in 100 countries, under 1,000 product classifications, by trade and by country.[14] Another source is *Kelly's Manufacturers and Merchants Directory*, which lists firms in the United States and other major trading countries in the world.[15]

Even if a workable random sample is drawn, inadequate means of transportation may prevent interviewing people as planned. For example, in developing countries, many areas, especially rural ones, are quite inaccessible. Thus, data gathering may have to be confined to urban areas. Further, only a small percentage of the population has telephones. The World Bank statistics indicate that there are only 4 telephones per 1,000 population in Egypt, 6 in Turkey, and 32 in Argentina. In many countries, the postal system is so inefficient that letters may not be delivered at all or may reach the addressee only after a long delay. In Brazil an estimated 30 percent of the domestic mail is never delivered.[16] In brief, it may be extremely difficult to obtain a proper random sample, especially in developing countries.

■■■■■■■■■■■■   **International Marketing Highlight 4.5**   ■■■■■■■■

Who Drinks More Wine?

According to a recent study, the Italians drink the most wine of any country—about 116 liters per capita a year, compared with 77 for the French and just over 9 for the British. But another study disagrees. It gives the French first place in the wine-drinking competition, finding that annual per capita intake in France is 70 liters and that the Italians drink only 62 liters a year. (The difference may well be in the way the population is defined or the way the questions were asked.)

No matter what the reason, the study by the French Inter-Professional Office of Wine (ONIVINS) says that the French have cut their wine consumption. More than half of the 12,400 people interviewed in this study said they abstain from drinking wine.

In 1980, according to ONIVINS, nearly one-third of the French drank wine daily, compared with only 18 percent in 1990. Families spend less time together and eat together less often, forcing wine to take a back seat to other options such as mineral water and soft drinks. The ONIVINS study also found that the French are choosing to drink higher-quality, when they choose to drink wine.

Source: The European, August 10–12, 1990.

Questionnaire Problems In many countries, different languages are spoken in different areas. Thus, the questionnaire has to be in different languages for use within the same country. In India, for example, 14 official languages are spoken in different parts of the country, although most government and business affairs are conducted in English. Similarly, in Switzerland, German is used in some areas and French in others. In the Republic of Congo, the official language is French, but only a small part of the population is fluent in French. Unfortunately, translating a questionnaire from one language to another is far from easy. In the translating process many points are entirely eclipsed, because many idioms, phrases, and statements mean different things in different cultures. For example, in Spanish there is no word that means "value" as we define it in English. Therefore, a U.S. restaurant chain conducting marketing research in Spain had to ask guests such questions as, "Do you think the quality of the food was equal to the price you paid?"[17] A Danish executive observed,

> Check this out by having a different translator put back into English what you've translated from the English. You'll get the shock of your life. I remember "out of sight, out of mind" had become "invisible things are insane."[18]
>
> This translation problem may be partially averted with the help of computers, but only partially; experience with computers shows that they cannot fathom the subtleties of language.[19]

Problem of Nonresponse Even if the interviewee is successfully reached, there is no guarantee that he or she will cooperate in furnishing the desired information. There are many reasons for nonresponse. First, cultural habits in many countries virtually prohibit communication with a stranger, particularly for women. For example, a researcher simply may not be able to speak on the phone with a housewife in an Islamic country to find out what she thinks of a particular brand. Second, in many societies such matters as preferences for hygienic products and food products are too personal to be shared with an outsider. In many Latin American countries, a woman would be embarrassed to talk with a researcher about her choice of a brand of sanitary pad or even, hair shampoo or perfume. Third, respondents in many cases may be unwilling to share their true feelings with interviewers because they suspect the interviewers may be agents of the government, perhaps seeking information for imposition of additional taxes. Fourth, middle-class people, in developing countries in particular, are reluctant to accept their status and may make false claims in order to reflect the lifestyle of wealthier people. For example, in a study on the consumption of tea in India, over 70 percent of the respondents from middle-income families claimed they used one of the several national brands of tea, a finding that could not be substantiated since over 60 percent of the tea sold nationally in India is unbranded, generic tea sold unpackaged.

Fifth, many respondents, willing to cooperate, may be illiterate, so that even oral communication may be difficult. In other words, their exposure to the modern world may be so limited and their outlook so narrow that the researchers would find it extremely difficult to elicit adequate responses from them. Sixth, in many countries, privacy is becoming a big issue. In Japan, for example, the middle class is showing increasing concern about the protection of personal information. Information that people are most anxious to protect includes income, assets, tax payments, family life, and political and religious affiliation.

Finally, the lack of established marketing research firms in many countries may force the researcher to count on ad hoc help for gathering data. How far such temporary help may be counted on to complete a job systematically can only be guessed.

Resolving the Problems

No foolproof methods exist for solving all the problems just discussed. Some suggestions, however, have been advanced: First, it has been proposed that the international marketing research effort be undertaken in conjunction with a reputable local firm. Such a firm could be a foreign office of a U.S. advertising firm like J. Walter Thompson, a U.S. accounting firm like Price Waterhouse, or a locally owned firm belonging to a third country, like a Japanese advertising agency in Italy. The resources of the cooperating firm would be invaluable—for example, its knowledge of local customs, including things like the feasibility of interviewing housewives while husbands are at work; its familiarity with the local environment, including modes of transportation available for personal interviews in smaller towns; and its contact in different parts of the country as sources for drawing a sample.

From the beginning, a person fully conversant with both sound marketing research procedures and the local culture should be involved in all phases of the research design. Such a person can recommend the number of languages the questionnaire should be printed in and what sort of cultural traits, habits, customs, and rituals to keep in mind in different phases of the research. A U.S.–educated marketer could serve in this function or anyone or with good business education or experience, preferably in marketing.

The questionnaire can first be written in English, then translated into the local language(s) by a native fluent in English. A third person should retranslate it back into English. This retranslated version can then be compared with the original English version. The three people involved should work together to eliminate differences in the three versions of the questionnaire by changing phrases, idioms, and words. Ultimately, the questionnaire in the local language should accurately reflect the questions in the original English questionnaire.

The persons hired to conduct the interviews should have prior experience if possible. A local cooperating firm could be helpful here. In any event, complete instructions and training should be given before work starts, the conducting of interviews should be practiced. Ways to ensure that the interviewers follow the instructions must be found for proper sampling control. For example, the researcher might accompany the interviewer sporadically.

Finally, the researcher should draw the best possible sample. If the sample is not random, the researcher should employ appropriate statistical techniques in analyzing the collected information so that the results reflect the reality of the situation.

Organization for International Marketing Research

International marketing research can be carried out at U.S. headquarters and in the host country. Marketing research at U.S. headquarters is useful both for short-term planning and budgeting and for strategy formulation. For example, yearly forecasts of sales for different products in different countries will be a part of the annual budget. But a study undertaken to determine if a new product successfully sold in the United States should be introduced in international markets would have a strategy focus.

Marketing research studies in host countries are concerned mainly with day-to-day operations, tactics to achieve designated goals, and short-term marketing planning. Thus, a study might examine the factors responsible for poor sales performance in the previous quarter. Or research might be undertaken to decide if a concentrated 6- or 10-week advertising campaign is preferable to spreading advertising over the whole year. Naturally, sales forecasting will be done to develop budgets. As mentioned earlier, the headquarters may also make sales forecasts. Thus, for discussion of annual plans and budgets, the host country manager would use his or her forecasts as the basis for resource allocation, while the headquarters' people use their forecasts to negotiate and approve the country budgets.

Marketing research is unquestionably an important function both at headquarters and in the host countries. The persons to take charge at the two different locations would vary from company to company. For example, at NCR a staff assistant reporting to the vice president of international marketing is responsible for marketing research at the corporate headquarters. The marketing research function for NCR in host countries is performed at different levels according to the importance of each country to the parent company. In Japan, in the U.K., and in Germany, NCR has large marketing research departments simply because the company is extremely active in these markets. On the other hand, in a country like South Korea, where NCR commitment is meager, marketing research study might be assigned to an outside consultant.

In addition to undertaking marketing research at the corporate level and in the host countries, in many companies marketing research is also conducted at the regional level. A company may divide its international operations into regions; for example, Western Europe, Far East, Latin America, Middle East, Africa, and South Asia. Each country manager in a region would report to the regional executive. Under such arrangements, the regional executive may seek marketing research information to formulate regional marketing strategy or to develop the marketing perspective of a country within the region. There may be a specific person responsible for marketing research in the region, or one of the staff persons may carry this responsibility.

What is important to recognize is that the process of gathering, analyzing, and reporting market-related information, which is in fact marketing research, may not necessarily be *called* marketing research. Moreover, marketing research responsibility may not necessarily be assigned to a marketing person. Of course, the extent of marketing research that a company undertakes would vary according to the style of management and the importance of a particular foreign country for a given product.

International Marketing Information System

Earlier in this chapter, three terms were introduced: *market research, marketing research,* and *marketing intelligence.* An international marketing information system is a formal way of structuring the information flow through these three modes. Large, complex organizations may do business in a great number of countries with any number of products and services. This complexity, combined with today's difficult and demanding business environment, makes it particularly important for international marketers to have adequate and timely information available in order to make the right moves.

The following mishap illustrates the critical need for information:

"I never dreamed this would happen to us," exclaimed the chairman of the American drug firm G.D. Searle & Co. (sales over $600 million) in an interview published in *Business Week.* The company was apparently unaware that it would be investigated by a Senate subcommittee on health involving charges that the company mishandled research data on two of its best selling products. It is obvious that this company—like many others—did not have an adequate "early warning" capability or intelligence system that could have enabled management to anticipate the crisis. One result of the threat: a corporate committee of social scientists was established to study economic and political trends and their potential effect on the company.

Another recent example of an intelligence mishap involved Westinghouse Corporation's agreement to sell utility companies 80 million pounds of uranium at an average contracted price of $10 a pound over a period of 20 years. At the time the agreement was signed, Westinghouse owned only about 20 percent of the contracted amount of uranium. Since then, its price rose to $40, so if the company would have fulfilled the terms of the agreement it could have lost about $2 billion. Obviously, top management was unaware that such an agreement was being negotiated, an intelligence failure concerning internal operations.[20]

Steps for Establishing an Information System

Exhibit 4.4 shows the essential steps for developing and maintaining an international marketing information system: determining information needs, identifying information sources, gathering information, analyzing information, and disseminating information.

Information will be needed at corporate headquarters, regional offices, and country locations. Some of it will be strategic information, and some will be operational information. It could also be grouped in the categories of market information, competitive information, foreign-exchange related data, resource information, prescriptive information (e.g., foreign taxes), and general-conditions information.

No generic framework for classifying information needs is suitable for all companies. Every company should work out its own information categories, based on its marketing information needs and the attitude of top management toward systematic information management. Whatever the ultimate system is—highly structured, computerized, primitive, unstructured, manual—it must be sophisticated enough and comprehensive enough to meet the information needs of that particular company.

Aspects of System Use

The information sources may be internal or external, international or domestic, secondary or primary. The information may be gathered by mail, telephone, or computer terminal through remote entry. Some information may be gathered regularly, and some may be collected on an ad hoc basis. Also, information may be gathered in a structured fashion or an open-ended one. In gathering information, duplication should be avoided, as it is wasteful in most cases to gather the same information from different sources. In certain cases, though, duplication can be used as a control device. The gathered information must be analyzed for use in the most convenient form and disseminated to all designated users. Some information may be made widely available to all managers. Other information may

EXHIBIT 4.4   Components of an International Marketing Information System

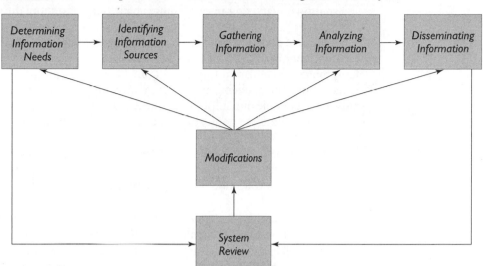

be restricted for senior people in the organization. Information may be disseminated on a regular basis or irregularly, or in some cases be available only on request.

The system design should be reviewed from time to time to ensure it still meets the demands placed on it. The review should also evaluate the cost/benefit relationship of the entire system. The review may recommend modifications in any one or more of the system components.

Most large, multimarket, multiproduct companies have some sort of multinational marketing information system in operation. It is difficult to say, however, how many of these systems can be labeled "sophisticated" or "advanced." The increasing popularity of the international data networks made available by such companies as Data Research Inc. and Predicasts indicates a trend toward the establishment of computerized information systems. These systems may serve information needs of marketing and of other functional areas of the business as well, in the following manner:

1. To aid in decisions relating to international market expansion, for example, whether new countries are potential candidates for market entry or whether existing products might be carried into new markets

2. To monitor performance in different countries and product markets based on criteria such as return on investment and market share. This way, existing or potential future problems can be detected and marketing tactics or strategies changed accordingly.

3. To scan the international environment in order to assess future world and country scenarios and to monitor emerging and changing environmental trends

4. To assess strategies with regard to the allocation of corporate resources and effort across different countries, product markets, target segments, and modes of entry to determine whether changes in this allocation would maximize long-run profitability.

Summary

The techniques and tools of international marketing research do not vary according to whether research is done in the United States or abroad. An international marketing research project essentially follows domestic procedures: problem definition, research design, data collection, analysis, and report preparation. However, several factors make international marketing research more challenging and more difficult, one being cultural differences.

Data are obtained from either secondary or primary sources. The United States offers a variety of secondary sources. Foremost among them is the U.S. Department of Commerce. Secondary information available in host countries may be plagued by problems of timeliness, reliability, and comparability. The collection of primary data abroad also poses possible difficulties such as the inability to draw a random sample, the unwillingness of the sample population to cooperate, and the inability to develop an adequate questionnaire.

Despite the inherent problems, a researcher can adopt measures to solve some, if not all, of the difficulties involved. Two helpful measures are the involvement of talented individuals in data collection and cooperation with respectable foreign marketing information sources.

The international research activity may be formally organized at home or in the host country, or at both locations. Further, the marketing research organization may be just a one-person department or a large entity in accordance with the scope of marketing activity in a country. A company deeply involved in business around the globe should establish an international marketing information system with formal structuring to determine information needs, to identify information sources, and to gather, analyze, and disseminate information.

Review Questions

1. What factors make conducting international marketing research more difficult than domestic marketing research?
2. What are the principal sources of secondary data in the United States?
3. What difficulties are associated with secondary data on marketing in host countries?
4. Discuss the problems a researcher may face in primary data collection overseas.
5. What factors account for the unreliability of secondary data in foreign countries?
6. What steps can be taken to resolve the problems of primary data collection in the developing countries?
7. What kind of companies should consider developing an international marketing information system?
8. What help can be expected from international agencies in the search for secondary data?

Creative Questions

1. Pizza Hut is interested in surveying consumers in France, Singapore, and Mexico. A consultant suggests conducting a telephone survey using the same questionnaire (initially written in English but duly translated into local languages). Evaluate the consultant's recommendation. Do you have any alternative recommendation for conducting the survey?
2. The U.S. government collects and disseminates an abundance of foreign trade data. Yet the marketing-related data is commonly not available. If you were to make a case to the U.S. government that it should provide data readily usable by marketers, indicate what type of data it should provide, in what format, and how current it should keep that data.

Endnotes

1. Jack Honomichl, "Research Growth Knows No Boundaries," *Marketing News,* August 17, 1998, p. 142. These 1999 figures have been extrapolated based on 1997 data. Also see "Market Research-Data Wars," *The Economist,* July 22, 1995, p. 60.

2. Ibid. Also see Cyndee Miller, "Research Firms Go Global to Make Revenue Grow," *Marketing News,* January 6, 1997, p. 1.

3. Earl Naumann, Donald W. Jackson, Jr. and William G. Wolfe, "Examining the Practices of United States and Japanese Market Research Firms," *California Management Review,* Summer 1994, pp. 49–69.

4. Charles F. Keown, "Foreign Mail Surveys: Response Rates Using Monetary Incentives," *Journal of International Business Studies,* Fall 1985, p. 153.

5. Susan P. Douglas and C. Samuel Craig, *International Marketing Research* (Englewood Cliffs, NJ: Prentice-Hall, Inc., 1983), p. 16.

6. *European Market Survey* (Pleasantville, NY: Reader's Digest Association, 1963).

7. Paul H. Berent, "International Research Is Different: The Case for Centralized Control," in *International Marketing Research: Does It Provide What the User Needs?* (Amsterdam: European Society for Opinion and Marketing Research, 1986), pp. 110–111.

8. Charles S. Mayer, "The Lessons of Multinational Marketing Research," *Business Horizons,* December 1978, p. 9.

9. "Product Pick-up Firm Samples International Supermarkets," *Marketing News,* March 1, 1985, p. 10.

10. *See* Ravi Parameswaran and Attila Yaprak, "A Cross-National Comparison of Consumer Research Measures," *Journal of International Business Studies,* Spring 1987, pp. 35–50.

11. "Grossly Distorted Picture," *The Economist,* February 5, 1994, p. 71.

12. Warren J. Keegan, *Multinational Marketing Management,* 4th ed. (Englewood Cliffs, NJ: Prentice-Hall, 1989), p. 223.

13. Philip R. Cateora, *International Marketing,* 5th ed. (Homewood, IL: Irwin, 1983), pp. 267–268.

14. *Boltin International* (Los Angeles, CA: Boltin International, an annual publication).

15. *Kelly's Manufacturers and Merchants Directory* (New York: Kelly's Directories Ltd., an annual publication).

16. Susan P. Douglas and C. Samuel Craig, *International Marketing Research* (Englewood Cliffs, NJ: Prentice-Hall, Inc., 1983), p. 224. Also see David Jobber and John Saunders, "An Experimental Investigation into Cross-National Mail Survey Response Rates," *Journal of International Business Studies,* Fall 1988, pp. 483–490.

17. Wallace Doolin, "Taking Your Business on the Road Abroad," *The Wall Street Journal,* July 25, 1994, p. A14.

18. Ferdinand F. Mauser, "Losing Something in Translation," *Harvard Business Review,* July–August 1987, p. 14.

19. J. Terence Gallagher, "A Problem of Translation," *The Asian Wall Street Journal Weekly,* September 30, 1985, p. 11c.

20. E. D. Jaffee, "Multinational Marketing Intelligence: An Information Requirements Model," *Management International Review* 19, no. 2 (1979): 53–60.

Appendix
Sources of Secondary Data

The following represents selected sources of information for international marketing purposes.

A. Information Available from International Agencies

    1. *The United Nations.* United Nations publications can be obtained from
       United Nations Publications
       Sales Office
       New York. NY 10017

       a. *Statistical Yearbook of the United Nations* (annual). A major source of world economic data, including information on population, manpower, agriculture, manufacturing, mining, construction, trade, transport, communications, balance of payments, consumption, wages and prices, national accounts, finance, international capital flows, housing, health, education, and mass communications.

       b. *Economic Survey of Europe* (annual). Review of current developments in the European economy. *Economic Bulletin for Europe,* issued twice annually; supplements *Survey.*

       c. *Economic Survey of Asia and the Far East* (annual). Review of current situation concerning agriculture, transport, trade, and balance of payments. *Economic Bulletin for Asia and the Far East,* issued three times annually; supplements the *Survey.*

       d. *Economic Survey of Latin America* (annual). Review of regional economic developments. *Economic Bulletin for Latin America,* issued twice annually; supplements the *Survey.*

       e. *Economic Developments in the Middle East* (annual). Review of developments concerning agriculture, industry, loom foreign trade, and balance of payments.

       f. *World Economic Survey* (annual). World economic report. A comprehensive review of world economic trends and issues.

       g. *World Trade Annual.* Information from the 24 principal trading countries of the world, providing statistics of trade by commodity and country.

       h. GATT publications (available from UN Publications Sales Office).

          i. Analytical Bibliography—Market surveys by products and by countries

          ii. *Guide to Sources of Information on Foreign Trade Regulations*

   iii. Compilation of Basic Information on Export Markets

   iv. *Compendium of Sources: International Trade Statistics*

   v. *Manual on Export Marketing Research for Developing Countries*

   vi. *World Directory of Industry and Trade Associations*

   vii. *Directory of Product and Industry Journals*

2. Organization for Economic Cooperation and Development (OECD) publications can be obtained from
   OECD Publications Office, Suite 1305
   1750 Pennsylvania Avenue, N.W.
   Washington, D.C. 20006

   a. OECD Economic Surveys. Each title in this series of economic studies is a booklet published annually by the OECD and pertaining to one of the 21 OECD member countries. Each booklet has information concerning recent trends of demand and output, prices and wages, foreign trade and payments, economic policy, and prospects and conclusions.

   b. *OECD Economic Outlook* (semiannual). Survey of economic trends and prospects in OECD countries, examining the current situation and prospects regarding demand and output, employment, costs and prices, and foreign trade for OECD as a whole and in some of the major countries. Trends of current balances, monetary developments, and capital movements as factors affecting international monetary developments are also considered.

   c. *Monthly Statistics of Foreign Trade.* This bulletin is intended to serve as a timely source of statistical data on the foreign trade by OECD member countries. The data cover not only overall trade by countries, but also a number of seasonally adjusted series, volume and average value indices, and trade by SITC sections.

3. International Monetary Fund (IMF) publications can be obtained from
   International Monetary Fund
   Washington, D.C. 20431

   a. *International Financial Statistics* (monthly). Statistical information on such financial matters as international liquidity, interest rates, prices, and money supply.

4. World Bank publications can be obtained from
   The World Bank
   1818 H Street, N.W.
   Washington, D.C. 20433

   a. *World Bank: Annual Report* (annual).

   b. *World Development Report* (annual). Reviews economy, assesses the impact of external factors on development, and considers future scenarios.

   c. *World Tables* (annual). Presents annual data for most of the World Bank's members in a four-page table for each economy.

   d. *Publications Update* (monthly). Lists various research publications of the World Bank. For example: William W. Ambrose, Paul R. Hennemeyer, and Jean-Pat, *Privatizing Telecommunications Systems: Business Opportunities in Developing Countries,* 1990.

5. International Chamber of Commerce (ICC) publications can be purchased at the following address
   The ICC Publishing Corporation, Inc.
   801 Second Avenue, Suite 1204
   New York, NY 10017

   a. *ICC/E.S. O. M.A.R. International Code of Marketing and Social Research Practice.* This code provides individuals and organizations with a set of rules so that marketing and opinion research can be conducted in accordance with accepted principles of integrity and fair competition.

   b. *International Code of Direct Mail and Mail Order Sales*

   c. *International Uniform Definitions for the Distributive T.* List of current definitions that permit international standardization of types of establishments, outlets, and selling methods.

   d. *Marketing: Discipline for Freedom*

   e. *Media Information for Advertising Planning*

   f. *Advertising Agencies: Their Services and Relationship with Advertisers and Media*

B. Information Available from U.S. Government Sources

   1. *U.S. Department of Commerce.* The following publication can be purchased by writing to
      The Superintendent of Documents
      U.S. Government Printing Office, Room 1617
      Publications Sales Branch
      Washington, D.C. 20402
      or:
      U.S. Department of Commerce
      Washington, D.C. 10130

      a. *A Basic Guide to Exporting.* Provides step-by-step approach to exporting; It is especially useful for firms with little or no export experience.

      b. *Foreign Trade Report FT410* (monthly). Provides a statistical record of shipments of all merchandise from the United States to some 100 countries.

      c. *International Economic Indicators* (quarterly). Lists trade trends for the United States and seven principal industrial countries.

      d. *International Demographic Data* (updated periodically). Details demographic profiles of developing countries and Eastern European economies.

      e. *Market Share Reports* (annual). Shows U.S. participation in foreign markets during the last five years. Covers 88 countries for 1,000 manufactured products.

      f. Overseas Business Reports (yearly). Some 60 percent of the reports are issued with background data on both developed and developing countries.

      g. *Foreign Economic Trends and Their Implications for the United States* (yearly). Some 150 reports are issued with country-by-country trade and economic statistics and trends.

      h. Global Market Surveys. Market research studies conducted in selected countries for specific U.S. products.

      i.   Country Market Sectoral Surveys. Reports showing the most promising export opportunities for U.S. firms in selected countries.

      j.   Trade Lists. Provide names and addresses of potential buyers, distributors, and agents for different industries in selected countries.

      k.   *Business America* (biweekly). Covers domestic and international news.

      l.   Country Studies. Each study classifies and analyzes the country's economic, military, political, and social systems and institutions, as well as the impact that cultural factors have on the country's lifestyle.

      m.   *European Trade Fairs: A Guide for Exporters.* Provides expert advice on participating in trade fairs.

      n.   *Custom Statistical Service for Exporters.* Includes current data and market trends on thousands of products in more than 200 nations. Data are arranged by time frames from one month to five years, and by dollar and unit value, quantity, growth rate, and market-share percentages.

2. Other Government Sources

      a.   *Aids to Business* (overseas investment). Explains how the Agency for International Development can assist U.S. firms interested in developing nations.

      b.   *Export Marketing for Smaller Firms.* Small Business Administration publishes guidelines for how small business firms can expand either their export or import market.

      c.   *Export-import Bank of the United States.* Describes U.S. export financing program.

      d.   *Agricultural Economy and Trade.* Published by the U.S. Department of Agriculture. Describes overseas business opportunities in the agricultural sector.

C. Information Available from Commercial Publishers

1. Books

      a.   Bartels, Robert. *Global Development and Marketing.* Columbus, OH: Grid Inc., 1981.

      b.   Buzzell, Robert D., John A. Quelch, and Christopher Bartlett. *Global Marketing Management: Cases and Readings,* 2nd ed. Reading, MA: Addison-Wesley Publishing Co., 1992.

      c.   Cateora, Philip C. *International Marketing,* 7th ed. Homewood, IL: Richard D. Irwin, Inc., 1990.

      d.   Cundiff, Edward W., and Marye Tharp Hilger. *Marketing International Environment.* Englewood Cliffs, NJ: Prentice-Hall, Inc., 1984.

      e.   Czinkota, Michael R., and Ilkka A. Ronkainen. *International Marketing,* 2nd ed. Chicago: Dryden Press, 1990.

      f.   Douglas, Susan P., and C. Samuel Craig. *International Marketing Research.* Englewood Cliffs, NJ: Prentice-Hall, Inc., 1983

      g.   Jain, Subhash C., and Lewis R. Tucker, Jr., eds. *International Marketing: Managerial Perspectives,* 2nd ed. Boston: Kent Co., 1986.

      h.   Jeannet, Jean-Pierre, and Hubert D. Hennessey. *International Marketing Management: Strategies and Cases.* Boston: Houghton Mifflin Co., 1988.

      i.   Kahler, Ruel. *International Marketing,* 5th ed. Southwestern Publishing Company, 1983.

j. Kaynak, Erdner. *Transnational Retailing.* Hawthorne, NY: de Gruyter, Inc., 1988.

k. Keegan, Warren J. *Global Marketing Management,* 4th ed. Englewood Cliffs, NJ: Prentice-Hall, Inc., 1989.

l. Kirpalani, V. H. *International Marketing.* New York: Random House, Inc., 1984.

m. Peebles, Dean M., and John K. Ryans, Jr. *Management of International Advertising.* Newton, MA: Allyn & Bacon, Inc., 1984.

n. Robock, Stefan H., and Kenneth Simmonds. *International Business and Multinational Enterprises,* 4th ed. Homewood, IL: Richard D. Irwin, Inc., 1990.

o. Terpstra, Vern. *International Marketing,* 4th ed. Hinsdale, IL: Dryden Press, 1987.

p. Thorelli, Hans B., and Helmut Becker, eds. *International Marketing Strategy,* rev. ed. New York: Pergamon Press, 1982.

q. Vernon, Raymond, and Louis T. Wells, Jr. *Manager in the International Economy,* 5th ed. Englewood Cliffs, NJ: Prentice-Hall, Inc., 1986.

2. Reference Material

a. *Business International Weekly Report.* New York:

Business International Corporation, weekly issue. Reports important events of interest to managers of worldwide operations.

b. Doing Business in Different Nations series. New York: Business International Corporation.

c. *Encyclopedia of Geographic Information Sources.* Detroit: Gale Research, 1990.

d. *European Markets: A Guide to Company and Industry Information Sources.* Washington, D.C.: Washington Researchers, 1989.

e. *European Statistics: 1987–88* and *International Marketing Statistics: 1989–90.* Detroit: Gale Research. Designed for market planners and researchers, provides information on social, economic, and consumer trends in 140 countries.

f. *International Marketing Data and Statistics* (annual). London: Euromonitor Publications, Ltd. Presents statistical information on all basic marketing parameters for over 100 countries.

g. *Exporter's Encyclopedia* (annual). Import regulations and procedures required for shipping to every country in the world, as well as information on preparing export shipments. Lists world ports, steamship lines, airlines, government agencies, trade organizations. Special sections on packing, marine insurance, export terms, and many other areas of foreign trade. Price includes twice-monthly supplementary bulletins and newsletters. Available from Dun and Bradstreet International, P.O. Box 3224, Church Street Station, New York, NY 10008.

h. *Multinational Business, Retail Business, Special Industry Reports.* New York: The Economist Intelligence Unit.

i. *Predibrief.* Cleveland, OH: Predicasts. Industry news reports for thirty-five countries.

j.   *Reference Book for World Traders.* Loose-leaf handbook covering information necessary for planning exports to and imports from all foreign countries, as well as market research throughout the world. Kept up to date by monthly supplements. Available from Croner Publications, Inc., 211–213 Jamaica Avenue, Queens Village, NY 11428.

k.   *Sources of European Economic Information,* 4th ed. Cambridge, England: Gower Publishing Co., Ltd., 1989.

l.   *The World in Figures,* 5th ed. London: The Economist Newspaper Limited, 1990.

m.   *World Advertising Expenditures,* 1990 edition. New York: Starch INRA Hooper Group of Companies, 1991.

n.   *Worldcasts.* Cleveland, OH: Predicasts. These are short-term and long-term economic forecasts in select industries for different countries.

o.   *The Europa Year Book,* vol. 1 and vol. 2 (annual). London: Europa Publications, Ltd. An authoritative reference work providing a wealth of detailed information on the political, economic, and commercial institutions of the world.

p.   *The Statesman's Year-Book* (annual). London: The Macmillan Ltd. A statistical and historical annual of the states of the world.

3.   Magazines and Newspapers
The Wall Street Journal
The New York Times
Nihom Keizai Shimbun, Japan
Financial Times, England
Frankfurter Algemine, Germany
Business Week
Fortune
Forbes
The Asian Wall Street Journal Weekly

4.   Service Organizations

An important source of foreign market information are service organizations such as banks and consultants. Most large international banks have periodicals and special reports on international market developments.

International Marketing Research: Internet Addresses

A. U.S. Government

1.   Agency for International Development
http://www.usaid.gov

2.   Customs Service
http://www.customs.ustreas.gov

3.   Department of Agriculture
http://www.usda.gov

4.   Department of Commerce
http://www.doc.gov

5.   Department of State
http://www.state.gov

6. Department of the Treasury
http://www.ustreas.gov

7. Federal Trade Commission
http://www.ftc.gov

8. International Trade Commission
http://www.usitc.gov

9. Small Business Administration
http://www.sba.gov

10. World Trade Centers Association
http://www.wtca.org

11. Export-Import Bank of the United States
http://www.exim.gov

12. National Trade Data Bank
http://www.stat-usa.gov

13. Office of the U.S. Trade Representative
http://www.ustr.gov/index.html

B. United Nations

1. All listings at
http://www.un.org

2. Industrial Development Organization
http://www.unido.org

C. Other

1. International Bank for Reconstruction and Development (World Bank)
http://www.worldbank.org

2. International Monetary Fund
http://www.imf.org

3. Inter-American Development Bank
http://www.iadb.org

4. Asian Development Bank
http://www.asiandevbank.org

5. European Community Information Service
http://www.europa.eu.int

6. Organization for Economic Cooperation and Development
http://www.oecd.org (France)
and
http://www.oecdwash.org (Washington, D.C.)

7. Organization of American States
http://www.oas.org

8. Commission of the European Union to the United States
http://www.eurunion.org

D. Periodic Reports, Newspapers, Magazines

1. Advertising Age
http://www.adage.com

2. Business Week
http://www.businessweek.com

3. The Economist
http://www.economist.com

4. Forbes
http://www.forbes.com

5. Fortune
http://pathfinder.com/fortune

6. Wall Street Journal
http://www.wsj.com

E. Indexes to Literature

1. New York Times Index
http://www.nytimes.com

2. Public Affairs Information Service Bulletin
http://www.pais.org

3. Wall Street Journal Index
http://www.wsj.com

PART 3

The Field of International Business

International Monetary System

CHAPTER FOCUS

After studying this chapter, you should be able to

■ Describe the development of today's international monetary system.

■ Explain how foreign exchange transactions are conducted.

■ Identify the problems associated with exchange rate fluctuations.

■ Discuss the balance-of-payments perspectives of the United States.

■ Examine current global monetary issues.

This chapter examines the subject of international business and trade in monetary terms. Trade settlements involve topics such as determination of foreign exchange rates, balance of payments, foreign exchange transactions, international financial flows, and international financial and trade institutions.

Each country has its own currency through which it expresses the value of its goods. For international trade settlements, however, the various currencies of the world must be transformed from one into the other. This task is accomplished through foreign exchange markets.

Periodically, a country must review the status of its economic relations with the rest of the world in terms of its exports and imports, its exchange of various kinds of services, and its purchase and sale of different types of assets and other international payments or receipts and transfers. Such an overall review is necessary to ascertain whether the country has a favorable or unfavorable monetary balance in relation to the rest of the world. In the post–World War II period, a number of institutions came into existence to monitor and assist countries in this endeavor. As a result of the establishment of these institutions, a new system of international monetary relations emerged in the late 1950s, one that went a long way toward increasing international trade. In the early 1970s, however, the weakening of the U.S. dollar caused the system to falter.

The all-important commitment of the United States to the monetary system of the 1950s and 1960s deserves mention here. In order to encourage worldwide monetary stability, the U.S. government agreed to exchange the dollar at the fixed price of $35 for an ounce of gold. With the value of the dollar stabilized, countries could deal in dollars without being constrained by currency fluctuations. Thus, the dollar became the common denominator in world trade. Because of the subsequent weakening of the dollar, and other related issues, the monetary stability of the world was disturbed and remained unsettled in the 1970s and early 1980s.

As the 1980s advanced, the U.S. economy stabilized, and the value of the dollar, against other currencies, climbed to an all-time high, adversely affecting the U.S. trade balance. In the fall of 1985 leading industrialized countries joined in the U.S. effort to intervene in the foreign exchange markets to decrease the value of the dollar. The dollar continued to stay weak in the remaining years of the 1980s and in the early 1990s. At the beginning of the year 2000, it appreciated a little bit and is expected to remain stable for the next few years.

Development of Today's International Monetary System

Post–World War II financial developments had long-range effects on international financial arrangements and on the role of gold. Moreover, this period saw problems of disequilibria brought about by adjustment of balance of payments. Following World War II, a keen awareness of the need to achieve economic prosperity grew among nations. The war years had shattered the economies of Europe and Japan, which therefore needed reconstruction. A number of countries were wresting political freedom from colonial rulers, particularly from Britain, and soon realized that political freedom alone was not sufficient. Economic prosperity was not only necessary for existence but mandatory for long-term survival and growth.

Countries realized that planned international cooperation fostered economic development and prosperity. Thus, immediately after the war, they agreed to a framework of international rules—a code of behavior—to maintain monetary discipline and to ensure that dissenting nations would not frustrate economic development efforts through counteractions.

Bretton Woods Conference

Negotiations to establish the postwar international monetary system took place at Bretton Woods, New Hampshire, in 1944. The general feeling at that time was that the economically disastrous interwar period and, to an extent, the precipitation of World War II resulted from a failure to include economic factors as a major consideration in post–World War I planning. Aiming to avoid the mistakes of the past and to set goals for economic prosperity the negotiators at Bretton Woods made the following recommendations:

- Each nation should be at liberty to use macroeconomic policies for full employment.
- Free-floating exchange rates were to be abandoned, as their ineffectiveness had been demonstrated during the 1920s and 1930s. The extremes of both permanently fixed and free-floating rates were to be avoided.
- A monetary system was needed that would recognize that exchange rates were both a national and an international concern.

International Monetary Fund

After long and careful deliberations, a monetary system was agreed upon at Bretton Woods. Member countries agreed to control the limits of their exchange rates in a predetermined way. Under the original agreement, exchange rates were permitted to vary by 1 percent above or below par. As a country's rate of exchange attained or approached either limit, called *arbitrage support points,* its central bank intervened in the market to prevent the rate from passing the limit. Market intervention required a nation to accumulate international reserves, composed of gold and foreign currencies, above normal trading requirements. The ***International Monetary Fund (IMF)*** was established at Bretton Woods to oversee the newly agreed upon monetary system.

In addition to the IMF, the *World Bank* was established to help developing countries in their economic development efforts. The World Bank family consists of the International Bank for Reconstruction and Development (IBRD); its concessional window, the International Development Association (IDA); the International Finance Corporation (IFC); the Inter-American Development Bank and its Fund for Special Operations (IDB/FSO); the Asian Development Bank and Fund (ADB/F); and the African Development Bank and Fund (AFDB/F). The World Bank makes loans to assist the growth of less developed countries around the globe, while the regional banks focus on the development needs in their geographic area.

More and more nations joined the original 55 IMF signatories, so that today there are over 150 members. With the passage of time, various changes have been made in the IMF system to ameliorate the difficulties that nations face. For example, if a nation's fixed parity ceases to be realistic, it can overvalue or devalue its currency. In such cases, the IMF agreed on orderly and reasonable changes in parity based upon the initiative of the country concerned. Such a system of alterable pass is often termed the *adjustable peg.*

The IMF has several major accomplishments to its credit:

- It sustained a rapidly increasing volume of trade and investment.
- It displayed flexibility in adapting to changes in international commerce.
- It proved to be efficient (even when there were decreasing percentages of reserves to trade).
- It proved to be hardy (it survived a number of pre–1971 crises, speculative and otherwise, and the down-and-up swings of several business cycles).
- It allowed a growing degree of international cooperation.
- It established a capacity to accommodate reforms and improvements.[1]

To an extent the fund served as an international central bank to help countries during periods of temporary balance-of-payments difficulties by protecting their rates of exchange. Because of that, countries did not need to resort to exchange controls and other barriers to restrict world trade.

As time passed, it became evident that the fund's resources for providing short-term accommodation to countries in monetary difficulties were not sufficient. To resolve the situation, the fund, after much debate and long deliberations, created *special drawing rights (SDRs)* in 1969. Sometimes called *paper gold*, SDRs special account entries on the IMF books designed to provide additional liquidity to support growing world commerce. Although SDRs are a form of fiat money not convertible to gold, their gold value is guaranteed, which helps to ensure their acceptability. Initially SDRs worth $9.5 billion were created. By the end of 1998 the IMF resources stood at $81.7 billion SDRs, of which $58.4 billion had been issued to member countries.[2]

Participant nations may use SDRs in a variety of ways: as a source of currency in a spot transaction, as a loan for clearing a financial obligation, as security for a loan, as a swap against currency, or in a forward exchange operation. A nation with a balance-of-payments need may use its SDRs to obtain usable currency from another nation designated by the fund. A participant also may use SDRs to make payments to the fund, such as repurchases. The fund itself may transfer SDRs to a participant for various purposes, including the transfer of SDRs instead of currency to a member using the fund's resources.

By providing a mechanism for international monetary cooperation, working to reduce restrictions to trade and capital flows, and helping members with their short-term balance-of-payments difficulties, the IMF makes a significant and unique contribution to human welfare and improved living standards throughout the world.

In the post–World War II period, in addition to IMF and the World Bank, a variety of other institutions came into existence to strengthen global trade and business and to promote economic development. These included the General Agreement on Tariffs and Trade (GATT) and the Organization for Economic Cooperation and Development (OECD). GATT (replaced by a new World Trade Organization) governed the trade of its member countries. OECD was organized for mutual cooperation in implementing the Marshall Plan and now promotes economic growth of its member countries.

The IMF and the Debt Crisis

In the 1970s developing nations all over the world found their efforts to manage their economic affairs swamped by a unique combination of adverse circumstances: dramatically increased oil prices, followed by worldwide inflation, a collapse in commodity prices, the worst world recession since the 1930s, and historically high interest rates. When oil prices shot up, these countries borrowed heavily at high interest rates to stave off economic dislocation.

Between 1974 and 1982 the two oil price shocks created a temporary savings surplus in high-income oil-exporting countries. Their surplus funds were recycled to developing countries. In addition to increasing their development aid, high-income oil-exporting countries placed much of their surplus oil revenue with international commercial banks in the form of short-term deposits. This action contributed to raising liquidity in the international banking system, because credit demand in the industrialized countries had been depressed by the oil price shocks. The liquidity drove real interest rates down. It prompted the banks in the industrialized countries to compensate for the slack in their traditional markets by lending more to developing countries.

Commercial lending to developing countries—along with official lending and aid—grew very rapidly during this period. As a result, the total medium- and long-term debt of developing countries rose fourfold in nominal terms, from about $140 billion at the end of 1974 to about $560 billion in 1982. By the end of 1998 their indebtedness had reached $2.4 trillion.[3] Developing countries were happy to take advantage of this unaccustomed access to cheap loans with few strings attached. They stepped up their commercial borrowing, which enabled them to maintain domestic growth and to finance major public investment programs, especially in the energy sector. With hindsight, it is clear that lending and borrowing decisions were often imprudent and resulted in excessive indebtedness in a number of countries. New funds were often channeled into low-yielding investments. In a number of countries, borrowings fueled a flight of capital that drained the pool of resources for investment even as the burden of foreign debt mounted.[4]

The debt crisis has had a profound impact on the economic performance of developing countries. One of the most urgent tasks facing the international community is to find ways of reducing the drag exerted by the continuing debt overhang on economic growth in the developing world. A framework to reduce the burden of debt must have two elements. First, the debtors need to grow faster and export more. Second, the cost of debt service must fall. With the right policies in both industrial and developing countries, these elements can go hand in hand.

While long-term solutions to the debt crisis are being examined, most countries have sought IMF assistance for debt relief. In the debt crisis, the fund assumed a new role as financial organizer for the troubled debtor nations. For example, the fund worked out a two-year program of austerity, currency devaluations, and domestic economic restructuring designed to produce sustained economic health for Brazil. It helped Brazil emerge from a $16 billion balance-of-payments deficit in 1982 to a $530 million surplus in 1984. The devaluations stopped capital flight and spurred exports, mainly of steel, shoes, textiles, and alcohol. In addition, steps to conserve energy slashed oil imports. Since then, Brazil has been able to service its debt of more than $100 billion.[5]

International Monetary Crisis in the 1970s

Toward the end of the 1960s the American economy began to deteriorate. Inflation continued to increase, and unemployment became widespread. Subsequently, President Nixon announced on August 15, 1971, that the United States would not redeem dollars officially held in gold. In addition, the dollar was devalued in 1971 and again in 1973. Thus, starting with 1971, the dollar's link with gold was broken. Without any attachment to gold, the U.S. dollar began to float. The United States hoped this would force its trading partners to revalue their currencies. It was commonly held that many strong foreign currencies were undervalued, giving them a substantial advantage against the dollar. Revaluation would have the effect of making the exports of revaluing countries like Japan and the then West Germany more expensive and their imports less expensive, thus reducing the U.S. balance-of-payments deficits.

Fixed versus Floating Rates

In the 1960s, most monetarists considered fixed exchange rates to be the backbone of international financial cooperation and the stability of the international monetary system. Floating, or "flexible," exchange rates were considered impractical. Today, however, all major nations have floating currencies.

In 1976, at an IMF meeting in Kingston, Jamaica, over 100 member nations reached consensus on amendments to the IMF Articles of Agreement that in effect accepted floating rates as the basis for the international monetary system.[6] The amended agreement, while reaffirming the importance of international cooperation and exchange rate stability, also recognized that such rate stability can be achieved only as the result of stability in underlying economic and financial conditions. Exchange rate stability of any lasting duration cannot be imposed externally by adoption of the pegged exchange rates and heavy official intervention in the foreign exchange market.

However, the merits attributed to floating exchange rates were not borne out. For example:

- When the floating exchange rates were introduced, it was said that balance-of-payments adjustments would be facilitated, but not only have imbalances not disappeared, they have become worse.

- It was thought that speculation would be curtailed. On the contrary, never has it assumed such proportions nor had such destabilizing effects as today.

- It was believed that market forces, left at last to their own devices, would determine the correct exchange-rate balance. But never have imbalances been so great, nor fluctuations so wide and erratic and so little justified by economic fundamentals.

- It was hoped that autonomy in economic and monetary policy would be preserved, allowing each country free choice of its monetary policy and rate of inflation. Facts have completely belied this prediction.

In the mid 1980s, the countries with primary responsibility for the world economy recognized the need for renewed international cooperation on monetary matters. Subsequently, in early 1987 the United States, Japan, France, Britain, Canada, Italy, and what was then West Germany concluded an accord called the *Louvre Agreements* on two complementary aspects: coordination of economic policy and more stable exchange rates. The seven signatories agreed to policies aimed at reducing their internal and external imbalances. For example, they agreed to intervene in exchange markets when necessary.

Since then, the Louvre Agreements have been reconfirmed and adjusted as required by economic and market developments. Economic policy commitments have been adapted and strengthened, including those of central banks. Thus, a first milestone was reached on the road to rebuilding an international monetary order, though it rested on the will and ability of governments to impose self-discipline.[7]

The IMF and the Mexican Debacle

In 1995 Mexico ran into deep economic problems, since the Mexican leaders pushed the country's borrowing too far ahead of its economic growth. The value of the peso went down 30 percent within a week, as foreign investors lost confidence in the country's economy.

How did Mexico get into a mess? Consider a person whose business is doubling every year but whose debt is tripling. When his creditors wake up and ask for some money back, he does not have the cash. It might take him a couple of years to raise it. Meanwhile he needs some more credit to keep his business going. This scenario fits Mexico well. Mexico has been growing consistently for half a dozen years, and its government finances were solid; the federal budget had been balanced three years running. So Mexico looked like a great place to invest. But foreign lenders, mainly American banks, pension, and mutual funds, overdid it. From 1991 through 1993 they loaned to Mexican enterprises and to the government $15 billion to $25 billion a year more than what Mexico was earning from its exports. Toward the end of 1994 these creditors recognized the problems and asked for some money back. But Mexico had no way to pay. The reason was that Mexico had $28 billion in dollar-denominated Treasury notes becoming due in 1995, of which $16 billion was owned by Americans.[8]

Most of the Mexican loans were owned by thousands of U.S. mutual and pension funds and retirement accounts. They had legal obligations to pay benefits to tens of millions of Americans, mostly small savers. There was no practical way to demand new loans from them. Therefore, the IMF and the U.S. government had to come to their rescue.

The IMF committed $17.8 billion to help Mexico in her currency crisis, while the U.S. government provided $40 billion in loan guarantees. The IMF help came with stringent measures to restore the country's economic health.

The IMF and the Asian Crisis

In the fall of 1997 the so-called growth economies of Southeast Asia, one after the other, ran into deep financial crisis. These included Thailand, Indonesia, South Korea, Philippines, and Malaysia. Particularly in the first three nations, the situation became serious enough for the IMF to come to the rescue. The collapse in their asset prices, the extent of financial and corporate insolvency, and the slowdown in the economic growth across the region showed no sign of abating.

The IMF put together a package of $57 billion for South Korea, $43 billion for Indonesia, and $17 billion for Thailand (see International Marketing Highlight 5.1). As a result of the vast sums of money that the IMF applied to the Asian problem, and the strict financial discipline that it required (tight government budgets, high interest rates, and liberalizing economic reforms), the Asian economies at the time of preparing this book had started to come back. Noteworthy are (1) important role that the IMF has come to play in rescuing nations in financial mess and (2) the need for nations to work together, since in a global economy problems are contagious. If one nation fails, others may not be far behind.

The world is undergoing tremendous changes in its economic and political spheres. In the midst of such changes, further adjustments and amendments are necessary to reform the international monetary system in future years (see International Marketing Highlight 5.2). For example, many nations argue that to cope with modern financial crisis, the IMF needs more cash. More cash can be obtained either by doubling members' subscriptions or by issuing new SDRs, the IMF's artificial currency. Alternatively, the IMF can borrow from international capital markets. But the merit of these ideas depends on the answer to a more fundamental question: What is the purpose of IMF intervention in a financial crisis?[9]

Apparently, there is a need for a new international monetary system, especially in light of the problems that Mexico and then the Southeast Asian nations faced. Perhaps a new system will emerge in the new century, based on the spirit of the Louvre Agreements. In their 1999 annual meeting in Washington, the IMF members reaffirmed their commitment to exchange rate stability. The members called for the creation of a representative committee of ministers from developing and industrialized countries to consider the reform and improvement of the international monetary system. In the not too distant future, a true international monetary system may emerge with a standard unit of value, automatic mechanisms, and sanctions that would be beyond the control of the countries involved. The time is ripe for dispassionate consideration of this issue.

International Marketing Highlight 5.1

The Fund's Sums

After committing $17.8 billion to rescue Mexico, how much money does the IMF have left in its coffers? The question sounds simple. But the answer is not, for the IMF's financial structure is fiendishly complex. For a start, its internal accounts are calculated in terms of SDRs—artificial assets created by the IMF and made up of a weighted basket of the world's top five currencies. At present, one SDR is worth $1.47.

The IMF's main source of capital is the subscriptions, or "quotas," that all its members pay. A country's quota depends on the size of its economy. The total amount of IMF quotas is 145 billion SDRs. But since countries pay part of their quota in their own currencies, and many of these are not freely convertible, the IMF's liquid resources stand at only 62.5 billion SDRs after its efforts to help the Mexicans. As some of these liquid resources have already been committed to countries in trouble, the IMF has an adjusted measure for what it calls "uncommitted usable resources." These total 48 billion SDRs.

The usual way to top-up the IMF's resources is to increase members' quotas, but this takes time. So in emergencies there are other potential sources of cash. Under a special agreement, the IMF can borrow up to 17 billion SDRs from industrialized countries and another 1.5 billion SDRs from Saudi Arabia. In extremis, it could sell some of its 104m ounces of gold, which are probably worth around $39 billion.

The IMF has some liabilities too. Every one of its members is entitled to receive a portion of its quota (the so-called "reserve tranche") with no questions asked. The IMF must always be in a position to honor these tranches, which add up to around $29 billion SDRs.

The reality, then, is that it is almost impossible to calculate how much the Fund could safely lend to a troubled country.

Source: The Economist, February 11, 1995, p. 67.

Foreign Exchange

An international marketer needs to transact financial transfers across national lines in order to close deals. The financial transfers from one country to another are made through the medium of foreign exchange. This section examines the framework for dealing in foreign exchange, with its problems and complexities.

The Meaning of Foreign Exchange

Foreign exchange is the monetary mechanism by which transactions involving two or more currencies take place. It is the exchange of one country's money for another country's money (see International Marketing Highlight 5.3). Assume a Mexican representative imports a machine from Cincinnati Milacron, a U.S. manufacturer. The machine costs $1.2 million in U.S. dollars. Commercial exchanges take place in Mexico in pesos, but Cincinnati Milacron wants to be paid in U.S. dollars, not pesos. The Mexican importer, therefore, must buy U.S. dollars against pesos, that is, obtain foreign exchange—or, more specifically, *dollar exchange*—to pay Milacron.

■■■■■■■■■■ International Marketing Highlight 5.2 ■■■■■■■■■■

Cooperation Remains the Watchword

The Louvre Accord may constitute the most important watershed in the post–Bretton Woods era. The major industrialized countries agreed not only to cooperate closely in foreign exchange markets but also to coordinate their macroeconomic policies toward commonly agreed goals—sustainable noninflationary growth and the elimination of external imbalances.

Monetary policy has been managed broadly within the framework of such international policy coordination. Fiscal policy, however, has been managed more independently, owing partly to domestic political constraints. As a result, monetary policy has been overburdened and its independence called into question.

We are confronted with a most difficult policy problem: how to incorporate fiscal policy discipline within the framework of international macroeconomic policy coordination. We have not solved this problem under either the Bretton Woods regime or the managed floating system.

Here, we should consider the issue of structural adjustment. It is, of course, important to promote more efficient resource allocation through structural reform, which may in turn contribute to achieving the aims of macroeconomic policy. At the same time, however, we should keep in mind that structural reforms are basically support measures, and not a substitute, for demand management policy. It is also important to understand that such reforms take time. This is what Japan has told the United States repeatedly in recent meetings and on other occasions. There may be no policymakers nowadays who have not become keen advocates of international policy coordination. We should be prepared to subordinate national interests to international objectives when necessary.

Source: Takeshi Ohta, "Beyond Bretton Woods," *Speaking of Japan*, March 1990, p. 18.

Terminology in Foreign Exchange

Transacting foreign exchange deals presents two problems. First, each country has its own methods and procedures for effecting foreign exchanges—usually developed by its central bank. The transactions themselves, however, take place through the banking system. Thus, both the methods of foreign exchange and the procedures of the central bank and commercial banking constraints must be thoroughly understood and followed to complete a foreign exchange transaction.

A second problem involves the fluctuation of rates of exchange that occurs in response to changes in the supply and demand of different currencies. For example, back in the 1960s a U.S. dollar could be exchanged for about five Swiss francs. In the early 1990s, this rate of exchange went down to as low as 1.3 Swiss francs for a U.S. dollar. Thus, a U.S. businessperson interested in Swiss currency has to pay much more today than in the 1960s. In fact, the rate of exchange between two countries can fluctuate from day to day. This produces a great deal of uncertainty, as a businessperson cannot know the exact value of foreign obligations and claims.

To appreciate the complexities of foreign exchange, several terms must be understood: gold standard, gold exchange standard, gold bullion standard, inconvertible currencies, hard and soft currencies. Understanding these terms also will provide a historical perspective on the making of payments across national boundaries.

Gold standard refers to using gold as the medium of exchange for effecting foreign commercial transactions. Before World War I, most countries followed the gold standard. Private citizens were permitted to own gold, and it could be shipped in and out of the country by individuals or banks without government interference. After World War I, the gold standard was abandoned because gold holdings were concentrated in a few countries, which made international trade difficult to manage.

After the gold standard was established, many countries adopted the *gold exchange standard,* which means that the foreign exchange rate of a currency was set in relation to that country's gold holdings. A country on the gold exchange standard is able to buy in the free market its own currency when it falls in value and to sell it when it increases beyond a predetermined point. This mechanism minimizes the effects of fluctuations in foreign exchange value.

Another way of maintaining a parity with gold is to be on the *gold bullion standard,* which amounts to holding an adequate quantity of gold in reserve in bar or bullion form to settle international transactions at the level of government. Under the gold bullion standard, private individuals are prohibited from possessing gold and it is no longer in coinage, but a government may deal in gold by buying and selling it.

After World War II, most nations prohibited conversion of currency into gold, hence the term *inconvertible currencies.* The phrase also refers to currencies that cannot be conveniently exchanged for other currencies. For example, currencies of a number of developing countries are inconvertible to U.S. dollars.

Currencies may also be labeled as *hard currencies* or *soft currencies:* hard currencies are those in great demand; soft are relatively easy to obtain. The currencies of the majority of developing countries are described as soft currencies as far as international transactions are concerned, whereas those of developed nations are hard currencies.

International Marketing Highlight 5.3

Foreign Exchange Market

Generally exporters prefer to be paid for their goods and services either in their own currency (Japanese in yen and Germans in marks, for example) or in U.S. dollars, which are accepted all over the world. For example, when the French buy oil from Saudi Arabia, they may pay in U.S. dollars, not French francs or Saudi dinars, even though the United States in not involved in the transaction.

The foreign exchange market is where the buying and selling of different currencies takes place. The market comprises a worldwide network of traders, connected by telephone lines and computer screens—there is no central headquarters. The three major centers of trading which handle more than half of all foreign exchange transactions are Great Britain, the United States and Japan. The transactions in Singapore, Switzerland, Hong Kong, Germany, France and Australia account for most of the rest of the market. Trading goes on 24 hours a day; 8 A.M. in London, the trading day is ending in Tokyo, Singapore, and Hong Kong. At 3 P.M. in London, the New York market opens for business. When it is 10 P.M. in London, the Tokyo market is already active.

The foreign exchange market is fast-paced, volatile and enormous. In fact, it is the largest market in the world. In 1996 an estimated $1 trillion was traded every day, roughly equivalent to every person in the world trading $190 per day.

Source: The Basics of Foreign Trade and Exchange (New York: The Federal Reserve Bank, 1997).

Exchange Rates

When countries were on the gold standard, the value of two currencies was determined on the basis of the gold content of each currency. (The technical term used to describe this procedure of determining relationship between two currencies is *par of exchange*.) For example, in the 1920s a U.S. dollar had 23.22 grains of pure gold, while the British pound sterling had 113.0016 grains. Since the latter currency had 4.8665 times more fine gold than the American dollar, it was worth $4.8665.

For those countries off the gold standard, exchange rates are regulated by the central banks. Most countries, however, attempt to maintain a steady exchange rate, which is necessary to promote foreign trade. The base price of a currency is determined by the supply and demand of a currency (see International Marketing Highlights 5.4).

The supply and demand of a currency is influenced by a variety of factors. For example, if a country continues to buy, year after year, more from other nations than it exports, the supply of its currency increases. Likewise, if a country spends overseas—say, to fight a war—its currency supply increases. Such increases adversely affect currency value, which is the base, or market, price.[10] (Exhibit 5.1 lists the factors affecting the supply and demand of the U.S. dollar.)

International Marketing Highlight 5.4

Big MacCurrencies: Can Hamburgers Provide Hot Tips about Exchange Rates?

The Big Mac index is based on the theory of *purchasing-power parity (PPP)*—the notion that a dollar should buy the same amount in all countries. In the long run,

EXHIBIT 5.1
Factors Affecting the
Supply and Demand
of U.S. Dollars

The Following Factors Increase the Supply of U.S. Dollars in World Markets	The Following Factors Increase the Demand for U.S. Dollars in World Markets
1. Imports of merchandise	1. Exports of merchandise
2. Imports of gold and silver	2. Exports of gold and silver
3. Payments to foreign ships for freight and passenger service	3. Foreign payments to U.S. shippers
4. American tourist expenditures abroad	4. Foreign tourist expenditures in the U.S.
5. Banking and all other financial charges payable to foreigners	5. Banking and other financial charges receivable from foreigners
6. Interest and dividends due on American securities held abroad	6. Interest and dividends due on foreign securities held here
7. New purchases of foreign securities	7. New sale of American securities abroad
8. Repurchase and redemption of American securities held abroad	8. Repurchase and redemption of foreign securities held here
9. Transfer of American balances to foreign banks	9. Transfer of foreign balances to American banks
10. U.S. government grants and loans	

according to this theory, currencies should move toward the rate that equalizes the prices of an identical basket of goods in each country. Our "basket" is a McDonald's Big Mac, which is now produced in over 100 countries. The Big Mac PPP is the exchange rate that would leave hamburgers costing the same in America as abroad. Comparing actual exchange rates with PPP provides one indication of whether a currency is under- or overvalued.

Massive discounting in America by McDonald's might have distorted the PPP calculations, except for the fact that the discounts did not include the Big Mac. So the annual burgernomics-fest can be served.

The first column in the table on page 141 shows local currency prices of a Big Mac; the second converts them into dollars. The average American price (including tax) is $2.42. China is the place for bargain hunters: a Beijing Big Mac costs only $1.16. At the other extreme, Big Mac fans pay a beefy $4.02 in Switzerland. In other words, the yuan is the most undervalued currency (by 52 percent) and the Swiss franc the most overvalued (by 66 percent).

The third column calculates Big Mac PPPs. For example, dividing the German price by the American price gives a dollar PPP of DM 2.02 (2.02 deutsche marks). The actual rate on April 7th was DM 1.71, implying that the deutsche mark is 18 percent overvalued against the dollar. But over the past two years the dollar has risen nearer to its PPP against most currencies. The yen is now close to its PPP of ¥121. Two years ago the Big Mac index suggested that it was 100 percent overvalued against the dollar.

Some critics find these conclusions hard to swallow. Yes, we admit it, the Big Mac is not a perfect measure. Price differences may be distorted by trade barriers on beef, sales taxes, or large variations in the cost of nontraded inputs such as rents. All the same, the index tends to come up with PPP estimates that are similar to those based on more sophisticated methods.

The Hamburger Standard

	Big Mac Prices		Implied PPP* of the Dollar	Actual Dollar Exchange Rate 7/4/97	Local Currency Under (-)/ Over(+) Valuation,† by Percent
	In Local Currency	In Dollars			
United States	$2.42	—	—	—	—
Argentina	Peso 2.50	2.50	1.03	1.00	13
Australia	A$ 2.50	1.94	1.03	1.29	220
Austria	Sch 34.00	2.82	14.0	12.0	117
Belgium	BFr 109	3.09	45.0	35.3	128
Brazil	Real2.97	2.81	1.23	1.06	116
Britain	£ 1.81	2.95	1.34	1.63	122
Canada	C $2.88	2.07	1.19	1.39	214
Chile	Peso 1,200	2.88	496	417	119
China	Yuan 9.70	1.16	4.01	8.33	252
Czech Republic	CKr 53.0	1.81	21.9	29.2	225
Denmark	DKr 25.75	3.95	10.6	6.52	163
France	FFr 17.5	3.04	7.23	5.76	126
Germany	DM 4.90	2.86	2.02	1.71	118
Hong Kong	HK $9.90	1.28	4.09	7.75	247
Hungary	Forint 271	1.52	112	178	237
Israel	Shekel 11.5	3.40	4.75	3.38	140
Italy	Lire 4,600	2.73	1,901	1,683	113
Japan	¥ 294	2.34	121	126	23
Malaysia	M $3.87	1.55	1.60	2.50	236
Mexico	Peso 14.9	1.89	6.16	7.90	222
Netherlands	Fl 5.45	2.83	2.25	1.92	117
New Zealand	NZ$ 3.25	2.24	1.34	1.45	27
Poland	Zloty 4.30	1.39	1.78	3.10	243
Russia	Rouble 11,000	1.92	4,545	5,739	221
Singapore	S$ 3.00	2.08	1.24	1.44	214
South Africa	Rand 7.80	1.76	3.22	4.43	227
South Korea	Won 2,300	2.57	950	894	16
Spain	Pta 375	2.60	155	144	17
Sweden	SKr 26.0	3.37	10.7	7.72	139
Switzerland	SFr 5.90	4.02	2.44	1.47	166
Taiwan	NT $68.0	2.47	28.1	27.6	12
Thailand	Baht 46.7	1.79	19.3	26.1	226

* Purchasing power parity: local price divided by price in the United States.
† Against dollar
Source: McDonald's.

The base, or market price, however, may not be the real value of a currency, since the central bank may set a different price in order to realize a stated set of objectives. For example, the value of the U.S. dollar was slowly deteriorating in the market in the 1980s, but President Regan refused to devalue it.

Many countries set a lower value on their currency to encourage exports or to seek balance-of-payment adjustments. In other words, long-term objectives may lead a country to set a different value on its currency than the current market value. Incidentally, the IMF assists nations in arriving at a realistic value for their currency in relation to long- and short-term goals. Frequently, the IMF pressures a country to value its currency at what seems to be an acceptable level. For example, it persuaded the Philippines to devalue its currency, the peso, in 1986 and India to devalue its rupee in 1991.

Conducting Foreign Exchange Transactions

Foreign exchange transactions may be conducted by governments via their central bank, brokers, commercial banks, or business corporations. Described here is the process that corporations follow. Assume Boeing wishes to buy $300 million worth of Rolls Royce (British) jet engines for use in its new series of airplanes. Boeing needs to buy the equivalent of $300 million in British pounds sterling to pay Rolls Royce for the engines. Boeing may buy the British currency either in the spot or forward market. In the spot transaction, the purchase is effected right away; forward buying is finalized at a predetermined future date. If the payment is to be made right away, Boeing will have no choice but to buy British pounds sterling on the spot. However, if payment is to be made at a future date, Boeing may transact a forward deal. A forward deal will be preferable if British currency is currently available at a rate that is expected to increase by the time the payment is due. The forward deal will enable Boeing to buy British pounds sterling at a future date at a currently agreed upon price.

Whether the purchase is to be made on the spot or in the future, Boeing Company will contact a number of commercial banks to seek price quotations for British pound sterling in terms of the U.S. dollar. Usually, different banks will quote different prices. For example, a multinational bank like the CitiGroup might have acquired British pound sterling balances when British currency was priced very low. That bank would be able to offer a better price to Boeing than, say, Bank of America, which might not have British pounds sterling on hand and would then have to buy them on the open market to satisfy Boeing's needs. The market might contain customers interested in exchanging British pounds sterling for another currency, or a British bank might be willing to lend the local currency.

Even when the British pounds sterling must be bought from the market, one bank might quote a better price than the other. It all depends on the size of the transaction, the importance of the customer to the bank, the direction of the currency market, future prospects of the currency, and the bank's present financial position.[11] Other things being equal, Boeing would choose the bank providing the best price.

Many MNCs pointedly seek the foreign currencies of the countries in which they are active by making deals at advantageous times.[12] For example, a U.S. corporation with excess cash on hand might buy a currency whose price is low in expectation of the price going up when the corporation needs U.S. dollars again. This way a corporation can make money dealing in foreign exchange transactions (see International Marketing Highlight 5.5).

■■■■■■   **International Marketing Highlight 5.5**   ■■■■■■

Shock from the Rise in Yen's Value

Sony's annual report for 1986 published an enviable listing of business achievements—new products, sales gains in major ranges, production and distribution rationalization, and strong performances by overseas subsidiaries. Yet the same report broke the bad news that net sales were down 7 percent, operating income had plummeted 75 percent, and net income had fallen 43 percent.

Where did the shock come from? Why the miserable results? Sony was the victim of a 40 percent rise in the yen's value against the dollar. Business excellence—doing all the right things, including protecting the value of revenues through forward currency contracts—had failed to shield the company from the ravages of foreign exchange rate turbulence.

Sony is not alone in having to inform its shareholders of disastrous results following adverse movements in exchange rates. Many other companies that are heavily dependent on international markets are also at the mercy of exchange rates. The auto industry is an obvious example. In 1987, Honda reported that "the strong yen . . . [made] it impossible to raise prices sufficiently to keep pace with currency movements . . . leading to significant declines in earnings." In 1986 Swedish forest products group MoDo cited the falling dollar's lead role in inducing a severe displacement of competitiveness in North American pulp markets. Volvo, Sanyo, Nissan, Matsushita, Philips, and Porsche have all suffered. Losses can come quickly and be painful.

Source: Staffan Hertzell and Christian Caspar, "Coping with Unpredictable Currencies," *The McKinsey Quarterly*, Summer 1988, p. 12.

Balance of Payments

The *balance of payments* of a country summarizes all the transactions that have taken place between its residents and foreigners in a given period, usually a year. The word *transactions* refers to exports and imports of goods and services, lending and borrowing of funds, remittances, and government aid and military expenditures. The term *residents* includes all individuals and business enterprises, including financial institutions, permanently residing within a country's borders, as well as government agencies at all levels. In other words, the balance of payments reflects the totality of a country's economic relations with the rest of the world: its trade in goods, its exchange of services, its purchase and sale of financial assets, and such important governmental transactions as foreign aid, military expenditures abroad, and the payment of reparation. Certain forces determine the volume of these transactions, how they are brought into balance, what problems arise when they fail to balance, and what policies are available to deal with those problems.

Recording Balance-of-Payments Transactions

Exhibit 5.2 highlights the U.S. balance-of-payments position for the year 1998. The transactions are recorded in three categories: current account, capital account, and addendum. The balance-of-payments record is made on the basis of rules of debit and credit, similar to those in business accounting. For example, receipts are entered as credits and payments as debits. Thus, exports, like sales, are entered as credits; imports, like purchases, as debits. All transactions affecting increases in assets, like direct investment abroad, or decreases in indebtedness, like the repayment of external debts, are recorded as credits. However, decreases in assets, like liquidation of foreign securities, and increases in liabilities, like borrowing abroad, are treated as debits.

The *current account* shows U.S. trade in currently produced goods and services. The positive or negative sign preceding each figure indicates whether the transaction represents a gain (+) or a loss (-) of foreign currency. In merchandise transactions, there was a negative balance (of trade) in 1998, meaning the import of goods exceeded the export of goods by $247.0 billion. Line 4 shows the net effect of expenditures incurred by U.S. military installations abroad and the amount of foreign currency earned by selling armaments. Line 5 shows that in 1998 America spent $78.3 billion less on services (tourism, shipping,

EXHIBIT 5.2

U.S. Balance-of-Payments Accounts: 1998 (in Billions of U.S. Dollars)

Current Account

(1) Balance of trade		−247.0
(2) Merchandise exports	+670.2	
(3) Merchandise imports	−917.2	
(4) Net military transactions		−4.4
(5) Net services		+78.3
(6) Net income from investments		−12.2
(7) Balance on goods and services (Lines 1 plus 4 plus 5 plus 6)		−176.5
(8) Unilateral transfers		−44.1
(9) Private	−26.7	
(10) U.S. government (nonmilitary)	−17.4	
(11) Balance on current account (Lines 7 plus 8)		−220.6

Capital Account

(12) Net private capital flows		+238.7
(13) Change in U.S. assets abroad	−285.6	
(14) Change in foreign assets in the U.S.	+524.3	
(15) Net governmental capital flows		+28.2
(16) Change in U.S. government assets	−7.2	
(17) Change in foreign official assets in the U.S.	−21.0	
(18) Balance on capital account (Lines 12 plus 15)		+210.5

Addendum

(19) Sum of Lines (11) and (18)	−10.1
(20) Statistical discrepancy	+10.1

Source: Statistical Abstract of the United States: 1998 (Washington, DC: U.S. Department of Commerce), pp 788–789.

other) than foreigners spent in the United States. Line 6 focuses on another major source of our foreign earnings, return on U.S. investments abroad.

The net result of all trading in goods and services is shown on Line 7. Lines 8–10 describe *unilateral transfers*, comprising private gifts to foreigners and official foreign aid. The current account balance ($220.6 billion in 1998) is shown on Line 11.

Lines 12–18 summarize transactions in the *capital account*. Line 12 shows that, on balance, Americans bought $238.7 billion more in assets abroad than private foreign investors bought in the United States (see the difference between Line 13 and 14).

The current-account deficit combined with the surplus in the capital account left the United States with a fairly large balance-of-payments deficit (see Line 19).

Since the two accounts should balance as a simple matter of arithmetic, the difference is considered a *statistical discrepancy* (Line 20). Although part of this discrepancy is attributable to errors in data collection and computation, the major portion reflects the U.S. balance-of-payments deficit.

The balance-of-payments record may not strictly follow double-entry bookkeeping in that not every transaction gives rise to equal and thus offsetting debit and credit entries. Discrepancies will occur when particular balance-of-payments entries do not represent the movement of funds, but rather the movement of a document or other proof of obligation. Further, some international payments are unilateral (one-sided), such as gifts, grants, and transfer payments. Payments of this type are entered as debits, and receipts as credits.

Finally, instead of using the 'T' account of standard accounting, the U.S. Department of Commerce posts all balance-of-payments transactions in a single column, with debits preceded by minus signs and credits by no sign at all.

"Surplus" or "Deficit" Balance-of-Payments

In Exhibit 5.2, with the help of the statistical-discrepancy item, the entries added up to zero. This is the usual way of striking the balance.

In the case of the United States, however, it is extremely difficult to compute the true balance-of-payments figure for two reasons. First, the U.S. dollar plays a key role in international trade and finance even after its devaluation. For this reason, a number of transactions take place in U.S. dollars between other nations exclusive of the United States. Second, foreign central banks, as well as the IMF, hold U.S. dollars as investments and as working balances to finance international trade and payments. With the complexities produced by these numbers, no single number can adequately describe the international position of the United States during any given period.

To illustrate the difficulty involved in compiling the "true" balance-of-payments figure for the United States, consider the following case. Official government statistics reveal that the United States has had continuous trade deficits since 1977. The trade deficit for 1999, for example, reached $271 billion. Further, with the exception of a very small surplus in 1980, the current account, a broader measure, has also been in deficit since 1977. Traditionally, nations with continuing balance-of-trade and current-account deficits experience a drop in the international value of their currencies. Indeed, this is the basic adjustment mechanism in a floating exchange rate system. Yet, the U.S. dollar continues to be strong.

U.S. Balance-of-Payments Position

Since World War II, the international transactions of the United States have shown enormous growth. In 1950 total receipts came to $10,203 million. Such transactions in 1960 amounted to $19,650 million; in 1970 to $42,969 million; in 1980 to $100,110 million; in 1990 to $143,000 million, and in 1999 to an estimated $242,000 million. Even after adjusting for inflation, these figures reflect a vast growth in international dealings by the United States with the rest of the world, as evidenced by the upsurge in U.S. private foreign investment, the rise in U.S. government expenditures abroad, and the emergence of the U.S. dollar as the world's principal reserve and trading currency.

In recent years the U.S. industry and government have adopted a variety of measures to improve its balance-of-payments position. U.S. exports have been encouraged at all levels. The U.S. economy has been restructured via new investments and technology, facilitating a rise in productivity that makes U.S. products more competitive abroad. Similarly, efforts have been made through persuasion and negotiations to limit Japanese exports. Finally, efforts to bring the value of U.S. dollar down by intervening in the financial markets has made U.S. products more competitive in export markets.[13]

Current and Emerging Issues

This section briefly examines the current strains on the world monetary system and attempts to project forthcoming events as we enter the next century. Although the world has overcome the crisis created by the 1973–1974 oil price increase, OPEC has lately shown an increase in its surplus, and if it takes measures to maintain this position, we might see a further increase in the price of oil and a need to recycle funds from oil exporters to the rest of the world. If, on the other hand, the price of oil declines, many oil-producing countries such as Nigeria and Mexico will face new difficulties on that account.

A large number of countries lived through the 1970s by means of heavy borrowing. At the same time, their ability to repay debts declined. International bankers in the last few years were stunned by the inability of these countries to service and repay their debts. Although IMF assistance has helped many nations (for example, Mexico, South Korea, Thailand, Indonesia), in meeting the immediate crisis, the debt problem is likely to linger for many years.

The private international bankers are already overcommitted, especially in developing countries. These institutions may be unwilling to accommodate the growing needs of the developing countries in the new millennium.

Lessons from the Asian Crash

The Asian companies and, in general, companies in the developing world will find it difficult to borrow money because of their past inability to repay loans. They must pay stiff risk premiums until lenders are confident that the money will not be frittered away and that no currency crisis will occur to destroy their ability to repay. The consolidation in the corporate sector is likely to spur the rise of a newer breed of Asian company—one that is smaller but more focused. Its forerunners are found among exporters that already have adjusted to the new rules of the global marketplace. In other words, the enterprises in developing countries need to abandon the favored practice of diversifying into a broad range of new industries. They should stay with a few core sectors and sell off the rest.[14]

Furthermore, the companies should not rely only on cheap labor. They must improve logistics, design, and inventory management to be globally competitive. Finally, they should team up with foreign partners to better understand the marketplace in the industrialized countries and serve the customers better and thus gain competitive strength.

Summary

After World War II, the nations of the world came to an important realization: for a secure future, national economies would have to be rebuilt or developed, and such a feat could be accomplished only through worldwide cooperation. Subsequently, a historic meeting of 55 nations took place at Bretton Woods, New Hampshire, to develop a monetary system that would ensure stable conditions for a healthy growth of the world economy. The IMF was originated to oversee the system. Essentially, the system controlled the limits on exchange rate movements in its member countries in a predetermined way. The exchange rates were permitted to vary by only 1 percent above and below par. As a country's rate of exchange attained or approached either limit, the country's central bank intervened in the market to prevent the rate from passing the limits.

The IMF not only reviews the status of different economies, but also gives advice on how a nation can achieve monetary stability.

In times of temporary balance-of-payments deficits, countries can approach the IMF for short-term loans to weather the difficult period. The IMF's short-term accommodation, however, has proved insufficient, and, therefore, SDRs have been created to provide additional liquidity.

The United States at one time guaranteed to convert the U.S. dollar into gold at a fixed rate of $35 per ounce of gold. This guarantee helped countries to trade. Indeed, many countries linked their national currencies to the U.S. dollar. In the early 1970s, however, the value of the U.S. dollar began to decline. Eventually, the United States devalued its dollar twice and abandoned the fixed parity between its dollar and gold. Since then, all currencies have floated free, and their values fluctuate on the basis of supply and demand.

A system of foreign exchange is necessary for transacting payments in foreign trade. When people import something, they must make payment to the exporter for it. Since the exporting country ordinarily has a different currency than the one used in the importing country, the importer must obtain the exporter's currency in order to pay for the imported good. The importer obtains the exporter's currency from its central bank. The central bank of the country sets an exchange value on its currency for the other currency. In this way, it is possible to determine how much the importer needs in local currency to pay the bank in order to receive the requisite amount of the exporter's currency.

The balance-of-payments concept refers to a systematic record of the economic transactions of a nation during a given period between its residents and the rest of the world. In general, if a nation exports more than it imports, it will have a favorable balance of payment; if the reverse is true, the nation will have an unfavorable balance of payment.

Review Questions

1. What reasons led nations to seek international monetary stability? How does such stability help promote world trade?
2. How did the Bretton Woods agreement provide a stable monetary environment?
3. What are special drawing rights (SDRs)? Why were they created?
4. What led the United States to devalue its dollar?
5. Why is it desirable for a country to maintain a stable foreign exchange rate for its currency?
6. Define *balance of payment*. How does it differ from balance of trade? How accurate are the U.S. balance-of-payment records?

Creative Questions

1. Has the role of the IMF (for example, maintenance of fixed exchange rates) in the world economy become less important since that organization was birthed at the Bretton Woods Conference? What new role might the IMF play to continue to be a viable institution?
2. In the interest of increasing its exports, can a country devalue its currency indiscriminately? Is there a point at which it may be counterproductive to devalue the currency? If so, explain why. Also, why don't the Japanese devalue the yen to help Japanese companies keep their export tempo?

Endnotes

1. *IMF Economic Reviews*, January–April 1999.

2. *The Economist*, February 21, 2000, p. 78.

3. *World Development Report* (Washington, DC: The World Bank, 1996).

4. "East Asia: Which Way to Safety?" *The Economist*, January 10, 1998, p. 62.

5. See *World Development Report 1999, Op. Cit.*

6. "Sisters in the Wood: A Survey of the IMF and the World Bank," *The Economist*, October 12, 1991, pp. 5–48.

7. See Edward Balladur, "Rebuilding an International Monetary System," *The Economist*, February 23, 1988, p. 28.

8. Rich Thomas, "How to Save Face—And Trade," *Newsweek*, February 6, 1995, p. 34.

9. "Why Can't a Country be Like a Firm?" *The Economist*, April 22, 1995, p. 79.

10. Robert G. Ruland and Timothy S. Doupink, "Foreign Currency Translation and the Behavior of Exchange Rates," *Journal of International Business Studies*, Fall 1988, pp. 461–476.

11. Arvind D. Jain and Douglas Nigh, "Politics and the International Lending Decisions of Banks," *Journal of International Business Studies*, Summer 1989, pp. 349–359.

12. Timothy A. Luehrman, "Exchange Rate Changes and the Distribution of Industry Value," *Journal of International Business Studies*, Fourth Quarter 1991, pp. 619–649.

13. "Exports: 'This Show Has Legs,'" *Business Week*, September 19, 1994, p. 48.

14. "What to Do About Asia," *Business Week*, January 26, 1998 p. 26.

CHAPTER 6

International Finance and Accounting

CHAPTER FOCUS

After studying this chapter, you should be able to

■ Explain the implications of financial decisions for international marketing strategy.

■ Describe the dimensions of international money management.

■ Discuss how international investment decisions are made.

■ Compare U.S. accounting practices with those of other nations.

Today's multinational enterprises must deal with an international monetary system full of complexities, challenges, and risks. Finance managers and treasurers in particular play a key role in managing worldwide money matters. It is important for international marketers to possess insight into multinational finance and accounting functions, because these functions usually have a significant impact on marketing. For example, without such an understanding of the financial side of international business, a marketing manager for an airplane manufacturer that is supplying 10 planes to a Mexican airline might accept routine negotiation for payment over three years in Mexican pesos. In contrast, a manager with international financial insight would foresee the depreciation of Mexican currency and opt for payment in U.S. dollars. The impact of the finance function on international marketing decisions can spell success or failure with each decision.

The financial objectives of a corporation typically constrain the latitude of a marketing manager. Marketers are affected by all aspects of their company's money management—the raising of money, the investing of money, the maintenance of liquidity, and even lesser factors like the repatriation of funds from subsidiaries to parent corporations. The decisions of marketing managers also are affected by accounting considerations.

Implications of Financial Decisions for Marketing

A discussion of the financial aspects of multinational business in a marketing text is entirely relevant in view of the fact that an enterprise ultimately ventures across national boundaries for the enhancement of its long-term profitability. Therefore, financial commitments and their results deeply affect the marketing perspective of a business. The close relationship between finance and marketing functions has long been recognized, but in the realm of international business, it is of heightened significance. Consider, for example, the effect on marketing of the parent corporation's *transfer pricing* policy (transfer pricing will be discussed thoroughly in Chapter 13). Decisions in setting prices for the transfer of goods, services, and technology between related affiliates in different countries are inevitably affected by fund positioning, income taxes, tariffs, and quotas; managerial incentives and evaluation; antitrust prosecution; the interest of joint venture partners; and corporate bargaining power with suppliers or financial institutions. Many of these sometimes conflicting considerations have both financial underpinnings and a direct or indirect impact on marketing.

Eventually, all marketing decisions that involve capital investment or other types of long-term financial commitment on the part of the parent corporation must be reviewed in the context of corporate international financial policy. For example, marketing wisdom might suggest improving the provision of after-sale services, which might entail manufacturing parts locally. But local manufacturing might require substantial investment and transfer of technology. In the context of overall financial goals, the parent may find it undesirable to invest in manufacturing spare parts and supplies in a host country. Or the parent may learn that another affiliate recently expanded capacity to manufacture the same parts, or that the political situation in the host country is discouraging to additional investments, and so on. In the end, the decision, which appeared potentially desirable based on marketing considerations, may be postponed or dropped when reviewed from the financial angle.

The financial strength of a company deeply affects marketing, particularly in the company's ability to maintain inventories. Making timely deliveries to customers could provide important competitive leverage in international business, particularly if inventory replenishment involves great distances and time. Similarly, marketing is affected by the company's ability to make economical bulk purchases of merchandise. Marketing decisions on promotional efforts in the mass media to strengthen the brand, commitment of resources to research and development for the timely introduction of new and improved products, and investment in developing cordial relationships with channels of distribution are all influenced by financial decisions. This intimate relationship between the two functions of finance and marketing means that marketers, especially international marketers, need a basic knowledge of financial matters (see International Marketing Highlight 6.1).

Few companies today, small or large, can afford to disregard the growing importance of overseas markets as a source of corporate growth. Increasingly interdependent trade flows and growing government involvement in economic affairs make financial management a complex function. The volatility of exchange rates adds to the complexity. Given the difficulties posed by these factors, plus the recent turbulent economic environment in a number of Asian nations in 1997–1998, setting global marketing strategies without the benefit of financial inputs is like looking through a pair of binoculars with one eye closed (see International Marketing Highlight 6.2).

The competitive challenges for all businesses have never been more daunting. There is enormous pressure to develop compelling products, services, and solutions for highly demanding customers while generating profitable growth. Three forces are converging to create both opportunities and risks for companies of all sizes:

- Globalization.
- Highly liquid capital markets.
- Shorter business life-cycles.

This pace of intense change is expected to continue. More than ever, cutting-edge strategy and superior execution separate the leaders from the laggards. Leading companies are transforming finance from a support function into a strategic weapon, creatively applying resources to those areas most critical to business performance. A well-equipped finance organization is a powerful strategic weapon that helps the enterprise generate growth and sustain shareholder value.

International Marketing Highlight 6.1

How Volkswagen Lost It All

To illustrate the impact of exchange rate changes, which is a financial impact on marketing, consider the case of Volkswagen (VW). In the 1960s VW experienced phenomenal growth. During 1960–1970, its annual sales increased from DM (deutsche mark) 4 billion to DM 15 billion and its exports increased manyfold. In the early 1960s exports represented half of total sales; toward the end of the decade, exports had become two-thirds of its total sales. VW emerged as the largest automobile exporter in the world.

Volkswagen's success in the U.S. market was highly remarkable. Since their introduction in the U.S. market in the early 1950s, VW's vehicles (particularly the Beetle) had filled an important market niche, catering to price-sensitive consumers. To many Americans, the Beetle was the ideal economy vehicle.

Volkswagen's commitment to the U.S. market was never in doubt. With service support and corporate commitment, annual sales increased from 200,000 vehicles in 1960 to 600,000 vehicles by the end of the decade. In the early 1960s the United States was VW's largest foreign customer, accounting for 30 percent of VW's exports; the U.S. market for imported cars was increasing; and VW was getting an increasing share of a growing market. By 1970, when imported cars constituted 14 percent of the U.S. car market, VW's market share in the U.S. was 6 percent, compared with 3 percent in 1960.

Then came the decline, and by 1973 the losses were huge. In October 1969 the DM was revalued, and its full effect was felt in 1970. The revaluation of the DM weakened the competitive position of VW in all the export markets. Volkswagen's net earnings dropped from DM 330 million in 1969 to DM 190 million in 1970. In some European countries, considerable losses in market share were experienced. The DM was again revalued in 1971 and 1972, and by 1972 its revaluation amounted to 40 percent over the 1969 figure. To partially offset currency change effects, VW prices were increased in the United States, and as a result VW lost its market share. In 1971 alone, the losses in the United States because of currency changes were estimated to be DM 200 million.

The early 1970s saw the gradual and regular strengthening of the DM and, with it, the weakening of VW's position. VW's fortunes were inextricably linked with those of the DM: as the DM rose, VW's profits fell. A strong currency clearly weakens the position of the country's exporters; this is particularly true if they are catering to price-sensitive markets. As its annual report of 1972 poignantly recorded, "Exports account for more than two-thirds of the Volkswagen AG's total sales. Of all the world's leading automobile manufacturers, VW is therefore the one most affected by variations in exchange rates."

Stuart Perkins, the chief executive of VW's American subsidiary, was so frustrated and exasperated by the havoc currency changes were playing on his sales that he exploded: "I used to call the sales people and ask how sales were doing. Last quarter, my first move was to call the financial people and ask how the D-mark-to-dollar exchange rate was doing."

The final collapse came in 1973, when VW incurred a loss of DM 807 million. Cash flow plunged from DM 1,671 million in 1972 to DM 618 million in 1973. Equity dropped to 24 percent of assets, from 31 percent the previous year. There was a steady decline in sales in the U.S. market, from a high of 570,000 vehicles in 1968 to 200,000 vehicles in 1976. VW ended 1975 in the red, with losses of DM 160 million.

Currency changes affected VW in three ways. First, the DM revaluation vis-à-vis the dollar made VW's position very uncompetitive in the United States, its biggest market. Second, the DM's revaluation in relation to other Western European currencies such as the pound sterling, the lira, and the French franc resulted in similar effects in those markets. VW found it increasingly difficult to compete in the United Kingdom, France, and Italy. Third, within the [former] West German market, VW had to face increasing import competition, especially from Renault and Fiat. Because of the weakening of the French and Italian currencies, these automobiles became very competitive on the German market.

International Marketing Highlight 6.2

Marketing Transaction Example

Suppose that J.T. Enterprises, a small manufacturer of wooden block sets, discovers an opportunity to sell 1,000 cases of blocks to a toy company in France. Under the terms of the sale agreement, the company will export the blocks to France and receive payment in French francs in approximately 60 days. The company must then sell the francs in exchange for U.S. dollars.

The French company has agreed to pay all shipping costs as well as the going rate of $100 per case of blocks. On the day of the sale agreement (September 4, 1992) the exchange rate between U.S. dollars and French francs is .20777, which means that one franc is worth 20.777 cents U.S. Or, put another way, it takes 1/.20777 or 4.813 francs to equal one dollar. Thus, the French toy company agrees to pay J.T. Enterprises 481.3 francs per case (4.813 × 100) or 481,300 francs for the entire order (481.3 × 1,000).

The company enters into the agreement with great confidence. The actual cost of manufacturing and packing the blocks for sale is $75 per case. Thus, the company expects to realize a profit of $25,000 ($100 − $75 × 1,000). But will the company actually realize this amount? Three possible situations could occur. First, the exchange rate could hold for the next 60 days. Second, the dollar could "weaken" in relation to the French franc within the next 60 days. And third, the dollar could "strengthen" in relation to the French franc in the next 60 days.

1. If the exchange rate between U.S. dollars and French francs holds at .20777, the company will indeed realize a profit of nearly $25,000. When it receives payment for the order, it can exchange 481,300 francs for $100,000 U.S. (with a slight amount of transaction costs).

2. If the dollar weakens relative to the French franc, then it takes less French francs to equal one U.S. dollar. This situation would be favorable to J.T. Enterprises. If, for example, the exchange rate was .26316 in 60 days, it would take only 1/.26316, or 3.800, francs to equal one U.S. dollar. Thus, the company could exchange 481,300 francs for $126,658 (481,300/3.800), and the profit realized would be approximately $51,658.

3. If, however, the dollar grows stronger relative to the French franc in the next 60 days, there will be a negative impact on the profit realized by J.T. Enterprises. For example, if the exchange rate fluctuates to .17241 on the day that the company receives its payment for the shipment, it will take 1/.17241, or 5.800 francs, to equal one U.S. dollar. Thus, when the company makes the currency exchange, it will receive only $82,983 (481,300/5.800), and profit realized will be approximately $7,893.

The company would be prudent to take measures to protect its anticipated profitability of $25,000 on the transaction. When a company fails to protect its profitability, it has what is known as an "open" position, meaning it is open, or exposed, to exchange rate risk. When a company ensures that it will receive the profit anticipated at the time of the sale agreement, it is said to have "covered" the exchange risk of the transaction.

Multinational Financial Management

The finance function has two principal aspects: (1) to provide the monetary wherewithal to do business and (2) to ensure an adequate financial return on the assets of the company commensurate with its objectives. Even in a strictly domestic business, the able management of funds and investment means solving all sorts of problems related to issues such as what financial return is adequate, how should the return be defined, what sources of funds should be tapped, when should funds be raised, and where should funds be used. In the international arena, the problems multiply. Finance management must not only deal with different currencies and their fluctuating rates, but also allow for the vagaries of the economic and political environments of nations with varying perspectives. This section briefly examines various facets of the finance function and relates them to conducting business across national boundaries.

Financial Objectives

Consider the financial objectives of an MNC that manufactures different types of parts and accessories for the automotive industry and related markets. The corporation's measure of performance is the return on capital employed. *Capital employed* is the sum of all assets plus the accumulated reserves for depreciation. In its financial goals, the corporation recognizes that not all operations are directly comparable, and states that targets for individual profit centers and operations will take into account the nature of the operation, its performance plans, and its record of achievement against them.

Target profit performance is stated to consist of

1. A competitive return on capital employed with a basic minimum pretax return of 15 percent, which shall be inflation-adjusted from time to time.
2. An annual growth rate of pretax profits of at least 12 percent.

New projects and further capital commitments are subject to a minimum hurdle rate of 25 percent return on capital unless deemed otherwise necessary or desirable by the corporation in view of legal requirements or the corporation's best long-term interest.

Emphasis on asset management at all levels will include annual targets for cash generation, capital expenditures, and balance sheet items, including inventory and receivables management. Particular attention is drawn to the differences between actual cash-generating capacity and book results. Each group and profit center is expected to develop not only net cash-generating capacity for its own requirements, but also sufficient funds for the corporation to meet its high-priority investment commitments and opportunities.

Thus, the company may require its subsidiaries to repatriate surplus funds to the corporate headquarters. As a guideline, the corporation intends each of its non–U.S.-dollar organizations to remit as dividends, or otherwise, an amount of its annual after-tax earnings equal to the same percentage that the corporation is currently paying from its consolidated after-tax income to its stockholders. Deviations from this policy may be expected when host country restrictions exist or when it is in the corporation's best long-term interest.

Financial limitations are identified as follows:

1. Investment in net working capital of less than 35 percent of annual sales; investment in net fixed assets of less than 25 percent of annual sales.
2. Dividend payments of approximately 40 percent of earnings.
3. No significant dilution of shareholders' ownership.

This company has nicely blended the financial objectives for both domestic and international business. From every business deal it expects a minimum inflation-adjusted pretax return of 15 percent, a minimum annual growth of 12 percent in pretax profits, and a 25 percent return on capital from new projects—the hurdle rate. The company intends to regularly repatriate profits and duly provide for exchange rate fluctuations. The objectives clearly recognize the legal/political constraints that may be imposed by host governments, and the company is willing to accept deviations from its objectives to comply with the local environment.

The financial limitations, stated as a part of the objectives, provide guides for sources and uses of funds. The company wants to make rather substantial, regular dividend payments of approximately 40 percent. This means internal funds in the form of retained earnings will be limited for investment in growth. Also, the company wants no significant dilution of shareholder's equity. It is possible, then, that equity capital will have to be considered as a last resort for raising money.

Financial objectives constitute the foundation for making financial decisions for a company. For example, in order to protect itself against exchange rate fluctuations, it might require managers in overseas subsidiaries to forecast regularly the exchange rates month-by-month for the upcoming six months. On the basis of those forecasts, corporate funds in a currency likely to be substantially depreciated would be utilized before funds in stronger currencies.

To illustrate this point, consider that in 1998 the Thai currency, the bhat, continued to decline, and all indications pointed toward a further depreciation of the currency. At the same time, the U.S. dollar continued to strengthen. Thus, in 1998 international financial managers had good reason to spend their bhat accumulations and save dollars.

Likewise, the goal to repatriate profits suggests that a financial manager in a foreign subsidiary can plan on meeting future investment needs only partially from retained earnings. According to the financial objectives, a new project proposed in a subsidiary outside the United States need not be put through the channels for final approval by the corporate management if it is not expected to meet the hurdle rate. Thus, financial objectives affect investment decisions as well.[1]

Money Management

Money management deals with sources and uses of funds, involving such considerations as how funds should be obtained (equity versus debt), in which currency a corporation or subsidiary should be responsible for raising funds, how the transfer of funds from one subsidiary to another or between a subsidiary and corporation should be handled, and in which financial instrument the funds should be invested as well as in which market. Prudent international money management requires minimizing the cost of funds and maximizing the return on investment over time by means of the best combination of currency of denomination and maturity characteristics of financial assets and liabilities. Such money management requirements are very complex in the international context. They require (1) the formulation and revision of capital structure decisions for different entities and (2) budgets for intracompany funds transfer.

Typically, a multinational enterprise is susceptible to three risks related to money management:[2] (1) the *political risk* of assets being taken over by the host country; (2) the *exchange risk* whereby the value of the U.S. dollar changes with reference to the host country currency; and (3) the *translation risk* whereby the corporate financial statements are required by the U.S. Securities and Exchange Commission (SEC) regulations to be based on historical costs rather than current value.

The goal of an international money manager is to obtain finances for foreign projects in a way that minimizes after-tax interest costs and foreign exchange losses. The *exchange rate parity theory* suggests that international differentials in interest costs are offset by changes in foreign exchange rates; that is, the expected value for net financing costs will be equal for all currencies over any given time period, provided foreign exchange markets are efficient. Thus, it makes no difference which currency is used to finance a foreign project.

Assuming the exchange rate parity theory holds, a number of considerations, such as tax policies, favor the use of host country financing. Many countries—Australia, Indonesia, South Africa, and Germany, for example—have no taxes on gains or losses arising from most long-term exchange transactions.[3] In some countries, gains and losses from long-term exchange transactions are subject to preferential capital gains tax rates or reserves treatment.[4] Furthermore, most countries apply some kind of surtax on foreign interest payments. These taxes are generally of the withholding sort and are usually available for rebate. A few countries—Argentina, for example—even impose a separate tax on foreign interest payments. These taxes increase the cost of borrowing in U.S. dollars or other foreign currency. Such policies encourage MNCs to prefer the use of host country financing. As a matter of fact, many firms require that all foreign projects be financed in the currency of the host country.[5]

The use of host country currency for financing limits the foreign exchange exposure and hence the risk.[6] Experience in India is relevant here.[7] Traditionally, foreign investors did not think that India provided an opportunity for raising capital locally. However, Honda Motor Company's issue was oversubscribed 165 times within a span of 72 hours. Similarly, Burroughs Corporation's stock and debenture issue was oversubscribed 30 times. In brief, even in many developing countries there is no shortage of local capital.

Translation risk still arises from foreign financing decisions. On the whole, however, such translation risk is less severe because, whereas exchange risk leads to a realizable gain or loss, translation risk is a paper gain or loss. Besides, the former is taxable, whereas the effects of translation risk rarely are.[8] Thus, an effective argument can be made for host country financing. But the argument is based on a variety of assumptions, both economic and noneconomic and if these assumptions fail, a company may be forced to seek funds in other markets than the host country.[9] In many developing countries, for example, the government may make it virtually impossible to raise money locally. In other situations, the local currency may be unusable.

Of course, money management involves many more facets than just host country financing. For our purposes here, however, such limited treatment of the subject is sufficient to provide a bird's-eye view of international money management.

Repatriation of Funds

In domestic business, an important financial decision made by a corporation is the establishment of *dividend policy*, that is, the amount of earnings to be distributed to the owners, the stockholders. Likewise, a multinational firm needs to formulate a strategy on remission of dividends from overseas affiliates to headquarters. According to Eiteman, Stonehill, and Moffett, the international dividend policy is determined by the following six factors:[10]

1. Tax implications.
2. Political risk.
3. Foreign exchange risk.
4. Age and size of affiliate.
5. Availability of funds.
6. Presence of joint venture partners.

Many countries—Germany, for example—tax retained earnings, which yields higher dividend payouts. Countries that levy withholding taxes on dividends paid to a foreign parent, on the other hand, discourage distribution of earnings in the form of dividends.

Taxes aside, in the case of countries exhibiting higher political risk, the parent might require the remission of all earnings minus funds needed for working capital and approved capital projects planned for the next few months. Such a perspective would more often apply to developing countries. Where political risk may not be an important factor, the dividend policy will be based on availability and use of funds. For example, if funds are needed in the United Kingdom, headquarters might decide to transfer its retained earnings from a German subsidiary to the United Kingdom rather than transferring funds from the United States. An alternative to this action would be the investment of funds in German marks.

Another factor that affects international dividend payment is foreign exchange risk. If the value of the host country currency is expected to decline substantially, other things being equal, common business wisdom will direct conversion of funds into a strong currency. Age and size of affiliates also influence the dividend policy. Research on the subject has showed that older affiliates provide a larger proportion of their earnings to the parent since their reinvestment needs decline with time. By the same token, recently established affiliates provide only marginal dividends. As far as size is concerned, larger firms usually have a formal policy for dividend payout, but small firms depend on ad hoc decisions.

Finally, if a foreign affiliate is formed as a joint venture, the interests of local stockholders force the company to follow a more stable dividend policy, because the worldwide corporate perspective cannot be pursued at the cost of valid claims by local investors who do not necessarily benefit from the global dividend strategy of the parent.

On the basis of the six factors just listed and discussed, a multinational firm may follow either a pooled strategy or a flexible strategy for distribution of earnings generated by foreign affiliates. The *pooled strategy* refers to a stated policy of remittance of profits to the parent on a regular basis. The *flexible strategy* leaves the decision on dividends to factors operating at the time. The flexible strategy permits the parent to make the most viable use of funds vis-à-vis its long-term global corporate objectives. Overall, the flexible approach in foreign earnings permits better utilization of the total financial resources available and eventually leads to a higher level of inflow of funds to the parent company in all forms—dividends, royalties, and various fees.

Making International Investments

Successful international companies continue to be interested in growth prospects, evaluating a variety of proposals from different sources that potentially could lead to investments abroad. These sources include company employees, unknown host country firms, licensees, distributors, and joint venture partners. Essentially, two processes of an investment proposal determine its fate: the selling of the proposal and its review. Proposal selling and reviewing go through a variety of formal and informal human interactions. The processes are significantly affected by the firm's internal politics—that is, factors such as who is backing the proposal, what the company's organization is, how company personalities interact—and by factors outside the firm. Ultimately, the winning strength of a proposal depends on the diligent work of those who prepare it (see Exhibit 6.1).

EXHIBIT 6.1
Checklist for
Preparing
International
Investment Proposal

1. Check with all the people whose approval is needed.
2. Check with all the people *they* will call on for advice.
3. If possible, determine who is most important for which aspects of the proposal (but be careful not to categorize people too narrowly).
4. Sell at the highest possible level—there's nothing like having the president's office behind you from the opening whistle.
5. Establish "people priorities"—who, in descending order, is most important for passing on the project. (This will by no means necessarily be in order of rank.)
6. Set up a flexible "people timetable"—who should be won over in what order.
7. Think ahead as to what each person is going to want to know about the project, and program that into the project analysis. (As one executive put it, you should "do *their* homework" for *them*.)
8. Measure your proposal against *all* stated corporate policy objectives; although sales and profit objectives are the easy ones, don't forget others.
9. Identify any potential enemies to your project and any points of potential resistance, and then establish strategies, or at least mental contingency plans, for dealing with them.
10. Make sure that the investment proposal format corresponds exactly to that used for domestic proposals so as to avoid having it appear to be exotic and thereby attract special detailed scrutiny regarding risk.
11. Give careful thought to any objections that may be raised against your proposal.
12. Be sure you know where your allies stand at all times.
13. In terms of the proposal itself, check carefully that you have not overlooked any obviously important details. Then check for more subtle omissions, and be particularly aware of problem areas and weak points. Have a good idea of the margin of error in the estimates.
14. Anticipate as many objections as possible, but don't be defensive and show your refutations of the objections too hastily.
15. At all times, carefully monitor the pulse of the project's momentum. Momentum can change abruptly. Be ready to facilitate steady progress and to forestall hitches.
16. Be particularly wary of dangerous "parabusiness" environmental criticism of overseas projects, that is, qualitative or essentially subjective, negative social and political judgments. (A domestic officer wishing to shoot down an international proposal may revert to the very thing that is seldom, or rarely, considered for domestic investment proposals, namely, a careful analysis of the political and social climate.)
17. Try to keep the project moving forward at a deliberate speed. Don't let it get stalled in excessive reviewing.

Selling Investment Proposals

Depending on the organizational arrangements of the company, the selling job begins at the middle-management level in the division or department responsible for the country where investment is being considered. When an opportunity arises that seems worthwhile, the manager involved, usually the manager of international development, begins checking with colleagues in manufacturing, marketing, and legal departments in a very informal fashion on such matters as sales projections, manufacturing estimates, patents, and taxes. The manager would also apprise superiors of the forthcoming proposal.

Throughout the early investigatory period that leads up to a formal presentation of the proposal to an international executive, it is important to concentrate on the really critical matters involved. Although these vary somewhat from industry to industry, the overriding emphasis should be put on marketing, because it is in this area that major problems occur. Once the investigation has been completed, a formal proposal is developed and submitted to the head of the section or department.

The section or department head will make a more detailed study of the proposed project with the objective of strengthening the proposal. The location of the investment, market estimates and sales forecasts, equipment costs, total capital required, sources of funding, raw materials availability, and human resources are examined.[11] On the basis of this examination, the proposal is completed for submission to the senior management. Accompanied by a letter, the final proposal includes an appropriations request, an engineering report, the project proposal, and financial analysis. The letter activates the formal review procedure, first through the finance committee, then through the board of directors.

Reviewing Investment Proposals

The review process of a investment proposal is shaped by the perspectives of a company's top management. Often the process and philosophy behind the review of investment opportunities change dramatically with a new person at the helm. In any event, most companies have a comprehensive system for reviewing investment proposals,[12] and all strive to determine whether the investment will provide long-term, lasting benefits for the owners. It is important that the chief executive or another top officer participate actively in the review process of individual major investment decisions in order to assess its value to the long-term strategic posture of the company.

The checklist in Exhibit 6.2 indicates the type of information needed for review of an international investment project. With this information, a framework for evaluation can be laid out. In the final analysis, the evaluation should provide the cost/benefit effects of the project for the host country, parent corporation, and foreign subsidiary.

International Accounting

Global economic interdependence and the existence of large, multinational enterprises create needs for measurement, information transfer, and evaluation of microinformation and macroinformation on an unprecedented scale. International accounting must address these issues. Traditionally, the flow of information between the parent and its subsidiaries was limited. In the last 20 years or so, however, the communication of accounting data across national boundaries has increased enormously. The rapid development of computer capability, as well as achievements in the field of air travel and telecommunications, has made it possible for an MNC to assemble detailed data from its worldwide operations on short notice. But, a challenge arises in determining exactly what information—out of the overwhelming abundance of information available—a parent corporation should request to serve both internal and external needs.

An international accounting system serves the same two basic purposes as domestic accounting. It provides information on the business conducted during a certain period

EXHIBIT 6.2
Checklist for
Reviewing
International
Investment Proposal

1. Carefully examine the record and predilections of the individual most directly responsible for the proposal. Is she chronically optimistic? Does she usually underestimate costs or overestimate future sales?

2. Who has been won over to her side? Why do certain managers support the proposal? Why do others oppose it?

3. Determine as best you can the politics of the situation, and try to discount each aspect in your analysis.

4. Systematically review all the estimates and projections of the proposal.

5. Look at the details, but also sit back and broadly scrutinize the project. Does it hang together, not only in its details but also as a whole? Does it fit in with the company's long-term objectives?

6. Give particularly close attention to the most crucial elements in your industry—marketing, manufacturing, technical know-how, or financing.

7. Look for holes. Errors of omission are sometimes harder to spot than outright mistakes.

8. Probe the weak or questionable assumptions that lie behind the figures.

9. Make sure you don't overlook anybody on the corporate staff, or elsewhere in the company, whose advice would be useful and who should see the proposal.

10. Don't let the proposal get "railroaded" through the process without sufficiently careful analysis.

11. Make sure that the difficulties—present and future—of doing business in the country and region in question are not minimized. What about the future effects of nascent regional trade groups? Any serious chance of low-price competition from new sources, for example, in the Pacific Rim or Eastern Europe?

12. Take a hard look at the broad political, social, and financial prospects of the country involved. Can you foresee the possibility of anything like an Iraqi attack on Kuwait or the currency turmoil in Southeast Asia?

13. Look at the overall conditions of doing business in the country involved. What are the chances of price controls, nationalization of retail outlets (such as pharmacies are in Sweden), greater mandatory fringe benefits, new labor legislation, work permit problems (as exist in Switzerland)?

14. Test the key assumptions of the proposal by subjecting them to a test of their elasticity, and test the overall flexibility of the project by projecting the effects of changes on the project. Suppose, for example, that the sales forecast is off by 10 percent. What will that do to profitability?

and the results obtained. The first purpose is achieved through the *income statement.* The second purpose is accomplished through the *balance sheet,* which shows the position of a business, its assets, and its liabilities at a particular time.

Accounting information is needed for the internal workings of the organization and to satisfy the requirements and expectations of the external community.

The internal contexts of an international corporation are obviously more complex and larger in scope than the external ones. For internal purposes, accounting information must meet the decision-making and control needs of *both* the parent company and its foreign subsidiary. Again, a challenge lies in determining how much of what information a corporation should compile in its internal accounting system. The external interest of corporate publics (e.g., stockholders, governments, financial communities, labor, customers, creditors, and employees) in *both* the parent and host country must also be served through accounting information. The external use of information creates the company image that will be presented to current and potential investors.[13]

International Accounting Reports

The income statement and the balance sheet are used all over the world. The emphasis placed on these statements, however, varies from country to country. In the United States the income statement is of primary interest. This is so because most large U.S. corporations are publicly owned, and stockholders" wealth depends primarily on stock market prices, which in turn are greatly affected by earnings per share. In Europe, as well as in Latin America and Asia, the major concerns are the ownership of wealth (rather than the generation of income) and the position of the firm in regard to its assets and the claims against them. This view makes the balance sheet of primary importance.

The format of an income statement and a balance sheet also varies among countries.[14] In the United States balance sheet liabilities appear on the right and assets on the left. In most European countries, the order is reversed. Along the same lines, non–U.S. balance sheets usually show fixed assets and stockholders' equity sections at the top, and current assets and current liabilities near the bottom. Such variations in format do not make a substantial difference in the information presented. But there are significant differences in the amount of information disclosed by various countries. By and large, U.S. companies disclose much more information than companies elsewhere.[15] This is largely due to the requirements of the SEC, as well as the listing requirements of the stock exchanges, particularly those of the New York Stock Exchange (NYSE) (see International Marketing Highlight 6.3).

International Marketing Highlight 6.3

Let the Investor Beware

So you want to invest overseas? That makes sense. After all, foreign stock markets often outperform the U.S. market. Now all you have to do is figure out what you're investing in.

It won't be easy. Disclosure and accounting rules overseas differ sharply from those in the United States—and also differ significantly among the foreign countries.

Only companies in the United States and Canada, for example, issue reports quarterly on profits and other key financial data. Most companies in Japan and Germany don't consolidate the financial data of majority-owned subsidiaries.

In some nations, the lack of a strong enforcement body like the Securities and Exchange Commission permits overseas companies to be more footloose and fancy-free with disclosures. Insider trading is often greeted with a wink by government regulators. In Holland, Spain, and France, where stock exchanges are relatively small, government regulation and oversight of company disclosures are very relaxed.

Source: The Wall Street Journal, September 22, 1989, p. R30.

Harmonization of International Accounting

Recent years have seen growing interest in facilitating the comparison of accounting information provided by multinational firms. Authorities on the subject, while rejecting the goal of complete standardization with totally uniform accounting, nevertheless recommend *harmonization,* which implies a reconciliation of different methods of presenting information to enhance international communication.[16]

Multinational firms raise capital in different countries. It is desirable, therefore, that investors and creditors be provided common information on which to base their investment decisions. The principal force behind the accounting profession's attempt at harmonization to facilitate the generation of common information has been the International Congress of Accountants (ICA). In its tenth meeting in Sidney in 1972, the ICA established the International Coordination Committee for the Accounting Profession (ICCAP) to provide leadership in the harmonization effort. One of the outcomes of ICCAP's efforts was the 1973 formation of the International Accounting Standards

Committee (IASC), which was formed to (1) develop basic standards to be observed in presenting audited financial statements and (2) promote worldwide acceptance and observance of these standards.

Very much in the manner of the Financial Accounting Standards Board (FASB) in the United States, the IASC issues international accounting standards. By 1992, the IASC had issued 44 standards.

The IASC has had only an indirect effect on the external financial reporting practices of U.S. multinational enterprises. The American Institute of CPAs (AICPA), for example, has pledged its best efforts to promote IASC standards. Yet the FASB, not the AICPA, presently sets U.S. accounting standards, and that organization has done little to harmonize its standards with those of the IASC, nor has the IASC attempted to harmonize its pronouncements with those of the FASB. As U.S. firms are bound by FASB, not IASC, standards, they are not presently required to disclose whatever differences exist between these two sets of standards.

The IASC appears to have more influence with financial institutions in other countries. For example, the World Federation of Stock Exchanges has asked member exchanges to require compliance with IASC standards. In addition, the London Stock Exchange requires that listed companies conform with IASC standards.

The ultimate success of the IASC in its harmonization effort depends primarily on the kinds of standards it issues. To be successful, it must issue statements that either develop broad accounting principles acceptable to most countries, including the United States, or gain the authority to require disclosures that would enable users to make valid comparisons of multinational enterprises.

America's accounting standards are among the world's most rigorous. The FASB claims that (1) the IASC standards are too flexible, giving firms too much discretion over what they report; (2) their meaning is often ambiguous; and (3) there are big uncertainties about how they will be enforced.[17] Thus, IASC standards are not likely to be accepted in the United States in the near future.[18]

Consolidation of Accounts

Most MNCs consolidate the accounting information from their different entities to present a single income statement and balance sheet for both parent and affiliates. The consolidation process is based on legal requirements of the parent company, information available from subsidiaries, and the practice established over time within the corporation. In the United States, MNCs are generally required by law to consolidate the accounts of a subsidiary if the parent owns 50 percent or more of the affiliate. In order to publish consolidated financial statements within a reasonable time after the end of the parent corporation's financial year, the U.S. multinationals usually require the affiliates to prepare their accounts earlier. For example, if the parent's financial year ends on December 31, the subsidiaries may end their financial year on October 31. This way subsidiaries' financial accounts will be available to the parent by December 31 for consolidation with its own.

Most corporations have standard procedures for the subsidiaries to report their accounting information. Thus, the management of subsidiaries must not only satisfy the legal accounting requirements of their host countries, but also make the information available in the format required by their corporate headquarters. Usually U.S. multinationals require their subsidiaries to submit quarterly accounts, comparing actual results against the standards. But some corporations request monthly accounts. Review meetings are held to examine the future outlook of the business on the basis of such periodic information. The recent trend has been to seek as much detailed information on the subsidiaries' activities as feasible, including, in addition to accounting information, data on markets, industry, climate, and economic environment.

National differences and delayed international standardization make it necessary for each multinational enterprise to deal individually with the issue of adequate reporting (see International Marketing Highlight 6.4). Unfortunately, varying national approaches to inflation accounting, new regional requirements for consolidation, demands for social accounting data, and uncoordinated actions by international "standardizing" organizations create additional problems. Consequently, there is a great need for new developments in accounting theory and practice to provide adequate multinational information.

■■■■■■■■■■■ **International Marketing Highlight 6.4** ■■■■■■■■■■■

A Computer Comparison

To illustrate how tough it is to compare profit performance in different nations, three accounting professors at Rider College in Lawrenceville, New Jersey, set up a computer model of an imaginary company's financial reports in four countries. Starting with the same gross operating profit of $1.5 million, the company had net profit of $34,600 in the United States, $260,600 in the United Kingdom, $240,600 in Australia, and $10,402 in Germany—all because of varying accounting rules in each country.

Although many companies have worldwide operations, their financial results in different countries aren't comparable. This is a serious problem for accountants who may be called upon to analyze a foreign company's financial statements.

The results of companies in Japan, Germany, Switzerland, and Spain are among the most difficult to compare with those of their U.S. counterparts. In Japan and Germany, many corporations don't consolidate results of their majority-owned subsidiaries; in Switzerland and Spain, some concerns set up hidden reserves, which result in lower reported profits.

Investing in Korean companies can also be tricky. Some Korean companies create "special gains and losses" that sometimes don't relate to company successes or failures.

Source: The Wall Street Journal, September 22, 1989, p. R30.

Summary

International marketing decisions are profoundly affected by the finance and accounting function; therefore, a brief review of their conduct in the international business field is in order. Essentially, international finance deals with the management of financial resources such as the sources and uses of funds and the remission of profits from subsidiaries. The underlying force behind financial decisions is a corporation's financial objectives. These objectives usually are defined in terms such as desired return on investment or assets, desired profit growth, hurdle rate (for accepting new projects), and proportion of earnings desired to be paid in the form of dividends.

After setting its financial objectives, a corporation can decide how to raise funds—whether to borrow money or to make a stock offering, where to raise money (in the United States or in another capital market) and who should trigger certain actions, the parent or a subsidiary. Two of the factors influencing international finance decisions are: (1) the varying and fluctuating exchange rates of different currencies, and (2) the restrictions imposed by host countries on the transfer of funds. Thus, before the source of funds can be settled, the exchange rates of the countries where the funds are to be raised must be predicted. Then funds can be raised to avoid exchange losses on the one hand and to minimize the cost of capital on the other.

Another factor that must be dealt with in money management is the political climate of the host country. If problems that may jeopardize the ownership of corporate funds appear likely, it might be desirable to transfer funds out of the country while there is still time, even at a substantial exchange loss.

Remission of profits from one country to another is determined by such factors as tax implications, political risk, foreign exchange risk, age and size of affiliate, availability of funds, and presence of joint venture partners. MNCs pursue either a pooled or flexible strategy in the matter of profit transfer from a subsidiary to the parent or to another subsidiary. The pooled strategy spells out profit to the parent by each subsidiary on a predetermined basis. The flexible strategy leaves the decision on remission of profits to the circumstances of the critical moment.

Marketing is affected by financial decisions in many ways, one being transfer pricing—the price that a subsidiary charges to another subsidiary belonging to the same parent for its goods, services, and technology. Another way that financial decisions affect marketing is that approval of projects that seem crucial from a marketing standpoint may be denied because they conflict with overall corporate financial objectives.

Most multinationals have a systematic procedure to receive, evaluate, and approve projects requiring capital expenditures. The selling of an investment project is followed by its review, in which the cost/benefit effects on the host country, parent corporation, and foreign subsidiary are evaluated.

In international accounting differing emphasis is placed on the income statement versus the balance sheet in different countries. For example, in the United States the income statement is considered of prime importance. In Europe, Asia, and Latin America, the balance sheet has greater significance.

Accounting systems and procedures, although essentially following the double-entry system, differ worldwide in various ways. Therefore, it is difficult to make comparisons. Efforts at harmonization of international accounting information are being spearheaded by the IASC.

Review Questions

1. Describe the meaning of money management in the international context.
2. What risks does a multinational enterprise sometimes face in international money management?
3. What are the arguments for and against raising capital in host country currency?
4. What factors determine international dividend policy?
5. What is transfer pricing, and what factors affect it?
6. What sorts of reports usually are included with a project proposal?
7. Explain why the income statement is considered more important than the balance sheet in the United States, whereas the reverse is true in Europe.
8. Why is more information usually disclosed by U.S. firms in their financial accounts than by their counterparts in Europe?

Creative Questions

1. The format of an income statement and a balance sheet in the United States varies from the conventions followed elsewhere in the world. What difference would it make if U.S. companies followed the practices of other nations? Would this practice make it easier for U.S. MNCs to consolidate their subsidiaries' accounts and interpret their performance?
2. What is a euro? Can a company raise money in euro? What are the pros and cons of such a decision?

Endnotes

1. *Crossborder Monitor*, December 16, 1998, p. 12.

2. Kwang Chul Lee and Cluik C. Y. Kwok, "Multinational Corporations vs. Domestic Corporations: International Environmental Factors and Determinants of Capital Structure," *Journal of International Business Studies*, Summer 1988, pp. 195–218.

3. *Investment, Licensing and Trading Conditions Abroad* (New York: Business International Corporation, no date).

4. See Alan C. Shapiro, *Multinational Financial Management*, 4th ed. (Boston: Allyn & Bacon, 1995).

5. J. S. Ang and Lai Tsong-Yue, "A Simple Rule for Multinational Capital Budgeting," *Global Finance Journal*, Fall, 1989, pp. 71–75.

6. Jongmoo Jay Choi, "Diversification, Exchange Risk, and Corporate International Investment," *Journal of International Business Studies*, Spring 1989, pp. 145–156.

7. "Indian Shares—Oversensitive," *The Economist*, February 9, 1994, p. 80.

8. Thomas G. O'Brien, "Accounting Versus Economic Exposure to Currency Risk," *The Journal of Financial Statement Analysis*, Summer 1997, pp. 21–28.

9. John D. Daniels and Lee H. Radebaugh, *International Business Environments and Operations*, 8th ed. (Reading, MA: Addison-Wesley, 1998), chapters 3–6.

10. David Eitemann, Arthur I. Stonehill, and Michael M. Moffett, *Multinational Business Finance*, 7th ed. (New York: Addison Wesley, 1995), chapter 19.

11. Joshua Mendes, "Go Abroad for Bigger Returns," *Fortune*, 1993 Investor's Guide, p. 88.

12. J. J. Pringle, "Managing Foreign Exchange Exposure," *Journal of Applied Corporate Finance* 3, (1991): pp. 73–82

13. William M. Abdallah and David E. Keller, "Measuring the Multinationals' Performance," *Management Accounting*, October 1985, pp. 25–30.

14. Timothy S. Doupink and Stephen B. Salter, "An Empirical Test of a Judgemental International Classification of Financial Reporting Practices," *Journal of International Business Studies* 24, no. 1 (1993): 41–60.

15. A. M. Agami, "Global Accounting Standards and Competitiveness of U.S. Corporations," *Multinational Business Review*, Spring 1993, pp. 38–43.

16. "MNCs Home Competitive Edge With Activity-Based Costing," *Business International*, January 29, 1991, p. 37.

17. Jeffrey E. Garten, "Global Accounting Rules? Not so Fast," *Business Week*, April 5, 1999, p. 26

18. "Accounting Standards: America v. the World," *The Economist*, January 17, 1998, p. 58.

CHAPTER 7

Regional Market Agreements

After studying this chapter, you should be able to

■ Present the rationale behind regional market agreements.

■ Discuss how market agreements affect international marketing.

■ Understand the historical perspectives of market agreements.

■ Discuss the European Community and its various aspects such as the Europe 1992 program and the Monetary Union.

■ Describe other agreements, especially the North American Free Trade Agreement.

A previous chapter discussed the worldwide postwar efforts to restore free trade. These efforts included the elimination of tariff barriers through the General Agreement on Tariffs and Trade (GATT) and stabilization of currencies through the International Monetary Fund (IMF). At the same time these efforts went forward on the international level, an interest in economic cooperation at the regional level also developed, resulting in different forms of market agreements. Regional economic cooperation is based on the premise that nations in a region connected by historical, geographic, cultural, economic, and political affinities may be able to strike more intensive cooperative agreements for mutually beneficial economic advantages than those in a more wide-ranging group.

An outstanding example of regional economic cooperation is today's *European Union (EU)*. Originally called the European Economic Community (EEC), in 1958, or simply the European Common Market, the name was changed in 1980 to European Community (EC), and then in 1992 to European Union. At the time of development of the Marshall Plan, the United States urged European nations to seek economic integration in coping with the problems of reconstruction. Such economic integration was expected to bring forth a Western European market as large as the U.S. market, one that would allow economies of scale via mass production. The self-interest of the United States was also involved in the push for European economic integration. The creation of a large, and to some extent homogeneous, market was certainly beneficial to U.S. corporations.

Economic cooperation has an effect on international marketing, varying according to the different forms of market agreements among nations. The international marketer should be aware of early attempts at regional cooperation and economic integration like that which led to the European Union, and of the cultivation of existing market agreements in different parts of the world.

Effects of Market Agreements on Marketing

Market agreements affect international marketing in a variety of ways. *First, the scope of the market is broadened.* For example, after the formation of the Common Market, the French market ceased to be just a French market; it became a part of the larger Common Market. Such an expanded market provides a *flexibility* that would not be feasible dealing with individual countries. For example, under one type of market agreement called a *free trade area agreement,* internal trade barriers among member countries are abolished and a company may move products from one country to another freely. This permits economies of scale not only in production but also in product promotion, distribution, and other aspects of business. Thus, the establishment of the Common Market allowed the Ford Motor Company to integrate its operations in Germany and Britain, and, as described in *Forbes,*

> A new management organization was created to make all the critical decisions for both the British and German companies. There were obvious operating economies in the arrangement—the duplicate dealer organizations in third markets could be eliminated, and responsibility went where the skill was: body development work was concentrated in Germany, power train development concentrated in Britain. The pooling cut the engineering bill in half for each company, provided economies of scale with double the volume in terms of purchase—commonization of purchase, common components—and provided the financial resources for a good product program at a really good price.[1]

Another company that benefited from the Common Market was Elizabeth Arden International. This global cosmetics and perfume company owned by Unilever recognized the need for pan-European integration early in the 1990s. At that time management created a project-team structure, with eight teams of 10–50 people (300 in all), led by a project director and reporting to a steering committee. The company spent two years on the effort, pursuing three specific objectives: build a pan-European business, not only to harmonize operations but to defend Arden against the activities of parallel importers and consolidation of the retail trade; optimize the business's tax position; and minimize indirect expenses, which at 30 percent of sales were unduly high.

The problem of excessive indirect costs stemmed mainly from duplication of processes within individual countries. But another cause was supply chain defects like the use of third-party distributors and stock movements that looked fine from a national standpoint but were blatantly inefficient when viewed at the pan-European level. Indeed, where inventories were concerned, poor information led to an increase in stock levels along the supply chain and high holding costs.

Marketing was also out of control, as national subsidiaries acted with little regard for coordination, resulting in high marketing costs and conflicting brand messages. Levels of customer satisfaction varied by country. Management decided that the time had come to take advantage of economies of scale and scope and to focus resources on the critical aspects of maintaining and expanding business. It decided that the answer would be to develop regionwide shared services.[2]

Since the formation of the EU, U.S. business activity in the region has grown significantly. U.S. investment in the EU increased fourfold during the 1970s. In 1998 U.S. investment in the EU was almost $420 billion, while EU investments in the United States amounted to nearly two-thirds of all foreign investments, about $380 billion.

A second way that market agreements affect international marketing is that they change the nature of competition. For example, before the formation of the Common Market, many American MNCs found little local competition in Western Europe, but afterward local companies were encouraged to expand quickly. They became factors in the market, through mergers and such, with the encouragement of member governments. In the computer field, for example, Siemens A.G. (German), Compagnie International pour L'Informatique (French), and Philips N.V. (Dutch) entered into a joint venture to compete effectively against IBM.

Despite IBM's best efforts, in 1985 the EU denied IBM the opportunity to join European firms for basic research to close Europe's technology gap with the United States and Japan. This research was sponsored to (1) use Esprit, a $1 billion program focusing on basic information technology and (2) encourage Britain's ICL, France's Bull, Italy's Olivetti, former West Germany's Nixdorf, and the Netherlands' Philips to cooperate with each other competing against giants such as IBM.[3] Such cooperation among businesses need not necessarily be among companies of different nations. In Italy, for example, Montecatini and Edison companies merged to form Montedison.

Third, market-agreement firms expand through mergers and acquisitions and thereby become highly competitive outside their market area as well. For example, after the formulation of the Common Market, French and German companies were able to compete aggressively against U.S. and Japanese multinationals worldwide. Consider Airbus Industrié, a consortium of French, German, English, and Spanish companies formed in 1970. This company grabbed 40 percent of newcraft orders in 1997 in a short span at the cost of American airframe manufacturers.[4]

Finally, market-agreement countries are able to make decisions favorable to all member-country companies. An individual country could never enforce certain measures that are desirable for the group. For example, Common Market antitrust policies could adversely affect an American company and its subsidiaries or licensees that previously had been given exclusive rights in, say, Italy and the Netherlands.

It is important to mention also that economic integration, while leading to a variety of benefits, can create some problems. Consider, for example, the potential for trouble with the freedom-of-labor movement within the EU. With relatively poor countries like

Greece and Portugal having joined the group, controversy over guest workers from these countries, in Germany in particular, has arisen. What is more, free entry for Spanish and Portuguese agricultural products has worsened the EU's agricultural problems, boosting output of such products as olive and citrus fruit and thus depressing prices. The lower prices are likely to put further pressure on the EU's budget, two-thirds of which is already spent on farm subsidies.

Another problem is the jeopardy into which existing agreements of a nation are thrown when it joins a market group. Entry into the EU caused Great Britain's commitments to the Commonwealth to diminish. Agricultural overproduction and inefficiencies are always potentially troublesome among member countries since no nation wants its output outpriced by cheap imports. Agricultural exports have been a chief issue of conflict between the United States and the EU, and to a large extent have been responsible for the delay in concluding the Uruguay Round deadlock, as was discussed in Chapter 2.

Many marketers erroneously thought that with the establishment of the Common Market, Western Europe would present a single homogeneous market. Instead, the market was simply enlarged. Within this enlarged, heterogeneous market, however, homogenous segments can be identified for the development of effective marketing strategy—each segment to be served by a unique marketing mix. These smaller markets are the ones that must be recognized and targeted.

Early Attempts at Regional Economic Integration

Current efforts toward regional economic integration among the nations of the world began with the creation of the *European Economic Community (EEC)* in 1958, born through a long history of trial and deliberation. In 1948 the *Organization for European Economic Cooperation (OEEC)* was established to administer the Marshall Aid program. Very soon it became obvious to all concerned that European nations would have to seek some form of economic cooperation in order to emerge as a large, autonomous market.

The drive toward European economic unity continued to gain momentum in the early 1950s, although many leaders doubted that perpetual cooperation, other than on an ad hoc basis, would ever be feasible. The proponents of the movement met with their first success with the establishment of the *European Coal and Steel Community (ECSC)* in 1952. The ECSC was created to develop a common market in coal, steel, and iron ore. The six countries participating in this effort were France, West Germany, Italy, Belgium, the Netherlands, and Luxembourg.

The success of the ECSC led these six nations to venture into the 1957 establishment of the EEC by the Treaty of Rome. Initially, the EEC was established as a *customs union* (discussed later in this chapter) that was gradually to include both industrial and agricultural goods and to lead to the abolition of restrictions on trade among member nations and the creation of common external tariffs. The EEC's organizers expected eventual economic union among the member countries to enable free movement of people, services, and capital, and gradual development of common social, fiscal, and monetary policies.

Simultaneously with the formation of the EEC, the *European Free Trade Association (EFTA)* was established in 1960 by the United Kingdom, Denmark, Sweden, Norway, Switzerland, Austria, and Portugal. These seven nations had been unable to come to agreement with the EEC.

With Europe as an example, regional agreements have come into existence all over the world—in Africa, in the Arab world, in Latin America, and in Asia. Communist countries also have made their own regional cooperative arrangements.

Bases of Economic Cooperation

Economic cooperation among nations is mainly dictated by economic, political, geographic, and social factors. Nations often cooperate with each other simply as a matter of economic necessity.[5] For example, 77 countries located distantly around the world have joined in a group called the *New International Economic Order (NIEO)*, which negotiates concessions from richer countries for the purpose of enhancing NIEO member trade.

Nations also may cooperate for political reasons. The *Commonwealth* is an interesting example of a political union of nations. Commonwealth countries are economically far apart from each other. For example, Australia is among the developed nations, while Pakistan is a developing country. Geographically, the Commonwealth countries are spread over different continents. Canada is in North America, Great Britain in Europe, Nigeria in Africa, and India in Asia. Even some political similarities of the past have vanished as these nations pursue different political modes: Burma is a military dictatorship; New Zealand, a democracy. The commonality of these nations is their historical partnership in the British Empire.

Geographic proximity is another factor that facilitates economic cooperation and integration among nations. Presumably countries in the same geographic region have a better appreciation of each other's strengths and weaknesses, and together they may come to realize synergies that would make them economically stronger. For example, a mass market is necessary for mass production. Nations located near each other are better able to develop a mass market. A notable example of such cooperation among nations in geographic proximity to one another is the EU.

Finally, countries also may associate with each other on the basis of social customs, traditions, taboos, and culture. Arab countries, for example, share a long Islamic heritage. Such bonds favor economic union.

Factors in Successful Economic Cooperation

What factors make for successful economic integration? Briefly, economic cooperation is likely to flourish when member countries have diverse products and raw materials. The most successful case of economic integration has been the EU. Nations belonging to the EU have more or less complementary economies, diverse industries, different natural resources, and varying agricultural bases. Further, it is desirable that member nations be of compatible economic status in terms of balance-of-payments position and level of development.

Types of Market Agreements

There are five principal forms of market agreements among nations: free trade area, customs union, common market, economic union, and political union. Such agreements are differentiated on several bases, as follows.

Free Trade Area

The *free trade area* type of agreement requires nations to remove all tariffs among the members. Let us assume three nations—A, B, and C—agree to a free trade area agreement to abolish all tariffs among themselves and permit free trade. Beyond the agreement, these nations may impose tariffs as they choose. For example, if Nation X trades extensively with Nation B, Nation B may have very low tariffs for goods imported from Nation X, while Nations A and C impose high tariffs on goods from Nation X. Under this type of agreement, Nation B is free to continue its *preferred* relationship with Nation X while Nation A and Nation C are at liberty to decide their own external tariff policies. *The European Free Trade Area (EFTA)* and the *Latin American Free Trade Area (LAFTA)* illustrate the free trade area type of agreement.

Customs Union

A *customs union,* in addition to requiring abolition of internal tariffs among members, further obligates the members to establish common external tariffs. To continue with the example of Nations A, B, and C, under a customs union agreement (instead of a free trade area agreement), Nation B would not be permitted to have a special relationship with Nation X. Nations A, B, and C would have to have a common tariff policy toward Nation X. A customs union agreement exists among Caribbean countries. Their cooperative effort started as a free trade area and later developed into a customs union. As mentioned earlier, the EU began as a customs union.

Common Market

In a *common market* type of agreement, members not only abolish internal tariffs among themselves and levy common external tariffs, but they also permit the free flow of all factors of production (capital, labor, technology) among themselves. In our illustration, Nations A, B, and C, under a common market agreement, not only would remove all tariffs and quotas among themselves and impose common tariffs against other countries such as Nation X, but also would allow capital, labor, and technology to move freely within their boundaries as if they were one nation. This means, for example, a resident of Nation A is free to accept a position in Nation C without a work permit. Likewise, an investor in Nation B is at liberty to invest money in Nation A, B, or C without restriction from either home or host government when transferring funds for investment.

Economic Union

Under the *economic union* arrangement, common market characteristics are combined with harmonization of economic policy. Member countries are expected to pursue common monetary and fiscal policies. Ordinarily this means synchronizing taxes, money supply, interest rates, and regulation of capital market, among other things. In effect, the economic union calls for a supranational authority to design an economic policy for an entire group of nations. The EU, to a great extent, can be called an economic union. This designation is justified by the fact that the union has a common agricultural policy and shares the European monetary system.

Political Union

A *political union* is the ultimate market agreement among nations. It includes the characteristics of an economic union and requires, in addition, political harmony among the members. Essentially, it means nations merging with each other to form a new nation.

In its pure form, an example of the political union does not exist. In the 1950s, however, Egypt, Syria, and Yemen formed a short-lived political union. To an extent, the Commonwealth of Nations and perhaps the newly formed Commonwealth of Independent States can be characterized as politically based agreements. In the future, in a very limited sense, the EU, with the European Parliament in place, could be considered a political union.

Market Agreements in Force

Most current market agreements are organized by geography. Some agreements are not formed according to region, however, but extend over different geographic areas of the world.

Europe

European nations have been by far the most aggressive in seeking economic integration. They have formed the EU, the EFTA, and the now defunct Council for Economic Assistance.

European Union (EU) Often called the *European Common Market,* the EU agreement came into existence in January 1958. Its purpose was to abolish over a 12-year period all customs, tariffs, and other economic barriers among the six member countries of the former: West Germany, France, Italy, the Netherlands, Belgium, and Luxembourg. In 1973 the United Kingdom, Denmark, and Ireland joined the EU. Greece became a full member in 1982. Spain and Portugal joined as full members on January 1, 1986. Austria, Finland

and Sweden became full members on January 1, 1995. As it stands today, the 15-member EU is the world's largest exporter, producing over one-fourth of world exports.

The EU represents a true customs union, having abolished all customs duties and restrictions on trade in industrial goods within the community while imposing common external tariffs and supporting free internal movement of labor and capital. In the area of agriculture, the EU has developed a protective common agricultural policy that consists of a support system designed to promote domestic agricultural production and guaranteed farm incomes.

The European Community's 1957 *Rome Treaty* called for the eventual formation of an economic union. Although some progress has been made toward this end in the form of a common antitrust policy, complete economic and monetary union, not to mention political union, has a long way to go. However, the name change from European Economic Community to European Community in 1980 and to European Union in 1992 indicated the broadened economic and political role this group was likely to play in the later years.

A number of other countries are linked with the Common Market as associate members. Turkey is one. The EU also has preferential trade agreements with a number of Mediterranean countries and with the countries in the EFTA.

Following the *Lomé* (capital of Togo) *Convention* in 1975 and its latest extension in 1990 (the fourth Lomé Convention), the EU agreed to a trading program with 66 *African, Caribbean, and Pacific (ACP)* countries that was valid for five years (1990–1995). The fourth Lomé agreement consolidated and built on the earlier Lomé agreements, and provided, in particular, trade opportunities and development aid to selected Third World countries from EU members.[6] It established a vast, privileged domain of cooperation among multiform (economic, commercial, and even cultural) northern (the members of the EU) and southern (the associated states of Africa, the Caribbean, and the Pacific) countries. At the time of preparing this book, a new agreement was in the works to replace the *Lomè IV* agreement that ended at the end of February 2000.

Today the EU is a viable world economic force with as large a market as that of the United States If the present trend continues, the EU will continue to grow as other countries join. In its meeting at Luxembourg in 1997, the EU decided to next offer membership in the group to the Czech Republic, Estonia, Hungary, Poland, Slovenia, and Cyprus.[7] At the Helsinki meeting in 1999, the EU invited another six countries, Bulgaria, Latvia, Lithuania, Malta, Romania, and Slovakia, to start negotiating for membership. Turkey, which has been waiting to join the group since 1969, was added to the official list of prospective members during the Helsinki deliberations.[8]

Because of the EU program, Western European nations are doing more together than ever. The Common Market is expanding, both in members and in terms of trade, after settling a protracted dispute over budgetary share. New agreements on matters important in future European development—space, broadcasting, and computer research—have been negotiated among countries and companies. But expanding trade has been, and continues to be, the greatest achievement of the Common Market.

The rate of expansion in European trade during the 1990s was seven times the rate of economic growth. This means several things. First, trade is acting as a propellant to Europe's overall economy—exactly what the continent's leaders had in mind when they launched the Common Market more than 42 years ago. The key provision of the treaty, the elimination of tariffs among member states, touched off a trade boom that continues to this day despite the severe recession of the 1990s.

Despite the tremendous achievements of the EU, in the mid-1980s the organization faced a variety of problems (see International Marketing Highlight 7.1). A critical examination showed that the EU had never really become a common market. After the first heady years, various kinds of nontariff barriers had once again begun to choke off trade among member nations. A common currency, even a single free capital market, remained little more than a goal for the distant future. Less soaring aims, like harmonizing economic policies and standardizing member countries' value-added taxes, also appeared remote. Freedom of trade in services hardly existed at all, and there was little consensus on how to bring it about. The EU's *common agricultural policy (CAP)*, which guarantees farmers high prices without limiting production, had produced huge surpluses that disrupted international markets and strained the EU budget. Yet farmers were not happy; their gripes about prices and market share erupted in violence.

The most disappointing failure was a lack of progress in creating a true common market in manufactured goods, the EU's original reason for existence. Before the EU's birth, Europe was a maze of protectionism. Tariffs and quotas were the most visible and significant barriers, backed by a host of regulations and other protectionist devices, some more than 100 years old. After the tariffs and quotas were eliminated, much of their protectionist function was gradually taken over by the nontariff barriers, many of which have proliferated over the years (see International Marketing Highlight 7.2).

International Marketing Highlight 7.1

Crazy Quilt of Regulations

If a commercial truck driver left New York and drove the 5,000 or so kilometers to Los Angeles, respecting all the applicable work and rest rules, he could drive the entire distance at an average speed of 60 kilometers per hour. If that same rule-obeying driver in the same heavy lorry were to leave the Midlands in the United Kingdom, pass by London, and drive down to Athens, also a distance of some 5,000 kilometers, he would be able to average only 12 kilometers per hour. It is worth noting that 12 kilometers per hour happens to be the speed of a horse and cart.

International Marketing Highlight 7.2

How Nontariff Barriers Hindered European Growth

A recent study by the EC Commission listed no fewer than 56 different categories of nontariff barriers, ranging from discrimination in government procurement contracts through national health and technical regulations to sheer customs chicanery at national borders. Many customs restrictions, such as taking currency in or out of France and Italy, are more stringent now than they were in the past. The time wasted getting goods through borders adds significantly to European industry's costs—as much as $1 billion a year. The total cost to industry of complying with all of the customs formalities is estimated at more than $10 billion, or between 5 percent and 10 percent of the value of the goods traded. This amounts to a substantial hidden tariff. In 1983, several truckloads of West German freezers were turned back at the French border for failing to have new certification documents in French, a requirement that had been introduced almost overnight. At the Italian border, customs officials often are simply unavailable, which halts truck traffic. Moreover, Italy still requires, as it did before 1958, that any pasta sold there must be made of durum wheat, not the soft wheat normally used for pasta-type products elsewhere. In Germany, a law whose origins go back several centuries specifies that beer sold there may be made only of barley malt, hops, and water. Since brewers in France, Belgium, and the Netherlands, like those in the United States, now use other grains or additives, this means that not a single bottle of Kronenbourg, Stella Artois, or Heineken can be sent across the Rhine.

Governments take action under many guises that discriminate against foreign products. France and Italy, for instance, impose disproportionately heavy taxes on big, powerful cars, which suits their automobile manufacturers, whose output is concentrated in the small-car end of the line. As buyers of goods and services—telecommunications equipment, for example, or pharmaceuticals for national health services—governments can be decidedly protectionist.

Source: European Community Press and Information Service, New York, March 1985.

The EU members realized that as markets and industries globalize, those constraints—physical, technical, and fiscal—are no longer endurable. Further, as the forces of globalization increased, the influence of European countries, both political and economic, had weakened. During the first half of the 1980s, Europe lost jobs at a rate of 0.5 percent per year, while its economy, roughly the same size as that of the United States, grew at 1.5 percent per year. At the same time, the unemployment rate in Europe climbed from 4 percent to around 6 percent. These numbers pointed to a troubling decline in the international competitiveness of European companies.

Thus, to create jobs, restore international competitiveness, and boost the value to European customers of the goods and services available to them, the EU members were led to adopt a new course, that is, _Europe 1992,_ or the _Internal Market Program._

In this program, the 12 member countries of the EU committed to integrating into a single internal market by the end of 1992. The result was to be a $4 trillion market of 340 million people. This Internal Market Program proposed sweeping changes in virtually every aspect of business life that were to greatly alter the way U.S. firms did business in Europe.

Initially described in a 1985 EU Commission White Paper, the Internal Market Program (or "Europe 1992") consisted of 285 legislative directives intended to eliminate present barriers to the free movement of goods, people, and capital among the 12 EU member states. Internal Market directives reached into every aspect of commercial activity, from eliminating border controls and duplicative customs documents, to setting uniform product standards, to establishing guidelines for company mergers.

The program concluded on time, although there have been a variety of hindrances relative to the national interests of member nations. For example, a German law discourages the import of parallel pharmaceuticals (drugs bought cheaply in one market and exported to where they are expensive) by requiring them to bear a certificate proving they meet German standards. The EU Commission, however, is getting tougher as it seeks to ensure that national governments effectively administer EU rules. To resolve the German pharmaceutical problem, the commission persuaded Germany to tell its customs offices to ignore the law.[9] By 1997, 85 percent of all regulations affecting business in the EU were EU regulations and directives instead of national laws.

European officials believe that the integration of the EU market has increased economic growth and employment, and led to greater consumption and imports. A study by the EU Commission predicted that the removal of existing barriers would result in a 5 percent increase in EU gross domestic product (GDP), more than $260 billion, through more economies of scale and greater economic efficiency.[10]

European industry has benefited most from the program. The ability to compete in a continental scale market and to avoid duplication of administrative procedures, production, marketing, and distribution systems has offered great advantages. In addition, a unified EU market offers tremendous opportunities to U.S. companies, both those located in Europe and those exporting. Of course, it also poses tougher competition, for U.S. companies, particularly in such industries as financial services, pharmaceuticals, telecommunications, electronics and computers.[11]

U.S. company sales in the 12-nation EU are over $650 billion, almost four times greater than sales to Japan. Achieving a single EU internal market should mean greater economic growth for Europe, which, in turn, should bring increased demand for American products. The uniformity of trade and financial regulations has allowed U.S. companies easier access to all the EU countries by eliminating the need to meet national registration requirements in each country. In other words, a product or service that meets the EU requirements in one member state can be freely marketed throughout the EU. U.S. industries are thus able to reach a greater number of European consumers at a lower cost.

The 1992 program dealt with three general objectives: the removal of physical barriers, the removal of technical barriers, and the removal of fiscal barriers through standardization of *value-added tax (VAT)* rates and excise taxes.

The removal of physical barriers meant eliminating the regulations and procedures that gave rise to such border controls as vehicle safety checks or animal and plant inspections. One important aspect of the program, and one with an immediate impact, was the adoption as of January 1, 1988, of a *Single Administrative Document,* which eliminated the need for duplicative customs documents for goods shipped to and within the EU.

Perhaps the most significant aspect of the program from the point of view of U.S. industry is the directives related to the removal of technical barriers. EU directives mandate the creation of uniform EU industrial standards, the opening of public procurement procedures, the removal of restrictions on trade in services and capital movements, and stricter guidelines against barriers to competition.

Another achievement of the EU is its 1991 historic accord on monetary and political union, the *Maastricht Treaty.* This treaty a milestone that will transform the way Europe does business. Exhibit 7.1 summarizes its main points. Like its precursor, the 1986 *Single Europe Act,* which paved the way for free trade within the EU after 1992, the accord promises to become a powerful force for even closer economic and political integration. The new *European Currency Unit,* to be called the *euro* (previously called the *ECU*), has the potential to become a strong rival to the dollar in international finance and trade.[12]

As per the Maastricht Treaty, EU created a *European Monetary Union (EMU)* on January 1, 1999. Of the 15 EU nations, 11 joined the union (see International Marketing Highlight 7.3). Britain, Sweden, Denmark and Greece have stayed out of it for the time

---

EXHIBIT 7.1
Major Points of Maastricht Treaty

Monetary Union: The EU would form a central bank by 1999 that would issue a single EU currency. Britain could opt out of monetary union.

Political Union: The EU states would forge common foreign and security policies, generally by consensus. In 1996 the EU reviewed political cooperation and formed a defense arm with a common defense policy.

New Policies: By replacing unanimity with majority voting at EU meetings, the EU gets more say in education, public health, culture, consumer protection, research and development, environment, and development cooperation. Britain had the right to opt out of decisions on social affairs.

European Parliament: The EU's 518-member assembly, primarily a consultative body, *would get some legislative say,* notably in internal trade, environment, education, health, and consumer protection.

Immigration: The EU would set goal of *common rules on immigration from outside* the EU, movement of immigrants within the community, and increased immigration-law enforcement. Decisions would require unanimity.

Citizenship: The EU would introduce "Citizen of the Union" guaranteeing free movement within the community, *granting after 1994 the right to vote and run in municipal elections in any EU nation.*

---

being. The currencies of member countries have been linked with fixed exchange rates, and the *European Central Bank (ECB),* headquartered in Frankfurt, Germany, runs the monetary policy for the entire Monetary Union.[13] The ECB is independent from governments, with a strict mandate of price stability.

To sum up, from January 1, 1999, the euro became the official EU currency. Starting from January 1, 2002, euro bills and coins will start circulating. Until July 2002, the curencies of individual countries—franc, gilder, lira, and so forth—will be simultaneously used along with euro. Thereafter those individual currencies will be phased out, and the euro will become the only currency in 11 of the 15 EU countries.[14]

International Marketing Highlight 7.3

Sex and the Single Currency

No one loves Europe's prospective single currency more than the Italians. Three-quarters are "very happy" about monetary union, say opinion pollsters. This year they uncomplainingly paid a hefty "tax for Europe" so that they could join it. There is even a prime-time television program, Maastricht Italia, devoted to extolling the euro. They love it, all right, but do they know what it is?

Not if you believe a survey recently published in *Il Mondo.* The newspaper said that only 21 percent of Italians know that the future single currency is called the euro. Slightly fewer get half-credit for identifying it as the ECU, a basket-currency that is the forerunner to the euro; and 59 percent haven't a clue what the object of their desire is called. They have even less idea where its headquarters will be. Only 0.2 percent managed to identify Frankfurt as the site of the future European central bank. Quite a few Italians, according to another poll, think the euro is a nickname for the European Union or a satellite television program.

Do Italians know less than other Europeans? Apparently. Though Eurobarometer, the EU's pollster, does not ask Europeans what the single currency is called "as widespread knowledge of the name euro is now taken for granted."

There is other evidence that ardor and ignorance go together. According to Eurobarometer, the countries that deem themselves well informed about monetary union (cool-headed northerners like Denmark, Finland, Germany and Britain) are the most euro-skeptic. The enthusiast (Italy, Greece, Spain) admit to being ill-informed. So eager are they nevertheless to join the euro that, according to OECD, Italy and Spain will have squeezed their budgets enough this year to qualify. These hot-blooded southerners are about to discover what happens when curbside seductions turn into lifelong commitments.

Source: The Economist, December 20, 1997, p. 74.

European Free Trade Association (EFTA) In 1959 EFTA was formed in Stockholm after a series of negotiations among those Western European countries that for one reason or another did not join the EEC. (Great Britain, for example, had certain arrangements with Commonwealth countries that hindered its joining the EEC.) Austria, Denmark, Norway, Portugal, Sweden, Switzerland, and the United Kingdom were the original seven members of the EFTA. Finland (as an associate) and Iceland joined later. Denmark and the United Kingdom ceased to be members in 1973, after joining the EU. That left EFTA with seven members: Austria, Finland, Iceland, Norway, Sweden, Switzerland, and tiny Liechtenstein.

The 12-nation EC, the world's largest trading bloc, and the seven-member EFTA agreed in October 1991 to form a new common market, the *European Economic Area (EEA).* The agreement (after it was approved by each of the 19 national parliaments) allowed for the free flow of most goods, services, capital, and people among its 19 member nations. It went into effect just as a single regional market was formed by the EU on January 1, 1993.[15]

The EEA, with the exception of Switzerland, consists of those countries whose voters narrowly rejected membership of the giant free trade area. The agreement also paved the way for several new countries to seek full membership in the EU, which is rapidly moving toward social and political as well as economic integration.

Of the seven members of EFTA, the two Nordic countries (Sweden and Finland) and Austria have joined the EU as full members in 1995. Switzerland and Norway by referendum on EU membership have decided to stay out. Iceland and Liechtenstein are still undecided. Thus for all intents and purposes, EFTA has splintered.

Council for Mutual Economic Assistance (CMEA) In 1949 communist countries, led by the Soviet Union, formed the *Council for Mutual Economic Assistance(CMEA)*, (sometimes called the *Council of Mutual Economic Cooperation COMECON)*, to coordinate trade and promote economic cooperation. Before it was disbanded on January 1, 1991, CMEA's membership included Bulgaria, Czechoslovakia, East Germany, Hungary, Mongolia, Poland, Romania, the Soviet Union, Cuba, and Vietnam. It was formed more as a political group than an economic association and was organized and tightly controlled by the Soviet Union.

Although some trade gains were recorded among its member nations, CMEA did not promote economic integration through product specialization in any significant way. This may be partly attributed to the fact that foreign trade among the centrally planned economies had been looked upon as a means of balancing shortages and surpluses generated by the domestic sector.[16]

Africa

Influenced by the EU, a number of African countries have attempted to draw up market agreements in order to benefit from economic integration and cooperation. There are several major African market groups. The *Afro-Malagasy Economic Union* was formed in 1974 with Cameroon, Central African Republic, Chad, Congo-Brazzaville, Dahomey, Ivory Coast, Mali, Mauritania, Niger, Senegal, Togo, and Burkina as members. The *East Africa Customs Union* was formed in 1967 with Ethiopia, Kenya, Sudan, Tanzania, Uganda, and Zambia as members. The *West African Economic Community (WAEC)* was established in 1972 with Ivory Coast, Mali, Mauritania, Niger, Senegal, and Burkina as its member countries. Another agreement has been the *Maghreb Economic Community* consisting of Algeria, Libya, Tunisia, and Morocco. The *Economic Community of West African States (ECOWAS)* was created with Benin, Cape Verde, Gambia, Ghana, Guinea, Guinea-Bissau, Ivory Coast, Liberia, Mali, Mauritania, Niger, Nigeria, Senegal, Sierra Leone, and Burkina as members.

Despite the fact that there are many market agreements in force in Africa, they have had no significant effect in promoting trade or economic progress, because most African nations are small and have no economic infrastructure to produce goods to be traded among themselves.

The *Economic Community of West African States (ECOWAS)* is a recent attempt by 15 African countries to seek economic cooperation for their mutual advantage. The agreement called for complete economic integration by 1992. However, Nigeria accounts for almost two-thirds of the community's exports, and its economic woes hindered smooth achievement of the goal of full integration.[17] Nevertheless, and despite the unique set of difficulties that the member countries have been going through, ECOWAS has survived. In 1994 the ECOWAS nations relaunched their efforts at economic reforms and trade liberalization. Although there have been problems, the regional economy ECOWAS covers offers significant opportunities for international marketers.

A recent development in the region is a 1996 trade protocol that provided for the establishment, within eight years, of a free trade area composed of all 14 Southern African countries. So far, only four—Botswana, Mauritius, Tanzania and Zimbabwe—have ratified the protocol. To speed things up, South Africa has proposed a system in which some 75 percent of current exports would enter the free trade area duty-free immediately and 87.6 percent within five years.[18]

Enormous scope exists to increase trade among the 14 states. Currently only 20 percent of trade is intraregional—compared with more than 50 percent in Asia and 70 percent in the EU—and even that is highly concentrated among a few nations.

Another hope is that the free trade area will result in increased capital flows, especially from South Africa to its smaller, poorer neighbors, where costs are significantly lower. Perhaps the most important attraction is a linkage to the EU that could help them gain improved access to the world's largest single market.

The snags are enormous, though. Because South Africa accounts for 75 percent of regional output, other partners want increased access to South Africa, yet are reluctant to offer reciprocity out of fear of killing their nascent manufacturing industries. Above all, political disputes continue to prevent economic union.

Latin America

Of all the developing areas of the world, Latin America has struggled the longest for the benefits of economic integration and cooperation. Market agreement attempts have been made to have certain countries specialize in certain industries, such as textiles, metal working, or shoe manufacturing, in order to derive benefits of scale and experience. The United States has played a major role in helping Latin American countries with market agreements. Unfortunately, the low level of economic activity and the political instability in the region have repeatedly been stumbling blocks.

Five major market agreements operate in Latin America: (1) the Latin American Integration Association (LAIA), (2) the Central American Common Market, (3) the Andean Common Market, (4) the Caribbean Community Common Market, and (5) Mercado Comun del Sur (Mercosur).

The *Latin American Free Trade Association (LAFTA),* originally formed in 1960, was renamed the *Latin American Integration Association (LAIA)* via the *Treaty of Montevideo* in August 1980. Its members are Argentina, Brazil, Chile, Mexico, Paraguay, Peru, Uruguay, Colombia, Ecuador, Venezuela, and Bolivia. LAFTA was the first attempt at economic cooperation among Latin American counties, but its large membership hampered its effectiveness. The fact that some member countries (Argentina, Brazil, Chile, Mexico, and Venezuela) are economically more advanced than others, like Uruguay and Bolivia, has made it difficult to make agreements for free trade among themselves. Even so, over the years the member-nations have lowered duties on select products and have taken steps to encourage trade in the region by keeping nontariff barriers under control.

The *Central American Common Market,* comprising Costa Rica, El Salvador, Guatemala, Honduras, and Nicaragua, was established in 1960. Its scope was more limited than that of LAFTA, and the countries, which are essentially on the same level of economic development, found the agreement mutually beneficial. However, it collapsed in 1969, when war broke out between Honduras and El Salvador after a riot at a soccer match involving the two countries. The members decided in 1992 to reestablish the Central American Common Market by 1995,[17] but even in 2000 the progress to date has been insignificant.

The *Andean Common Market* was created in 1969 by Bolivia, Chile, Colombia, Ecuador, Peru, and Venezuela as a subgroup of LAFTA. Chile is no longer a member, while Panama holds associate status in the group. The group decided to form a customs union by 1996 and work toward joining NAFTA or MERCOSUR (discussed later) by the year 2000.

The *Caribbean Community and Common Market (CARICOM)* was formed in 1968 with Barbados, Guyana, Jamaica, Trinidad and Tobago, Antigua, Dominica, Grenada, Montserrat, St. Kitts-Nevis-Anguilla, St. Lucia, St. Vincent, and Belize as the members. CARICOM countries have worked out a common external tariff structure and are continuing their efforts to establish a single-market economy. The group has negotiated trade concessions from the United States under the auspices of the *Enterprise for Americas Initiative (EAI)*.

MERCOSUR originated with a trade agreement signed in March 1991 by Uruguay, Brazil, Argentina, and Paraguay. It was officially launched on January 1, 1995 with a combined income providing an internal market of $500 billion.[19] MERCOSUR represents the beginning of the process of integration of 200 million consumers into one single market accounting for 75 percent of South America's GDP.[20]

MERCOSUR is a full- fledged customs union. The agreement allows for the free movement of goods and services and production factors among member countries and establishes a *common external tariff (CET)* for third countries. The maximum CET on most imported goods is 20 percent.[21] (See International Highlight 7.4.)

Of the aforementioned agreements, LAIA has been the least effective and indeed is almost defunct, while MERCOSUR offers that most hope for integration in the area. The ultimate dream of most Latin American countries is to join, together or alone, with the *North American Free Trade Area (NAFTA)* of Mexico, Canada, and the U.S.

■ International Marketing Highlight 7.4 ■

What MERCOSUR Has Done

The Free Trade Area In a transition phase between 1991 and 1994, MERCOSUR's members cut tariffs sharply on trade with each other; today most goods go tariff-free inside MERCOSUR, though there are some far from trivial exceptions: cars and sugar (which are subject to special arrangements) and groups of products considered sensitive by each member, 950 items for Uruguay, 427 for Paraguay, 221 for Argentina and 29 for Brazil. Internal tariffs on these products are to be cut progressively to zero by 2000 (1999 for Brazil and Argentina), by which time cars and sugar are supposed to be brought into the free trade scheme. But, unlike NAFTA, MERCOSUR as yet lacks agreements to achieve eventual free trade in services, or to deal with such issues as intellectual property and government procurement.

The Customs Union Against most expectations, at the end of 1994 MERCOSUR agreed to embark on the second stage of its integration project: to create a customs union in which, as in the European Union (but not in NAFTA), members apply a *common external tariff (CET)* to imports from third countries. From January 1, 1995, a CET set at 11 different levels, from zero to 20 percent, was applied to most imports. In this case, a larger group of products has been temporarily excluded: each country was allowed to exempt 300 items (299 for Paraguay) whose tariffs will converge (through annual increases or decreases) at the CET by January 2001 (2006 for Paraguay, which will have to raise its tariffs). A second group of products also is subject to special arrangements: tariffs on imported capital goods are to converge by 2001 at a CET of 14 percent, and on computers and telecommunications equipment at 16 percent by 2006. During 1995 two further changes were made. To support its anti-inflation plan, Brazil was allowed temporarily to cut tariffs below CET levels on 150 products (since reduced to ten), while the others were allowed to do this for 50 products. Secondly, because of global financial markets' concern over fiscal and balance-of-payments deficits in developing countries after the Mexican crisis, Argentina imposed a general 3 percent duty on imports from outside MERCOSUR, besides raising its tariffs on capital goods and telecoms equipment, while Brazil increased its list of CET-exempt products by 150 for a year, and raised tariffs on consumer electronics and cars.

Toward a Common Market In December 1995 MERCOSUR agreed on a five-year program under which it hopes to perfect the free trade area and customs union. This involves standardizing many trade-related rules and procedures, and moving toward harmonizing its members' economic policies. But since there is no commitment to allow free movement of labor, creating a true common market remains a fairly distant aspiration.

Free Trade Agreement with Chile During 1996 tariffs on most MERCOSUR/Chilean trade will be cut on both sides by 30 percent; from 2000 they will then fall to zero over four years. A small group of Chile's food and agricultural imports from MERCOSUR will have special treatment: tariffs on most of these will start falling in 2006 and reach zero by 2011, though wheat, flour, and sugar will retain their existing tariffs (from zero to 31 percent, depending on world prices) until at least 2014. To qualify for tariff preferences, goods must have MERCOSUR or Chilean content of at least 60 percent.

Source: The Economist, October 12, 1996

Asia

Asia is a vast continent with a large population. In the past, meager industrial development combined with the diversity and size of the region gave little reason for market arrangements. Nonetheless, many years ago Japan and the Pacific countries, Australia and New Zealand, along with the United States and Canada, created the *Pacific Basin Economic Council* to encourage intraregional trade, but it failed to develop into a market agreement.

In Southeast Asia, though, the emerging countries of Indonesia, Malaysia, the Philippines, Singapore, and Thailand have made a first attempt at establishing a market agreement. With these countries as members, the *Association of South East Asian Nations (ASEAN)* became operational in 1978. Brunei and Vietnam became members later. Cambodia, Laos, and Myanmar have become associate members and participate in such functional programs of the group as science and technology, tourism, and human resources development.

The association seeks closer economic integration and cooperation through the establishment of complementary industries and investment incentives to nonmember countries. Although the group initially had setbacks in meeting its goals, it now shows slow progress. To further integrate their economies, the ASEAN members in 1993 signed an agreement to establish *ASEAN Free Trade Area (AFTA)* by 2003. This agreement calls for lowering of tariffs and elimination of nontariff barriers over a 15-year period.[22] AFTA is on track to become the most populous free-trade zone in the world by 2003, easily surpassing the EU and NAFTA.

When ASEAN was first established, it was an unlikely partnership of five underdeveloped economies—Indonesia, Malaysia, the Philippines, Thailand, and Singapore. The main raison d'etre for the organization was to act as a regional buttress against communism. Now, nearly two decades later, ASEAN has grown beyond its preoccupation with the political conflict in Indochina. AFTA is the linchpin of its members' ambitions to form an economic bloc.[23]

An interesting development in Asia is the emergence of a new group called *Asia-Pacific Economic Cooperation (APEC)* among 18 nations, who had their first meeting in 1993. APEC, whose membership includes China, Japan, Australia, New Zealand, Brunei, Canada, Chile, Hong Kong, Indonesia, South Korea, Malaysia, Mexico, Papua New Guinea, the Philippines, Singapore, Taiwan, Thailand, and the United States had a combined GDP of

$15.1 trillion in 1998, nearly equal to the $16.2 trillion GPD of the *Group of Seven (G-7)*— (United States, United Kingdom, Germany, France, Italy, Canada, and Japan. By the year 2003 APEC will be larger than the G-7 and will dominate U.S. trade; 40 percent of U.S. foreign commerce will by then be with APEC nations, twice that with Europe.

APEC is committed to pursue free and open trade and investment, as well as economic and technical cooperation within the region. Developed countries in APEC seek to provide free access to their markets by 2010. Although the agreement is not binding, the developing countries are expected to fulfill its requirements by 2020.[24]

The Indian subcontinent region, with a population of over 1 billion people, provides another possibility for a regional market group. In December 1985, seven nations of the region (India, Pakistan, Bangladesh, Sri Lanka, Nepal, Bhutan, and Maldives) put aside their differences and launched the *South Asian Association for Regional Cooperation (SAARC)*. SAARC's initial purpose has been limited to cooperation in noncontroversial areas such as agriculture, rural development, telecommunications, postal services, transport, science and technology, meteorology, tourism, and sports. Important elements like the formation of a common market or a free trade zone have been omitted. Unfortunately, the chronic enmity between India and Pakistan makes the trade agreement difficult. In spite of this, there are hopeful signs that some sort of trade agreement in South Asia may occur in the next few years. This optimism is based on the fact that seven nations in the region (Bangladesh, Bhutan, India, Maldives, Nepal, Pakistan, and Sri Lanka) entered into a *South Asian Preferential Trade Arrangement* (SAPTA) in December 1995. SAPTA may lead to a full-fledged trade agreement once the nations realize the benefits of market cooperation. As a large nation in the region, India must take the lead if ever a South Asian free trade agreement is to become a reality.[25]

Countries in the Arab region have already made some progress in making market agreements. Several market groups are operating there. One of these is the *Arab Common Market (ACM)* formed in 1964 with Egypt, Iraq, Kuwait, Jordan, and Syria as members. This group planned to achieve free internal trade within 10 years, but it has not yet achieved this goal. External tariffs are likely to be regulated sometime early in this century.

U.S.–Canada Free Trade Agreement

On January 2, 1988, President Reagan and Prime Minister Mulroney of Canada signed the U.S.–Canada *Free Trade Agreement (FTA)*. This historic agreement represents the culmination of efforts stretching back more than 100 years. FTA was designed to strengthen an already extensive trading relationship and enhance economic opportunity on both sides of the common border.

Each year the United States and Canada exchange more goods and services than any other two countries in the world. Bilateral trade in goods and services exceeded $325 billion in 1999. The elimination of tariffs and most other barriers to trade between the two countries under the FTA has increased economic growth, lowered prices, expanded employment, and enhanced the competitiveness of both countries in the world marketplace.

Although the FTA does not eliminate all trade problems between the two nations, it does provide a consultative framework for managing these problems before they create serious economic and political friction. Predictably, industries in both the United States and Canada have undergone some structural readjustment to adapt to changing market conditions. The less restricted trade permitted by the FTA has spurred both economies to higher growth rates, increased efficiency, and improved competitiveness with other trading partners.[26]

The agreement came into force one year after it was signed, on January 1, 1989. The two governments have established a joint Canada–U.S. Trade Commission to oversee its implementation. A secretariat in each capital (Washington, D.C., and Ottawa) is the principal government office responsible for that country's implementation of the agreement.

North American Free Trade Agreement (NAFTA)

On January 1, 1994, the U.S.–Canada–Mexico free trade agreement emerged as the *North American Free-Trade Agreement (NAFTA)*. NAFTA created the largest market in the world: 370 million consumers and $7 trillion in output. It bodes well for U.S. and Canadian marketers, who stand to gain much in meeting the long pent-up demands of newly affluent Mexicans. The Mexicans have been able to attract a variety of manufacturing to their country. Following are NAFTA's key provisions.[27]

- America and Canada are to phase out tariffs on *textiles and apparel* over 10 years. Mexico is to eliminate many tariffs in this sector immediately.

- All tariffs on *cars and car parts* are to be eliminated over 10 years.

- In *agriculture,* Mexico and America phased out 57 percent of trade barriers immediately, 94 percent will be eliminated after 10 years, and 100 percent after 15 years. Similarly, Mexico and Canada would phase out tariffs. The U.S.–Canada FTA remains unchanged.

- Pemex, Mexico's state oil company, will keep its constitutional monopoly over most of the country's *oil industry.* However, foreigners could invest in petrochemicals, electricity generation, and coal mines. Procurement contracts for Pemex and Mexico's state electricity commission are opened for foreigners.

- Foreign *banks and securities brokers* are to have unrestricted access to Mexico from the year 2000 on. Some restrictions remain on sales of policies in Mexico by American and Canadian *insurers,* but with gradual freeing of direct investment.

- *Lorry-drivers* are able to cross the Mexican border freely beginning in 1999.

- Most of Mexico's trade barriers on *telecommunications equipment* have been eliminated. Basic voice services remain protected, but with foreigners authorized to provide value-added telephone services.

- Modest agreement has been reached to open *central-government procurement* to competition. However, this provision need not bind lower layers of government.

- *Intellectual property* is protected to U.S. standards.

- NAFTA *investors* generally receive national treatment, with freedom to seek binding arbitration from an international forum. However, special protection is given to Mexican energy and railway industries, American airline and radio communications industries, and Canadian culture.

- Each country applies its own *environmental standards,* provided such standards have a scientific basis. Lowering of standards as a lure to investment is "inappropriate."

- Two *commissions* have been established with power to impose fines and remove trade privileges (as a last resort) when environmental standards or legislation involving health and safety, minimum wages, or child labor have been ignored. Governments pay the fines, and only after a long bureaucratic process.

The way the three economies (U.S., Canadian, and Mexican) complement each other allows for greater room for growth and efficiency gains from free trade. Increased economic ties through NAFTA have resulted in net growth for the three partners. Nevertheless, at the time of this writing, there has been a fierce debate in the United States about the usefulness of NAFTA. The critics argue that NAFTA has led to huge U.S. trade deficits with Mexico and Canada. For example, in 1993 before NAFTA went into force, the United States had a trade surplus with Mexico amounting to $1.7 billion and a trade deficit of $11.0 billion with Canada. Since then, the United States has regularly incurred trade deficit with Mexico, while the deficit with Canada hit high, the worst showing since 1986. In 1997 the United States had a trade deficit of $16 billion and $13 billion with Canada and Mexico, respectively. In addition, NAFTA, it is claimed, has cost over 300,000 U.S. jobs, and has depressed wages and caused the flight of industry and investment to Mexico.[28]

On the other hand, according to NAFTA supporters, the accord prompted a major increase in U.S. exports to Canada and Mexico, stimulated domestic industrial production, and helped cushion the blow of Mexico's economic collapse. NAFTA proponents acknowledge the trade deficits, but blame them on a slow-growing Canadian economy and the 1994 peso crisis that plunged Mexico into economic turmoil.

At the time NAFTA was signed, the United States had expected to extend the agreement to include additional countries and ultimately to create a hemispheric trade pact, the *America Free Trade Agreement,* which would attempt to meld five separate free trade pacts involving countries in North and South America. Chile has been talked about as the first country to be invited into NAFTA. To move ahead, the Clinton administration needed the fast-track authority by which Congress votes yes or no on trade pacts but cannot change the terms. Unfortunately, in 1997 the Congress declined to grant the fast-track authority. Contrary to expectations, President Clinton did not make another attempt to seek the congressional authority, so during his term Chile might not become a member of NAFTA. Meanwhile, both Mexico and Canada have separately made trade agreements with Chile without waiting for the United States.

Regional trade agreements have promoted growth for the EU, Mexico, and others. Even when trade agreements occur among economies with different levels of development, the net result has been positive. The accession of Greece, Spain, and Portugal to the EU did not depress real wages within the EU. In fact, during the 1980s, real manufacturing wages rose in the Federal Republic of Germany, France, and the United Kingdom by at least 20 percent. EU programs have resulted in the continued lowering of barriers to trade and investment and have prompted a renewal of economic and job growth. Similarly, NAFTA, which concluded in 1996, has powered the region's economic growth, productivity, and global competitiveness into the twenty-first century.[29] (See International Marketing Highlight 7.5.)

■■■■■■■■■   **International Marketing Highlight 7.5**   ■■■■■■■■■

Rush Hour Replaces Siestas

The U.S. has a new "New South." It's called Mexico.

Four decades ago, U.S. industry migrated to Georgia, Alabama and other Southern states in search of cheap land and labor, eventually transforming what was once a largely rural backwater into one of the country's most economically vibrant regions. In a single generation, millions of Southerners vaulted from poverty to the middle class, and the South became an important market for the very goods it was producing. A similar process is now unfolding in Mexico. In the five years since the passage of NAFTA U.S. manufacturers have hired 600,000 new workers in Mexico, a pace of job creation almost identical to what took place in the U.S. Southeast in the 1960s and the 1970s. Once-sleepy towns are turning into cities, with malls and multiplexes reminiscent of the U.S. Sun Belt. And laborers, who once sought a better life across the border, are now settling in the arid north of Mexico to work in factories that have become critical to the global production plans of U.S. firms.

Source: The Wall Street Journal, October 29, 1999, p. A1

Other Forms of Agreements

We have discussed the important types of market agreements extant among nations in different regions of the world. In addition to these, various nations have made a variety of other arrangements for their economic benefit. For instance, four different forms of agreement are the Commonwealth of Nations, the Commonwealth of Independent States, commodity agreements, and producer cartels. Although the *Commonwealth of Nations* was mentioned in relation to political union, it is not, strictly speaking, a political union. The only political bond among the Commonwealth nations existed in the past when they constituted part of the British Empire. On the economic front, the member nations accord one another preferential treatment by agreeing to import from each other on a selective basis. Still, this situation has changed greatly since its beginnings in the post–World War II period, partially on political grounds and partially in response to individual economic interest.

The *Commonwealth of Independent States (CIS)* is a confederation of 11 countries that were previously part of the Soviet Union.[30] The shape that this agreement will ultimately take is difficult to say since its scope is not clear, but there is little doubt that it would be dominated by Russia, which has half of the former superpower's people and most of its resources and industrial base. Some people are skeptical that the CIS will survive long. Most of the member republics, especially Ukraine, are deeply suspicious of Russian intentions.

Another significant type of market agreement is the **commodity agreement.** Some of these agreements have been entered into under the auspices of GATT to stabilize the price of commodities such as textiles, coffee, olive oil, sugar, tin, cocoa, and wheat. The underlying purpose of commodity agreements, which are made between producing and consuming countries, has been to prevent excessive price fluctuations that would be detrimental to the developing countries.[31]

The term *producer cartel* refers to a unilateral agreement among producers of a commodity, or suppliers of a natural resource, to deal collectively as a group with the buyers for purposes of trading the commodity. The producer cartel became a popular mode of economic cooperation among producers of strategic commodities after the success of the OPEC petroleum cartel. Since 1975 a number of producer cartels have been organized by countries exporting bauxite, phosphate, chromium, rubber, and copper. However, it is unrealistic to expect other cartels to duplicate OPEC's record.

Summary

In the post–World War II period, nations came to realize that the task of economic reconstruction and expansion could be achieved more smoothly through cooperation among nations. The cooperation took two forms: global and regional. Global cooperation was reflected in steps such as the establishment of the World Bank, the IMF, and the GATT. Chapters 2 and 5 examined these efforts.

Regional cooperation took the form of economic integration through market agreements among nations in geographical proximity to each other. Five types of market agreements are free trade area, customs union, common market, economic union, and political union. Market agreements are based on commonality of interest among nations. For example, developing countries share the common objective of economic development. Likewise, political systems and culture may influence nations to enter into economic cooperation. However, geographic proximity turns out to be the basis for market agreements more often than any other reason for cooperation. Other things being equal, nations located in the same region are usually influenced by common social and economic environments.

Historically, the economic cooperation among nations that influences governments today first emerged in Europe. Six European countries—former West Germany, France,

Italy, the Netherlands, Belgium, and Luxembourg—agreed to form what is now called the EU. Its example was followed by the establishment of market agreements in other parts of Europe and elsewhere throughout the world.

From the marketing viewpoint, the importance of market agreements lies in the potential generation of markets. Inasmuch as mass production can be justified only by mass markets, market agreements boost industrial development and economic activity. For example, the EU is about equal in size to the U.S. market. Thus, certain economies of scale that previously could not be achieved in Western Europe are now feasible as a result of the formation of the EU.

Review Questions

1. What factors lead nations to work toward economic integration?
2. What role did the United States play in the establishment of the EEC?
3. Why did Great Britain not join the EEC at the time of its creation, but did so later?
4. List the differences between the arrangements of a free trade area and a customs union.
5. Is economic integration workable among developing countries?
6. Explain why Japan might be hindered in establishing a market agreement in the Pacific region based on your general knowledge of the factors that promote such arrangements.
7. In what way has the unification of the European market in 1992 benefited U.S. business and industry?

Creative Questions

1. Do regional market agreements contradict multilateral agreements? Why do we need the regional agreements if we have the latter? Are there any major provisions in NAFTA that have not been covered by the Uruguay Round agreement?
2. Is a market agreement among the Indian Ocean countries (i.e., India, Pakistan, Iran, South Africa, and others) feasible? What problems discourage such an agreement? How can these problems be resolved?

Endnotes

1. "Common Marketing for the Common Market," *Forbes,* July 1, 1972, p. 23. Also see John Drew, "European Markets: A Business Overview," *Europe,* July–August 1984, pp. 18–19.

2. "Elizabeth Arden Whips up a New Formula," *Country Monitor,* July 7, 1999, p. 12.

3. "IBM Finds a Club that Doesn't Want It as a Member," *Business Week,* February 11, 1985, p. 42.

4. "Up, Up and Away: At Last for Airbus?, " *Business Week,* February 9, 1998, p. 58.

5. See Bela Balassa, *The Theory of Economic Integration* (Homewood, IL: Irwin, 1961), pp. 1–21.

6. "Lomé IV Convention," *Development Forum,* May–June 1989, p. 20.

7. "The Luxembourg Rebuff," *The Economist,* December 20, 1997, p. 17. Also see "Turkey and the EU," *The Economist,* December 20, 1997, p. 74.

8. "The European Union Decides It Might One Day Talk Turkey," *The Economist,* December 18, 1999, p. 42. Also see "EU Enlargement," *The Economist,* December 18, 1999, p. 148.

9. Francine Lamoriello, "Completing the Internal Market by 1992: The EC's Legislative Program for Business," *Business America,* August 1, 1988, pp. 16–18.

10. *Business International,* November 27, 1989, p. 365.

11. *The Economist,* April 10, 1993, p. 74. *Also see Crossborder Monitor,* August 17, 1994, p. 3.

12. "A Little EMU Enlightenment," *The Economist,* February 22, 1997, p. 88.

13. "A Common Currency in Europe will Bring Big Changes to Many," *The Wall Street Journal,* March 24, 1997, p. A1. Also see: "Is Europe's Currency Coming Apart?," *The Economist,* June 7, 1997, p. 13.

14. Thomas Kamm, " As the Euro's Arrival Nears, Europe Braces For Lots of Headaches," *The Wall Street Journal,* November 30, 1998, p. A1. Also see: *Talking About Euro* (Brussels, Belgium: Information Program for the European Citizen, 1997).

15. Alan Riding, "Europeans in Accord to Create Vastly Expanded Trading Bloc," *The New York Times,* October 23, 1991, p. A1. Also see "Tearing Down Even More Fences in Europe," *Business Week,* November 4, 1991, p. 50.

16. "COMECON's Crumbling Credit-Worthiness," *The Wall Street Journal,* September 18, 1985, p. 31.

17. Thomas V. Greer, "The Economic Community of West African States," *International Marketing Review,* Vol. 9. No. 3, 1992, pp. 25–39.

18. "Free Trade Accord?," *Crossborder Monitor,* December 2, 1998, p. 10.

19. "Growing Markets Lure Companies to Mercosur Region," *Crossborder Monitor,* June 8, 1994, p. 1.

20. "Remapping South America," *The Economist,* December 12, 1996.

21. MERCOSUR and Beyond: The Imminent Emergence of the South American Markets (Austin, TX: CIBER - University of Texas, 1996).

22. *The Asian Free Trade Area* (Singapore: Intercedent, 1997).

23. *Crossborder Monitor,* July 23, 1994, p. 8. Also see: Minoru Murofushi, "A Business Agenda for APEC," *Asia–Pacific Review,* vol. 3, Nov. 2, Fall/Winter 1996, pp. 21-36.

24. *APEC Means Business* (Singapore: Asia Pacific Economic Cooperation Secretariat, 1996).

25. Subhash C. Jain, "Prospects for a South Asian Free Trade Agreement: Problems and Challenges," *International Business Review,* 8 (Nov. 4, 1999), pp. 1-15.

26. Alan Freeman, "Free-Trade Pact Creates Winners, Losers," *The Wall Street Journal,* February 7, 1989, p. A20.

27. "Depending on the View, NAFTA Glass Half Full or Half Empty," *The Wall Street Journal,* March 9, 1997, p. A13. Also see: "Singing the NAFTA Blues," *Business Week,* December 9, 1996, p. 54; and Sidney Weintraub, "Extend the Benefits of Free Trade," *The Wall Street Journal,* February 26, 1998, p. A16.

28. "The Americas: The Free-Trade Winds Die Away," *The Economist,* November 22, 1997, p. 35.

29. Joel Millonan, "What Southeast was to U.S. companies, Mexico is Becoming," *The Wall Street Journal,* October 29, 1999, p. A1.

30. "How Long Can Yeltsin Hold It All Together?" *Business Week,* January 13, 1992, p. 49.

31. Steve Mufson, "Third World Pleas on Commodity Prices Get No Sympathy in Developed Nations," *The Wall Street Journal,* October 2, 1985, p. 34.

PART 4

Environmental Factors Affecting International Marketing

CHAPTER 8

Economic Environment

CHAPTER FOCUS_____

After studying this chapter, you should be able to

- Describe the macroeconomic and microeconomic environment.

- Explain the effect of the economic environment on international marketing strategy.

- Analyze the components of the economic environment of a country.

- Describe the emerging opportunities in developing countries.

This chapter deals with the phenomenon of economic environment. In most cases, economic environment can be viewed from two different angles: the macro view or the micro view. From a macro view, people's wants and needs and the economic policy of a country establish market scope and economic outlook. A microenvironmental view focuses on a firm's ability to compete within a market.

Different countries provide varying market potential based on their population. However, "potential" does not guarantee a realizable opportunity for any given firm. For example, a low level of economic activity in a country may force most of its people to live modestly. In such a country, many foods and services taken for granted in the industrialized countries are considered luxuries and would be marketable only to the elite. In addition, even if there is a market for a given product or service, the competition from both existing and other potential businesses may make it difficult for a new firm to establish itself.

Not only does the economic environment of a country, both from the macro and micro viewpoints, largely define the marketing opportunity in that country, but the economic environment of a firm's home country, to an extent, also influences marketing overseas. Hence the economic situation of the United States at any given time will affect the international activity of U.S. firms.

This chapter begins with an examination of the factors that compose macro- and microeconomic environments. This explanation is followed by an illustration of the economic environment's impact on international marketing strategy. Finally, a framework for measuring economic potential and conducting opportunity analyses is furnished.

Macroeconomic Environment

A country's economy is based on its sources of domestic livelihood and the allocation of those resources. Because not all of the world's economies operate at the same level of efficiency, it is necessary to form a clear idea of the economic situation of a particular host country in order to make good marketing decisions. Such economic perspectives of a country refer to its macroeconomic environment.

Population and Income

The most basic information to be considered is that which describes the nature of the population, because the people, of course, constitute the market. Exhibit 8.1 shows the population of different countries of the world, but population figures alone provide little information useful for marketing, since people must have an adequate income to become viable customers. Thus, Exhibit 8.1 also shows population combined with per capita GNP, providing an estimate of *consuming capacity*. An index of consuming capacity depicts the absolute, or aggregate, consumption for different countries. The consumption can be satisfied either domestically or through imports.

The information in Exhibit 8.1 should be interpreted cautiously because it makes no allowances for differences in the purchasing power of different countries. This point may be illustrated with reference to Thailand. Although its per capita GNP is lower than that of the United States, the Thai baht goes much further than the U.S. dollar. A few years ago, for example, one dozen eggs cost only $.79 in Bangkok, while in New York they cost $1.15; an apartment rented for $950 in Bangkok, while the rent for an equivalent apartment in New York was $1,680; the taxi fare for a five-mile ride in New York and Bangkok came to $8.12 and $1.83, respectively.[1]

Two conclusions are obvious, however: (1) aggregate consuming capacity depends on total population as well as per capita income, and (2) advanced countries dominate as potential customers. In Chapter 1, it was noted that the U.S. MNCs are mainly active in

EXHIBIT 8.1
Consuming Capacities
of Selected Countries

Country	Population (in Millions)	Per Capita GNP (in U.S. Dollars)	Index of Consuming Capacity
United States	270	29,340	7,921,800
Japan	126	32,380	4,079,880
Germany	82	25,850	2,119,700
France	59	24,940	1,471,460
United Kingdom	59	21,400	1,262,600
Italy	58	20,250	1,174,500
Brazil	166	4,570	758,620
Canada	31	20,020	620,620
India	980	430	421,400
Netherlands	16	24,760	396,160
Australia	19	20,300	385,700
Mexico	96	3,970	381,120
Argentina	36	8,970	322,920
Switzerland	7	40,080	280,560
Belgium	10	25,380	253,800
Turkey	63	3,160	199,080
Denmark	5	33,260	166,300
Thailand	61	2,200	134,200
South Africa	41	2,880	118,080
Israel	6	15,940	95,640
Philippines	75	1,050	78,750
Peru	25	2,460	61,500
New Zealand	4	14,700	58,800
Ecuador	12	1,530	18,360
Paraguay	5	1,760	8,800
Uganda	21	320	6,720

Source: World Bank Report 2000 (Washington, DC, The World Bank, 2000).

Western Europe, Japan, and Canada—advanced countries with high population and high per capita income. In contrast, despite a large population, Bangladesh does not offer a realizable market potential. This is true also of other developing countries.

It must be noted that many developing countries are slowly emerging from their traditional poverty. Thus, it would be shortsighted to write them off. As a matter of fact, there is an interesting development taking place in the economic arena as far as the United States is concerned: Western Europe and Japan are becoming more competitive with the United States, while developing countries are becoming potential markets. Indeed, U.S. exports to developing countries as a group already substantially exceed exports to its traditional trading partners.

Structure of Consumption

Nations' overall patterns of consumption can be viewed not only on the basis of potential but also on the basis of structure. In other words, it is important not only to measure the volume of consumption among various nations, but to note the characteristics of that consumption, which reveal its structure. Particularly conspicuous in this respect are differences in emphasis. Depending on economic factors, a country may have to emphasize producer goods over consumer goods. Also, what are considered necessities in one economy may be luxuries in another. In addition, consumption in most advanced countries is characterized by a higher proportion of expenditures devoted to capital goods than consumption in developing countries, where substantially more is spent on consumer goods.

When a less developed economy decides to become technically and economically more advanced, an extraordinary percentage of national income must be diverted to capital goods, especially if that economy is unable to attract substantial amounts of foreign currency in the form of direct investment, loans, or other aid. This is one important reason why less developed countries find the transition period to economic advancement so difficult.

The structural differences with regard to expenditures among nations can be explained by a theory propounded by the German statistician Engel. The *law of consumption (Engel's law)* states that poorer families and societies spend a greater proportion of their incomes on food than well-to-do people.[2] Exhibit 8.2 substantiates Engel's law on a global scale. Shown is the percentage of per capita income spent for food, housing, clothing, and other purposes in selected countries. Developing countries like the Philippines and Sri Lanka spend a larger percentage on food than countries like the United States. Further, in any country, rural people spend a larger percentage on food than urban dwellers (not shown in the exhibit). Housing, in particular, receives a much smaller share of income in developing countries than in the advanced nations (see International Marketing Highlight 8.1).

The structure of consumption varies among developed countries, too. While the average American home covers 1,583 square feet and the typical European dwelling is more than 1,050 square feet, Japanese families manage with 925 square feet. The U.S. nuclear

EXHIBIT 8.2   Consumption Expenditures of Selected Countries

Country (Base Year)	Food & Beverage	Clothing & Footwear	Housing & Operations	Household Furnishings	Medical Care & Health	Transportation	Recreation	Other*
Industrial Market Economies								
Belgium	19.7	6.8	17.7	10.7	10.6	13.1	6.6	14.8
Canada	16.2	5.7	22.4	9.7	4.2	15.8	11.3	14.7
France	19.4	6.2	17.8	8.2	10.5	6.8	8.1	13.0
Japan	20.8	6.1	18.6	6.3	10.4	10.7	10.6	16.5
Sweden	22.3	8.4	23.5	6.8	2.7	17.9	10.5	8.0
United Kingdom	21.1	6.7	18.4	7.2	1.3	18.3	10.1	17.0
United States	13.3	7.7	17.4	6.3	12.4	16.4	11.7	14.8
[Former] West Germany	23.6	8.6	19.8	9.7	3.1	16.4	10.7	8.2
Middle-Income Countries								
Mexico	37.4	8.2	12.6	12.4	4.0	9.1	5.6	10.8
Philippines	60.0	5.3	3.1	13.5	n.a.	2.3	n.a	15.8
Republic of Korea	36.8	4.7	9.9	6.1	7.2	11.2	11.9	12.3
Low-Income Countries								
India	53.5	13.1	11.1	4.9	2.4	7.5	3.2	4.3
Sri Lanka	52.7	10.1	4.2	5.5	1.3	18.3	4.1	3.9

Other includes expenditures for personal care, restaurants, and hotels.
Note: The expenditures are expressed as percentages of total consumption in constant prices.
Source: United Nations Statistical Yearbook, 1993-1994.

family boasts 2.2 cars on average; comparable households in the European community average 1.3 cars. In Japan, the average is 0.88. And while food costs absorb 26 percent of the typical Japanese household's income, the amount is less than 15 percent for the average American family, and about 20 percent for the Europeans.[3] As shown in Exhibit 8.3, while the average person in England eats 13 pounds of cereal a year, per capita consumption in France is just 1 pound, and in Japan less than one-fourth of a pound. Americans eat about 10 pounds of cereal each per year.

International Marketing Highlight 8.1

Acquiring a Vacation Spot

One CEO visited North Africa and fell in love with Morocco. Imagining frequent trips to this desert kingdom, he established a Marrakesh subsidiary for his firm, which manufactures kitchen cabinets. Unfortunately, he neglected to notice that most Moroccans don't have indoor kitchens, much less kitchen cabinets. The branch operation was a total failure. The lure of exotic climes had distorted this executive's previously sound business judgment.

Source: Charles F. Valentine, *The Arthur Young International Business Guide* (New York; John Wiley & Sons, 1988), p. 22.

Other Economic Indicators

Population, income, and expenditure data provide basic insights into the economies of different nations. For a certain point in time, however, a variety of other aspects of economic environment may be pertinent in a given case. This economic information may be found in categories such as

- Production indicators (such as the production of raw steel, automobiles, trucks, and electric power; crude-oil refinery runs, coal production, paper-board production, lumber production, and rail freight traffic).

EXHIBIT 8.3
Food Consumption Differences among Nations: 1995

Country	Food Market and Habits		
	Per Capita Cereal Consumption (in Pounds)	Per Capita Frozen-Food Consumption (in Pounds)	Percent of Homes with Microwave Ovens
United States	9.8	92.4	80
Britain	12.8	48.2	43
[former] West Germany	2.0	33.4	21
Denmark	4.6	53.9	—
Sweden	—	51.7	—
France	1.1	40.5	16
Norway	—	38.3	—
Netherlands	—	34.8	8
Switzerland	—	33.2	—
Spain	0.4	—	13
Ireland	15.4	—	—
Australia	12.3	—	—
Canada	8.7	—	—
Belgium	—	—	10
Italy	—	—	3
Japan	0.2	18.6	—

Source: Kellogg Co. Annual Report, 1996.

- Prices (such as the price of gold, finished steel, aluminum, wheat, cotton, industrial raw materials, and foodstuffs).
- Finance (such as corporate bond yield, prime commercial paper, value of local currency with reference to U.S. dollars, money supply).
- Other indicators (such as index of industrial production, retail sales, installment credit debt, and wholesale and retail inventories).

It is neither necessary nor possible for a marketer to gather information about and review all these indicators from each country.[4] At any given time, the choice of economic indicators to be examined is determined by the purpose of the project at hand. For example, a company contemplating manufacturing tires abroad needs to look into the foreign country's automobile and truck production data for a number of previous years as well as the data for those countries that are likely to import tires from the foreign country. A processed-food manufacturer, on the other hand, would be interested in such information as inflation rate, foodstuff prices, and retail sales data. In brief, marketers should examine only those economic indicators that are relevant to their marketing decisions. Relevancy can be determined in part by the marketer's domestic operations but should also reflect the new situation in the foreign country.

Concept of Economic Advancement

Developing countries are becoming important markets as their economies advance. According to the concept of *international product life cycle* examined in Chapter 2, more and more developing countries may become significant markets. It would be desirable for a marketer, therefore, to keep informed about countries slowly reaching the point where market potential will become worthwhile. GNP per capita, adjusted for purchasing power parity, may be relied on as a measure of the economic viability of a market. It provides a reasonable estimate of the market in cases where detailed analysis is not feasible.

Economic advancement is characterized by such factors as comparatively small allocation of labor force to agriculture; energy available in large amounts at low cost per unit; high level of GNP and income; high levels of per capita consumption; relatively low rates of population growth; complex modern facilities for transportation, communication, and exchange; a substantial amount of capital for investment; urbanization based on production as well as exchange; diversified manufacturing that accounts for an important share of the labor force; numerous tertiary occupations; specialization of both physical and mental labor; surpluses of both goods and services; and a highly developed technology that includes ample media and methods for experiment. These factors can be utilized to examine economic standing. Needless to say, a large variety of information is needed to categorize countries on an economic development scale. For many characteristics, hard data may not be available, in which case judgment becomes the determining factor.[5]

Generally, the conditions in underdeveloped economies are the reverse of those that characterize economic advancement. This fact raises an interesting question. Can poor countries be converted into advanced countries by reversing the conditions that hamper economic progress? The answer, however, is not a simple yes, because economic development is not a simple, discrete process. Many historical, geographic, political, and cultural factors are intimately related to the economic well-being of a nation. For example, no wars have been fought on U.S. soil in the last 100 years, a fact contributing to this country's present economic greatness.

Economic Systems

The economic system of a country is another important factor that a marketer must understand. Traditionally, there are two types of economic systems: state-owned and capitalist. The state-owned, or Marxist, system is pursued in communist countries, where all activities related to production and distribution are controlled by the state. The capitalist system predominates in the Western World, but no country exhibits a pure form of capitalism today. The "invisible hand" of the marketplace propounded by Adam Smith is not given completely free reign, even in the United States, where some laws and conditions are imposed on various businesses. (The nature of some of these laws and controls are examined in Chapter 11. Most countries have mixed economic systems in which certain industries are allowed to run freely while others are strictly or partially controlled. The nature of the economic system affects the political/regulatory control of the economy.

An interesting development of the recent past is an economic system that is new to the modern world and links economic life with religion.[6] Some Muslim countries have adopted a national economic perspective based on Islam. This trend, led by Iran, is still emerging, and it is difficult to say how far it will go or what impact it will have on marketers (see International Marketing Highlight 8.2).

International Marketing Highlight 8.2

Turning the Prophet's Profits

Islamic banks and investment funds are increasingly popular with Muslim savers. Can they continue to grow?

There are now more than 100 specialized institutions that invest money according to strict Islamic principles, ranging from mass-market savings banks in Geneva. Even some western banks are embracing the concept: last month the Citibank opened the first western-owned Islamic bank. Based in Bahrain, Citi Islamic Investment Bank has startup capital of $20 million.

Islamic banks are still puny by international standards. Taken together, their assets are somewhere between $25 billion and $30 billion. But they are growing fast. Some of the biggest, such as Kuwait Finance House and Pakistan's Muslim Commercial Bank are growing their assets by about 10 percent a year. The potential market—1 billion or so Muslims—is huge.

Islam's religious revival is the industry's motor. True believers obey *sharia*, Islam's holy law. This places several demands on Muslim savers. They must not finance activities prohibited by the Koran, such as gambling and the consumption of alcohol. Nor are they allowed to receive interest. ("Those who benefit from interest," warns the Koran, "shall be raised like those driven mad by the touch of the devil.")

To abide by those strictures, Islamic banks have developed alternative financial contracts. The most common of those is *murabaha*, a form of so-called "cost-plus" financing. This works as follows. Say a company wants to purchase $100 million of equipment. Instead of lending it the money for three months at 2% interest, an Islamic bank will buy the equipment itself. It will then sell it to the firm for $102 million, with payment deferred for three months. The bank will then claim that it is charging a profit mark-up rather than an interest rate.

Source: The Economist, August 24, 1996, p. 58.

Mutual Economic Dependence   The U.S. economy is profoundly related to the economies of other nations, particularly those of the advanced countries. The U.S. market is so large that despite its ability to supply most of its needs from domestic output, it is also deeply embroiled in international trade. Thus, what happens in Western Europe cannot be ignored by the United States. Although there may be a time lag, happenings there are bound to ultimately affect the U.S. economy. It has been estimated that a recession in Western Europe affects the United States after a lag of about six months. Thus, when performing an economic analysis of a country, an international marketer needs to consider the economic perspectives of the overall world economy, particularly those of its major trading partners and the host country.

The depth of economic analysis needed varies from case to case. For example, if the enterprise concerns Saudi Arabia, economic development in the Pacific region can be discounted. In contrast, if a project is related to Japanese industries, the economic environment in emerging countries of Southeast Asia must be reviewed.

Microeconomic Environment

Microeconomic environment refers to the environment surrounding a specific product or market rather than a country's overall economic environment. An examination of a microenvironment indicates whether a company can successfully enter a specific market. Essentially, then, the microeconomic environment concerns competition.

Sources of Competition

A U.S. company may face competition in an international market from three different sources: local business, other U.S. corporations, and foreign companies.[7] For example, if Ford Motor Company were to consider entering the German market, it would compete against General Motors, Volkswagen, and Honda Motors of Japan. Different competitors, however, might aim to satisfy different types of demand: existing, latent, or incipient. *Existing demand* refers to a product bought to satisfy a recognized need. *Latent demand* applies in a situation where a particular need has been recognized, but no products have been offered. *Incipient demand* describes a projected need that will emerge when customers become aware of it sometime in the future.

Consider demand in the computer industry. Overall, IBM may be strong in, let us say, Spain. But a firm like Dell Computers may choose to enter the Spanish market to serve latent demand there. As a result, Dell avoids direct confrontation with IBM, which is serving existing, not latent, demand, at least in the short run. Competition can also be analyzed according to the characteristics of products: breakthrough, competitive, and improved. A *breakthrough product* is a unique innovation that is mainly technical in nature, such as the digital watch, VCR, and personal computer. A *competitive product* is one of many brands currently available in the market and has no special advantage over the competing products. An *improved product* is not unique but is generally superior to many existing brands.

The nature of the competition that a company faces in entering an overseas market can be determined by relating the three types of products to the three types of demand. Upon examining the competition, a company should be able to ascertain which product or market it is most capable of pursuing.

For example, let us assume Procter & Gamble is interested in manufacturing hair shampoo in Egypt and seeks entry into the emerging Arab market. The company finds that in addition to a number of local brands, Johnson & Johnson's baby shampoo and Helene Curtis Industries' Suave Shampoo are the *competitive* products in the market. Gillette has recently entered the market with its Silkience brand, which is considered an *improved* product. Most of the competition appears to be addressing the *existing* demand. No attempts have been made to satisfy *latent* demand or *incipient* demand.

After reviewing various considerations, Procter & Gamble may decide to fulfill latent demand with an improved offering through its Head & Shoulders brand. Based on market information, the company reasons that a hair problem most consumers face in that part of the world is dandruff. No brand has addressed itself to that problem. Even Gillette's new entry mainly emphasizes silkiness of hair. Thus, analysis of the competition with reference to product offerings and demand enables Procter & Gamble to determine its entry point into the Arab market.

Competitive Advantage

The [preceding analysis—according to type of product (breakthrough, competitive, or improved) and type of demand (existing, latent, or incipient)—is sufficient to reveal an open space in the market for entry. But competitors might follow right on the heels of Procter & Gamble's entry steps. Thus, further analysis is needed to figure out the *competitive advantage* the company has over rivals, existing and potential. The following questions could be raised to analyze the competition:

- Who is the competition now, and who will it be in the future?
- What are the key competitors' strategies, objectives, and goals?
- How important is a specific market to the competitors, and are they committed enough to continue to invest?
- What unique strengths do the competitors have?
- Do they have any weaknesses that make them vulnerable?
- What changes are likely in the competitors' future strategies?
- What are the implications of competitors' strategies on the market, the industry, and one's own company?

The best way to examine the competition is to draw up a demographic profile of the industry. Markets dominated by small, single-industry businesses or small national competitors differ significantly from those dominated by multi-industry companies, and those in turn are different from markets controlled by multinational or foreign companies.

A simple listing of major competitors is not enough information. Their goals, and if possible, their total financial situations should be learned, including their serious problems as well as their advantages and opportunities—that is, their relative strengths and weaknesses. Exhibit 8.4 lists areas to be assessed for competitive strengths and weaknesses. Note that most areas of strength either are related to the excellence of personnel or are resource-based. Not all factors have the same significance for every product or market. Therefore, it is desirable first to recognize the critical factors that could directly or indirectly bear on a product's performance in a given market. Adequate distribution might be critical in a

---

EXHIBIT 8.4
Assessing Competitor's Areas of Strength

1. Excellence in product design and/or performance (engineering ingenuity).
2. Low-cost, high-efficiency operating skill in manufacturing and/or in distribution.
3. Leadership in product innovation.
4. Efficiency in customer service.
5. Personal relationships with customers.
6. Efficiency in transportation and logistics.
7. Effectiveness in sales promotion.
8. Merchandising efficiency—high turnover of inventories and/or of capital.
9. Skillful trading in volatile price movement commodities.
10. Ability to influence legislation.
11. Highly efficient, low-cost facilities.
12. Ownership or control of low-cost or scarce raw materials.
13. Control of intermediate distribution or processing units.
14. Massive availability of capital.
15. Widespread customer acceptance of company brand name (reputation).
16. Product availability and convenience.
17. Customer loyalty.
18. Dominant market share position.
19. Effectiveness of advertising.
20. High quality of salesforce.

---

developing country with inadequate means of transportation and communication, whereas development of new products through research and development might be strategic to gain the competitive edge in Western Europe.

An example of strength is provided by the BMW car company. It is commonly known that selling foreign cars in Japan is not easy. Yet BMW sells almost 100,000 cars annually to the Japanese, and that number is expected to be four times as high by the year 2010. With Japanese consumers' increasing interest in luxury cars, a new market segment had been emerging but was not being tapped by the Japanese companies. BMW took advantage of the situation. Avoiding the pitfalls that make doing business in Japan difficult, it established a comfortable niche for itself. After establishing its own dealer network and expanding it, the company advertised heavily, set up a service-and-parts system, and lowered interest rates to a single digit (5 percent) when the consumer interest rates were 15 percent. In brief, despite the fact that Japan is a difficult market to enter, analysis of the microeconomic environment showed that BMW could successfully seek entry.[8]

Japanese auto companies, in turn, have captured a major share (in 1998, approximately 31 percent) of the U.S. auto market. Let us assume Ford Motor Company decides to retaliate by exploring the possibility of entering the Japanese market. Despite all its strengths and experience in international business, Ford may find itself greatly constrained in its endeavors. In the past, cost was a major factor in U.S. auto competition with Japan. Because of U.S. wage-price and managerial efficiency differentials, the Japanese companies were able to build a car and ship it to the United States for $2,000 to $2,300 less than it would cost Detroit to produce an equivalent vehicle. Now, because of (1) the appreciation of the yen against the dollar and (2) U.S. companies' attempts to overhaul their operations, cost differential is not significant anymore. Yet U.S. companies may find it difficult to match Japanese selling methods—one-half the cars sold there are peddled by door-to-door salesmen. Such sales tactics, coupled with high-quality vehicles, stack the odds against Ford Motor Company.[9] Thus, even if Ford were to assemble cars in Japan, other things being equal, it would still be severely handicapped in its lack of selling experience in Japan. In this instance, analysis of the microeconomic environment paints a discouraging picture for Ford's entry into the Japanese market.

Economic Environment and Marketing Strategy

The overall macroeconomic climate of the host country as well as the microeconomic environment surrounding the product or market has a significant effect on marketing strategy. The macroeconomic environment sets the limit of activity in different sectors of the economy. Thus, when the economy is booming, there will be plenty of jobs, consumers will be optimistic, and cash registers will ring often. In a booming economy situation, the international marketer will have more opportunity in the marketplace, although marketplace opportunities may attract new competition. However, when an economy is down, unemployment may rise, interest rates may go up, sales could be more difficult to generate, and the international marketer's decisions will take a different shape.

Impact of Macroeconomic Environment

Brazil, one of the countries emerging into a developed economy, provides a case where there should be ample opportunities for U.S. international marketers. Yet, at the dawn of the new century, the Brazilian economy was beset by a variety of problems that restricted the realization of opportunities there. The turmoil in the financial markets makes the outlook for 2000–2002 risky. If the government avoids a devaluation, the austerity measures required to support the national currency, the real, and to cut the fiscal deficit will have a negative impact on consumer confidence. The economy may not grow more than 2 percent to 3 percent annually. The private consumption and investment are likely to be hurt. Moreover, Brazilian exports to the United States and other markets have been noncompetitive in price.

But the monetary reforms that the country introduced in the past few years should help. For example, the launching of the new currency, the real, helped slash inflation from 50 percent a month in June 1994 to just under 5 percent in 1997. The revival of consumer credit could trigger a spending surge, giving new strength to many industrial sectors.[10]

Betting on Brazil's recovery, U.S. investors have sent billions of dollars flowing into that nation's stock market. At the end of 1997 Brazil had received more U.S. direct investment than any other country, amounting to $18.0 billion against Mexico's $16.4 billion. Thus, the long-run economic outlook for Brazil may be promising.

The health of an economy affects consumer confidence, which is then reflected in consumer buying plans. A favorable economic climate generates a spirit of optimism that makes consumers more willing to spend money. The reverse occurs when economic conditions are unfavorable. In Brazil's case, 1998–1999 was not an exciting period. Although inflation has been under control, the credit restrictions have had a negative impact on consumption. Things might stabilize in a year or so, and then opportunities should develop. A recent survey by Price Waterhouse confirmed that 93 percent of the company's U.S. clients consider Brazil to be Latin America's most attractive investment target.[11]

Although economic climate affects all businesses, some are affected more deeply than others. International marketers should calculate the extent to which their business is susceptible to economic conditions. For example, in a booming economy, consumers tend to buy durable goods. Thus, the economic environment in Brazil during 2000 seemed unattractive for consumer goods manufacturers interested in entering the market.

It should be noted, however, that current economic environment is just one variable. Even if the short-run economic environment is not conducive to profits, a company might wisely enter an overseas market based on good long-term economic prospects in that country and such other favorable factors as growing political stability or the existence of low wage scales. The long-run perspective is the most important one, provided a firm has sufficient resources to endure waiting for the future favorable environment. From that standpoint, Brazil is an attractive market to enter.

Impact of Microeconomic Environment

The following example shows how the microeconomic environment of a product/market affects marketing strategy: A very successful U.S. company, for many years a leader in its field, launched a cheaper version of its traditional product almost simultaneously in the United States and in Europe. The product design, pricing, and advertising copy—in fact, the whole marketing approach—were quite similar in both areas. The strategy was very successful at home, but in Europe sales fell far below expectations. What was the cause of the trouble? The company had neglected several significant differences between the two market areas:

1. In the United States it had a major share of the market, while in Europe it was an insignificant factor.
2. At home, the company's product concept was in the mature phase of its life cycle, while in Europe it was at its beginning.
3. In the United States roughly 85 percent of all households knew the company and its products, whereas in Europe the awareness level was barely 5 percent, and few customers understood the nature of this innovative product.
4. As a result, the advertising copy that featured a low price without explaining the product concept was meaningful to most U.S. consumers but unsuitable for most of the European market.

It is evident from this illustration that the U.S. company got into problems in Europe because its competitive strength there was meager (small market share), the product, relatively speaking, was new to the market (starting life cycle position), and the product presented an unfamiliar concept. In other words, the company did not orient its marketing program with the product/market environment existing in Europe.

Impact of Domestic Economic Environment

Although international marketers should be concerned with economic environment overseas, they should also be sensitive to economic perspectives of the home market, just as the reverse is true for domestic marketers. Indeed, firms react to changing domestic and international economic environments and can be expected to shift their relative emphasis in promoting domestic versus foreign trade. During 1990, as the recession deepened in the United States, U.S. companies appeared to put greater stress on foreign markets than on U.S. markets. Similarly, in 1993, as the dollar fell, companies became more anxious to tap export markets.[12] During slack conditions in the U.S., overseas markets provide a realistic alternative for maintaining business tempo.[13] However, to develop perpetual foreign markets, firms cannot simply shift gears in favor of overseas markets when something goes wrong in the domestic market and then abandon foreign markets once the domestic economy picks up again. Such tactics are harmful to long-term market development abroad, plus they damage the reputation of the business.

Analysis of Economic Environments

Given the perspectives of macro- and microeconomic environment, an opportunity analysis may be performed to determine if it is worthwhile to seek entry into a foreign country's market. A conceptual scheme is helpful for analyzing economic environment in practice in order to assess marketing opportunities. The conceptual scheme requires consideration of such variables as those shown in Exhibit 8.5. With the use of these variables, analysis of marketing opportunity centers on two sets of criteria: cost/benefit criteria and risk/reward criteria.*

Cost/Benefit Criteria Analysis

Cost-benefit criteria answer a series of questions that stress markets, competition, and the financial implications of doing business in a foreign country.

Markets Will people want our products? More importantly, will they want them enough to pay a price that will yield us a profit? Is the market large enough for the firm?

Competition What kind of competition will we have to face, and will the rules apply equally to all? Concern about equal treatment within a market arises from the *altered marketplace competition* that exists in many countries because of host governments that own or subsidize competitors. In such cases, the foreign business usually is at a disadvantage even when it is pitted against inefficient local business.

Financial Examination How many resources (and how much of each type of resource) must be committed, and what will they cost? What return may be expected, and how long might it take to recover the investment?

---

* Inasmuch as this chapter deals with economic environment only, the risk/reward criteria will be examined here solely with reference to economic situation. The risk/reward analysis should be extended by relating it to cultural environment (Chapter 9) and the political environment (Chapter 10).

EXHIBIT 8.5
Considerations
in the Evaluation
of Economic
Environments

Financial Considerations

1. Capital acquisition plan
2. Length of payback period
3. Projected cash inflows (years one, two, and so forth)
4. Projected cash outflows (years one, two, and so forth)
5. Return on investment
6. Monetary exchange considerations

Technical and Engineering Feasibility Considerations

7. Raw materials availability (construction/support/supplies)
8. Raw materials availability (products)
9. Geography/climate
10. Site locations and access
11. Availability of local labor
12. Availability of local management
13. Economic infrastructure (roads, water, electricity, and so forth)
14. Facilities planning (preliminary or detailed)

Marketing Considerations

15. Market size
16. Market potential
17. Distribution costs
18. Competition
19. Time necessary to establish distribution/sales channels
20. Promotion costs
21. Social/cultural factors affecting products

Economic and Legal Considerations

22. Legal systems
23. Host government attitudes toward foreign investment
24. Host attitude toward this particular investment
25. Restrictions on ownership
26. Tax laws
27. Import/export restrictions
28. Capital flow restrictions
29. Land-title acquisitions
30. Inflation

Political and Social Considerations

31. Internal political stability
32. Relations with neighboring countries
33. Political/social traditions
34. Communist influence
35. Religious/racial/language homogeneity
36. Labor organizations and attitudes
37. Skill/technical level of the labor force
38. Socioeconomic infrastructure to support families

In addition to these cost/benefit criteria, the level of training and skills of a national workforce are important considerations. So is the availability of educated, experienced local managers. Most MNCs have learned the value of having local or regional executives in host countries. For example, Sperry Rand Corporation in Japan shares a joint venture that is manned entirely by Japanese workers and executives.[14] Furthermore, transportation, the communications system, and the availability of local resources (especially energy) should be considered. This list could go on and on, but enough has been said to illustrate some of the assessable conceptual factors influencing market-entry decisions.

Risk/Reward Criteria Analysis

Risk/reward criteria emphasize the overall constantly changing mix of situations in the social, political, and economic climates of a host country. In terms of economics, the macroeconomic characteristics of a nation will almost always affect the specific economics of business. The national economic objectives of the country, therefore, also figure in a firm's decision to explore entry there.

For example, the firm needs to know how *fiscal policy* (control of the nation's economy through taxes) translates into business taxation, and how *income policy* (wage/price guideposts) may affect wage and price controls. The firm also needs to know about a country's *monetary policy* (control of the nation's economy through increasing or decreasing interest rates by the central bank). Does the country's policy place restrictions on international cash transactions, such as the repatriation of profits? What is the outlook, for example, for the cost and availability of credits? Is the currency strong, and, more important, what is the inflation situation?

Social/Cultural and Political Factors Although it is convenient to categorize a country's environment into social/cultural, political, and economic aspects, they each overlap, and they all influence the intelligent analysis of any one aspect.

In the social area, the demographic characteristics of the population should be taken into account. The general level of education is an important indicator of the society's development, the likelihood of its accepting new ideas, and possibly its attitude toward a foreign investor. The standard of living and the general expectations of the country tell marketers a great deal. Is the society a progressive one or a static one? Does it aspire to development, or is it frozen into old social patterns and mores? Are its expectations pragmatic or unrealistic? Class structure, where it exists, also yields useful information.

The political area reflects both the social and economic situations, and vice versa. However, some political aspects are particularly relevant to economic analysis:

- What kind of political system does the country have? Is it a democratic/parliamentary society? Or is it authoritarian and possibly repressive?

- Is the national leadership popular or unpopular? The answer might indicate the probability of radical change.

- By our standards, are the national policies successful or unsuccessful?

- What is the level of insurgency, if any? It might range all the way from random, occasional violence to organized guerrilla warfare or foreign-supported insurgency. One of the biggest changes in international business has been the necessity of physical and ideological defense in foreign countries.

If there is a common denominator of both the cost/benefit and risk/reward equations, it is the desirability of stability. That is not to suggest that business should want some imposed stability at the price of reduced performance. Rather, what is desired is a reasonable level of stability already existing in all of the areas just discussed. The aim should be to ensure that capital investment is recovered over a reasonable period, generates a satisfactory profit, and provides a base for the further expansion of international business.

An Illustration

Decisions related to foreign market entry, expansion, and conversion, as well as phasing out from foreign markets, call for a systematic framework for analysis, as discussed previously. Various approaches are available to assess international marketing opportunities.[15] Illustrated here is one method of putting a framework into practical use, consisting of three phases:

1. Appropriate national markets are selected by quickly screening the full range of options without regard to any preconceived notions.
2. Specific strategic approaches are devised for each country or group of countries based on the company's specific product technologies.
3. Marketing plans for each country or group of countries are developed, reviewed, revised, and incorporated into the overall corporate concept without regard to conventional wisdom or stereotypes.

Phase One: Selecting National Markets There are over 180 countries in the world; of these the majority may appear to offer entry markets. Many countries go out of their way to attract foreign investment by offering lures ranging from tax exemptions to low-paid, amply skilled labor. These inducements, valid as they may be in certain individual cases, have repeatedly led to hasty foreign market entry.

A good basis for decision is arrived at through a comparative analysis of different countries, with long-term economic environment having the greatest weight. First, certain countries, on account of their political situations (for example, Libya under Qadhafi) would be considered unsuitable for market entry. It might help to consult an index that rates different countries for business attractiveness. The final choice should be based on the company's own assessment and risk preference.

Next, markets that are either too small in terms of population and per capita income or economically too weak should be eliminated. For example, a number of countries with populations of less than 20 million and annual per capita incomes below $2,000 are of little interest to many companies because of limited demand potential.

The markets surviving this screening are then assessed for strategic attractiveness. A battery of criteria should be developed to fit the specific requirements of the corporation. Basically, the criteria should focus on the following five factors (industry/product characteristics may require slight modifications):

1. Future demand and economic potential of the country in question.
2. Distribution of purchasing power by population groups or market segments.
3. Country-specific technical product standards.
4. "Spillover" from the national market (via standards, regulations, norms, or economic ties) to other markets (for example, the MERCOSUR Pact provides for duty-free exports from Brazil to Uruguay).
5. Access to vital resources (qualified labor force, raw materials sources, suppliers).

There is no reason to expand the list, since additional criteria are rarely significant enough to result in useful new insights. Rather, management should concentrate on developing truly meaningful and practical parameters for each of these five criteria, so that the selection process does not become unnecessarily costly and the results are fully relevant to the company concerned. For example, a German flooring manufacturer, selling principally to the building industry, selected the following yardsticks:

1. *Economic potential:* new housing needs; GNP growth.
2. *Wealth:* per capita income; per capita market size for institutional building or private dwellings (the higher the per capita income, market volume, and share of institutional buildings, the more attractive the market).
3. *Technical product standards:* price level of similar products—for example, price per square meter for floor coverings (the higher the price level, the more attractive the market tends to be for a technically advanced producer).
4. *Spillover:* area in which the same building standards (especially fire safety standards) apply (for example, the U.S. National Electrical Manufacturers' Association standards are widely applicable in Latin America, and British standards apply in most of the Commonwealth countries).
5. *Resource availability:* annual production volume of PVC (an important raw material for the company).

Using these criteria, the German manufacturer in our example based its analysis of economic potential on two factors: housing needs and economic base (see Exhibit 8.6). In specifying these criteria, the company deliberately confined itself to measures that (1) could readily be developed from existing sources of macroeconomic data, (2) would show trends as well as current positions, and (3) would match the company's particular characteristics as closely as possible.

Since German producers of floor covering employ a highly sophisticated technology, it would have been senseless to give a high ranking to a country with only rudimentary pro-

EXHIBIT 8.6   Assessing Country Economic Potential:
The Case of a Building Industry Flooring Supplier

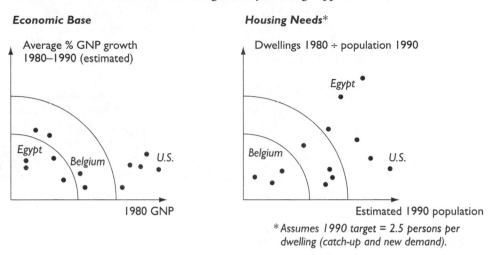

Economic Base

Average % GNP growth
1980–1990 (estimated)

Egypt   Belgium   U.S.

1980 GNP

*Housing Needs**

Dwellings 1980 ÷ population 1990

Egypt

Belgium   U.S.

Estimated 1990 population

*Assumes 1990 target = 2.5 persons per
dwelling (catch-up and new demand).

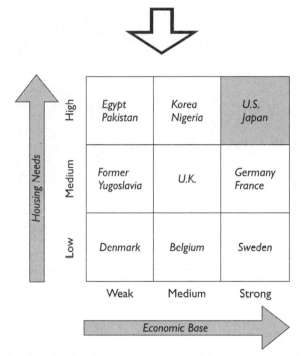

	Weak	Medium	Strong
High	Egypt Pakistan	Korea Nigeria	U.S. Japan
Medium	Former Yugoslavia	U.K.	Germany France
Low	Denmark	Belgium	Sweden

Housing Needs

Economic Base

Examples: Sweden—needs only in replacement sector, Pakistan—economically too weak to meet needs.

duction technology in this particular facet. Companies in other industries, of course, would have to consider other factors—auto registrations per thousand population, percentage of households with telephones, density of household appliance installations, and the like.

The resulting values are rated, for each criterion, on a scale of 1 to 5, so that by weighing the criteria on a percentage basis, each country can be assigned an index number indicating its overall attractiveness. In this particular case, the result was that, out of the 49 countries surviving the initial screening, 16 were ultimately judged attractive enough—on the basis of market potential, per capita market size, level of technical sophistication, prevailing regulations, and resource availability—to warrant serious attention.

Interestingly, the traditionally German-favored markets of Austria and Belgium emerged with low rankings from this strategically based assessment because the level of potential demand was judged to be insufficient. Some new markets such as Egypt and Pakistan were also downgraded as offering an inadequate economic base. Likewise, even such high-potential markets as Italy and Indonesia were eliminated for objective reasons (in the latter case, the low technical standard of most products).

Phase Two: Determining Marketing Strategy After a short list of attractive foreign markets has been compiled, the next step is to group these countries according to their respective stages of economic development. Here the criterion of classification is not per capita income, but the degree of market penetration by the generic product in question. For example, the floor covering manufacturer already mentioned grouped the countries into three categories—developing, take-off and mature—as defined by these factors (see Exhibit 8.7):

EXHIBIT 8.7   Grouping Countries by Phase of Development

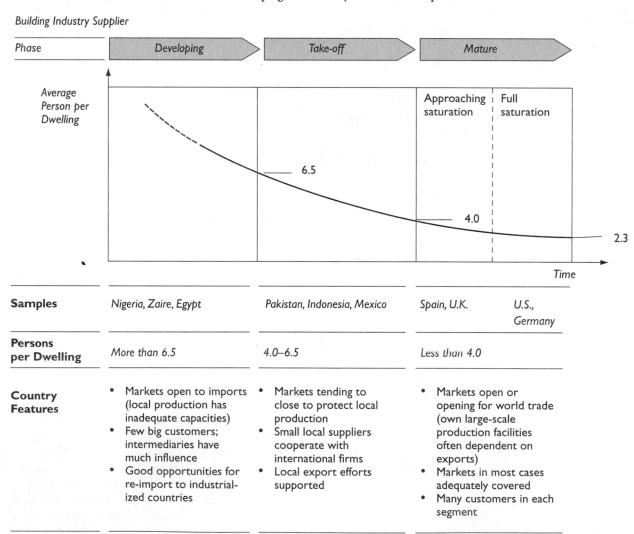

	Developing	Take-off	Mature	
Samples	Nigeria, Zaire, Egypt	Pakistan, Indonesia, Mexico	Spain, U.K.	U.S., Germany
Persons per Dwelling	More than 6.5	4.0–6.5	Less than 4.0	
Country Features	• Markets open to imports (local production has inadequate capacities) • Few big customers; intermediaries have much influence • Good opportunities for re-import to industrialized countries	• Markets tending to close to protect local production • Small local suppliers cooperate with international firms • Local export efforts supported	• Markets open or opening for world trade (own large-scale production facilities often dependent on exports) • Markets in most cases adequately covered • Many customers in each segment	

1. *Accessibility of markets:* crucial for the choice between export and import production.
2. *Local competitive situation:* crucial for the choice between independent construction, joint venture, and acquisition.
3. *Customer structure:* crucial for sales and distribution strategy.
4. *Re-import potential:* crucial for international product/market strategy.

The established development phases and their defining criteria must be very closely geared to the company situation, since it is these factors, not the apparent attractiveness of markets, that will make or break the company's strategic thrust into a given country.

This being the case, for each country or group of countries on the short list, management should formulate a generic marketing strategy with respect to investment, risk, product, and pricing policies—that is, a unified strategic framework applicable to all the countries in each stage of development. This step should yield a clear understanding of what the respective stages of economic development of each country entail for the company's marketing strategies (see Exhibit 8.8).

Companies are too often inclined to regard "overseas" as a single market, or at least to differentiate very little among individual overseas markets. Another common error is the assumption that product or service concepts suited to a highly developed consumer economy will work as well in any foreign market. This is rarely true. Different markets demand different approaches.

Across-the-board strategic approaches typically result in ill-advised and inappropriate allocation of resources. In less developed markets that could be perfectly well served by a few distributors, companies have in some cases established production facilities that are doomed to permanent unprofitability. In markets already at the take-off point, companies have failed to build the necessary local plants and instead have complained about declining exports only to finally abandon the field to competitors. And in markets already approaching saturation, companies have often sought to impose domestic technical standards where adequate standards and knowledge already exist or tried to operate like minireplicas of parent corporations, marketing too many product lines with too few salespeople.

Again and again, product-line offerings are weighted toward either cheaper or higher-quality products than the local market will accept. Clearly, the best insurance against such errors is to select strategies appropriate to the country.

Phase Three: Developing Marketing Plans In developing detailed marketing plans, it is first necessary to determine which product lines fit local markets and to allocate resources accordingly. A rough analysis of potential international business, global sales, and profit targets based on the estimates worked out in Phase One will help in assigning product lines. A framework for resource allocation can then be mapped out according to rough comparative figures for investment quotas, management needs, and skilled-labor requirements. This framework should be supplemented by company-specific examples of standard marketing strategies for each group of countries.

Exhibit 8.9 illustrates the resource allocation process. Different product lines are assigned to different country groups, and for each country category different strategic approaches are specified, for example, support on large-scale products, establishment of local production facilities, cooperation with local manufacturers.

The level of detail in this resource allocation decision framework will depend on a number of factors: company history and philosophy, business policy objectives, scope and variety of product lines, and the number of countries to be served. Working within this decision framework, each product division should analyze its own market in terms of size, growth, and competitive situations; assess its profitability prospects, opportunities, and risks; and identify its own current strategic position on the basis of market share, profit sit-

■■■■■■■■■   **EXHIBIT 8.8**   Developing Standard Strategies

Phase	Developing	Take-Off	Mature
Basic strategy	Test market; pursue profitable individual projects and/or export activities	Build base; allocate substantial resources to establish leading position in market	Expand/round off operations allocate resources selectively to develop market niches
Elements of Strategy			
Investment	Minimize (distribution and services)	Invest to expand capacity (relatively long payback)	Expand selectively in R&D, production, and distribution (relatively short payback)
Risk	Avoid	Accept	Limit
Know-how transfer (R&D)	Document know-how on reference projects	Use local know-how in product technology and/or production engineering	Transfer know-how in special product lines; acquire local know-how to round off own base
Market share objective	Concentrate on key projects possibly build position in profitable businesses with local support	Extend base with new products, new outlets, and/or new applications	Expand/defend
Cost leadership objective	Minimum acceptable (especially reduction of guarantee risks)	Economies of scale; reduction of fixed costs	Rationalize; optimize resources
Product	Standard technology; simple products	Aim for wide range, "innovator" role	Full product line in selected areas; products of high technical quality
Price	Price high	Aim for price leadership (at both ends)	Back stable market price level
Distribution	Use select local distributors (exclusive distribution)	Use large number of small distributors (intensive distribution)	Use company salesforce (selective distribution)
Promotion	Selective advertising with typical high-prestige products, aiming at decision makers	Active utilization of selective marketing resources	Selected product advertising

uation, and vulnerability to local risks. Each product division will then be in a position to develop country-specific marketing alternatives for servicing each national market.

Top management's role throughout is to coordinate the marketing strategy development efforts of the various divisions and constantly monitor the strategic decision framework.

This three-phase approach exhibits a number of advantages.

- It allows management to set up, with a minimum of planning effort, a strategic framework that gives clear priority to market selection decisions, thus making it much easier for the divisions to work out effective product-line strategies, unhampered by the usual "chicken or egg" problem.

EXHIBIT 8.9   Specimen Framework for Resource Allocation

Phase	Specimen Countries	Resource Allocation by Product Division					
		PVC Floor Coverings	Carpeting	Suspended Ceilings	Wall Paneling	PVC Tubes	Plastic Coated Roof Insulation
Developing: "test marktet"	Nigeria	Intensive	None	Moderate	None	Intensive	Intensive
(Share of total resources: 20%)		Specific Plans: • Develop own plastics-processing facilities • Acquire plastics processors					
Take-off: "Build base"	Indonesia	Moderate	None	None	None	Moderate	Moderate
(Share of total resources: 50%)		Specific Plans: • Give support in key projects • Cooperate with state-owned construction organization					
Mature: "Expand/round off operations"	Spain	Moderate	Moderate	Intensive	Intensive	None	None
(Share of total resources: 30%)		Specific Plans: • Develop local facilities for tufting and paneling • Acquire/cooperate with suppliers using unique product and production technology • Develop own distribution channel • Extend range to provide complete interior equipment program (system concept)					

- Division managers can foresee, at a fairly early stage, what reallocations of management, labor, and capital resources are needed and what adjustments may have to be imposed from the top because of inadequate resources.
- The company's future risk profile can be worked out in terms of resource commitment by country group and type of investment.
- The usual plethora of "exceptional" (and mostly opportunistic) product/market situations is sharply reduced. Only the really good opportunities pass through the filter; exceptions are no longer the rule.
- The dazzling-in-theory but unrealistic-in-practice concept of establishing production bases in low-wage countries, buying from the world's lowest-cost sources, and selling products wherever the best prices can be had is replaced by a realistic country-by-country market evaluation.
- Issues of organization, personnel assignment, and integration of overseas operations into corporate planning and control systems reach management's attention only after the fundamental strategic aspects of the company's overseas involvement have been thoroughly prepared.

This three-phase approach enables management to profitably concentrate resources and attention on a handful of really attractive countries instead of dissipating its efforts in vain attempts to serve the entire world.

Opportunities in the Developing World

The framework just discussed is applicable for analyzing the economic environment in both developed and developing countries. However, further examination of opportunities in developing countries is appropriate for two reasons. First, more and more developing countries are pursuing a growth path. South Korea, Taiwan, Singapore, and Hong Kong were first; Brazil and China followed. Now India and Eastern European countries have been opening up (see International Marketing Highlight 8.3). Several other nations are following suit as well. The developing world is beginning to rely on the market mechanism to attract investment and technology and become industrialized.

The second reason why opportunities in developing countries should be even more closely examined than those in advanced countries is that government plays a bigger role in business decisions in developing countries. This necessitates dealing with the bureaucrats approach foreign investment with much less sophistication and confidence than do private-sector executives.

These characteristics suggest that in analyzing opportunities in developing countries, a company should place more emphasis on long-term potential than on short-term gains (see International Marketing Highlight 8.4). In addition, extra attention should be paid to political and social variables since they will greatly influence the scope and nature of the market and are likely to differ in at least some respects from those of the home country. Business conditions vary so much from one country to the other that a comparative (i.e., multicountry) analysis may be difficult. Moreover, reliable and timely information is less available in developing countries than in advanced ones; thus, there is no way to systematically evaluate such factors as sociopolitical conditions. Instead, broad guidelines and a general feel for the situation are necessary, for which a trusted native could be of immense help.

For example, it has been estimated that basic packaged-foods sales take off when GDP per head increases to $5,000.[16] Based on this guideline, only a few Asian countries qualify for packaged foods. However, many of these nations are already more affluent than the aggregate figures imply. In countries such as Indonesia and Thailand, a rising middle class can afford to indulge itself. Besides, Asia has a higher percentage of younger people, a trend likely to continue for the next 30 years or so. That is important, because young people are more willing to change their living habits than older ones.

International Marketing Highlight 8.3

Scents and Sensibility

Avon Products is increasingly focusing on what its CEO calls "Avon Heaven," the developing countries that in 1995 accounted for 38 percent of the firm's sales and 49 percent of its pretax profits. Developing countries might have been designed for Avon. First, the retailing infrastructure tends to be underdeveloped—and, apart from a very basic distribution network, Avon needs no infrastructure. Second, the products sold by local vendors tend to be of poor quality. And, third, women in most developing countries are eager to work to supplement the family income: they call on three or four times as many clients as their western counterparts.

But what really appeals to Avon is how little cash it has to spend to generate big profits. In Russia, the firm has invested less than $500,000 but its 16,000 representatives sold a net $30 million of products in 1996, up from nothing in 1993. From this, Avon skims an operating profit margin of around 30 percent. Avon imports all the products it sells in Russia from its British operations. When net sales hit about $50 million a year, the firm may manufacture locally.

Source: The Economist, July 13, 1996, p. 57

In general, many U.S. firms' overall approach to foreign-investment decision making regarding developing countries is much less sophisticated than that for developed countries. The former is often characterized by a lack of breadth in consideration of important variables, a biased perspective, and inadequate preparation. The key to future improvement of opportunity analysis in developing countries may lie in the motivation generated by the inevitable increase in competition. In the past, for example, the sheer power, dynamism, and momentum of U.S. business virtually ensured its success in almost any developing nation. As competition, particularly from Japan, becomes more significant, the recognition of shades of difference and finer distinctions with regard to opportunities becomes more important as well.

■■■■■■■■■■■■■■■   **International Marketing Highlight 8.4**   ■■■■■■■■■■■■■■■

Procter & Gamble's Foreign Formula

The day after a 34-year-old Peruvian became manager of Procter & Gamble Co.'s Peru subsidiary in September 1988, the economy hit the skids. By the end of the year, inflation had soared to 2,000 percent. Key managers fled. Leftist terrorists kidnapped or murdered business leaders. The P&G subsidiary's sales plunged more than 30 percent, and the unit posted a loss. Money became tight. But while many MNCs pulled out of Peru. P&G remained. Now, the consumer-products company is expanding there.

Throughout Latin America, P&G is shaking the stranglehold of government controls and its own strict U.S. culture. The Latin American division began as a fledgling detergent company but now is a $1 billion business that contributes 15 percent of P&G's international sales. The company expects the division, which has subsidiaries in 9 countries and sells in 10 others through distributors, to double its revenue again in five years. The division's profit margins exceed its international average.

P&G's success is attributed to an important lesson: U.S. management and marketing plans often don't work outside the United States. For example, Ace detergent, launched in Mexico in the early 1950s, was clobbered by local competitors. Developed for U.S. washing machines, the product had a low-suds formula. But at that time, many Mexicans washed their clothes in the river or in a basin of water, and they judged detergent by its suds.

Eventually, the formula was changed. Similarly, P&G switched from cardboard boxes to plastic bags, which kept the detergent drier and were cheaper. Besides, many consumers shop every day and can afford only small amounts of detergent each time. Now, one top seller throughout Latin America is the 100-gram bag, enough to wash just one basket of clothes.

Source: The Wall Street Journal, June 5, 1990, p. 1.

Summary

The economic environment of a foreign country must be examined before an international marketer decides to enter its market. A country burdened with economic problems may lack stability and become vulnerable to political radicalism. On the other hand, a growing and burgeoning economy usually stimulates business activity and offers new opportunities. Thus, a careful review of economic conditions, both short-and long-term, is a prerequisite for a decision about entering an overseas market.

The economic environment can be divided into macro- and microeconomic aspects. Macroenvironment describes the overall economic situation in a country and is analyzed using economic indicators such as population, GNP per capita, index of industrial production, rate of economic growth, inflation rate, balance-of-trade surplus (deficit), interest rates, unemployment data, and the like. The economic system of a country is also part of the macroenvironment. Two extreme types of economic systems are the capitalist system and state control. The latter is mainly found in socialist countries; most western countries pursue a mixed form of capitalism.

Microenvironment refers to economic conditions relevant to a particular product or market. Analysis of microeconomic environment is largely performed with reference to competition. A firm should properly identify different sources of competition and examine its own strengths and weaknesses relative to major competitors. Equipped with a competitive advantage over its rivals, a firm will be able to develop a workable marketing mix.

International marketers should examine not only the economic environment of a country, both macro- and micro-, before preparing to enter its market, but should also take into account the impact of the economic environment of their own country. For example, many U.S. firms enter the international market during a recession to sustain their business, only to withdraw as the domestic scene improves.

Conceptual schemes or frameworks are helpful for analyzing economic environment. Analysis can be performed with reference to cost/benefit and risk/reward criteria. Cost/benefit criteria include markets, competition, and financial implications of doing business in a country. Risk/reward criteria include the broad social, economic, and political climates of a nation. The successful application of a conceptual scheme yields a marketing strategy that will foster the development of market plans appropriate to a particular foreign market at a particular time. The conceptual scheme can be used to analyze opportunities in developed and developing economies. In many cases, however, lack of adequate information on developing countries may require decision makers to depend more on the "feel" of the situation than on actual data.

Review Questions

1. Should all the different types of economic indicators be used to examine the macroeconomic environments of different countries? Discuss what should be used and why.
2. Discuss the following statements: "Although advanced countries offer an immediate market opportunity, the competitive activity is excessively keen there. It may, therefore, be more advantageous for a firm to gain a permanent foothold in one or more developing countries, since often there is no competition to reckon with."
3. Present a scheme for analyzing the economic environment of Mexico from the viewpoint of an appliance manufacturer.
4. What relevance does Engel's law have in the analysis of economic environment for overseas business?
5. How can a firm determine its competitive advantage overseas?
6. Illustrate how the economic perspectives of different countries are related.

Creative Questions

1. A company is interested in selling telecommunications equipment (telephone exchanges, etc.) to India, which has 990 million people and only 7 million phone lines. What kind of economic analysis would you conduct to determine the viability of this opportunity in India?
2. The product life cycle theory alleges that the nature and number of competitors vary at different stages. During the early stages (introduction, growth) of the product life

cycle the product has little or no competition, whereas at later stages (maturity, decline), the competition becomes tougher. Does this mean that if a company enters a growth market overseas, it need not undertake competitive analysis?

Endnotes

1. "A Snapshot of Living Standards," *Fortune*, July 31, 1989, p. 92.

2. Gunnar Myrdal, *The Asian Drama: An Inquiry into the Poverty of Nations* (New York: Pantheon, 1968).

3. Bill Saporito, "Where the Global Action is," *Fortune*, Autumn–Winter 1993, p. 63.

4. *The Economist*, April 2, 1994, p. 100. Also see "The Myth of the Japanese Middle Class," *Business America*, September 12, 1988, p. 49.

5. The most up-to-date statistics on a worldwide basis are available from the World Bank. See *World Development Report—2000* (New York: Oxford University Press, 2000).

6. Benjamin R. Barber, "Jihad vs. McWorld," *The Atlantic*, March 1992, pp. 53–56, 58–63.

7. See Jonathan Friedland, "U.S. Phone Giants Find Telmex Can Be a Bruising Competitor," *The Wall Street Journal*, October 23, 1998, p. A1.

8. Information was obtained from BMW Marketing Division in Germany.

9. Valerie Reitman, "In Japan's Car Market, Big Three Face Rivals Who Go Door-to-Door," *The Wall Street Journal*, September 28, 1994, p.1.

10. "Upbeat in Brazil," *Country Monitor*, February 9, 2000, p. 1.

11. *Crossborder Monitor*, January 21, 1998, p. 2.

12. "U.S.-Based MNCs say Weak Dollar Is Nothing to Cry About," *Crossborder Monitor*, July 20, 1994, p. 1.

13. C.P. Rao, M. Krishna Erramilli, and Gopala K. Ganesh, "Impact of Domestic Recession on Export Marketing Behavior," *International Marketing Review* 7, no. 2 (1990). 54–65.

14. See Jeremy Main, "How to Go Global and Why," *Fortune*, August 28, 1989, p. 70.

15. V. Kumar, Antonie Stam, and Erich A. Joachimsthaler, "An Interactive Multi-Criteria Approach to Identifying Potential Foreign Markets," *Journal of International Marketing* 2, no. 1 (1994): 29–52. Also see Marie E. Wicks Kelly and George C. Philippatos, "Comparative Analysis of the Foreign Investment Evaluation Practices by U.S.–Based Manufacturing Multinational Companies," *Business Studies*, Winter 1982, pp. 19–42; Robert Weigand, "International Investments; Weighing the Incentives," *Harvard Business Review*, July–August 1983, pp. 146–153; and Philip Kotler and Liam Fahey, "The World's Champion Marketers: The Japanese," *Journal of Business Strategy*, Summer 1982, pp. 3–13.

16. "Adam Smith and the Wok," *The Economist*, December 4, 1993, p. 15.

CHAPTER 9

Cultural
Environment

CHAPTER FOCUS_____

After studying this chapter, you should be able to

■ Explain the meaning of culture, and describe its various aspects.

■ Describe the impact of culture on product, price, promotion, and distribution decisions.

■ Analyze cultural implications for a product or market.

■ Discuss cultural adaptation.

■ Explain the process of cultural change.

Doing business across national boundaries requires interaction with people nurtured in different cultural environments. Values that are important to one group of people may mean little to another. Some typical U.S. attitudes and perceptions are at striking variance with those of certain other countries. These cultural differences deeply affect market behavior. International marketers, therefore, need to be as familiar as possible with the cultural traits of any country they want to do business with. International business literature is full of instances where stereotyped notions of countries' cultures have led to insurmountable problems. More than any other function of a business, marketing perhaps is most susceptible to cultural error, since marketing by definition requires contact with the people of the country concerned. Practically all marketing decisions are culture-bound.

The effect of culture on international marketing ventures is multifaceted. The factoring of cultural differences into marketing mix decisions to enhance the likelihood of success has long been a critical issue in overseas operations. With the globalization of worldwide commerce, cultural forces have taken on additional importance. Naiveté and blundering in regard to culture can lead to expensive mistakes. And although some cultural differences are instantly obvious, others are subtle and can surface in surprising ways.

This chapter begins by examining the meaning of culture and goes on to explore its profound effect on marketing outside the U.S. Various elements of culture are discussed. A framework for analyzing culture is introduced. The impact of the sociocultural fabric of the host nation on different marketing decisions is explored. Following this, a procedure for cultural adaptation overseas is recommended. Finally, the impact of foreign business on local culture as an agent of cultural change in the host country is examined.

The Concept of Culture

It was the middle of October, and a marketing executive from the U.S. was flying to Saudi Arabia to finalize a contract with a local company to supply hospital furnishings. The next day, he met the Saudi contacts and wondered if they would sign the deal within two or three days, since he had to report the matter to his board the following Monday. The Saudi executive made a simple response: "Insha Allah," which means "if God is willing." The American felt completely lost. He found the carefree response of the Saudi insulting and unbusinesslike. He felt he had made an effort by going all the way to Saudi Arabia in order for them to question any matter requiring clarification before signing the contract. He thought that the Saudi executive was treating a deal worth over $100 million as if it meant nothing.

During the next meeting the American was determined to put the matter in stronger terms, emphasizing the importance of his board's meeting. But the Arabs again ignored the issue of signing the contract. "They were friendly, appeared happy and calm, but wouldn't sign on the dotted lines," the American later explained. Finally on orders from the president of his company, he returned home without the contract.

Why did the Saudi executives not sign the sales contract? After all, they had agreed to all the terms and conditions during their meeting in New York. But in Riyadh they did not even care to review it, let alone sign it.

Unfortunately, the U.S. executive had arrived at the wrong time. It was the time of Ramadan, holy month, when most Muslims fast. During this time, everything slows down, particularly business.[1] In western societies, religion is for most people only one aspect of life, and business goes on as usual most of the time. In the Islamic countries, religion is a total way of life for the majority of people. It affects every facet of living. Thus, no matter how important a business deal may be, it will probably not be conducted during the holy month. This U.S. executive was not aware of Muslim culture and its values and therefore scheduled a business meeting for the one time of year when business was not likely to be conducted.

Culture includes all learned behavior and values that are transmitted to an individual living within the society through shared experience. The concept of culture is broad and extremely complex. It involves virtually every part of a person's life and touches on virtually all human needs, both physical and psychological. A classic definition is provided by Sir Edward Tylor: "Culture is that complex whole which includes knowledge, belief, art, morals, law, custom, and any other capabilities and habits acquired by [individuals as members] of society."[2]

Culture, then, develops through recurrent social relationships that form patterns that are eventually internalized by members of the entire group. It is commonly agreed that a culture must have these three characteristics:

1. It is *learned*, that is, people over time transmit the culture of their group from generation to generation.
2. It is *interrelated*, that is, one part of the culture is deeply connected with another part, such as religion with marriage, or business with social status.
3. It is *shared*, that is, the tenets of the culture are accepted by most members of the group.[3]

Another characteristic of culture is that it continues to evolve through constant embellishment and adaptation, partly in response to environmental needs and partly through the influence of outside forces.[4] In other words, a culture does not stand still, but slowly, over time, changes.

A nation may embody more than one culture, each exhibiting fundamental differences. Canada has a dual culture: English-speaking and French-speaking. Two distinctive cultures also exist in Israel: a so-called western group consisting of European and U.S. immigrants, whose culture corresponds to their backgrounds, and a so-called Oriental group consisting of immigrants from Asian and African countries, most of them Arab-speaking Muslim societies. The contrasts between the two groups have been described this way by Abraham Pizam and Arie Reichel:

> The Oriental set of values corresponds to the values generally attributed to traditional societies described as: compulsory in their force, sacred in their tone and stable in their timelessness. They call for fatalistic acceptance of the world as is, respect for those in authority, and submergence of the individual in collectivity.
>
> In contrast to this, the norms and values of Israelis of western ancestry can be described as stressing acquisitive activities, an aggressive attitude toward economic and social change, and a clear trend toward a higher degree of industrialization. The oriental Israeli immigrants, having arrived later than the western immigrants, were expected to be absorbed in a western society, having a strong emphasis on specificity, universalism, and achievement.[5]

Cultural Field

Knowledge of a culture can be gained by probing its various aspects—but which aspects? Since culture is such a vast concept, it is desirable to develop a field for cultural understanding. From the viewpoint of a marketer, one way of gaining cultural understanding is to examine the following cultural elements within a country: material life, social interactions, language, aesthetics, religion and faith, pride and prejudice, and ethics and mores.[6]

Material Life

Material life refers to economics, that is, what people do to derive their livelihood. The tools, knowledge, techniques, methods, and processes that a culture utilizes to produce goods and services, as well as their distribution and consumption, are all part of material life. Thus, two essential parts of material life are knowledge and economics.

Material life reflects the standard of living and degree of technological advancement. Suppose a large proportion of a hypothetical population is engaged in agriculture. Agricultural operations are mainly performed by manual labor; mechanization of agriculture is unknown. Modern techniques of farming such as use of fertilizers, pesticides, and quality seeds are unfamiliar. The medium of exchange is a barter system, markets are local, and living is entirely rural. Such a composite description suggests that the society is primitive. Opportunities for multinational business in a primitive environment will be limited.

By contrast, consider a society in which the manufacturing industry serves as the major source of employment, and agriculture supports about one-tenth of the population. People live in urban centers and have such modern amenities as television, cars, VCRs, newspapers, and so on. Money is the medium of exchange. In such a culture, business across national boundaries would make sense.

The material life of any given society will fall on a continuum between traditional and industrialized poles. That position indicates a society's overall way of life and can be analyzed to determine opportunities for an international marketer. For example, Brazil and Pakistan are both developing countries, but the study of material life in the two countries would show that Brazil is ahead of Pakistan, offering market opportunities for electrical appliances, stereos, and television sets. In Pakistan, which is still emerging from total dependence on farming, agricultural tools would be more important.

Social Interactions

Social interactions establish the roles that people play in a society and their authority/responsibility patterns. These roles and patterns are supported by society's institutional framework, which includes, for example, education and marriage.

Consider the traditional marriage of a Saudi woman. The woman's father chooses the husband-to-be. After agreeing on a small payment for the bride, the two men hold hands in front of a judge to finalize the marriage. The woman sees her husband for the first time when he comes to consummate the marriage. The social role assigned to women in the strict Islamic world is one of complete dependency on men, whose authority and command cannot be questioned. A woman's place is always in the home. Outside the home, if women are seen at all, they are veiled. Karen Elliott House described the Islamic male and female ways this way:

> Moslems [sic] believe in the segregation of men and women, with the exception of husbands and wives and close family members. Men who are strangers to the family are not even supposed to see a man's female relatives. Moslems are not receptive to the western concept of liberation of women. Males are more privileged. It is not uncommon, as an example, to witness some Moslem males traveling by air in the first-class section of an airliner and their wives in the back, flying economy.[7]

Social roles are also established by culture. For example, a woman can be a wife, a mother, a community leader, and/or an employee. What role is preferred in different situations is culture-bound. Most Swiss women consider household work (e.g., washing dishes, cleaning floors) as their primary role. For this reason, they resent modern gadgets and machines.

Behavior also emerges from culture in the form of conventions, rituals, and practices on different occasions such as festivals, marriages, informal get-togethers, and times of grief or religious celebration.

Likewise, the authority of the aged, the teacher, and the religious leader in many societies is derived from the culture (see International Marketing Highlight 9.1). The educational system, the social settings (celebrations and festivities), and customs and traditions prescribe roles and patterns for individuals and groups. A good example is the caste system in India. A person's social and occupational status is determined by birth in a certain family or community. Such is the strength of social heritage that, despite caste discrimination being declared unconstitutional and legally punishable, the system still prevails, especially in rural areas.

With reference to marketing, social interactions influence family decision making and buying behavior and define the scope of personal influence and opinion. In Latin America and Asia the extended family is considered the most basic and stable unit of social organization. It is the center for all economic, political, social, and religious life, providing companionship, protection, and a common set of values with specifically prescribed means for fulfilling them. In contrast, the nuclear family (husband, wife, and children) is the focus of social organization in the U.S.

An empirical study by Chin Tiong Tan and James McCullough showed how cultural differences affect the husband-wife influence in buying decisions.[8] A Singapore husband, it was discovered, played a more dominant role than his U.S. counterpart in family decision making. Similar results were obtained in a study of Dutch and U.S. housewives.[9] The U.S. wife played a more autonomous role than the Dutch wife in family decision making. Thus, social roles vary from culture to culture and are likely to affect buying behavior.

International Marketing Highlight 9.1

"The Flower Day"

Although professors in Thai universities receive very low salaries, they are greatly respected, at least in part because until around 1900, all educators were Buddhist monks. One day a year, there is a ceremony at each Thai university called "The Flower Day," which an American Fulbright professor describes this way: "Today students paid homage to their professors—a symbolic celebration of rather common significance to them. I found it an astonishing phenomenon. In a large auditorium, student representatives from each department crawled up, in the manner of Asian supplication, and gave beautiful floral offerings to their *Aacaan* (professors). Their choral chants asked for blessing and showed gratitude. Their speeches asked for forgiveness for any disrespect or nonfulfillment of expectation. They promised to work diligently. In a moment of paradox, I remembered I must not forget to pay the premium on my professional liability insurance this year."

Language

Language as part of culture consists not only of the spoken word, but also symbolic communication of time, space, things, friendship, and agreements. Nonverbal communication occurs through gestures, expressions, and other body movements.

The many different languages of the world do not literally translate from one to another, and understanding the symbolic and physical aspects of different cultures' communication is even more difficult to achieve. For example, a phrase such as "body by Fisher" translated literally into Flemish means "corpse by Fisher." Similarly, "Let Hertz put you in the driver's seat" translated literally into Spanish means "Let Hertz make you a chauffeur."[10] Nova translates into Spanish as "it doesn't go." A shipment of Chinese shoes destined for Egypt created a problem because the design on the soles of the shoes spelled "God" in Arabic. Olympia's Roto photocopier did not sell well because "roto" refers to the lowest class in Chile, and "roto" in Spanish means "broken."[11]

In addition, meanings differ within the same language used in different places.[12] The English language differs so much from one English-speaking country to another that sometimes the same word means something entirely opposite in a different culture. "Table the report" in the U.S. means postponement; in England it means "bring the matter to the forefront."

Language differences can affect all sorts of business dealings, contracts, negotiations, advertising, and labeling. A dentist's store sign in Hong Kong read, "Teeth extracted by the latest methodists." A tailor's store sign in Jordan advised, "Order your summer suits.

Because in big rush we will execute customers in strict rotation."[13] Coca-Cola Co., gained some important language information that warned it not to use the diet name in France: the word "diet" suggests poor health there. Instead, the company called its Diet Coke Coca-Cola Light.

Symbolic communication poses some cross-cultural dangers, too. To be on time for an appointment is an accepted norm of behavior in the U.S. A person is looked down upon if he or she fails to be on time. But in many other cultures, people are not particular about time and an appointment for 11 AM means *about* that time (see International Marketing Highlight 9.2). Greetings vary from culture to culture, encompassing the handshake, hug, nose rub, kiss, and placing the hands in praying position. In Chile, women typically greet everyone, even strangers, with a kiss on one cheek. In Brazil, it is kisses on both cheeks. In Spain, in business circles, one had better become friends before kissing or even patting someone on the shoulder.[14] Lack of awareness concerning a country's accepted form of greeting can lead to awkward encounters and sometimes offended feelings.

------ **International Marketing Highlight 9.2** ------

Being on Time

Attitudes toward punctuality vary greatly from one culture to another and unless understood can cause confusion and misunderstanding. Romanians, Japanese, and Germans are very punctual, while many of the Latin countries have a more relaxed attitude toward time. The Japanese consider it rude to be late for a business meeting, but it is acceptable, even fashionable, to be late for a social occasion. In Guatemala, on the other hand, a luncheon at a specified time means that some guests might be 10 minutes early while others may be 45 minutes late.

Aesthetics

Aesthetics include the art, drama, music, folkways, and architecture endemic to a society. These aspects of a society convey its concept of beauty and modes of expression. For example, different colors have different meanings worldwide. In western societies, wedding gowns are usually white, but in Asia, white symbolizes sorrow.

The aesthetic values of a society show in the design, styles, colors, expressions, symbols, movements, emotions, and postures valued and preferred in a particular culture. These attributes have an impact on the design and promotion of different products.

Likewise, space, and the way that a person occupies it, communicates something about social position in the terms of each culture. A large office on the top floor of a building in the U.S. means that the person occupying that office is important in an organizational hierarchy. Such a conclusion elsewhere would not always be right. Japanese executives usually share an office.

In the U.S., worldly possessions and material things are often used as symbols of success. A Lincoln Continental or a Mercedes automobile signifies achievement. However, in many countries, owning such expensive automobiles would not command respect. Particularly in the Islamic countries, an emphasis on material possessions is frowned upon.

In many situations the symbolic language of communication is more important than the actual words, and people respond accordingly. Therefore, an international businessperson must understand nonverbal cultural differences to avoid communicating the wrong message.

Religion and Faith

Religion influences a culture's outlook on life, its meaning and concept. Islam considers emphasis on material wealth ignoble. In Christianity, particularly in western cultures, the ideal of people taking dominion of the earthly environment has combined with the Calvinist ethic of hard work and success to promote the idea of the acquisition of wealth as a measure of achievement. Hinduism, while it places no sanction on the acquisition of wealth, is fatalistic about the acquisition of riches. In general, the religion practiced in a society influences the emphasis placed on material life, which in turn affects the attitudes toward owning and using goods and services. Religious traditions may even prohibit the use of certain goods and services altogether.[15] For example, Hinduism prescribes vegetarianism, with special stress on abstinence from beef. Islam forbids the eating of pork.

A fatalistic belief leads Asians to choose an auspicious time to buy a car or to plan a wedding. Car salespeople in Japan deliver a car to a consumer on a lucky day; contractors check for an auspicious day before breaking ground; and insurance salespeople are careful to pick a good day for obtaining a customer's signature on a life insurance policy.[16]

Religion also influences male-female roles, as well as societal institutions and customs such as marriage and funeral rites. Islam assigns women an inferior role and restricts their activities to the household. Whereas a Muslim man may have more than one wife, a woman must practice monogamy.

Religion affects patterns of living in various other ways. It establishes authority relationships, an individual's duties and responsibilities both in childhood and as an adult, and the sanctity of different acts such as hygiene. In the name of religion, Iranians in 1979 disrupted their whole country.[17] The Catholic church officially continues to prohibit the use of birth control devices. Animism, a religion emphasizing magic and practiced in many parts of Africa, demands human sacrifices.

In general, organized religion and faith inevitably motivate people and their customs in numerous ways. The impact of religion is continuous and profound (see International Marketing Highlight 9.3). Consequently, international marketers must be sensitive to the religious principles of each host country (see International Marketing Highlight 9.4).

International Marketing Highlight 9.3

Cultural Diversity

When a manager from the dominant U.S. culture saw two Arab-American employees arguing, he figured he had better stay out of it. But the employees *expected* a third-party intermediary, or *wasta* in Arabic, and without one the incident blew up.

The expectation goes back to the Koran and Bedouin tradition. While the dominant American culture is likely to take an individualistic, win-lose approach and emphasize privacy, Arab-Americans tend to value a win-win result that preserves group harmony but often requires mediation.

A Latino manager starts a budget-planning meeting by chatting casually and checking with his new staff on whether everyone can get together after work. His non-Latino boss frets over the delay and wonders why he doesn't get straight to the numbers. Latino culture teaches that building relationships is often critical to working together, while the dominant American culture encourages "getting down to business."

Source: The Wall Street Journal, September 12, 1990, p. B1.

International Marketing Highlight 9.4

Laziza Rises Again

The Arab world is not a good place to sell beer. Islam, the main religion in all Arab countries, prohibits alcohol, and many states—Saudi Arabia, Kuwait, and several of the United Arab Emirates, among others—ban it outright. Elsewhere, booze is sold only in windowless bars in posh hotels, or by bureaucratic state-owned firms. Even Lebanon, the country with the loosest living and freest markets in the region, consumes a mere 3.5m cases of beer each year. Big western exporters have little time for the area. So why is Laziza, a long-defunct Lebanese beer brand, relaunching itself with plans for a grand expansion?

The answer lies in a clever marketing ploy. From its founding in 1931 until stray civil-war shells peppered the company's brewery and forced a halt in production in 1990, Laziza was Lebanon's foremost brand of beer. Many of the Gulf Arabs who poured into Beirut in the 1960s and 1970s for a spot of debauchery acquired a taste for it. Their successors, who have taken to visiting Lebanon again since the end of the civil war in 1991, are doubtless also succumbing to the charms of Lebanese beer. But they could not indulge the habit at home until Georges Khawam, grandson of Laziza's founder, hit on the idea of relaunching the brand with a nonalcoholic line for export.

Laziza reappeared in Beirut's stores and bars in May, where it has quickly captured a third of the market, according to Mr. Khawam. Within a year, he hopes to be selling in Saudi Arabia, Bahrain, Qatar, Syria, Jordan and the UAE. He is also shipping to Britain and France, where the Arabic name (meaning delicious or delightful) and Lebanese pedigree should appeal to expatriate Arabs. Since he has subcontracted local production to Bavaria, a Dutch-owed brewery, his investment has been small; but if the Arabs get a taste for Laziza he might even consider spending the $15m needed to refurbish the old shell-scarred brewery in Beirut.

Source: The Economist, June 26, 1999.

Pride and Prejudice

Even the culture most backward in the eyes of a westerner will foster a certain pride in its people about its traits and ways. Indeed, developing countries sometimes evince more pride—and prejudice— than developed countries. The Chinese are jealous of their cultural heritage, and they speak of it with great emotion. So do the Egyptians of their heritage. In contrast, many Americans express feelings of being deprived of cultural history in a country so young and diverse by nature (see International Marketing Highlight 9.5).

Cultural pride and prejudice make many nations reject foreign ideas and imported products. But the reverse also occurs: a perception of greatness attributed to another culture may lead to the eager acceptance of things reflecting that culture. For example, the Japanese are proud of their culture and economic achievement and prefer to buy Japanese manufactures. Yet the words *Made in the U.S.A.* marked on a product communicate quality and sophistication to the Japanese as well as to people in many developing countries. The Japanese respond to names. They like dealing with people of standing. It is for this reason that Mead Corporation, which has successfully operated in Japan for 35 years, had Nelson Mead, the son of the founder, handle that business.

███████████ International Marketing Highlight 9.5 ███████████

Cultural Islands

Japan: Boasts the strongest work ethic, exhibits the greatest concern about the work ethic of employees from other nations, and strongly supports free trade.

South Korea: Strongly favors protectionism, puts country ahead of company, encourages a corporate responsibility toward employees, and expresses optimisim about the future.

India: Expresses optimism about the future and strongly favors protectionism.

Hungary: Favors a different corporate organization than that found in other countries and emphasizes economic regeneration.

Source: Rosabeth Moss Kanter, "Transcending Business Boundaries: 12,000 World Managers View Change," *Harvard Business Review,* May–June 1991, p. 153.

Ethics and Mores   The concept of what is right and wrong is based on culture.[18] To be straightforward and openly honest are considered morally right in the U.S., even if feelings are hurt. In Latin cultures, however, people avoid direct statements that would embarrass or make another uncomfortable. Thus, even if a Latin businessman does not mean to do business, he would appear to participate, only later to excuse himself from the transaction process.

In an empirical study of U.S., French, and German managers substantial differences were noted on ethical issues. On an issue that may benefit the firm at the expense of the environment, the French and German managers were more likely to side with their employers and participate in what they perceived as a relatively minor infraction of environmental law. The American managers were less likely to approve a production run that would result in illegal air pollution.[19]

The differences in mannerisms between the Japanese and the Koreans also illustrate this point. The Japanese are formal and reserved; the Koreans informal and outgoing. A Korean saleswoman puts her hand on a customer's shoulder as she walks him to the door; a Korean executive invites a business acquaintance home to meet the family. Such acts of familiarity would be very unusual in Japan.[20]

John L. Graham noted that culture has significant influence on the process of business negotiations conducted by the executives in the U.S., Japan, and Brazil.[21] His study revealed substantial differences in bargaining style across the three cultures. Brazilians made fewer commitments and more demands. Their first offers were more greedy. Americans were more apt to offer a fair price, one that was closer to the eventual solution. Japanese consistently asked for higher profit solutions when making the initial offer in a negotiation. (see International Marketing Highlight 9.6).

Culture and Marketing

Culture influences every aspect of marketing. Exhibit 9.1 illustrates the linkages between culture and marketing action. A marketing-oriented firm makes decisions based on customer perspectives which determine customers' actions and are shaped by customers' lifestyles and behavior patterns. The products that people buy, the attributes that they value, and the principals whose opinions they accept, are all culture-based choices. It is not an overstatement to say that a person's perspectives or resources, problems, and opportunities to a considerable extent are generated and conditioned by culture (see International Marketing Highlight 9.7).

■■■■■■■ **International Marketing Highlight 9.6** ■■■■■■■

Why Can't People Do Things the American Way?

Bill Hastings, the assistant director of marketing for a small American manufacturing company, visited Bangkok to investigate the possibility of distributing the company's products in Southeast Asia. Bill traveled with Cheryl Acosta, field director for the company's international operations. Neither of them had any prior experience in Asia. Bill, in fact, had never traveled outside the U.S. Both executives felt mildly apprehensive about being neophytes in the field, but they felt great excitement, too, as if they were the first explorers in an uncharted area. (Neither acknowledged that their counterparts in other companies probably had had years of international experience and had developed a mastery of Southeast Asian business practices.)

Bill and Cheryl attempted to complete a 12-country marketing study in six weeks. Bill figured that once he obtained the facts and made a quick decision on how to proceed, sales would start rolling in. But they found the environment baffling and made little head-

EXHIBIT 9.1   Impact of Culture on Marketing Decisions

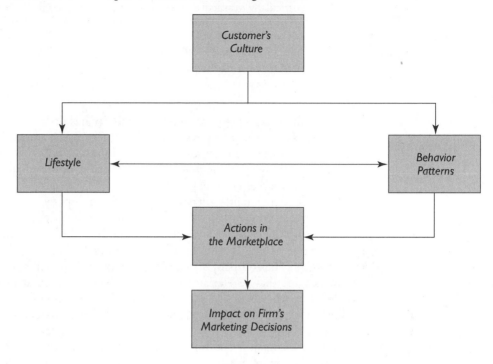

way. Frustrated, they impulsively recommended a plan to headquarters that ended in a fiasco one year later.

"I can't understand what happened," Bill reflected in the aftermath. "The same method worked just fine when we started operations in Los Angeles."

A good example of cultural impact is found in the foods that people prefer. Of all the universals that constitute "culture," few, if any, are so ingrained and consistently reinforced as food habits. The daily physiological requirement of nutrition in some form exists for every human inhabitant in any society or culture—there is no escape from eating for an extended period. Food consumption, acquisition, and preparation also are interrelated with many of the other universals of the culture, including religious observances and ceremonies, feasting, folklore, and the division of labor.

International Marketing Highlight 9.7

Embarrassment in the Air

United Airlines' experiences in the Pacific market show how embarrassing cultural mistakes can be. One of the airline's officials reported the following:

> The map we inserted into our sales promotion brochure left out one of Japan's main islands. Our magazine ad campaign, "We Know the Orient," listed the names of Far Eastern countries below pictures of local coins. Unfortunately, the coins didn't match up with the countries.
>
> I leave to your imagination how Chinese businessmen felt taking off from Hong Kong during the inauguration of our concierge services for first-class passengers. To mark the occasion, each concierge was proudly wearing a white carnation . . . a well-known Oriental symbol of death.
>
> Perhaps the most embarrassing mistake was our in-flight magazine cover that showed Australian actor Paul Hogan wandering through the Outback. The caption read, "Paul Hogan Camps It Up." Hogan's lawyer was kind enough to phone us long distance from Sydney to let us

know that "camps it up" is Australian slang for "flaunts his homosexuality." The Paul Hogan story is particularly instructive. Americans often assume that the folks Down Under are just like Americans because we all speak English. This does not make for happy customers. Australians expect real cream in their coffee—not artificial whitener. And the American hand gesture for "thumbs up" has quite a different meaning Down Under. It does *not* mean "OK."

Source: John R. Zeeman, "Service—The Cutting Edge of Global Competition: What United Is Learning in the Pacific," a presentation before the Academy of International Business, Chicago, Illinois, November 14, 1987.

The human perception of edibile desirability has little to do with actual nutritional fulfillments. Culture creates the system of communication among humans about edibility, toxicity, and repleteness in regard to food. Cultural pressures easily overrule physiological necessities, making it impossible for an individual from one culture to predict the food preferences of another culture.

Consider McDonald's entry into India. The company had to deal with (1) a market that is 60 percent vegetarian, (2) an aversion to either beef or pork among the minority meat eaters, (3) a hostility to frozen meat and fish, and (4) the general Indian fondness for spice with everything. To satisfy such tastes, McDonald's had to do more than provide the right burgers. The company serves vegetarian burgers as well as chicken and fish burgers, and makes sure that vegetarian burgers are cooked in a separate area in the kitchen using separate utensils. Sauces like *McMasala* and *McImli* are on offer to satisfy the Indian taste for spice. The company also introduced a spiced version of its fries.[22]

Although the trend is slowly shifting, drink preferences vary markedly across Europe: Germans still consume six times as much beer per capita as Italians, and the French six times as much wine per capita as the British.[23] And despite their geographic closeness, Japan and Korea couldn't have more different coffee markets. The average Japanese drinks 800 cups of coffee a year, a Korean about a quarter of that.[24] Marketing is also influenced by cultural customs in gift giving, which likewise vary from country to country. As explained by Kathleen Reardon, customs concerning gift giving are extremely important to understand. In some cultures, gifts are expected, and failure to present them is considered an insult, whereas in other countries, offering a gift is considered offensive. Business executives also need to know when to present gifts—on the initial visit or afterward; where to present gifts—in public or in private; what type of gift to present; what color it should be; and how many to present.

Gift giving is an important part of doing business in Japan. Exchanging gifts symbolizes the depth and strength of a business relationship to the Japanese. Gifts are usually exchanged at the first meeting. When presented with a gift, companies are expected to respond by giving a gift.

In sharp contrast, gifts are rarely exchanged in Germany and are usually not appropriate. Small gifts are fine, but expensive items are not a general practice.

Gift giving is not a normal custom in Belgium or the U.K., either, although in both countries flowers are a suitable gift if invited to someone's home. Even that is not as easy as it sounds. International executives must use caution to choose appropriate flowers. For example, avoid sending chrysanthemums (especially white) in Belgium and elsewhere in Europe since they are mainly used for funerals. In Europe, it is also considered bad luck to present an even number of flowers. Beware of white flowers in Japan where they are associated with death, and purple flowers in Mexico and Brazil.[25]

These descriptions are merely summaries; they do not encompass all trends, etiquettes, and traditions observed in the respective cultures. Each country warrants an indepth report to provide meaningful data for planning a thorough marketing strategy.

Cultural differences always affect decision making when it comes to the product and its price, as well as to the way it is distributed and promoted. Lack of familiarity with the business practices, social customs, and etiquette of a country can weaken a company's position in the market, prevent it from accomplishing its objectives, and ultimately lead to failure.[26]

The Product

Two similar products are introduced into a country. One does extremely well; the other flops. Why? Although the performance of a product/market depends on a variety of factors, in many cases *failure is directly traceable to cultural blunders*. For example, Kentucky Fried Chicken was received well in France (as in Germany and the U.K.), but McDonald's stumbled.[27] The British prefer a wood handle on their umbrella while we in the U.S. find the plastic handle satisfactory, a fact that umbrella manufacturers have learned to heed. Procter & Gamble's Head & Shoulders shampoo did well in the U.K., the Netherlands, and Germany, but flopped in France because in France dandruff is a socially embarrassing problem that nobody wants to admit having.

A product that has been highly profitable in the U.S. may not achieve the same success elsewhere, because the product attributes desired in the U.S. may not be desired in another part of the world. The Campbell Soup Company found out the hard way that the condensed soups so popular and acceptable in the U.S. were not liked in England. Accustomed to ready-to-eat soups, the English consumer found it hard to believe that water or milk could be added to soup without spoiling the taste.[28] Phillip Morris ran into difficulties because of taste differences among nations. One of its popular brands was a dismal flop in Canada despite adequate promotion. Canadians have a preference for Virginia-type tobacco blends, which are different from what the popular brand had to offer.[29]

Sometimes a product that is unacceptable in its U.S. form may succeed if it is adapted to the culture of the new market. Mister Donut's success in Japan is the result of a series of minute but sensible modifications. Their coffee cup is smaller and lighter, to fit the finger size of the average Japanese consumer. Even their donuts are a little smaller there than those in the U.S. Similarly, Japanese mothers found the Beechnut babyfood jar too big. After the jar was made smaller, the sales increased. After years of painstaking market research, P&G finally realized that Japanese parents are very concerned with keeping their babies clean, and they change their children's diapers far more often than Americans do. In response, P&G devised Ultra Pampers, a more-absorbent diaper that keeps the child drier and makes frequent changing a less-messy task. P&G also discovered that in land-starved Japan, shelf and closet space is almost as precious to housewives as their children, so it made the diapers thinner so the same number fit in a much smaller box. The popularity of the new diapers spread rapidly, and today Ultra Pampers is the market leader in Japan.[30]

Another good example is the Barbie doll of cultural adaptation. This all-American best-seller did not do very well in Japan for a long time. Finally, Mattel Toys, its creator, gave the manufacturing license to Takara, a Japanese company. Takara's own survey revealed that most Japanese girls—and their parents—thought the doll's breasts were too big and the legs unrealistically long. After correcting these minor defects, and converting the Barbie doll's blue eyes to dark brown, Takara started selling the same doll under the same brand name and concept, and found that its production could not keep up with the demand. Takara sold some 2 million Barbie dolls in just two years. According to a Takara executive, dolls in Japan are a reflection of what girls want to be. With the target customer group in Japan being eighth-graders, the doll had to look more Japanese than the original version.[31]

In India, the Barbie doll had a slightly different problem. In a conservative country like India, the concept of a boyfriend was unacceptable, so Ken did not accompany her. However, since brothers and sisters in India are much closer than in Western societies, Mattel created Mark as Barbie's brother for the Indian market.

The positioning of a product in different countries should be in line with the cultural traits of each society[32] (see International Marketing Highlight 9.8). Renault's strategy in different countries illustrates the point. In France, the Renault car was introduced as a little "supercar" that was fun to drive both on highways and within the city. In Germany, where auto buying is viewed as a serious matter, the emphasis was put on safety, modern engineering, and interior comfort. In Italy, road performance—road-handling capacity and acceleration—was stressed. In Finland, the focus was on solid construction and reliability. For Holland, the Renault car had to be redesigned, because the Dutch consider a small car cheap and mechanically inferior.[33] The same principle about positioning and culture applies to the personal computer. American computer companies learned early on that they could not simply target Europe as one market, but must court each country market separately, acknowledging cultural differences. The French, for example, are very nationalistic, looking for more French-made parts in the product. The German market focuses mostly on high quality.[34]

Cultural attitudes toward risk sometimes require different marketing tactics. In Mexico, where consumers are influenced by fatalism, the belief that humans have little control in life events, the use of product warranties to reduce the risk of negative outcomes associated with purchases is less effective than in the U.S.[35]

■■■■■■■■■ International Marketing Highlight 9.8 ■■■■■■■■■

The Marlboro Man

What do college students in different countries think when considering Marlboro cigarettes? A researcher at Northwestern University posed this question and put it to the test by researching college students in five countries: Brazil, Japan, Norway, Thailand, and the U.S. Small samples of students in each country participated in a word-association test by responding to the statement: "Smoking a Marlboro cigarette . . ."

Responses were sharply mixed. Thai students considered smoking a Marlboro cigarette to be relaxing. Norwegian students most closely linked smoking Marlboros to disease, and Brazilians associated the brand with pollution. U.S. students responded to "Smoking a Marlboro cigarette . . ." with words like "cowboy," "horse," and "macho"—all relating directly to Marlboro's longstanding advertising campaign. The Japanese associated smoking Marlboros with social occasions.

These different images point out that products and brands mean different things around the world because the cultural contexts in which they are interpreted vary greatly. This means that creative advertising needs to be adjusted to accommodate the specific cultural context in which it is placed. For example, because Japanese consumers associate Marlboro cigarettes with being sociable, it would be best for Marlboro advertisements in Japan to show the cowboy with other cowboys rather than by himself. In Thailand, where consumers perceive cigarettes to be suggestive of relaxation, it would be most effective to show the cowboy in a subdued context rather than chasing wild horses.

Source: Lenore Skenazy, "How Does Slogan Translate," *Advertising Age*, October 12, 1987, p. 84.

Distribution   The cultural dimensions of a nation make certain distribution arrangements more viable. For example, in the U.S., Sears, Roebuck & Co. merchandises a big percentage of products under its own brand name. In Mexico, however, Sears has done two things differently in order to respond to pride aspects in the local culture. First, it buys over 90 percent of its items from national manufacturers. Second, it carries U.S. national brands made in Mexico to cater to well-to-do customers who like to distinguish themselves by using U.S. brands.

Channels of distribution may need to be modified to suit local conditions. Avon uses door-to-door and other direct-selling methods in the U.S. with great success. Americans appreciate the opportunity to make buying decisions in the privacy of their homes or workplaces. Such arrangements, however, did not work abroad. European women considered calls by Avon representatives to be intrusions on their privacy, and the representatives felt uncomfortable as well.[36] The company faced a similar problem in Japan. To solve the problem, it had to reassign each saleswoman to her own neighborhood and social group, a milieu in which she already knew her customers or could get to know them easily.[37]

Another case of culture affecting the mapping of sales territories involved a French company in Africa. It decided to divide the sales territories based on market potential (respecting local administrative boundaries), something it had done successfully in the Western European market. This type of territory structure, however, did not allow for the fact that the African countries contained a number of tribes, each with a particular person authorized to buy in the community. The territory arrangements overlapped with these tribal areas and created a great deal of confusion in the assignment of sales responsibilities.[38]

Promotion

Promotion practices, particularly advertising, are perhaps most susceptible to cultural error. Examples abound where advertising copy and design were culturally repugnant and therefore totally ineffective. In Thailand the Warner-Lambert Company used its U.S. ad for Listerine showing a boy and a girl being affectionate with each other. This type of appeal was ineffective since the boy-girl relationship shown was ultra-modern and hence against the cultural norms of Thailand's conservative society. A slight modification—two girls talking about Listerine—had a positive effect on sales.[39]

Colgate Palmolive Company introduced its Cue toothpaste in France only to find out later that *cue* in French is a pornographic word.[40] Pepsi ran into difficulties in Germany for using its U.S. ad, "Come alive, you're in the Pepsi generation," which in German meant "Come alive out of the grave."[41] Pepsodent's promise of white teeth backfired in Southeast Asia, where betel nut chewing was an acceptable norm, and therefore, yellow teeth were taken for granted.[42] A P&G soap commercial showed a Japanese husband in the room as his wife was bathing. The Japanese considered it an invasion of privacy and distasteful.[43] An airline ad campaign urged Hispanics to fly *en cuero*. It is hard to figure out what the airline had in mind, given that the phrase means stark naked.[44]

Ajax's white tornado was not perceived as a symbol of power in many countries, Ultra Brite's sexy girl throwing kisses was ineffective in Belgium, and the company was forced to drop the theme "Give your mouth sex appeal."[45] Carlsberg had to add a third elephant to its label of Elephant beer for an ad in Africa since two elephants are a symbol of bad luck there.[46]

Usage of color in ads must be attuned to cultural norms as well. In Japan, as in many Asian countries, the color white is for mourning; purple is associated with death in many Latin American countries; and brown and gray are disliked in Nicaragua[47] (see International Marketing Highlight 9.9).

International Marketing Highlight 9.9

Taboos Around the World

- Never touch the head of a Thai or pass an object over it, as the head is considered sacred in Thailand. Likewise, never point the bottoms of the feet in the direction of another person in Thailand or cross your legs while sitting, especially in the presence of an older person.

- Avoid using triangular shapes in Hong Kong, Korea, or Taiwan, as the triangle is considered a negative shape in those countries.
- Remember that the number seven is considered bad luck in Kenya, good luck in Czech Republic, and has magical connotations in Benin.
- Red is a positive color in Denmark but represents witchcraft and death in many African countries.
- A nod means "no" in Bulgaria, and shaking the head from side to side means "yes."

Source: Business America, Vol. 112, no. 2 (Special Edition 1991): 26–27.

Pricing

The price that a customer is willing to pay for a product may depend more on its perceived than its actual value. Since the value of goods imported from a western country is often perceived as much higher than that of domestic products in developing countries, the imported goods often command an inflated price. A story is told of an East Indian who on a trip to England bought an expensive sweater for his wife from a London department store. He was disappointed to find, on closer inspection, after returning home, that the sweater had been manufactured in India. What had seemed a reasonable price for an English product was too high for a domestic one. Perceived value, not actual value, was the determinant of acceptable price.

An empirical investigation by Philippe Cattin and his colleagues showed that U.S. and French purchasing managers attached varying degrees of importance to products manufactured in different countries.[48] For example, *Made in England* appeared to be favorably perceived by the French, promising more luxurious and more inventive products, than *Made in the U.S.A.* On the other hand, *Made in Germany* products were more highly regarded by American than French consumers.

It would appear that in countries where the image of the exporting country is high, a premium price can be charged. However, where a national image is weak, an international business could do well to deemphasize "made in" information and perhaps seek market entry through a joint venture or some other form of close association with a domestic firm.

Cultural Analysis—The Primacy-of-Host-Country Viewpoint

The analysis of cultural differences is necessary for the formulation of international marketing strategy. Conceptually, cultural analysis may be based on any of the following three approaches: ethnocentrism, assimilation, and primacy-of-host-country viewpoint.

The *ethnocentrism approach* assumes, "We are the best." Many U.S. companies assume that what is good at home will work in foreign markets as well. The examples discussed in the previous section illustrate how ethnocentrism can lead to costly mistakes. The *assimilation approach* is somewhat similar, assuming that since the U.S. is a cultural melting pot, the cultural traits demonstrated in U.S. society are relevant anywhere. The third viewpoint, the *primacy-of-host-country approach*, bases decisions on the cultural traits of the host country. This approach considers domestic information inappropriate to successful operation in markets outside the U.S. The discussion that follows assumes the primacy-of-host-country viewpoint.

Assessment of Culture

An assessment of a country's culture for marketing's sake involves analyzing the people's attitudes, motivations, perceptions, and learning processes. Exhibit 9.2 summarizes more specifically the cultural determinants. The information contained in this exhibit attempts to relate cultural traits to marketing decisions. For example, simply knowing about the religion or morality of a culture is not enough. What must be analyzed is whether or not

EXHIBIT 9.2   Outline of Cross-Cultural Analysis of Consumer Behavior

1. **Determine relevant motivations in the culture.** What needs are fulfilled with this product in the minds of members of the culture? How are these needs presently fulfilled? Do members of this culture readily recognize these needs?

2. **Determine characteristic behavior patterns.** What patterns are characteristic of purchasing behavior? What forms of division of labor exist within the family structure? How frequently are products of this type purchased? What size packages are normally purchased? Do any of these characteristic behaviors conflict with behavior expected for this product? How strongly ingrained are the behavior patterns that conflict with those needed for distribution of this product?

3. **Determine what broad cultural values are relevant to this product.** Are there strong values about work, morality, religion, family relations, and so on, that relate to this product? Does this product connote attributes that are in conflict with these cultural values? Can conflicts with values be avoided by changing the product? Are there positive values in this culture with which the product might be identified?

4. **Determine characteristic forms of decision making.** Do members of the culture display a studied approach to decisions concerning innovations or an impulsive approach? What is the form of the decision process? Upon what information sources do members of the culture rely? Do members of the culture tend to be rigid or flexible in the acceptance of new ideas? What criteria do they use in evaluating alternatives?

5. **Evaluate promotion methods appropriate to the culture.** What role does advertising occupy in the culture? What themes, words, or illustrations are taboo? What language problems exist in present markets that cannot be translated into this culture? What types of salespeople are accepted by members of the culture? Are such salespeople available?

6. **Determine appropriate institutions for this product in the minds of consumers.** What types of retailers and intermediary institutions are available? What services do these institutions offer that are expected by the consumer? What alternatives are available for obtaining services needed for the product but not offered by existing institutions? How are various types of retailers regarded by consumers? What alternatives are available for obtaining services needed for the product but not offered by existing institutions? How are various types of retailers regarded by consumers? Will changes in the distribution structure be readily accepted?

Source: James F. Engel, Roger D. Blackwell, and David T. Kollat, *Consumer Behavior*, 3rd ed. (Hinsdale, IL: Dryden Press, 1978), p. 90.

the product slated to be introduced into the country has any direct or indirect connotations that conflict with the cultural patterns of the society. Similarly, an examination of advertising themes, phrases, words, or expressions should confirm viability of promotional decisions.

The cultural values of a nation may be studied through either observation or fieldwork. *Observation* requires living in a culture over a long period in order to become deeply involved in its pattern of living. *Fieldwork*, on the other hand, involves gathering information on a set of variables relative to the culture. Although the observation method may be more desirable for a fuller understanding of the culture, from the standpoint of business it is impractical. The study of culture in the realm of international marketing must be based on fieldwork.

One way to conduct the cultural analysis of a country for the purpose of making marketing decisions is to answer the specific marketing-related questions raised by Engel and his colleagues in Exhibit 9.2.

A different way of understanding foreign cultures is recommended by Edward T. Hall.[49] His framework, which he calls a *map of culture*, is a two-dimensional matrix containing different human activities, which he calls *primary message systems*. These activities are interaction, association, subsistence, bisexuality, territoriality, temporality, learning, play, defense, and exploitation. Exhibit 9.3 explains briefly the 10 primary message systems.

■■■■■■■■■■■■■ ■   **EXHIBIT 9.3**   Primary Message System of Edward Hall's Map of Culture

1. *Interaction.* The interaction with the environment through different modes such as speech and writing.
2. *Association.* The structure and organization of society and its various components.
3. *Subsistence.* The perspective of activities of individuals and groups that deal with livelihood and living.
4. *Bisexuality.* The differentiation of roles and functions along sex lines.
5. *Territoriality.* The possession, use, and defense of land and territory.
6. *Temporality.* The division and allocation of time and its use for various activities.
7. *Learning.* The patterns of transmitting knowledge.
8. *Play.* The process of enjoyment through relaxation and recreation.
9. *Defense.* The protection against natural and human forces in the environment.
10. *Exploitation.* The application of skills and technology to turn natural resources to people's needs.

Source: Excerpt from *The Silent Language* by Edward T. Hall, © 1959 by Edward T. Hall. Used by permission of Doubleday, a division of Bantam, Doubleday, Dell Publishing Group, Inc.

A person interested in learning about a culture need not study all 10 aspects, but by examining any one of them fully can gain an adequate understanding of the culture. Hall explains it this way:

> Since each [aspect] is enmeshed in the other, one can start the study of culture with any of the 10 and eventually come out with a complete picture. For example, to understand buyer behavior, a marketer could analyze the culture by examining the association aspect; association intersects with all other nine aspects just as they intersect with association. With each intersection, a variety of questions can be raised to gain cultural understanding. To illustrate the point, the intersection of association with learning may be examined by seeking answers to such questions as: How do different groups of the society learn about new things? Whose opinions are respected in each group? Similarly, the intersection of learning with association would be revealed in connection with such problems as how learning takes place through different sources in different groups.

The use of Hall's framework for international marketers is shown in Exhibit 9.4 in an analysis of the play activity for a toys and games company. Presumably, perspectives of play vary from one culture to another. To suit the marketing program to the cultural traits of the local market, Hall's framework creates 18 categories of questions (see Exhibit 9.4). For example, categories 13 and 14 deal with learning as it emerges in play and play as it leads to learning.

Hall's approach provides an overall perspective on the culture through analysis of one or two primary message systems. In relation to the needs of business, this system works well, because the time and expense for a comprehensive cultural perspective are not required. Only the particular element of the culture directly related to a particular international marketing decision needs to be analyzed.

Cultural Adaptation

Cultural adaptation refers to the making of business decisions appropriate to the cultural traits of the society. In other words, decision makers must ensure that native customs, traditions, and taboos will offer no constraint to implementation of the marketing plan.

Although the necessity for cultural adaptation is widely recognized, its practice is hindered by the tendency to use a **self-reference criterion** (SRC), i.e.: Whenever people are faced with unfamiliar situations, their own values are the measure for their understanding and response to the circumstances. For example, if someone in the U.S. is late for an appointment, that person will most likely feel guilty about it and apologize for being late—

EXHIBIT 9.4   Business Application of Edward Hall's Map of Culture

Intersections of Play and Other Primary Message Systems	Sample Questions Concerning Cultural Patterns Significant for Marketing Toys and Games
1. Interaction/play	How do people interact during play as regards competitiveness, instigation, or leadership?
2. Play/interaction	What games are played involving acting, role playing, or other aspects of real-world interaction?
3. Association/play	Who organizes play, and how do the organization patterns differ?
4. Play/association	What games are played about organization—for example, team competitions and games involving kings, judges, or leader-developed rules and penalties?
5. Subsistence/play	What are the significant factors regarding people such as distributors, teachers, coaches, or publishers who make their livelihood from games?
6. Play/subsistence	What games are played about work roles in society such as doctors, nurses, firemen?
7. Bisexuality/play	What are the significant differences between the sexes in the sports, games, and toys enjoyed?
8. Play/bisexuality	What games and toys involve bisexuality—for example, dolls, dressing up, dancing?
9. Territoriality/play	Where are games played, and what are the limits observed in houses, parks, streets, schools, and so forth?
10. Play/territoriality	What games are played about space and ownership—for example, Monopoly?
11. Temporality/play	At what ages and what times of the day and year are different games played?
12. Play/temporality	What games are played about and involving time—for example, clocks, speed tests?
13. Learning/play	What patterns of coaching, tuition, and training exist for learning games?
14. Play/learning	What games are played about and involving learning and knowledge—for example, quizzes?
15. Defense/play	What are the safety rules for games, equipment, and toys?
16. Play/defense	What war and defense games and toys are utilized?
17. Exploitation/play	What resources and technology are permitted or utilized for games and sport—for example, hunting and fishing rules, use of parks, cameras, vehicles, and so forth?
18. Play/exploitation	What games and toys about technology or exploitation are used—for example, scouting, chemical sets, microscopes?

Source: Stefan H. Robock and Kenneth Simmonds, *International Business and Multinational Enterprises*, 4th ed. (Homewood, IL: Irwin, 1989), p. 426.

the value of punctuality and the importance of time have been instilled. The same person visiting an Arab country will be unhappy and angry with an Arab businessperson who arrives late and fails even to apologize. But punctuality is not given the same priority in the Arab world as in the U.S. To the Arab, a 9:00 AM meeting means *about* 9:00 AM. Indeed, it may mean simply some time in the morning. This is only one example of how the tendency toward SRC acts as a stumbling block to cultural adaptation.

Framework for Adaptation

A four-step procedure is recommended for checking the influence of SRC in business adaptation:

- *Step 1*. Define the business problem or goal in terms of the cultural traits, habits, or norms of the U.S.
- *Step 2*. Define the business problem or goal in terms of the foreign cultural traits, habits, or norms. Make no value judgments.
- *Step 3*. Isolate the SRC influence in the problem, and examine it carefully to see how it complicates the problem.
- *Step 4*. Redefine the problem without the SRC influence, and solve for the optimum business goal situation.

To illustrate the implementation of this four-step procedure, consider this hypothetical question: What automobile would be appropriate for the Pakistani market?

Step 1. In the U.S., the automobile is a necessity for most people. Two cars per family is an accepted concept. Highway systems are designed for speeds of up to 80 miles per hour, but the legal limit for many highways is 65 miles per hour. Gasoline of high octane without lead is conveniently available. Consumers look for comforts in the automobile such as air conditioning, AM/FM radio, cruise control, and leg room. Manufacturing techniques are sophisticated, and foreign exchange problems are unknown. Purchasers have a choice of buying either domestic or foreign-made automobiles. Introduction of yearly models of different cars is an accepted practice. Imports have achieved a significant share of the U.S. market and continue to challenge the viability of the domestic industry.

Step 2. Pakistan is a developing country. Over 60 percent of the people are illiterate and live in villages with muddy roads. Even in urban areas, the lack of modern roads restricts speed to 35–40 miles per hour. Gasoline is very expensive—the equivalent of almost $5 for a U.S. gallon—and it is only 60 octane. The country is committed to a thoroughly Islamic way of life. Islamic thinking is finding its way into economic, political, educational, and family life. The western attitude toward acquisition of goods and toward materialistic life is frowned upon. The rich have to live inconspicuously. The bicycle is the major mode of individual transportation and may be compared to having a good used car in the U.S. Some people, a little more well-to-do, drive scooters, smaller versions of the motorcycle. Automobile ownership is a symbol of status and achievement. Ownership of an imported car is the equivalent of owning a Mercedes in the U.S. With per capita GNP of $480 (1998 estimate), discretionary income is minimal.

Step 3. Review of Steps 1 and 2 brings out the significant differences between the two countries. Even the cheapest American car, say, a Geo, would not match Pakistan's needs. In brief, an automobile manufacturer interested in entering Pakistan may not be able to successfully penetrate the market simply by modifying a U.S. model. Pakistan's needs call for a new product concept.

Step 4. The company seeking to enter the Pakistan market will be obliged to design an entirely new car. Such a car should be simple in all aspects: lightweight; few, if any, castings; and no compound body design; capable of giving very high mileage, say, 80–100 miles per gallon, with cruising speeds up to 40 miles per hour. The car could simply be made of scrap iron with a low-powered engine and no frills. Such a car should be manufactured using local materials with minimum dependence on imported technology or parts. In other words, foreign exchange requirements of the project should be minimal. Overall, the price for the car would have to be around $4,000.

Pakistan is not the only country that needs such a car. A large majority of developing countries offer potential opportunities for a product of this type. Unfortunately SRC criteria, so deeply ingrained among western auto manufacturers, have interfered with the development of an automobile for poorer nations.

Areas of Adaptation

Essentially, there are three areas of foreign business adaptation: product, institutional, and individual. The *product* may be marketed abroad as is; or it may be modified to fit the foreign country's climate, electrical specifications, color preferences, and the like; or it may be completely redesigned to match local requirements—a $5,000 automobile for the developing countries would be an example. *Institutional* behavior includes adaptation of the organization and business interactions to match the host's perspective. Thus, the U.S. firm in Spain might allow the workers time for a siesta during the day.

Most important, the adaptation of *individuals'* responses to foreign situations should strive to be free of SRC. Such adaptation may be required in all regards—the meaning of time, social behavior, play behavior, family interactions, and more. For example, adaptation may require that the female spouse of a U.S. executive not accompany him to a dinner party in an Islamic country. Unfortunately, in international situations, each culture is so deeply imbued with its own values that only what is normally seen and done appears appropriate and right.

Appropriate adaptive behavior is necessary to the successful conduct of foreign business, but adaptation should not be misinterpreted to mean that a person should adopt the foreign country's attitudes and traits for his or her own. Rather, one should, by inhibiting SRC, gain understanding and develop a spirit of tolerance and appreciation of different cultures. Neglect of cultural factors will at best limit marketing success and at worst lead to failure.

Cultural Change

International marketers must not only become familiar with the culture of a prospective market and then orient the marketing mix accordingly, they must also be prepared for the fact that over time *cultures do change*.

This characteristic of culture brings up interesting possibilities. Products and services that were at one time acceptable may become unacceptable at a later time because of cultural change. For example, back in the 1950s the filter cigarette was rejected in many Southeast Asian countries because its basic for-health's-sake promotion over regular cigarettes made no sense in countries where the average life span was 30 years. After 10 years, the filter cigarette slowly began to gain more acceptance. To an extent, the shift in attitude toward this product may be attributed to cultural change.

Basis of Cultural Change

Different anthropologists specify different reasons for cultural change. Although it may be disputed, one way of looking at cultural change is through economic development linked to Maslow's hierarchy-of-needs theory. Maslow ranked five human needs from lowest to highest, with lowest needs being the ones that people try to satisfy first: *physiological needs* (food, water, shelter, sex); *safety needs* (protection, security, stability); *social needs* (affection, friendship, acceptance); *ego needs* (prestige, success, self-esteem); and last, *the need for self-actualization* (self-fulfillment).[50]

Maslow's theory as applied to cultural change goes this way: As a country begins to move from a subsistence economy, where fulfillment of physiological needs has been the major goal, to a situation where basic needs are easily achievable, new needs take precedence. This change forces cultural adjustments. In other words, as the economic well-being of a society satisfies one level of needs, it gives rise to new needs whose satisfaction requires cultural change.

Consider the role of an Asian homemaker. In a village economy, she would be fully confined to her home. However, a job for her husband in a factory in a nearby city enables the family to move to town. This move assures the family of basic needs fulfillment. There will be no more dependence on the farm for survival, but instead a weekly check. At this time, safety needs become important. Safety requires buying groceries at the factory store as soon as they are available. In many developing countries items such as cooking oil, sugar, and bar soap are often in short supply. Thus, while the husband is at work, the wife must shop. This new role for the wife represents a cultural change that results from economic prosperity. No longer are her activities confined within the home; now she can go out alone to shop, something that would have been culturally prohibited before.

Whether all aspects of a culture change when a single aspect changes is a question that may be answered by referring to Hall's classification of cultural aspects into formal, informal, and technical.[51] *Formal* aspects constitute the core of a culture. They are the most deeply rooted and are extremely difficult to change. Formal aspects are taught as absolute rights and wrongs. Nonobservance of formal aspects cannot be forgiven.

Informal aspects are traits that one learns by being a member of the society. Everyone is supposed to be aware of these aspects. If an informal aspect is not adhered to, an expression of disapproval or concern would be shown, but accommodation is feasible in relation to informal aspects.

Technical aspects are transmitted in the form of instruction and have reasons behind them. Change can be most easily accomplished in technical cultural aspects. So long as change can be reasoned in a logical fashion, no emotions stand in the way.

The definition of formal, informal, and technical cultural aspects will vary from country to country. For example, take the case of cigarette smoking among middle-class teenage girls. In India this matter would be concerned with a formal aspect of the culture and completely rejected. In Latin America it would be in conflict with an informal aspect of the culture. While parents might not like their daughters smoking, they might tolerate it after registering their disapproval. In Germany and Sweden a young girl's smoking could be categorized as a technical aspect. Parents might, on technical grounds, oppose smoking for health reasons. Once it is agreed that the cigarettes will be low-tar, there might be no objection to the girl's smoking.

MNCs as Agents of Change

A family's move from village to town, from farm work to factory work, illustrates how industrialization forces cultural change. A country may industrialize by exploiting its indigenous resources. But in the modern era, an important source of industrialization is the MNC. An MNC rapidly and effectively transfers features of one cultural society to certain sectors of another, perhaps very different society. In this process, it is uniquely capable of forcing cultural change.

MNCs transmit home country values in two ways: (1) through the vast network of affiliates, which introduce, demonstrate, and disseminate new behaviors while increasing and shaping the manufacturing sector of host countries, and (2) through the business service structure, including advertising and business education.

Millions of people in host countries work for foreign affiliates of MNCs. In early 1998 50 million people were directly employed by MNC affiliates in other countries. Today that number is even higher. These people, while living in their own culture, spend their working lives in a foreign environment. Foreign affiliates are in most cases highly integrated with the parent corporation. They are subject to close headquarters control through a variety of mechanisms, notably majority equity ownership, managerial control in key decision areas, and the presence of expatriate managers among the senior employees of the affiliate. Thus, the working life of the affiliate to a large extent reflects the values common in the corridors of the parent corporation. These affiliate employees may initiate, learn, and internalize new values and become channels to further diffuse these values in the host country culture at large.

The advertising media of MNCs is another avenue of transmitting cultural values in host countries. The move of manufacturing companies to foreign countries is frequently accompanied by a simultaneous move by advertising agencies. Of the top six advertising agencies in the world, five are based in the U.S. Therefore, MNC affiliates in their marketing efforts abroad have easy access to the agencies handling parent company business. These foreign agencies transmit and reinforce attitudes that fit nicely with the requirements of the MNCs. Change in the acceptance of advertising has been influenced by American practices. Today most European countries permit commercials on their broadcasting networks.

The role of advertising in the context of international marketing was summarized well by Paul C. Harper, Jr.:

> It should be noted that advertising does more than merely sell products and form consumption patterns; it informs, educates, changes attitudes, and builds images. For purposes of illustration, we may quote the statement of a marketing manager who answered the basic marketing ques-

tion, "What do we sell?" in the following way: "Never a product, always an idea." In other words, the function of advertising agencies is to seek "to influence human behavior in ways favorable to the interests of their clients," to "indoctrinate" them.[52]

Another interesting development is the spread worldwide of U.S. business education. Business schools, especially the Harvard Graduate School of Business Administration, have trained thousands of foreign students through professional education in business. Additionally, many U.S. business schools have aided in the establishment of similar institutions in host countries. The Harvard Business School alone has helped Switzerland, Japan, France, Turkey, India, the U.K., and a number of other countries in creating institutions for offering advanced education in business. In all these schools, staff and alumni from Harvard are an influential, if not dominant, group within the faculty, and in most cases, teaching and reading reflect a decidedly U.S. business philosophy. The coming generation of top managers in Europe, all more or less similarly trained to put the commercial interests of their enterprises above other considerations, are increasingly divorced from their particular national framework and reflect to various degrees the business philosophy of the top U.S. schools.[53]

These students, whether actually instructed in the U.S. or their homeland, generate and support ideas, values, and viewpoints that conform to the cultural traits revered in U.S. business circles. At the product/market level, they demand products and services in market categories where international marketers have traditionally had more experience. Included is a range of products from nutritious and more hygienically packaged goods to various kinds of household furnishings, appliances, and entertainment-oriented products. Also, new products are more easily accepted by people who have been educated by U.S. institutions.

Summary

The cultural traits of a country have a profound effect on people's lifestyle and behavior patterns, and these are reflected in the marketplace. *Culture* is a complex term, and its precise definition is difficult. Broadly defined, it refers to all learned behavior of all facets of life and living transmitted from generation to generation. Cultural differences among countries can be striking or subtle and should be zealously examined by the international marketer.

The study of culture includes material life (the means and artifacts people use for livelihood); social interactions between individuals and groups in formal and informal situations; language (spoken/written words, symbols, and physical expressions that people use to communicate); aesthetics (art, drama, music); religion and faith; pride and prejudices; and ethics and mores. Cultural traits account for such differences among nations as color preferences, concept of time, and authority patterns. For example, in western countries a bride's gown is usually white, but in the Far East women wear white during mourning.

Cultural differences have impact on marketing decisions regarding product, price, distribution, and promotion. One framework for analyzing culture is provided by Engel's questions used to seek information on the cultural differences of national societies. Another is Hall's cultural map, with its two-dimensional matrix using 10 human activities to generate a cultural analysis.

To conduct business successfully across national boundaries, marketers must adapt their products and promotion to local cultures. A four-step process for facilitating cultural adaptation guides the international marketer to avoid the influence of self-reference criteria (SRC). The tendency toward SRC reinforces the idea that what is good at home is good—and relevant—anywhere else as well. This type of thinking poses a big stumbling block to cultural adaptation.

A discussion of culture must also deal with cultural change. Cultures do change, though change is usually slow. Industrialization is an important factor behind cultural change. MNCs, through involvement in the industrialization process, serve as change agents in foreign cultures. Their worldwide networks of affiliates transmit the values of the parent corporation's culture. Cultural change also takes place as a result of advertising media and the internationalization of business education.

Review Questions

1. What elements of culture may be most relevant to marketing? Why?
2. How might a marketer of cosmetics assess significant cultural traits for his or her business in the Muslim world?
3. Americans share a variety of common traits with the English. Based on this assumption, will it be safe to conclude that the two societies have a more or less common culture?
4. Illustrate how an international marketer can use Hall's map of culture.
5. How has the spread of professional education in business affected local culture?
6. Describe how MNCs influence host country culture through their network of affiliates.
7. How could aesthetics, as an element of culture, affect marketing decisions in the international context?
8. Should an international marketer deliberately attempt to seek cultural change in a society?
9. Discuss this statement: "It is economic not cultural differences that count. Given the economic environment and income levels of the U.S., people in any country, Muslim or Christian, would follow the U.S. lifestyle and materialistic living."

Creative Questions

1. China has a large population, and its economy is booming. However, in 1998 cola consumption in the country was only 10 servings (8 oz. per serving) per capita. For a comparison, the consumption in the U.S. in the same year was 360 servings per capita. Apparently, there is a huge potential for soft drinks in China. Are there any cultural barriers that may become hurdles in realizing this potential? Discuss the nature of these barriers, and explain how they could affect cola consumption.
2. What cultural adaptations are required to make U.S. cars more acceptable in Japan?

Endnotes

1. "Making Do During Ramadan," *Business Week*, April 8, 1991, p. 18A.

2. Edward B. Tylor, *Primitive Culture* (London: John Murray, 1871), p. 1.

3. Edward T. Hall, *Beyond Culture* (Garden City, NY: Anchor Books, 1977), p. 16. *Also see* Edward T. Hall, "Learning the Arabs' Silent Language," *Psychology Today*, August 1979, p. 54.

4. Subhash, C. Jain and Lewis R. Tucker, "The Influence of Culture on Strategic Constructs in the Process of Globalization: An Empirical Study of North America and Japanese MNCs." *International Business Review*, 4, no. 1 (1995): 19–37.

5. Abraham Pizam and Arie Reichel, "Cultural Determinants of Managerial Behavior," *Management International Review* 2 (1977): 66.

6. Martin J. Gannon, *Understanding Global Cultures* (Thousand Oaks, CA: 1994), pp. 3–18.

7. Karen Elliott House, "Saudi Marriage Mores Are Shaken as Women Seek a Stronger Voice," *The Wall Street Journal*, June 8, 1981, p. 1. *Also see* "Marriage-Minded Japanese Turn to Mama," *The Asian Wall Street Journal Weekly*, August 24, 1981, p. 13.

8. Chin Tiong Tan and James McCullough, "Ethnicity and Family Buying Behavior." Paper presented at the Annual Meeting of

the Academy of International Business, Cleveland, Ohio, October 1984.

9. Robert T. Green, Bronislaw J. Verhage, and Isabell C. M. Cunningham, "Household Purchasing Decisions," *Working Paper* (Austin, TX: Univ. of Texas, 1993).

10. David A. Ricks, "How to Avoid Business Blunders Abroad," *Business*, April–June 1984, pp. 3–11.

11. David A. Ricks, "International Business Blunders: An Update," *B&E Review*, January–March 1988, p. 11.

12. Vern Terpstra, *International Marketing* (Hinsdale, IL: Dryden Press, 1983). *Also see* Robert Howells, "Culture Clash: An American's Guide to English," *The Wall Street Journal*, October 30, 1984, p. 34.

13. Ricks, "International Business Blunders," p. 12.

14. Susan Barciela, "Know the Customs of the Country," *The Hartford Courant*, March 14, 1994, p. 7.

15. Gillian Rice, "Philosophy and Practice of Islamic Ethics: Implications for Doing Business in Muslim Countries," Working Paper #96-5 (Glendale, AZ: The American Graduate School of International Management, no date).

16. "Before Buying Insurance, Consult This Calendar," *The Asian Wall Street Journal Weekly*, October 10, 1988, p. 8.

17. *See* Youssef M. Ibrahim, "Revolutionary Islam of Iran Is Neutralized by Policies of Bahrain," *The Wall Street Journal*, August 11, 1987, p. 1; and Karen Elliott House, "Rising Islamic Fervor Challenges the West, Every Moslem Ruler," *The Wall Street Journal*, August 7, 1987, p. 1.

18. Fred Seidel, "Comparative Business Ethics in Europe," Working Paper, E.M. Lyon, France, 1999. Also see: Alexander L. Nill, "Marketing Ethics in a Cross-Cultural Environment: A Communicative Approach," Discussion Paper series No. 99–1, Thunderbird Research Center, 1999.

19. Helmut Becker and David J. Fritzsche, "A Comparison of the Ethical Behavior of American, French and German Managers," *Columbia Journal of World Business*, Winter 1987, pp. 87–96.

20. Lee Smith, "Korea's Challenge to Japan," *Fortune*, February 6, 1984, p. 94.

21. John L. Graham, "The Influence of Culture on Business Negotiations," *Journal of International Business Studies*, Spring 1985, pp. 81–96.

22. "Spice with Everything," *The Economist*, November 22, 1997, p. 81.

23. *The McKinsey Quarterly*, No. 4, 1991, p. 6. *Also see* Philip R. Harris and Robert T. Moran, *Managing Cultural Differences*, 2nd ed. (Houston, TX: Gulf Publishing Co., 1987).

24. Damon Darlin, "Coke, Nestlé Launch First Coffee Drink," *The Wall Street Journal*, October 25, 1994, p. 42.

25. *See* Kathleen Reardon, *International Business Gift-Giving Customs* (Jamesville, WI: The Parker Pen Company, 1981). *Also see* Michael Lynn, George M. Zinkham, and Judy Harris, "Consumers Tipping: A Cross-Country Study," *Journal of Consumer Research* 20 (1993): 478–488.

26. Tevfik Dalgic and Ruud Neijblom, "International Marketing Blunders Revisited—Some lessons for Managers," *Journal of International Marketing* 4, no. 1 (1995): 81–92.

27. Susan Douglas and Bernard Dubois, "Looking at the Cultural Environment for International Marketing Opportunities," *Columbia Journal of World Business*, Winter 1977, p. 102. *Also see* Ian R. Wilson, "American Success Story—Coca-Cola in Japan." in Mark B. Winchester, ed., *The International Essays for Business Decision Makers* (Dallas: The Center for International Business, 1980), pp. 119–127.

28. "The $30 Million Lesson," *Sales Management*, March 1967, pp. 31–38. *Also see* Henry Lane, "Systems, Values, and Action: An Analytic Framework for Intercultural Management Research," *Management International Review* 3 (1980): 61–70.

29. Robert D. Buzzell, "Can You Standardize Multinational Marketing?" *Harvard Business Review*, November–December 1968, pp. 102–113.

30. *Fortune*, November 6, 1989, p. 86. *Also see* Patriya Tansuhaj, et al., "Across National Examination of Innovation Resistance," *International Marketing Review* 8, no. 3 (1991): 7–20.

31. Kenichi Ohmae, *Triad Power* (New York: The Free Press, 1985), pp. 102–104.

32. Jennifer L. Aaker and Bernd Schmitt, "The Influence of Culture on the Self-Expressive Use of Brands," CIBER Working Paper, No. 98-27. Anderson Graduate School of Management, UCLA.

33. Susan Douglas and Bernard Dubois, "Looking at the Cultural Environment for International Marketing Opportunities," *Columbia Journal of World Business*, Winter 1977, pp. 106–107.

34. L. Erik Calonius, "As a Market for PCS, Europe Seems as Hot as the U.S. Is Not," *The Wall Street Journal*, August 19, 1985, p. 1.

35. Robert J. Hoover, Robert T. Green, and Joel Saegart, "A Cross-National Study of Perceived Risk," *Journal of Marketing*, July 1978, pp. 102–108.

36. Susan Douglas and Bernard Dubois, "Looking at the Cultural Environment for International Marketing Opportunities," *Columbia Journal of World Business*, Winter 1977, p. 107. *Also see* Erdener Kaynak and Lionel A. Mitchell, "Cultural Barriers to the Full-Scale Acceptance of Supermarkets in Less-Developed Countries," a paper presented at the Annual Meeting of the Academy of International Business, New Orleans, October 1980.

37. Gary A. Knight, "International Marketing Blunders by American Firms in Japan—Some Lessons for Management," *Journal of International Marketing* 3, no. 4 (1995): 107–129.

38. Douglas and Dubois, "Looking at the Cultural Environment."

39. R. S. Diamon, "Managers Away From Home," *Fortune*, August 15, 1969, p. 50.

40. Howe Martyn, *International Business—Principles and Problems* (New York: Collier-Macmillan, 1964), p. 78.

41. *Advertising Age*, May 9, 1960, p. 75.

42. Matt Miller and Sundeep Chakravarti, "For Indians, a 2,000 Year-Old Habit of Chewing Red Goo Is Hard to Break," *The Wall Street Journal*, May 12, 1987, p. 28.

43. *Fortune*, November 6, 1989, p. 86.

44. "Catch As Catch Can," *World* 2 (1992): 2.

45. S. Watson Dunn, "Effect of National Identity on Multinational Promotional Strategy in Europe," *Journal of Marketing*, October 1976, pp. 54–55.

46. J. Douglas McConnell, "The Economics of Behavioral Factors on the Multinational Corporation," in Fred C. Allvine, ed., *Combined Proceedings* (Chicago: American Marketing Association, 1971), p. 264. *Also see* Arndt Sorge and Malcom Warner, "Culture, Management and Manufacturing Organization: A Study of British and German Firms," *Management International Review* 1 (1981): 35–48.

47. Charles Winick, "Anthropology's Contribution to Marketing," *Journal of Marketing*, July 1961, p. 59. *Also see* D. E. Allen, "Anthropological Insights into Customer Behavior," *European Journal of Marketing* 5 (1971): 45–47.

48. Philippe Cattin, Alain Jolibert, and Colleen Lohnes, "A Cross-Cultural Study of 'Made-in' Concepts," *The Journal of International Business Studies*, Winter 1982, pp. 131–142. *Also see* Victor V. Cordell, "Competitive Context and Price as Moderators of Country of Origin Preferences," *Journal of the Academy of Marketing Science*, Spring 1991, pp. 123–128.

49. Edward T. Hall, *The Silent Language* (Garden City, NY: Doubleday, 1959), pp. 61–81.

50. *See* Abraham H. Maslow, *Motivation and Personality* (New York: Harper & Row, 1954).

51. Hall, *The Silent Language*.

52. Paul C. Harper, Jr., "The Agency Business in 1980," *Advertising Age*, November 29, 1978, p. 35.

53. *See* Robert S. Greenberger and Ian Johnson, "Chinese Who Studied in U.S. Undercut Dogmas at Home," *The Wall Street Journal*, November 3, 1997, p. A24.

CHAPTER 10

Political

Environment

After studying this chapter, you should be able to

■ Describe how political situations affect international marketing decisions.

■ Identify sources of political problems.

■ Discuss different ways that governments may intervene in the affairs of foreign firms.

■ Explain how the political perspectives of a country can be examined.

■ Compare alternative strategies a company may pursue in response to political intervention.

A thorough review of the political environment of a country must precede commitment to a new market there. A rich foreign market may not warrant entry if the political environment is characterized by instability and uncertainty. Political changes and upheavals may occur after an international marketer has made a commitment and has an established business. The revolution in Iran, for instance, exposed U.S. companies to potential losses of $1 billion and drove home the lesson that the political situation in a country must be reviewed on a continuing basis.

Political environment connotes diverse happenings such as civil difficulties (for example, the conflict between the rival tribes in the African country of Sudan); acts of terrorism against businesses (for example, kidnappings and arson); and conflicts between countries in a particular region, which may be one-time occurrences like the war between India and China or perennial problems like the enmity between the People's Republic of China and Taiwan.

Political stability has been found to be one of the crucial variables that companies weigh when considering going overseas. If risks of violence, expropriation, restriction of operations, or restrictions on repatriation of capital and remittances of profits are high in a particular country, it is necessary to know how to monitor that country's ongoing political situation. This chapter examines the effects of political conflicts and difficulties in foreign countries on overseas business and discusses ways to analyze politics and measure risk. Strategic responses to political change available to multinational marketers also are covered.

Politics and Marketing

A few years ago the French president François Mitterrand invited Apple Computer executives to lunch at his residence, Élysée Palace. The Apple executives jumped at the invitation, since for months they had been trying to sell their personal computers to the French government. The French government had authorized a $156 million purchase of teaching computers for the French school system, but Apple's foreign citizenship had hindered its efforts to get a piece of the order.

During the private, two-hour lunch, with a translator present, the Apple executives praised the government's computer program and offered to help in any way they could. But President Mitterrand rebuffed them. Later one aide said that the president had invited the Apple executives to discuss technological cooperation with French companies, not the educational computer purchase program.[1]

How Apple tried, and failed, to get a significant share of the computer order is a revealing tale of international marketing and politics. The total order, for 120,000 microcomputers, was the biggest single purchase of educational computers in Europe and part of an ambitious campaign to teach almost everybody in France how to use computers. Although Apple at that time was the largest vendor of professional microcomputers in France, when the list of suppliers for the new program was announced, Apple received no order.

The head of Apple's subsidiary near Paris, a Frenchman, blamed the company's exclusion on lobbying by competitors and Apple's U.S. nationality: "The color of our passport is wrong."

On hearing about Apple's difficulties, the U.S. government complained to France about what it considered the unfair handling of the microcomputer order, raising the possibility of retaliatory moves in U.S. government contracting procedures. Other than registering its annoyance, the U.S. government did not pursue the matter, perhaps for political reasons.

Whether such nationalistic buying got French students the best equipment is a matter of debate. Yet this event clearly brings out the political underpinnings of international marketing.

The political perspectives of both home and host countries are inextricably involved in marketing decisions.[2] Certainly U.S. politics have significantly affected the U.S. automotive industry. Stringent requirements such as fuel efficiency standards have burdened the industry in several ways. On the other hand, governments around the world help the competitiveness of their domestic industries through various fiscal and monetary measures. Such political support can play a key role in an industry's search for markets abroad.

The U.S. auto industry would benefit from U.S. government concessions favoring U.S. automotive exports. European countries rely on *value-added taxes (VATs)* to help their industries. These taxes are applied to all levels of manufacturing transactions up to and including the final sale to the user, unless the final sale is for export, in which case the taxes are rebated, thus effectively reducing the price in international commerce. Japan imposes a *commodity tax* on selected lines of products, including automobiles. In the event of export, the commodity tax is waived. The U.S. has no corresponding arrangement. Thus, when a new automobile is shipped from the U.S. to Japan, it receives no rebate or relief of its U.S. taxes upon export and also must bear the cost of the Japanese commodity tax (15 or 20 percent depending on the size of the vehicle) when it is sold in Japan[3] (see International Marketing Highlight 10.1).

The competition facing U.S. manufacturers, therefore, both at home and in international markets, is potent and resourceful. Moreover, a number of these overseas competitors are wholly or partly state-owned and thus respond to the direction of their governments, which depend heavily on their export business for the maintenance of employment and the earning of foreign exchange. This fact makes politics profoundly important.

The ways in which politics may affect international marketing are varied. For example, in January 1985, Ford Motor Company divested itself of its auto operations in South Africa to take a 40 percent minority position.[4] At about the same time, Japan liberalized tobacco imports by lifting restrictions on price, distribution, and the number of retail outlets that can handle their products, thus encouraging foreign suppliers to intensify their marketing efforts.[5] In July 1985, Mexico approved the long delayed, once rejected, 100 percent IBM-owned microcomputer plant to encourage more foreign investment.[6] After waiting for several years, toward the end of 1988, PepsiCo got the Indian government's approval for a joint venture there.[7] In 1991, after much politicking, the French government permitted IBM to link up with France's state-owned computer maker, Groupe Bull, to develop high-speed RISC computer technology.[8]

International Marketing Highlight 10.1

Politics of Smoking

The federal government officially discourages cigarette smoking in the U.S. But if people in other countries are going to smoke anyway, why shouldn't they puff away on American tobacco?

Armed with this logic, the Reagan administration strong-armed Japan, South Korea, and Taiwan to dismantle their government-sanctioned tobacco monopolies. This opened lucrative markets and created such growth for U.S. cigarette makers that skyrocketing Asian sales did much to offset the decline at home.

However, Thailand, with a government tobacco monopoly of its own, has been fighting U.S. pressure to open up, and U.S. tobacco companies approached the Bush administration to take up trade sanctions against the Thais. That raises many questions about U.S. trade policy, including: Should Washington use its muscle to promote a product overseas that it acknowledges is deadly? Are trade disputes to be decided by lawyers and bureaucrats on the basis of commercial regulations, or should health and safety experts get into the act? Should the U.S. use trade policy to make the world healthier, just as it does to save whales, punish Cuba, or promote human rights?

Source: Business Week, October 9, 1989, p. 61.

Conceptually, multinational enterprises are affected by politics in three areas: (1) the pattern of ownership in the parent company or the affiliate, (2) the direction and nature of growth of the affiliate, and (3) the flow of product, technology, and managerial skills within the companies of the group. Take the case of China. The impact of politics on the strategies adopted by MNCs there leads to one important conclusion: the strategic choices made by MNC affiliates are a response more to political environment than to the interaction of market forces or to technological innovation. In other words, the government can substantially influence the strategy of MNC affiliates in ways that were thought impossible even a few years ago.

In India many MNC affiliates had to diversify into areas where neither the parent company nor the affiliate had the core capabilities. Competence ceased to be an important factor in strategy formulation compared with the need to comply with political directives and regulations. In general, the transfer of product and technology from the parent company in order to exploit new markets in the host country meets with obstruction from the government unless the technology is in the areas specified by regulation.

Sources of Political Problems

Exhibit 10.1 shows that the two main sources of political problems for firms doing business in foreign countries are political sovereignty and political conflict.

Political Sovereignty

Political sovereignty refers to a country's desire to assert its authority over foreign business through various sanctions. Such sanctions are regular and evolutionary, and therefore predictable. An example is increases in taxes over foreign operations. Many of the developing countries impose restrictions on foreign business to protect their independence (economic domination is often perceived as leading to political subservience). These countries are jealous of their political freedom and want to protect it at all costs, even if it means going at a slow economic pace and without the help of MNCs. Thus, the political sovereignty problem exists mainly in developing countries.

The industrialized nations, whose political sovereignty has been secure for a long time, require a more open policy for the economic realities of today's world. Today governments are expected simultaneously to curb unemployment, limit inflation, redistribute income, build up backward regions, deliver health services, and avoid abusing the environment. These wide-ranging objectives make developed countries seek foreign technology, use foreign capital and foreign raw materials, and sell their specialties in foreign markets. The net result is that these countries have found themselves exchanging guarantees for mutual access to one another's economies. In brief, among the developed countries, multinationalism of business is politically acceptable and economically desirable.

Political Conflict

Many countries in different parts of the world undergo *political conflict* of various sorts—turmoil, internal war, and conspiracy that can be irregular, revolutionary, and/or discontinuous. *Turmoil* refers to instant upheaval on a massive scale against an established regime (for example, the Islamic fundamentalists' mass protest against the shah of Iran). *Internal*

EXHIBIT 10.1   Politics and Foreign Business

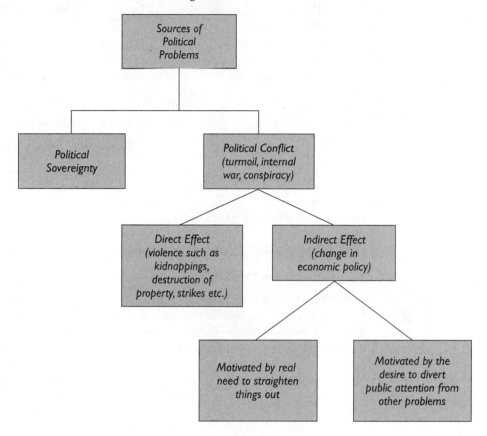

war means large-scale, organized violence against a government, such as guerrilla warfare (for example, Vietnam's actions in Cambodia). *Conspiracy* represents an instant, planned act of violence against those in power (for example, the assassination of Egyptian President Anwar Sadat).

Political conflict may or may not have an impact on business. For example, while the ouster of the shah of Iran incurred heavy losses for U.S. business there, the murder of Anwar Sadat made no difference to international business in Egypt at that time.

Political change sometimes leads to a more favorable business climate. For example, after the Peronist regime was overthrown in Argentina, the new government's policy was so favorable toward multinationals that the previously nationalized firms were returned to their owners. Similarly, Sukarno's departure from the Indonesian scene improved the business climate there, as did Nkrumah's absence from Ghana. After the assassination of Prime Minister Rajiv Gandhi in 1991, India's policy became highly favorable for international business. Suddenly U.S. multinationals found India an attractive place to do business.

It is important to make a distinction between political risk and political conflict. Political conflict in a country may lead to unstable conditions, but those conditions may or may not affect business. Therefore, political risk may or may not result from political unrest. Businesses must analyze each occurrence of political conflict and assess the likelihood of its impact on business.[9] Consider the case of the Philippines. During 1988 Communist threats posed insurmountable problems for foreign companies, although the economy had been doing well. For example, Dole's banana plantation there was attacked and two warehouses destroyed. Yet, in the interest of long-term opportunity, Dole officials refused to take any drastic steps.[10]

Sometimes the conflict is in response to a particular political event that subsides with time, such as when disgruntled French farmers ransacked a Coca-Cola plant in a series of demonstrations brought on in part by U.S. pressure on Europe to reduce agricultural subsidies.[11]

The effect of political conflict on business may be direct or indirect. *Direct effects* would be violence against the firms in such forms as kidnapping an executive, damaging company property, striking, and the like. Overall, direct effects are usually temporary and do not result in huge losses (see International Marketing Highlight 10.2). *Indirect effects* occur because of changes in government policy. Such changes may come from a new attitude on the part of an existing government or from a new government. The changes may be motivated by a sincere desire to straighten things out or simply to divert public attention from other domestic problems plaguing the country.

International Marketing Highlight 10.2

Executives in Peru Don't Leave Home without It

Herbert Dunn, a former police officer and SWAT-team member in the U.S., came to Peru in 1984 as a security consultant. He now teaches local executives how to defend themselves in a terrorist attack—a common occurrence in Peru.

With two major terrorist groups and a variety of smaller ones carrying out bombings, killings, and kidnappings, security is an obsession here. In 1990 alone, political violence claimed 3,384 lives—more than were lost in Lebanon's civil war in 1990—and caused material damage estimated by one research firm at $3 billion. That's about 15 percent of Peru's gross domestic product.

Many top businesspeople, some journalists, and even usually sedate political scientists don't leave home without a revolver. Visitors to corporate headquarters routinely check their guns, along with IDs, upon entering. Factories are fortified bunkers, surrounded by high walls and barbed wire, with armed guards looking out from watchtowers.

Even some of Lima's Kentucky Fried Chicken outlets have three armed guards at the entrance—not, as one resident jokes, to guard the quality of the product, but to keep the stores standing after two bomb attacks this year. Terrorists "seem to have an obsession about fried chicken," says Bustavo Gorriti, a journalist. "They must think it's the food of choice of the American plutocracy."

Source: The Wall Street Journal, April 10, 1991, p. 1.

It is important to understand the nature of political conflict in foreign countries and the motivation behind government actions. If a change in government policy is merely for symbolic purposes, it represents less risk to foreign businesses. Also, when new policy is expressed through the imposition of certain constraints, requirements, or controls on foreign businesses, it is important to assess the host government's administrative ability. Does that government have the capacity to promulgate and enforce the new policy? If such capabilities are lacking, the new policy will remain a well-intentioned effort that produce no actual affects on foreign businesses.

Political Intervention

Carefully chosen overseas markets provide substantial opportunity but often with the risk of intervention by host governments seeking to further their own interests. Nations are not monolithic, or even bipartisan. Rather, they are composed of different groups, each of

which is intent on maximizing its individual interests. In countries where foreign investment plays a significant role in the economy, the goals of special interests frequently bring
on interference in the operations of foreign firms. If a foreign company is prominent in
the economy of such developing countries as Zambia, Guinea, Iran, and Tanzania, the
possibilities of government intervention are relatively great. Although such intervention is
certainly not limited to developing countries, it is more likely there than in developed
countries, which generally respond to foreign enterprise by establishing their own multinationals to challenge the foreign firms both on the home front and abroad. Developing
countries may have to intervene directly in the operations of MNCs operating in their
lands in order to pursue their own special interests.

Political intervention can be defined as a decision on the part of the host country government that may force a change in the operations, policies, and strategies of a foreign
firm. The intervention may range from some sort of control to complete takeover, or an-
nexation, of the foreign enterprise. The magnitude of intervention would vary according
to the company's business in the country and the nature of the intervention.

There are different forms of intervention: expropriation, domestication, exchange
control, import restrictions, market control, tax control, price control, and labor restrictions. The likely effects of these on marketing mix variables comprise the following:[12]

- **Product:** local content law, technology content, restrictions on the sale of some
  products, products' functional range, design of products, useful life, adaptability
  to local conditions, patent life, local manufacturing and assembling.
- **Place:** territory assigned, type of dealership, minority representation, payments to
  agents, products handled by different outlets.
- **Price:** transfer pricing, price ceiling and price floor, price paid for local raw materials, price contracts, price paid for imported raw materials.
- **Promotion:** local production of commercials, local artists, type of message, type
  of copy, availability of media, time restrictions on the use of certain media.

Expropriation   Of all the forms of political intervention, *expropriation* is most pervasive. As defined by
Eitemen and Stonehill, it is

> Official seizure of foreign property by a host country whose intention is to use the seized prop-
> erty in the public interest. Expropriation is recognized by international law as the right of sover-
> eign states, provided the expropriated firms are given prompt compensation, at fair market value,
> in convertible currencies.[13]

Other terms used interchangeably with expropriation are nationalization and socialization. *Nationalization* refers to a transfer of the entire industry within that country from
private to public ownership, with no discrimination as to foreign ownership or local ownership. *Socialization*, also referred to as communization, differs from nationalization in
that it is a transfer of all the industries within the country. *Confiscation* means expropriation without compensation.

Traditionally, patterns of expropriation have been differentiated according to industry,
geographic region, type of ownership, technology, degree of vertical integration, asset size,
and politicoeconomic situation. In an older study, Latin America accounted for 49 percent of all expropriations between 1960 and 1976, followed by the Arab countries with 27
percent, black Africa with 13 percent, and Asian nations with 11 percent.[14] A study by the
United Nations of foreign firm takeovers between 1960 and 1974 showed that two-thirds
of all takeovers were accounted for by just 10 nations, including Argentina, Chile, Cuba,
Peru, Algeria, Libya, and Iraq.[15]

For a long time it was believed that ownership shared with host nations through joint
ventures was advantageous. This belief has been proved wrong. For example, David G.

Bradley found that joint ventures with host country governments, as opposed to wholly-owned foreign subsidiaries, have a greater rate of expropriation.[16]

Technology can serve as the defense against expropriation, if the technology of the enterprise cannot be duplicated by the host country or cannot be made operable by the expropriators. Further, if a firm is vertically integrated with the parent firm so that the parent controls either the supplies for production or the market for the product, the firm is then an unlikely target for expropriation. Asset size also makes a difference here. A firm with total assets in excess of $100 million has a 50 times greater chance of being expropriated than a firm with assets of less than $1 million.[17]

The politicoeconomic backdrops against which expropriations have taken place have been associated with sweeping and violent upheavals that transformed the basic government structure and politicoeconomic ideologies of the nations involved. Signs of such upheavals being imminent should serve as a warning of expropriations being likely.

Recent trends show that expropriation activity has decreased over time. Many developing countries now protect foreign direct investors from expropriation. This change reflects their governments' shift away from an emphasis on ideologies and politics to a more functional need for economic development. In light of this trend, expropriations have become more selective, directed toward those foreign-owned enterprises whose policies or aspirations have collided with the economic plans and priorities of the developing nation. A recent study on the subject supports the conclusion that expropriation is unlikely to resurface in the near future as a source of MNC–developing country contention.[18] The broad-scale movement in developing countries to privatize state-owned enterprises also indicates that governments will not be eager to replace private-sector activity with state ownership. In sum, for the near future, significant expropriation activity is unlikely.

Domestication

Domestication, which can be thought of as *creeping expropriation*, is a process by which controls and restrictions placed on the foreign firm gradually reduce the control of the owners. Although domestication may lead ultimately to expropriation, in a way it offers a compromise to both parties. The MNC continues to operate in the country while the host government is able to maintain leverage on the foreign firm through imposing different controls. Domestication involves several measures, including

- Gradual transfer of ownership to nationals.
- Promotion of a large number of nationals to higher levels of management.
- Greater decision-making powers accorded to nationals.
- More products produced locally rather than imported for assembly.
- Specific export regulations designed to dictate participation in world markets.

From the viewpoint of the host country, domestication is preferable to expropriation. It provides the host country enough control to carefully scrutinize and regulate activities of the foreign firm. In this way, any truly negative effects of the MNC's operations in the country can be discovered and prompt corrective action taken, either through negotiations or through legislation and decree for further control.

Other Forms of Intervention

In addition to expropriation and domestication, there are various other means of government intervention in foreign enterprise, usually in the form of legislative action or a decree enacted in the best national interest. Although such intervention usually applies to both domestic and foreign businesses, a deeper probe often reveals that certain aspects of the law or decree are irrelevant for domestic business and are meant specifically to control foreign business. For example, a clause in a decree restricting repatriation of profits to stockholders outside the country would be meaningless for native companies. Following is a discussion of exchange control, import restrictions, market control, tax control, price control, and labor restrictions.

Exchange Control Countries having difficulties with the balance of trade often impose restrictions on the free use of foreign exchange. For example, import of luxuries from outside the country may be restricted. Similarly, restrictions may be placed on the remittances from the country involving hard currency. This type of *exchange control* may also be an effort to encourage domestic industry.

Exchange-control measures affect foreign business in two ways. First, profits and capital cannot be returned to the parent company at will. Second, raw materials, machinery, spare parts, and the like cannot be liberally imported for operating purposes.

Many developing countries utilize exchange control to regulate their hard-currency balances. The need for such regulations is one important reason for restrictions on imports of consumer goods (for example, cars, appliances, clothing, perfumes) in most emerging countries. Sometimes even developed countries may resort to exchange control. One example is France in 1981 after the socialist government took over.[19]

Import Restrictions Another type of government intervention, *import restrictions,* is primarily for the support of native industries. Consider a foreign pharmaceutical company traditionally importing certain compounds and chemicals from the parent company. If the host country places restrictions on imports, the company may be forced to depend on local sources of supply for these new materials. Such dependence on local supply can create two types of problems for the foreign firm. First, the local product may be of inferior quality, which would affect the quality of the finished product. Second, locally the product may be in such short supply that the pharmaceutical manufacturer cannot acquire it in adequate quantity.

Presumably, governments legislate import restrictions with the total industry and not a particular company in mind. Thus, the difficulties likely to be faced by a foreign company do not figure in the discussion. Further, when a country wants to encourage domestic industry as a matter of industrial policy, import restrictions are adopted with the realization that the local product will be inferior, at least initially. Strictly from the point of view of the government, import restrictions seem reasonable, but they ordinarily jeopardize the functions of foreign business.

Market Control The government of a country sometimes imposes *market control* to prevent foreign companies from competing in certain markets. For example, until recently Japan prohibited foreign companies from selling sophisticated communications equipment to the Japanese government. Thus, AT&T, GTE-Sylvania, and ITT could do little business with Japan.

The Arab boycott of companies doing business with Israel was an interesting example of market control. The Arab states had not accepted Israel's right to exist and hoped that the boycott eventually would bring about its collapse. Although many companies had given in to Arab demands, the U.S. government adopted strict laws to prevent companies from becoming susceptible to the Arab blackmail.

As another example of market control, in April 1998 China ordered all direct-sales operations to cease immediately. Alarmed by a rise in pyramid schemes by some direct sellers and uneasy about the big sales meetings that direct sellers hold, Beijing gave all companies that held direct-selling licenses six months to convert to retail outlets or shut down altogether. The move threatened Avon's China sales, of about $75 million a year, and put Avon, Amway, and Mary Kay's combined China investment of roughly $180 million at risk. It also created problems for Sara Lee Corp. and Tupperware Corp., which had recently launched direct-sales efforts in China.[20] (China withdrew the order after a little arm-twisting from Washington, and also because over 20 million Chinese were involved in direct sales, with more turning to the business as unemployment rose.)

Tax Control Governments may also impose *tax control* by means of excessive and unconventional taxes on foreign business. For example, a new form of excise tax for which there is no precedent may be placed on the output of a foreign firm. Such taxes are imposed for three reasons. First, an out-of-the-way burden on foreign companies is an indirect way of warning them that they are not wanted in a country any longer. Second, when a country is in dire need of new revenues, an additional tax burden on foreign companies appears not only politically prudent but economically convenient. And third, taxes can be retaliatory when a government learns that foreign corporations have abused differences in international taxation and have deprived the country of due revenue.

Taxes per se do not hinder foreign enterprise. However, problems do arise over excessively discriminatory taxes or taxes imposed at variance with the company's agreement with the government. For example, the host government may have agreed to give a tax holiday to a company—say, for five years—to establish its operations in the country. Three years later, though the government may choose to reverse its position for some reason, such as a new government's refusing to live with the agreement entered into by its predecessor.

Price Control For the sake of the public interest in difficult economic times, countries often resort to *price controls.* Even in the U.S., the price-control weapon has been used many times. President Nixon imposed price controls in the early 1970s to fight inflation. Likewise, many states control the price that a vendor may charge for milk. Until recently the price of gasoline was regulated.

Countries use price-control devices in various ways to improve their economies, by setting an official price on essential products such as drugs, heating oil, sugar, and cereals. Price control becomes a special problem if it is imposed randomly—for example, if a price limit is placed on a company's finished product, but the prices of the raw materials used in the production of that product are left to market forces. If the product of a particular foreign company has been singled out for price control without any economic rationale, such a measure amounts to undesirable intervention in the working of a foreign firm.

Labor Restrictions In many nations, labor unions are very strong and have great political clout. In these countries *labor restrictions* are an effective form of government intervention. Using its strength, labor may be able to talk the government into passing very restrictive laws that support labor at heavy cost to business. Traditionally, labor unions in Latin America have been able to prevent layoffs, plant shutdowns, and the like, even when business could not afford to meet such demands. Labor unions are gradually becoming strong in Western Europe. Germany and a number of other European nations require labor representation on boards of directors.

Foreign firms may find it difficult to accommodate labor demands transformed into laws. Even where there are no labor laws to comply with, there may be labor problems. Problems can reach such a level that the foreign enterprise is left with no other choice but to leave.

Political Perspectives

Given today's climate of global economic and political change and the experience of widespread nationalizations and expropriations in the 1960s and 1970s, there is a growing recognition in the business world of the need for a company to "look before it leaps" when considering entry into a foreign country. Any multinational marketer would be well-advised to make a thorough analysis of political risks as well as risks peculiar to the company's industry in foreign settings.

History shows that far and away the riskiest ventures are those in developing countries, where appeals to nationalism are most damaging to multinationals. On the other hand, these countries cannot simply be ignored by international marketers. For the U.S., the developing countries are increasingly important both economically and politically. They are major suppliers of raw materials, including, of course, oil; moreover, they constitute the most rapidly growing U.S. export markets. From 1994 to 1999 U.S. exports of capital goods to developing countries almost doubled, from less than $72 billion to more than $145 billion. In fact, taken as a group, developing countries (excluding OPEC countries) now account for more U.S. exports than the Western European countries.

During the recessionary period of the early 1990s, while U.S. exports to industrial countries stagnated or declined, exports to developing (including oil-exporting) countries continued to expand. Without that demand for U.S. goods, unemployment and production figures would have been far worse. In 1998 about 28 percent of $860 billion in direct overseas U.S. investments was in developing countries. The developing countries also accounted for around 42 percent of the $637 billion in U.S. bank claims on foreigners. Profits and interest from these investments and loans play an important role in offsetting U.S. trade deficits.

The political perspectives of a nation should be examined according to

- Type of government.
- Stability of government.
- Quality of host government's economic management.
- Change in government policy.
- Host country's attitude toward foreign investment.
- Host country's relationship with the rest of the world.
- Host country's relationship with parent company's home government.
- Attitude toward assignment of foreign personnel.
- Extent of anti-private-sector influence or influence of state-controlled industries.
- Fairness and honesty of administrative procedures.
- Closeness between government and people.

The importance of these factors varies from country to country. Nevertheless, it is desirable to consider them all to ensure a complete knowledge of the political outlook for doing business in a particular country.

Type of Government

World governments can be grouped in four categories: democratic republics, communist dictatorships, dictatorships, and monarchies. In each category there is a spectrum of variation. *Democratic republics* are formed through regular elections and have party systems. In the U.S. and England, two major political parties are active. Italy and France have several political parties. In Mexico, one dominant party controls. Although economic policies are an important issue in democracies, different parties hold different views on how the country's economy can be strengthened. In England, the two major parties, Labour and Conservative (or Tory), have different economic approaches. A Labour government usually seeks greater government control, while a Tory government stands for programs similar to those of the Republican party of the U.S.

Communist dictatorships control all business activity. Such governments exist in Cuba, the People's Republic of China, Vietnam, North Korea, and Burma. Communist countries maintain various types of ties with foreign business. Because China desires to achieve economic progress through using western technology and skills, the business climate there has been favorable. On the other hand, Myanmar (formerly Burma) has totally isolated itself from the rest of the world. The attitude of the Chinese government swings with changing events. It is convinced that the best way for the country to survive is to keep the screws on political dissent while it energizes the economy with free-market reforms.

Dictatorships are authoritarian regimes. These governments are run either by military dictators as in Pakistan or by civilian dictators as in Libya. Military dictators often eventually adopt a civilian posture, usually by holding an election that gives the appearance of a government elected by popular vote.

Authoritarian governments can be further categorized according to economic philosophy. They may be left-wing or Marxist-oriented, or right-wing and directed toward free enterprise. Angola and Nicaragua reflect, for instance, left-wing characteristics, whereas both Pakistan and Nigeria follow right-wing policies.

Finally, *monarchies* are governments in which the ruler derives power through inheritance. A country may have a monarchy and yet be democratic such as Great Britain, whose Queen Elizabeth II is titular head of the country but not head of the British government. But in many countries, the government is actually run by the monarch. Saudi Arabia and Jordan have monarchies. The shah of Iran was a reigning monarch. A monarch may have political inclinations to either the left or the right.

Any review of a country's political system and its impact on foreign business must remain free of stereotyped notions. Political philosophies change over time. Thus, what a government or a party stood for in the 1980s may not hold true in the year 2000. Both current and emerging perspectives need to be analyzed.

Government Stability

Many countries have frequent changes of government. In such a climate, a foreign business may find that by the time it is ready to implement an agreement, the government with whom the initial agreement was arranged has changed to one that is not sympathetic to the commitments made by its predecessor. Consequently, it is important for international marketers to examine, before making agreements, whether the current government is likely to continue to be in office for a while (see International Marketing Highlight 10.3). In a democratic situation, the incumbent party's strength or the alternative outcomes of the next election can be weighed to assess the likelihood of change. In other situations, a variety of symptoms could point toward governing instability:

- Public unrest (demonstrations, riots, or other demonstrations of social tension).
- Government crises (opposition forces trying to topple the government).
- Armed attacks by one group of people on another, or by groups from a neighboring country.
- Guerrilla warfare.
- Politically motivated assassinations.
- Coup d'état.
- Irregular change in top government leaders.

A report covering these points should be prepared to present evidence of a government's stability or instability.

Government Economic Management

Another factor to examine is the quality of the host government's economic management. A country that manages its economic affairs according to sound economic principles, whether through free economics or socialist policies, will, all things being equal, provide a more favorable environment than a country governed by political emotions and abrupt practices. The economic environment of a country should be studied in the political context with reference to

- The ability of the government to sustain its internal and external debt.
- The country's pursuit of stable and diversified economic growth.
- The country's ability to generate an adequate amount of foreign exchange.
- The nature of the various fiscal and monetary means used to steer the economy.
- The quality of the long-term planning of economic policy and its implementation.

As an example, a country that continues to live on borrowed funds, either from private sources or international agencies like the IMF, and frequently defaults on payments demonstrates poor economic management.

■■■■■■ International Marketing Highlight 10.3 ■■■■■■

Change in Command

Sam Parry was the assistant director of a corporate team investigating the prospects of a manufacturing venture in a small Caribbean country. After six weeks in the field, the team received a request from the government to address the head of state and his cabinet about their proposal. The team spent several days preparing a presentation. At the last minute, however, the project director was called away; she assigned Sam to address the assembled leaders in her place.

Sam had spent enough time helping to prepare the presentation that he felt comfortable with it. He even practiced his introduction to the prime minister—the honorable Mr. Tollis—and to the prime minister's cabinet. Finally, the day arrived for the address. Sam and the team were received at the governmental palace.

Once settled into the prime minister's meeting room, Sam opened the presentation. "Honorable Mr. Tollis," he began, "and esteemed members of the cabinet. . . ."

Abruptly, the prime minister interrupted Sam. "Won't you please start over?" he asked with a peeved smile.

Sam was taken aback. He hadn't expected his hosts to be so formal. They always seemed so casual in their open-necked short-sleeved shirts while Sam and his team sweated away in their suits. But Sam soon regained his composure. "Most honorable Mr. Tollis and highly esteemed members of the cabinet. . . ."

"Be so kind as to begin again," said the prime minister, now visibly annoyed.

"Most esteemed and honorable Mr. Tollis—"

"Perhaps you should start yet again."

Shaken, Sam glanced desperately at his team, then at the government officials surrounding him. The ceiling fans rattled lightly overhead.

One of the cabinet ministers nearby took pity on Sam. Leaning over, the elderly gentleman whispered, "Excuse me, but Mr. Tollis was deposed six months ago. You are now addressing the honorable Mr. Herbert."

Source: Charles F. Valentine, *The Arthur Young International Business Guide* (New York: John Wiley & Sons, 1988), p. 400.

Change in Government Policy

More than anything else, MNCs dislike frequent policy changes by host countries. Policy changes may occur even without a change in government. It is important, therefore, for the foreign business to analyze the mechanism of government policy changes. Information on the autonomy of legislatures and study of the procedures followed for seeking constitutional changes can be crucial.

Attitude Toward Foreign Investment

Many nations look upon foreign investment with suspicion. This is true of both developed and developing countries. Take, for example, Japan, where it is extremely difficult for a foreign business to establish itself without first generating a trusting relationship that enables it to gain entry through a joint venture. Developing countries are usually afraid of domination and exploitation by foreign business. In response to national attitudes, these nations legislate a variety of laws and regulations to prescribe the role of foreign investment in their economies.[21] It is appropriate, therefore, to review a host country's regulations and identify underlying attitudes and motivations before deciding to invest there. Indirectly, the success of other multinational businesses in a country indicates a favorable climate.

International Stance of Government

Countries that maintain amicable political relationships with the rest of the world and have respect for international law and order show political maturity. These countries can be expected to behave in a responsible fashion. Iran serves as a negative example: in the post-shah period the government behaved erratically, without regard for international treaties and obligations. Uganda during Dada's regime did the same. Usually, extreme cases can be easily identified. For less spectacular situations, membership in regional and international organizations as well as adherence to bilateral and multilateral principles and agreements provides evidence of a country's relationship with other nations.

Relationship with Parent Company's Home Government

In theory, MNCs have no political alignment. Yet a company originating in the U.S. will continue to be known as a U.S. company even though it may derive a major portion of its revenues and profits from operations outside the U.S. Nestlé, for example, generates close to 50 percent of its revenues in the U.S. and only 4 percent in its home country, Switzerland. Nevertheless, it is identified as a Swiss company.

Thus, the relationship between the host country government and the parent company government will affect, either directly or indirectly, the MNC. International marketers should therefore trace the history of the relationship between the host country's government and the home country government before deciding to enter a market. Do the two governments agree on issues debated in international agencies? Are there any points of discord? Are there reasons to believe that relations between the two countries will improve or deteriorate in the future? (see International Marketing Highlight 10.4).

Attitude Toward Foreign Managers

A company making an investment in a foreign country needs to make sure that its business there is managed effectively. Among other factors, a crucial determinant of success in overseas operations is the assignment of experienced persons to key positions. But in a country where appointment of local nationals to key positions is a requirement, and where qualified nationals are in short supply, there are bound to be difficulties.

Anti-Private-Sector Influence

An interesting development of the post–World War II period has been the increased presence of government in a wide spectrum of social and economic affairs that were previously ignored by government. In the U.S., concern for the poor, the aged, minorities, consumers' rights, and the environment has spurred government response and the adoption of a variety of legislative measures. In a great many foreign countries, such concerns have led governments to take over businesses to be run as public enterprises. Sympathies for public-sector enterprises, successful or not as businesses, have rendered private corporations suspect and undesirable in many countries. Also, public-sector enterprises are not limited to developing countries. Great Britain and France have many government corporations, from airlines to broadcasting companies to banks and steel mills. An example is Airbus Industrié, a civilian aircraft manufacturer owned by the British, French, German, and Spanish governments.

Obviously, in nations where there is an ongoing bias against home-grown private businesses, an MNC cannot expect a cordial welcome. In such a situation, an MNC must contend with the problems that arise because of it being a private business as well as a foreign one. Sound business intelligence and familiarity with the industrial policy of the government and related legislative acts and decrees should provide clarification of the role of the private sector in any given economy.

International Marketing Highlight 10.4

Copyright Struggle in New York

A copyright squabble in 1988 between two small companies in New York's Chinatown over videotapes of Taiwanese soap operas illustrates how a relationship between governments could erupt into a political problem. U.E. Enterprises Inc., accused of pirating the Taiwanese television programs, claims that Taiwanese nationals no longer are entitled to copyright protection as a result of the decision by the U.S. to recognize the People's Republic of China as the "sole legal government" of China in 1979. That decision, the defendants claim, negated the U.S.–Taiwan Friendship, Commerce and Navigation Treaty of 1948, which is the legal framework for trade as well as copyright agreements between the U.S. and Taiwan. The defendant's case relies on a complex argument that a law passed by Congress in 1979, purporting to maintain normal trade relations with Taiwan after recognition of the People's Republic, is constitutionally invalid because it effectively amended the treaty by changing the parties from the Republic of China to the "governing authorities of Corp., E-II Holdings Inc.'s Samsonite Unit, Walt Disney Co., and many others from the pirating of their products in Taiwan. Because of this the case received wide publicity.

Although the judgment was against U.E. Enterprises, the case highlights the significance of political relations between countries.

Source: The Wall Street Journal, October 25, 1988, p. B8.

Administrative Procedures

Every country has its own unique administrative scheme. The scheme emerges from such factors as experience, culture, the system of reward and punishment, availability of qualified administrators, and style of leadership. Additionally, the availability of modern means of transportation and communication helps to streamline government administration. Businesses often complain about the U.S. federal bureaucracy and its states' agencies, but if they were to compare U.S. administration with other nations', they would be pleasantly surprised to learn that government in the U.S. is far more efficient than elsewhere. It is not extraordinary in many African countries for administrators to be altogether unavailable, the telephones not to work, or files to be forever lost. Similar difficulties would not be unusual in either Asia or Latin America. Such hindrances, in addition to the usual red tape, make business dealings uncomfortable and unpleasant. Although a company would probably not bypass an overseas opportunity solely because of this factor, knowledge about the inefficiency of administrative machinery might warn its managers to lengthen schedules and perhaps engage the services of a local broker or an agent.

Closeness of Government to People

Iran's 1979 crisis suggests that economic development cannot be imposed on a nation; rather, it must evolve over time. The breakneck speed with which the shah of Iran invested billions of dollars in development in the late 1960s and early 1970s created a fragile society. The shah imposed a modern infrastructure, an industry dependent on foreign technology, and a western lifestyle on a Muslim society that was opposed to change. This swift modernization, with GNP per capita increasing from $200 to over $2,000 in a decade's time, triggered a reaction that led to the shah's fall. The people, in other words, could not absorb modernization quickly enough to adapt their lives accordingly, and they revolted. Religious priests became the leaders of a people disillusioned by western living and material progress.

The Islamic revolution in Iran provides a classic case of how the distance between government and people can lead to the total disruption of a country. Many political scientists have noted the similarities between Saudi Arabia's modernization and Iran's. There also, a tribal nomadic society is being transformed seemingly overnight into an industrial society with modern amenities and facilities.[22] To an extent, South Vietnam presented a similar problem. The government kept developing programs, with U.S. aid, that widened the distance between the government and its people.

It is sometimes difficult to ascertain whether the people and the government of a country are in accord. The U.S. government, despite all its resources, failed to foresee that the shah would fall. However, contact with journalists, religious leaders, and the intelligentsia of a country can provide some insights into the feelings of ordinary citizens toward their government and its programs. In traditional societies, where a windfall such as oil revenues suddenly offers an opportunity for multinational business, it would be prudent to investigate the sentiments of the people before making major commitments.

Political Models

On the basis of the factors discussed so far, a country can be categorized as having one of the following political slants: state-centric international politics, pluralistic national politics, bureaucratic organizational politics, or transnational politics. Each of these political model systems presents different kinds of risk for doing business.

The *state-centric model* of international politics assumes that national governments seek power and status in relation to one another, that they do so in the context of a competitive, decentralized international political system, and that they utilize whatever internal political resources are available in pursuit of their international objectives. National governments' actions are thus assumed to be functions of the officials' desire for international power and status and of their reactions to political pressures exerted by other national governments.

The *pluralistic model* of national politics assumes that national governments are responsive to the diverse and conflicting interests and pressures of multiple interest groups within a political system. Group interests and pressures are expressed through electoral processes but are especially important in legislative and administrative processes, where they take the form of lobbying activities. National governments' actions are thus assumed to be functions of the officials' desire to remain in office or of their reaction to internal political pressures.

The *bureaucratic organizational politics behavior model* assumes that national governments' actions are the result of organizational processes within government bureaucracies. Intragovernmental conflicts, then, are generated by the differing policy preferences of individual officials and agencies. These variances arise from conflicting organizational interests, differences in career experiences, differences in ties to domestic clientele groups, and other factors. This model also suggests that government policies are slow to change because of bureaucratic inertia.

The *transnational politics model* emphasizes the increasingly important role played in world politics by organizations other than those of national governments. Thus, not only MNCs but also international organizations and nongovernmental associations such as transnational interest groups are all assuming greater influence, often at the expense of national governments.

Each model contains numerous variables and and is based on propositions about relationships among these variables. Each one is also evident in an abundance of impressionistic case studies, systematic quantitative studies, and historical narratives. Even this abbreviated discussion suggests the utility of these models in political risk assessment, for they can be used to develop a lengthy and systematic list of potential sources of political risk.

Political Risk Assessment (PRA)

Political risk assessment (PRA) is useful for three reasons:

1. To identify countries that may turn out to be the Irans of tomorrow. (PRA should sound a warning signal of mounting political risks so that a firm can protect itself by minimizing its exposure.)
2. To identify countries unnecessarily discounted as politically unsound, for example, Cambodia, and to identify countries where political conditions have changed for the better, for example, Vietnam and Haiti.
3. To provide a framework to identify countries that are politically risky, but not so risky as to be automatically ruled out. (Most developing countries fall into this category.)

PRA Methods   Corporations utilize any number of methods to analyze political risk. The currently favored approaches are (1) qualitative ones known as the grand-tour approach, old-hand approach, and delphi technique, and (2) quantitative methods.

Grand Tour In the *grand-tour approach,* an executive or a team of executives visit the country in which investment is being considered. Usually, prior to the visit, there is some preliminary market research. Upon arrival, there are usually meetings with government officials and local businesspersons. The results of this type of visit can be very superficial, representing only selected pieces of information and therefore possibly camouflaging undesirable aspects of the market.

Old Hand The *old-hand approach* relies on the advice of an outside consultant or a person deemed to be an expert. Usually such persons are seasoned educators, diplomats, local politicians, or businesspersons. The capability and experience of the advisor is the factor determining the quality of this report.

Delphi Technique In the *delphi technique,* a group of experts are asked to share their opinions independently on a given problem, in a form that can be scored in order to produce a statistical distribution of opinion. The experts are shown the resulting distribution and given the chance to alter their original views. The process is repeated several times. For some problems, it has been found that the average opinion of the group at the last round is usually more nearly correct than any of the individual views in the beginning.
To use this method, a group of experts would be asked to rate different political factors, for example, the stability of government, the role of its armed forces, and its political conflicts. Based on the final expert opinion, a go or no-go decision can be made.

Quantitative Methods In addition to the foregoing qualitative methods, many businesses have tried *quantitative methods* to judge political risk. A quantitative method involves developing a mathematical relationship among a series of quantifiable factors in order to predict (within specified probability ranges) the likelihood of certain events. Banks have utilized this technique before granting loans to foreign countries. This technique requires collection of different forms of quantitative data, complex analysis of data using an appropriate computer program, and expert interpretation of the results.

PRA Models

PRA has become a fact of U.S. corporate life. The surge of interest in PRA began with the unexpected fall of the shah's regime in Iran and was reinforced by the overthrow of apparently secure governments in Nicaragua and South Korea. Several independent PRA consultants are available to help corporate clients develop general PRA summaries or provide studies of specific countries. The best-known risk raters are the Economist Intelligence Unit (EIU), a New York–based subsidiary of The Economist Group, London; BERI S.A.'s Business Risk service (BRs); and Bank of America's Country Risk Monitor.

EIU's Country Risk Service (CRS) assesses composite country risk through four types of risk to investors: political risk (22 percent of the composite), economic policy risk (28 percent), economic structure risk (27 percent), and liquidity risk (23 percent). The *political risk* component includes two subcategories: (1) political stability, represented in five indicators—war, social unrest, orderly political transfer, politically motivated violence, and international disputes—and (2) political effectiveness, with six indicators—change in government orientation, institutional effectiveness, bureaucracy, transparency/fairness, corruption, and crime.

Economic policy risk is determined with 27 variables in five categories: monetary policy, fiscal policy, exchange rate policy, trade policy, and regulatory environment. Economic structure risk incorporates global environment, growth, current account, debt, and financial structure groupings with 28 variables. *Liquidity risk* employs 10 variables. In each of the four categories, numerical scores are converted to letter grades ranging from A to E.

BERI provides a complete picture of country risk based on a set of quantitative indices developed and refined over a 25-year period. A comprehensive *Profit Opportunity Recommendation (POR)* is an average of three ratings, each on a 100-point scale. *The Political Risk Index (PRI)* is composed of ratings on 10 political and social variables. The *Operations Risk Index (ORI)* includes weighted ratings on 15 economic, financial, and structural variables. The third index is the *R Factor,* also a weighted index, covering the country's legal framework, foreign exchange, hard currency reserves, and foreign debt. The POR thus represents all aspects of country risk. Risk is calculated for the present, as well as one-year and five-year time frames.

In its *Country Risk Monitor,* Bank of America evaluates country risk on the basis of economic ratios. For 80 countries, an ordinal ranking is created for each of the ratios. A rank of 1 indicates the least difficulty or problem; a rank of 80 is associated with the most difficulty. The ranks are then averaged across the 10 variables, and a comprehensive ranking of the averages is created to provide a picture of relative risk. The *Country Risk Monitor* provides rankings for the current year, historical data for the previous four years, and projections for the next five years.

Consider Brazil's ratings in 1999. BERI gave Brazil an overall score of 74 (out of 100), ranking it 42nd out of 147 countries, a significant improvement over 1997, when the score was 62. Bank of America, however, expressed a rather dim view of Brazil in its 1999 forecast. EIU put Brazil in category C, giving it a total score of 58 (which is a slight improvement over the 1997 score of 54).[23] The reason behind this improved showing is easy to see. Inflation is down and the country has liberalized the economy to become attractive to foreign investors.

Too often, consultants' reports are of dubious usefulness to subsidiary managers, since they are mainly oriented to corporate headquarters. The objectives of a good PRA system should not be limited to collecting and evaluating information but rather should aim to select the best political intelligence for decision making. Toward this end, a specific study tailored to a particular purpose is more useful than a general one. Although there is some debate about the usefulness of the indexing services, their client lists include a number of Fortune 500 companies.

Strategic Response

When a company has become susceptible to political risk or has been politically victimized, it must make an effort to salvage its position. Whereas there is little a company can do to ward off internal violence or political instability in the host country, it can employ a number of tactics to discourage expropriation or to generally strengthen its position (see International Marketing Highlight 10.5). As one author has stated,

> In sum, host governments should not be seen by MNC top managers exclusively as an impediment to global strategic freedom, to be avoided at all cost. Occasionally they may provide enough of a helping hand—through privileged market access, export credits, and subsidies—for smaller MNCs to face global competition, to make it worthwhile for those smaller, often weaker, MNCs to relinquish wholeheartedly some strategic freedom to gain competitive strength through government support. Host governments can thus either hamper or help global strategies, depending on their policies and on the strategic options of the affected firms. It is important, therefore, to make an analysis of host government goals, policies, and actions an integral part of the strategy formulation process in a global business.[24]

International Marketing Highlight 10.5

How Big Mac Kept from Becoming a Serb Archenemy

During most of the 78-day air war against Yugoslavia, while NATO kept the bombs dropping, McDonald's kept the burgers flipping.

Vandalized at the outset by angry mobs, McDonald's Corp. was forced to temporarily close its 15 restaurants in Yugoslavia. But when local managers flung the doors open again, they accomplished an extraordinary comeback using an unusual marketing strategy: They put McDonald's U.S. citizenship on the back burner.

To help overcome animosity toward a quintessential American trademark, the local restaurants promoted the McCountry, a domestic pork burger with paprika garnish. As a national flourish to evoke Serbian identity and pride, they produced posters and lapel buttons showing the golden arches topped with a traditional Serbian cap called sajkaca (pronounced shy-KACK-a). They also handed out free cheeseburgers at anti-NATO rallies. The basement of one restaurant in the Serbian capital even served as a bomb shelter.

Now that the war is over, the company is basking in its success. Cash registers are ringing at prewar levels. In spite of falling wages, rising prices and lingering anger at the U.S., McDonald's restaurants around the country are thronged with Serbs hungry for Big Macs and fries. And why not, ask 16-year-old Jovan Stojanovic, munching on a burger. "I don't associate McDonald's with America," he says. "Mac is ours."

Source: The Wall Street Journal. September 3, 1999, p. B1

Strategic Choices

Essentially, a company has three strategic responses to political difficulties in a host country: to *adapt*, to *withdraw*, or to take *counteractive measures*.[25] For example, in the 1970s IBM completely withdrew from India because the company could not live with the restrictions imposed by the government on freedom of strategy in product development, pricing, and other areas. Nestlé, on the other hand, accepted India's infringements in return for continued presence in the market. CPC International, du Pont, and Brown Boveri (a European company) likewise seek market presence rather than complete withdrawal.

The third choice, counteractive response, amounts to making a new move to gain a competitive advantage based on company strengths and the needs of the host government.

For example, Honeywell merged its French subsidiary, Honeywell Bull, with the French government company, Compagnie International pour L'Informatique, which was losing money. This arrangement gave Honeywell access to the French market and qualified it to receive French government grants for R&D (see International Marketing Highlight 10.6). Thus it may be perfectly rational to stay in the country even if, or perhaps because, the competitors have left. In the long run, staying, but with a minimum commitment, may provide greater freedom of operation once the political situation stabilizes.[26]

■■■■■■■ **International Marketing Highlight 10.6** ■■■■■■■

Managing Government Intervention

Bristol-Myers pursued the counteractive strategy in Indonesia. It had successfully marketed one of its nutritional products in Indonesia, which was centrally obtained from its Nijmegen facility in Holland. This worked well for Bristol-Myers, since the Indonesian market wasn't developed enough to justify the cost of building a plant there to service this market. The problem started when the Indonesian government decided to close its borders to the "finished product" that Bristol-Myers had introduced so successfully into the market. Bristol-Myers had to decide whether to find an alternative that could circumvent the new regulation or withdraw from the Indonesian market. Bristol-Myers decided to follow the former route. The concerned product was composed of a highly sophisticated powder that was blended with a heat-sensitive key raw material and canned. Bristol-Myers solved the problem by ascertaining what the Indonesian government really meant by "finished product." It worked closely with the ministry of health and the ministry of economics in Indonesia to come up with a mutually acceptable solution: Bristol-Myers was permitted to import a "base" powder that it would blend with an indigenous raw material. Bristol-Myers successfully subcontracted with an Indonesian company to produce and blend the raw material with the base. The "finished product" was subsequently canned, carried the Bristol-Myers label, and continued to be sold in Indonesia.

Keep in mind, however, that no single strategy works best in a single country or even in a single industry. If the MNC's managers are flexible and imaginative in responding to government demands, the consequences could be surprisingly favorable. Encarnation and Vachani found that new product lines and markets, risk diversifications, and higher earnings were among the benefits MNCs operating in India enjoyed in the wake of that country's "hostile" equity laws. Some, for example, negotiated for manufacturing licenses and other concessions in exchange for "Indianization." Others successfully sought entry to new markets, hitherto forbidden.[27] The choice, of course, among the three options of adapting, withdrawing, or taking counteractive measures depends on the bargaining power of the company in respect to the bargaining power of the host government.

MNCs' Bargaining Power

The bargaining power of MNCs stems from such factors as technology, economies of scale, and product differentiation. Companies with *technology* badly needed by the host country and unobtainable on comparative terms elsewhere can bargain from a leverage position. For example, in the late 1970s Indonesia desperately sought to boost its oil exploration activity. This goal required sophisticated technology, and Indonesia was willing to go to any length to get it. In other words, oil companies negotiated with the Indonesian government on very favorable terms since they had the necessary technology.[28]

Similarly, Mexico willingly permitted IBM to establish a wholly owned microcomputer plant because the Mexican government was concerned that without a major microcomputer plant, the local market would consists of outmoded and overpriced products. If a company like IBM entered the market, it could pull other companies in the production chain along with it. Technology can provide effective bargaining power.

Economies of scale, which a foreign firm might realize through its worldwide production and distribution arrangements, can also yield a unique bargaining strength. If the low cost of the local multinational firm's output is directly related to its worldwide network or vertical integration (via the establishment of specialized plants in various countries and the transfer of components or end products among them), the host country will hesitate to intervene out of fear that any intervention would cancel out the benefits that the firm derives from being a part of the network. In the case of Marcona Mining's iron milling operation in Peru, such intervention did just that. The firm signed long-term supply agreements with its customers stipulating that in the event of nationalization, the contracts with its Peruvian subsidiary would be considered void and Marcona Mining would supply its customers from its other milling operations. When the firm was expropriated, the Peruvian government found it had no outlet for iron ore concentrate. As the trade in this commodity is based almost entirely on long-term controls, there was no well-developed spot market to which the Peruvian government could turn.

Product differentiation (i.e., differentiation based on the nature of the product and product quality/performance attributes, and not on consumer perceptions) can serve as another area of strength in foreign firms' bargaining with the host governments. For example, a firm producing high-quality agricultural machinery will have greater leverage in dealing with a host government than will a cosmetics manufacturer.

To sum up, firms with technical, operational, and managerial requirements that are within the reach of the abilities of the host nation will have little bargaining power. Such firms are more likely to experience intervention than those in complex fields. Hence, there is considerable local pressure on governments in Kenya, Indonesia, Brazil, and India to restrict such areas as consumer goods manufacturing, retailing, importing and exporting, and distribution to nationals only.

Bargaining Power of Host Country

The bargaining power of the host country mainly depends on two factors: control of market access and inducements. The host country controls access to the market by restricting entry for other competitors or by opening up rights to restricted markets. For example, Spain attracted Ford Motor Company by making it feasible for the company to sell enough cars there. Similarly, Japan has permitted foreign companies to sell communications-related products to its government, which may serve as an incentive for such firms as Western Electric to become more active in that market.

In addition, host countries may offer such inducements as R&D funds, tax holidays, market information, land subsidies, and financial concessions (repatriation arrangements) to attract the businesses sought. For example, ITT's European units have received large government grants to develop communication equipment tailored to local conditions.

Strategic Response

The strategic response a company makes to intervention by the host country should depend on the bargaining power on each side. The following strategies are recommended for improving the odds in international investing:

- Seek joint ventures with local private parties.
- Concentrate proprietary research, product development, and process technology in the home country.
- Ensure that each new investment is economically dependent on the parent corporation in the U.S. (For example, establish the parent as the sole supplier of essential materials.)

- Avoid local branding or establish a single global trademark.
- Adopt a low-profile, multiplant strategy, with a number of investments in different countries.

To conclude, the major benefits to a host country from a foreign investment usually appear at the beginning. Over time, the incremental benefits become smaller and the costs more apparent. Unless the firm continually renews these benefits by introducing more products, say, or by expanding output and developing export markets, it is likely to be subject to increasing political risks. The common government attitude is to ignore the past and instead ask what will be done for it in the future. In a situation where the firm's future contributions are unlikely to evoke a favorable government reaction, the firm is advised to concentrate on protecting its foreign investments by striking a balance between the company's goals and those of its host. For example, a company may introduce higher technology products and thereby foster the government's economic plans.

Summary

An international marketer needs to examine carefully the political environment of a country before making major commitments in that country. The political situation of a country may or may not be conducive to profitable business there.

Political problems related to foreign business occur mainly because of political sovereignty, a country's desire to assert its authority, and political conflict—either internal conflicts such as civil war or external ones with another country. Such troubles may lead a country to intervene politically in the affairs of private business, particularly those of foreign firms. Intervention may range from some form of control to complete takeover, or expropriation, which is the official seizure of foreign property by a host country. Other forms of intervention include exchange control, import restrictions, market control, tax control, price control, and labor restrictions. At one time, political intervention mainly occurred in developing countries. Now, even industrially developed countries seek to control foreign enterprises in various ways.

The possibility of political intervention makes it necessary for a foreign marketer to carefully analyze the political situation of a country before investing there. This analysis can be made through study of the country's type of government (republic, dictatorship, and so forth); stability of government; economic management by government; frequency of changes in government policy; attitudes toward foreign investment, other governments, the parent company's home government, foreign managers, and private business; viability of administrative procedures; and closeness between the government and its people. On the basis of the preceding factors, the foreign firm can determine the political risk of doing business with a given country. Various methods or models can be employed for political risk assessment.

In theory, a company should not enter a politically unsafe country. However, situations sometimes change within a country after entry has been made. For example, traditionally Iran provided a workable environment, but beginning in 1978 it became an extremely high-risk country. What can a company do if problems arise after it has entered a market? Three strategic responses to political intervention are (1) adapt, accepting infringements and molding the business operations to suit the foreign government's requirements; (2) withdraw and call it quits even if this means suffering a loss of property; or (3) attempt counteractive measures such as proposals to provide the government with what it wants and at the same time allow the company a few concessions.

In the final analysis, the host government's willingness to grant concessions to the foreign enterprise would depend on the MNC's bargaining leverage. For example, a host gov-

15. *Transnational Corporations in World Development: Third Survey* (New York: United Nations, 1983).

16. David G. Bradley, op. cit.

17. Ibid.

18. Michael S. Minor, "The Demise of Expropriation as an Instrument of Old LDC Policy, 1980–1992," *Journal of International Business Studies* 25, no. 1 (1994): 177–188.

19. "Europe's Economic Malaise," *Business Week*, December 7, 1981, p. 74.

20. "Ultimatum for the Avon Lady," *Business Week*, May 11, 1998, p. 33.

21. "Indian Tobacco: Raj Pickle," *The Economist*, April 1, 1995, p. 56.

22. Douglas Jehl, "Saudis' Heartland is Seething with Rage at Rulers and U.S.," *The New York Times*, November 5, 1996, p. 1A.

23. *The Economist*, January 10, 2000, p. 48.

24. C. K. Prahalad and Yves L. Doz, *The Multinational Mission* (New York: The Free Press, 1987), p. 68.

25. Yves L. Doz and C. K. Prahalad, "How MNCs Cope with Host Government Intervention," *Harvard Business Review*, March–April 1980, pp. 149–157.

26. Amjad Hadjikhari and Jan Johanson, "Facing Foreign Market Turbulence: Three Swedish Multinationals in Iran," *Journal of International Marketing*, no. 4 (1996): 53–74.

27. D. J. Encarnation and Sushil Vachini, "Foreign Ownership: When Hosts Change the Rules," *Harvard Business Review*, September–October 1985, pp. 152–160.

28. "Foreign Countries Offer Wide Range of Incentives to Invest," *The Asian Wall Street Journal Weekly*, August 24, 1981, pp. 12–14.

ernment would be willing to concede to the terms of a multinational enterpri
in business that is of strategic national importance and that cannot be replace
other hand, a company manufacturing consumer goods such as bar soaps and
may not have much bargaining power with the host government.

Review Questions

1. Why is it necessary for international marketers to study political environment
can foreign politics affect marketing decisions?
2. What are the underlying causes of political unrest? Discuss.
3. Discuss different ways in which a host government may intervene in the affair
multinational firm.
4. Define *expropriation*. What can a company do to counteract expropriation?
5. What factors should a company study to gain insight into a country's politics?
6. Why is it desirable to undertake political risk assessment?
7. What responses can a company make to government intervention in a forei
country?

Creative Questions

1. In 1999 the Clinton administration extended "most favorite nation" (MFN) trading
status to China despite that country's poor record in respecting human rights. What
political factors influenced this decision? Should America have compromised its policy on human rights for economic gains? What influence is this decision likely to have
on other nations with questionable records on maintaining human rights?
2. According to *The Economist*, causes of war have not disappeared from the face of the
earth. One possibility is a general war between Islamic nations and the West. Such a
war would have three potential ignites: ideology, skin color, and conflict of interest.
Examine this proposition, suggesting ways such a war could be averted.

Endnotes

1. Richard L. Hudson, "Apple Computer vs. French Chauvinism:
Politics, Not Free Trade, Wins in the End," *The Wall Street Journal*, February 22, 1985, p. 34.

2. *See* Roberto Friedmann, "Political Risk and International
Marketing," *Columbia Journal of World Business*, Winter
1988.

"Toyota's Fast Lane," *Business Week*, November 4, 1985, p. 42.
Also see "Asian Auto Makers Find a Back Door to the U.S. Mar-
et," *Business Week*, December 9, 1985, p. 52; "Import or Die,"
e Economist, February 19, 1983, pp. 11–12.

Screws Are Tightening on U.S. Companies," *Business*
February 11, 1985, p. 38.

Cigarette Makers Aim for Bigger Share of Japan Mar-
Asian Wall Street Journal Weekly, October 28, 1985,

"Mexico Hopes Its Approval of IBM Plant En-
Foreign Investment," *The Wall Street Journal*,
25.

7. Anthony Spaeth and Amal Kumar Naj, "PepsiCo Accepts
Tough Conditions for the Right to Sell Cola in India," *The
Wall Street Journal*, September 20, 1988, p. 44.

8. *Business Week*, February 10, 1992, p. 43.

9. See "Mr. Tatum Checks Out, " *The Economist*, November 9,
1996, p. 78.

10. Lynne Reaves, "U.S. Marketers Fend Off Turmoil in Philippines," *Advertising Age*, May 16, 1988, p. 10.

11. *Fortune*, November 2, 1993, p. 18.

12. Humayun Akhtrer and Robert F. Lusch, "Political Risk and the
Evolution of the Control of Foreign Business: Equity, Earnings
and the Marketing Mix," *Journal of Global Marketing*, Spring
1988, p. 117.

13. David K. Eiteman and Arthur I. Stonehill, *Multinational Business Finance* (Reading MA: Addison-Wesley, 1979), p. 186.

14. David G. Bradley, "Managing Against Expropriation," *Harvard
Business Review*, July–August 1977, pp. 75–84.

CHAPTER 11

Legal Environment

CHAPTER FOCUS

After studying this chapter, you should be able to

- Describe two types of legal systems.

- Discuss jurisdiction of laws.

- Compare some relevant host country laws, U.S. laws, and international laws and conventions.

- Explain how companies may use arbitration to resolve conflict in a foreign environment.

Multinational enterprise in its global exercise must cope with widely differing laws. A U.S. corporation not only has to consider U.S. laws wherever it does business, but also must be responsive to the host country's laws.[1] For example, without requiring proof that certain market practices have adversely affected competition, U.S. law nevertheless makes them violations. These practices include horizontal price fixing among competitors, market division by agreement among competitors, and price discrimination. Even though such practices might be common in a foreign country, U.S. corporations cannot engage in them. Simultaneously, local laws must be adhered to even if they forbid practices that are allowed in the U.S. For example, in Europe a clear-cut distinction is made between agencies and distributorships. Agents are deemed auxiliaries of their principal; distributorships are independent enterprises. Exclusive distributorships are considered restrictive in European Union (EU) countries. The foreign marketer must be careful in making distribution arrangements in, say, France, so as not to violate the regulation concerning distributorship contracts.

Worldwide, different countries pursue legal systems of varied complexity and dimension. In some countries, laws provide only a broad guide, and the interpretation is left to the courts. In other countries, laws spell out virtually every detail. A foreign enterprise, therefore, has to be scrupulous in learning and heeding all local laws and regulations.[2] From the marketing standpoint, a U.S. company should be especially careful in obeying laws pertaining to competition, price setting (such as price discrimination, resale price maintenance), distribution arrangements (such as exclusive dealership), product quality (such as wholesomeness, packaging, warranty and service, patents and trademarks), personal selling (such as white-collar employment/labor laws), and advertising (such as media usage, information provision).

In addition, there are both host country and U.S. laws concerned with taxes, tariffs, licensing, and other areas related to business that should be understood and complied with, along with certain international laws and conventions that affect marketing decision making in the global context. The international marketer should also understand the use of arbitration as an alternative to legal recourse.

The impact of law on marketing is illustrated by an Italian law allowing wine coolers to be sold there. Although Italy had been producing wine coolers for export for years, existing law had prohibited wine from being mixed with other ingredients, basically to protect consumers from tampered wine. The new law prevents the beverage from being called a wine cooler. Instead, it is to be described as a wine-based "fantasy" beverage with a minimum of 75 percent wine and grape juice. The Italian word *fantasia* also means multicolored. No artificial flavors, sugar, or water are allowed. Both Riunite and Cantina Sociale di Foggia launched their wine beverages in Italy within days of official publication of the laws.[3]

International Legal Perspectives

Two important aspects of international legal systems are pertinent to marketing: the philosophical bases of the laws and the jurisdiction of these laws.

Common Law versus Code Law

Philosophically, two types of legal systems may be distinguished: common law and code law. *Common law* is based on precedents and practices established in the past and interpreted over time. Common law was first developed in England, and most of the countries that at one time or another formed a part of the British Empire follow this system. *Code law* is based on detailed rules for all eventualities. Code law was developed by the Romans and is popularly practiced by a number of free world countries. Most countries of the free world may be divided into those that follow common law, as do Great Britain, U.S., Australia, India, and Kenya, and those that have code law, as do Italy, France, Germany, Mexico, and Switzerland.

It is important for an international marketer to be familiar with the genesis of a country's law, for it frequently has far-reaching effects on all kinds of decisions. For example, the *right to a property* (which would cover such things as trademarks) in a common-law country would depend on the history of use of the property—that is, in the case of a trademark dispute which party actually used the trademark on its package and in its advertising campaign. According to code law, however, the right of property would be based on which party actually registered the trademark. Assume two companies, say Alpha and Beta, are claiming rights to a trademark. Alpha registered the trademark but never used it. On the other hand, Beta has been using it all along in various commercial ways without ever bothering to register it. In a common-law country, the trademark would belong to Beta Company. In a code-law country, it would be the property of the Alpha Company.

Similarly, so-called *acts of God* in contractual obligations are interpreted differently in the two legal systems. Consider a Japanese company that enters into contracts with firms in England and Italy to deliver certain electronic equipment on a specified date. When a hurricane on the high seas destroys the Japanese shipment, the company cannot fulfill the contract. In both England and Italy, this is considered an act of God, and the Japanese company is not held liable for not meeting the contractual terms. But now assume the shipment is destroyed by a breakdown in the air conditioning of the building where the goods are stored. In this case, the common law might not release the Japanese exporters from noncompliance, because air conditioning failure during summer heat can be expected and therefore is not an act of God. Under code law, however, both circumstances would most likely be considered acts of God.

The division between code-law and common-law countries, broad in nature, narrows in actual practice. Some common-law countries also have specific codes, particularly in the area of commerce, that must be followed. Furthermore, although two countries follow the same system, the interpretation in a particular case may differ based on the experiences and precedents in the two environments. Thus, air conditioning failure might be considered an act of God in Kenya, even though it is a common-law country, because air conditioning is limited there and the climate is sultry most of the year.

Jurisdiction of Laws

Remarkably enough, although business across national boundaries is an accomplished fact, there is no international body to make rules and oversee their fulfillment by different parties. Thus, a business incorporated in a particular country carries the burden of complying with the laws of both the incorporating nation and the host country. A large U.S. manufacturer with subsidiaries incorporated or registered in different parts of the world is liable to the laws of all the nations where it does business.

Major problems can occur when laws of more than one country must be respected and these laws have conflicting values. If a contract contains a *jurisdiction clause* stipulating which country's legal system should be used to settle disputes, the matter can be settled accordingly; but in the absence of such a clause, legal and counterlegal actions, presumably in different courts, perhaps in different countries, may follow. Should the laws of the country where the agreement was made prevail, or the laws of the country where the contract has to be fulfilled? Each party naturally would like to settle the issue according to the legal system that favors its position. Sometimes arbitration, which will be discussed in a later section, can settle the dispute.

Consider the Bhopal tragedy, in which over 2,000 people died from a gas leakage accident in a Union Carbide plant in India in 1984. The Indian government would have liked the question of compensation to survivors settled in the U.S. courts, because the U.S. courts have been more liberal than the Indian courts in granting compensation to victims in such cases. Union Carbide would have preferred that the case be settled in the Indian courts, in the hope that its liability would be reduced substantially. In the end, the case was settled in India (for readers' interest, it was an out-of-court settlement).

Host Country Laws

Countries enact laws to control foreign businesses in their economies, and some of these laws are discriminatory against foreign goods and businesses. On the other hand, laws are sometimes designed to allow reciprocity with nations on good trading terms with the country. Extremely favorable laws may be passed to attract foreign investment.

In general, the legal environment of a country for foreign commerce depends on that country's economic objectives and its obligations and position in relating to world-wide commerce. In some situations, though, the laws have political aims as well. For example, a government may decide to restrict all imports in order to promote a feeling of national unity among the people and their political supporters. Or different political considerations may cause a country to liberalize its laws pertaining to foreign business. In 1988, in the wake of a high U.S. trade deficit and under pressure from Washington, Taiwan reduced tariffs on some 3,500 items by an average of 50 percent, including telecommunications, medical equipment, pharmaceuticals, sophisticated electronic equipment, forest products, agricultural goods, and cigarettes.[4] South Korea and Japan, other trading partners of the U.S. with whom it had a substantial negative trade balance, have been similarly tilting their trade policy toward the U.S. Japan has finally scrapped its Staple Food Control Act that restricted free trade in rice. As a result, U.S. rice should be easy to sell in Japan. Also, the freer competition should bring down the price for the Japanese consumers, which has been roughly nine times the world market price.[5]

Laws that bear on entry into foreign markets take several forms, including tariffs, antidumping laws, export/import licensing, investment regulations, legal incentives, and restrictive trading laws.

Tariffs

A *tariff* is a tax that a government levies on exports and imports. The tax on exports is called *export duty*. The tax on imports is called *import duty* or *customs duty*. The purpose of export duty is to discourage selling overseas to maintain adequate supply at home.

The import duty is levied for different reasons: to protect home industry from being outpriced by cheap imports, to gain a source of revenue for the government, and to prevent the dilution of foreign exchange balances through consumer goods purchased by a few privileged people. In developing countries, where new industries cannot compete with imports from the Western World and resources are limited, the import duty serves as an important measure to promote economic development. Although the usual reasons for levying import duties do not apply for the U.S. and other industrialized countries, the influx of Japanese imports, particularly automobiles, has led many concerned groups to recommend heavy import duty on Nissans, Toyotas, and Hondas.

An import duty may be assessed either according to the value of the product (called *ad valorem*), or on a unit basis (called *specific duty*), or both. Computation of a specific duty is easier because the price factor does not come into the picture as it does in ad valorem duty.

A related term, *subsidy*, is relevant here. A subsidy is a reverse tariff. Many countries provide a subsidy for local manufactures for export abroad. For example, South Korea provides a subsidy to its steel manufacturers to compete effectively in the world market. A subsidy may also be provided to local products to make them competitive against imports. The U.S. government subsidizes certain types of steel to protect the U.S. industry against imports.

Antidumping Laws

Dumping is a type of pricing strategy for selling products in foreign markets below cost, or below the price charged to domestic customers. Dumping is practiced to capture a foreign market and to damage rival foreign national enterprises. In the 1980s foreign car manufacturers were charged with dumping cars in the U.S. Japanese television manufacturers and steel companies have been similarly charged. In recent years the U.S. government has accused India, France, and Brazil of dumping stainless steel wire rods and forged stainless steel flanges.[6]

Host governments often pass laws against dumping with a view to protecting local industries. Dumping can be a problem for developed and developing countries alike. The U.S. Treasury Department found that 23 of 28 foreign automakers had been dumping cars in the U.S. It demanded that the foreign manufacturers increase their car prices. Subsequently, Volkswagen, for instance, raised its car price an average of 2.5 percent.

In the same way, on the recommendation of the International Trade Commission, under the provisions of the 1974 Trade Act, the Treasury Department set minimum steel import price levels to enable U.S. manufacturers to compete against Japanese steelmakers.[7] Among the developing countries, Brazil has passed antidumping legislation against imports from the U.S. and Japan. Similar laws exist in South Korea, Taiwan, India, and Nigeria (see International Marketing Highlight 11.1).

In theory, the practice of dumping cannot be criticized. A business should be free to set any price it finds would be beneficial in the long run; thus, different prices may be set in different markets, based on the demand and the competition. The argument against dumping, however, is that price differentials are intended strictly to weaken competition and over the long run hurt everyone. Particularly in international business, dumping inhibits the orderly development of national industry. From this viewpoint, attacks on rival markets by dumping amount to destructive as well as unscrupulous means of securing market position. It is for this reason that countries pass *antidumping laws*.

International Marketing Highlight 11.1

Dump, Counterdump

The United States is the terror of the memory-chip industry. Over the years its trade officials have charged Japan, South Korea, and Taiwan with dumping, sparking trade wars, disrupting the industry, and, according to some, exacerbating shortages that have at times kept prices artificially high. Now, for the first time, Taiwan's semiconductor industry association is charging America's Mircron, along with the American subsidiaries of South Korea's LG and Samsung, with selling these chips, known as DRAMS, below cost in the Taiwanese market.

The Taiwanese allege that Micron is damaging local producers by selling chips more cheaply in Taiwan than at home. So far Taiwan has produced little evidence that this is so—and Micron denies it. But then again Taiwan's law is such that not much evidence is needed; there is, for instance, no requirement to prove a link between alleged dumping and injury. If the semiconductor association prevails, Taiwan could impose special tariffs on Micron and the American arms of the two South Korean firms, much as America has done to Japanese and South Korean producers in the past. In fact, things will probably not get so far; instead, most analysts see this Taiwanese action as a retaliation for the antidumping case against Taiwan that America started last year. If America dropped those charges, no doubt Taiwan would drop its charges against the U.S.

Source: The Economist, May 15, 1999, p. 66.

Export/Import Licensing

Many countries have laws on the books that require exporters and importers to obtain licenses before engaging in trade across national boundaries. For example, Singapore requires importers of video games to obtain an import permit from the Board of Film Censors to distribute their product in Singapore.[8] The purpose of an *export license* may be simply to allow for the statistical tracking of export activities. Licensing may also help to ensure that certain goods are not exported at all, or at least not to certain countries. Chapter 17 discusses U.S. government prohibition of exportation of certain high-tech and defense-related goods to certain countries. Readers may recall the debate in the Congress in 1993 about the sale of Cray's super computers and nuclear power plants to China, which finally was approved.[9]

Import licensing is enforced to control the unnecessary purchase of goods from other countries. Such restraints save foreign exchange balances for other important purposes like the import of pharmaceuticals, chemicals, and machinery. India, for example, has strict licensing requirements against the import of cars and other luxury goods.

Foreign Investment Regulations

One of the primary aims of laws and regulations on foreign investment is to limit the influence of MNCs and to achieve a pattern of foreign investment that contributes most effectively to the realization of the host country's economic objectives. There are several broad areas of legislation concerned with foreign investment: administration of the investment process, screening criteria, ownership, finance, employment and training, technology transfer, investment incentives, and dispute settlement.

General Motors (GM) Corporation's problems in Germany show how varying investment laws can pose difficulty. GM sold its unprofitable Terex subsidiary, which made earthmoving equipment, to IBH Holding AG of Mainz in 1980. Over the next two years, before IBH declared bankruptcy in 1983, GM made four equity investments in the increasingly troubled German holding company. In return, the automaker received immediate repayments of millions owed to it by IBH. Such a maneuver, called "round-tripping," is generally considered illegal, unless properly disclosed, in Germany—though not in the U.S. The Germans contend that this round-tripping could hide a company's true financial condition and thus mislead investors and creditors.

Criminal investigation was launched against GM and its chairman Roger Smith. It took two years for the problem to be settled and GM to be exonerated of any wrongdoing. Before making a routine visit to Germany in 1986, Mr. Smith directed GM attorneys to seek assurances from a German prosecutor's office that he would not be arrested. He further requested the audit committee of the GM board to conduct its own review to satisfy itself that he had acted properly.[10]

Legal Incentives

Investment incentives enacted to attract foreign investment are an important part of government policy in most developing countries. In a few cases, incentive schemes are still the only significant regulation of foreign investment. Also, in certain countries foreign private investment is the main or sole beneficiary of incentives, because local capital and entrepreneurship cannot undertake the kind of investment encouraged by the incentives. On the other hand, other countries restrict incentives to local enterprises, joint ventures, or enterprises with a minority foreign participation.

Depending on the basic approach to investment regulation, incentives may be awarded automatically to all enterprises meeting the conditions specified in the relevant legislation, or incentives may be granted for a specific performance or contribution to the host country's economy such as export promotion and diversification, the development of a backward area, the transfer of modern technology, the encouragement of applied research in the host country, and so forth. Incentives also are often awarded on the basis of case-by-case negotiation in accordance with ad hoc criteria.

The main incentive to the establishment of an enterprise is ordinarily an income-tax holiday of several years' duration. Some governments are inclined to reduce the length of such tax holidays when they involve important tax revenue losses. Tax measures such as accelerated depreciation (often used in developed countries as a stimulant to investment) have proved less effective for various reasons as incentives in the economic environment of developing countries, where the main interest is in new investment rather than the encouragement of expenditure on plant replacement. Other fiscal incentives obtainable in developing countries include the waiver of import duties on equipment and materials essential for production, exemptions from property taxes, and numerous minor tax concessions granted by the provinces or localities where the enterprise is located.

Restrictive Trading Laws

In addition to the tax incentive laws, many governments adopt measures that restrict imports or artificially stimulate exports. Usually such laws are referred to as *nontariff barriers* to international trade. There are several major types:

- *Government participation in trade:* subsidies, countervailing duties, government procurement, and state trading.
- *Customs and entry procedures:* valuation, classification, documentation, and health and safety regulations.
- *Standards:* product standards, packaging, and labeling and marking.
- *Specific limitations:* quotas, exchange controls, import restraints, and licensing.
- *Import charges:* prior import credit restrictions for imports, special duties, and variable levies.

    For example, suppose Germany imposes an 11 percent value-added tax on a domestic product and a 13 percent tax adjustment at the border on a product of identical price and quality imported from the U.S. German buyers would choose the German product over the U.S. import because the tax is 2 percent lower. If a German exporter were given a rebate of 13 percent, he would be able to sell at 2 percent below U.S. price levels and would benefit from an equivalent export subsidy.[11]

- *Other measures:* voluntary export restraints whereby agreement is made between two trading countries to limit the exports of a specific product to a particular level, such as the agreement between Japan and the U.S. in the 1980s to limit Japanese car exports to the U.S.; and orderly marketing agreements, which are specific agreements between trading partners to negotiate trade restrictions (see International Marketing Highlight 11.2).

━━━━━   **International Marketing Highlight 11.2**   ━━━━━

Tough Move on Gum Control

Like spitting, public chewing may wind up on the wrong side of the law in the sternly ruled island republic of Singapore. The government has banned the manufacture, sale, and importation of chewing gum. Mere possession of the stuff is not illegal yet, but offending sellers face fines of up to $1,200, and importers could get a year in jail. Gum, explains a government spokesman, "causes filthiness to our public facilities."

Singapore's subway trains have been halted several times recently when wads of chewing gum jammed their doors. The gum lobby argues that gum does not clog doors, people do. The government is unmoved.

Gum fanciers arriving from abroad must declare any gum they have with them on their customs forms. They will be allowed to bring in small amounts for their personal use, but the government reserves the right to define how much that may be.

Source: Time, January 13, 1992, p. 31.

U.S. Laws

Both U.S. corporations and their U.S. officers working abroad remain liable to the laws of the U.S. For instance, individuals must comply with U.S. Internal Revenue Service (IRS) laws, and corporations are bound by U.S. antitrust laws. One application of the U.S. antitrust laws to an American company overseas is the Gillette Company case. Many years ago, the Justice Department sought an injunction against Gillette for its acquisition of shares in Braun AG of Germany. The Justice Department held that Gillette's acquisition of Braun would restrict competition in shaving devices in the U.S., given the fact that Braun makes electric razors and that Braun had previously relinquished to a third company its rights to sell in the U.S. market until 1976.[12] (For readers' interest, Gillette acquired Braun AG in late 1980s.)

Some laws, however, have been specially enacted to direct multinational marketing activities, such as the Foreign Corrupt Practices Act (FCPA) of 1977. Basically, the intention of these laws is to protect American economic interests, ensure national security, maintain recognized standards of ethics, and promote fair competition.

Laws Affecting Foreign Trade

The U.S., relative to other nations, has a liberal attitude toward exports and imports. Nevertheless, there are many regulations that a U.S. exporter must be aware of in the conduct of business. First of all, the government prohibits trading with some nations, for example, Iran, Cuba, and, until recently, Vietnam. Also, exportation of several products, among them defense-related equipment, must be cleared with the U.S. Department of Commerce by obtaining a license permitting shipment (licensing requirements will be discussed in Chapter 17). The Omnibus Trade and Competitiveness Act of 1988 affects U.S. exporters in many ways, as discussed in Chapter 2.

The U.S. government imposes some restrictions, via the IRS, on pricing for intracompany foreign transactions. The IRS ensures that prices are not underestimated to save U.S. taxes. For example, a U.S. corporation may export certain goods to its subsidiary, say, in Germany, at a very low price. This would reduce the corporation's U.S. taxes. It is for this reason that the IRS is authorized to review pricing and demand change, if necessary, in such company-to-company overseas transfers.

In regard to imports, the U.S. markets traditionally are open to all nations with few restrictions. For health and safety reasons, food products from many developing countries are usually the subject of those restrictions. For example, in 1985 the Food and Drug Administration detained Sri Lankan tea imports for special testing following terrorist threats to contaminate that nation's black tea with cyanide. Sri Lanka provides about 11 percent of U.S. tea imports, or about 21 million pounds of black tea annually. As another example, for several weeks in 1989, Chilean grapes and other fruits were prohibited from entering the U.S., since some of these products had been poisoned.

Although the federal government basically subscribes to free trade and has supported through GATT (now WTO) the worldwide effort toward this goal, various legislative and nonlegislative measures have been adopted to protect domestic U.S. industry. Protectionism increased in the 1970s when more and more U.S. companies showed signs of crumbling, often from an inability to compete in the world market. The textile, tire, and auto industries cut production or closed down entire factories, largely because U.S. consumers purchased imports. Consequently, workers and industries applied continuing pressure for tougher tariffs and trade quotas. Thus, for some products, like automobiles, import duties were increased. For other products, like textiles, quotas were imposed on imports from various countries. For steel, the government set minimum prices on imports to make domestic steel competitive.

Antitrust Laws

As noted earlier, the U.S. antitrust laws apply to U.S. corporations in their international dealings as well as in their domestic transactions. More specifically, U.S. businesses must carefully ascertain if antitrust laws would be violated in any way in the following situations:

- When a U.S. firm *acquires* a foreign firm.
- When a U.S. firm *engages in a joint venture* abroad with another American company or a foreign firm.
- When a U.S. firm *enters into a marketing agreement* with a foreign-based firm.

The Justice Department has become very strict in the application of U.S. antitrust laws on foreign operations of U.S. corporations. Justice Department enforcement takes several forms.

- In 1980 it initiated criminal grand jury probes into allegations that U.S. and foreign competitors illegally set the prices of uranium, phosphate, and ocean shipping rates.
- In 1985 it reviewed the overseas licensing agreements of some two dozen multinationals to see whether their prices or territorial arrangements unreasonably prevented overseas producers from selling in the U.S.
- In 1990 it investigated oil company reactions to the new two-tier pricing system for foreign crude oil along with other aspects of their relations with oil-producing countries.
- In 1997 it examined the "marketing" merger between Texaco and Shell Oil and its impact on U.S. gasoline prices.

The antitrust laws are being legislated outside the U.S. as well, especially in EU countries. In 1999 Italy's competition authority nailed Coca-Cola for its anticompetitive practices. It has been claimed that Coca-Cola and CCBI, its affiliated bottler, along with six other local bottlers, not only dominate the Italian market, but have also abused this power to damage their competitors. One prong of Coke's strategy targets wholesalers. They are bound in by a complicated system of exclusivity bonuses and discounts, which are designed less to boost sales of Coke than to oust Pepsi from the market. To illustrate, a Roman wholesaler was lured into a 4 percent extra discount for exclusively carrying Coke by ousting Pepsi.[13] At the time of preparing this book the matter was still pending.

Foreign Corrupt Practices Act (FCPA)

The FCPA, passed by Congress in 1977, has stringent antibribery provisions prohibiting all U.S. companies on file with the Securities and Exchange Commission (SEC) from making any unauthorized payments. These payments include those made to foreign officials, political parties, or candidates. The law prescribes a $1 million penalty to a corporation for violation of the law. Corporate officers connected with illegal payments may be fined $10,000 or be subjected to a five-year imprisonment, or both.

How FCPA can create hindrances is illustrated by the Coca-Cola Company's deal with the former Soviet Union. In 1986 Coca-Cola signed a $30 million six-year agreement to expand its business in the U.S.S.R. Until then, Coke was sold only in Moscow shops for tourists, and the company's Fanta orange soda was available in only a few other cities. Published reports indicated that the Coca-Cola Company paid bribes to people in the Soviet Union to crack the Soviet market. Subsequently, a federal grand jury initiated an investigation to determine if the allegations of wrongdoing were correct. Although the company was finally proved innocent, it had to endure subpoenas of its documents and other inconveniences to prove its innocence.[14]

In part, the FCPA is an effort to extend American moral standards to other countries. The act also seeks to enlist U.S. MNCs as instruments of U.S. foreign policy. The FCPA, therefore, marks a major attempt by the U.S. government to enforce a series of noneconomic foreign policy objectives through private enterprise, which has traditionally been considered to have only economic purposes. The FCPA places American corporations doing business abroad in an awkward position. On the one hand, they must comply with the U.S. law, and on the other, they have to compete with other foreign countries whose governments do not prohibit such payments. In some nations where American business is conducted, bribery is commonplace; the FCPA could weaken the competitive position of U.S. corporations in such countries (see International Marketing Highlight 11.3).

In addition to the fact that the FCPA adversely affects U.S. trade, critics of the act argue that the U.S. should not try to force its moral principles and concepts of right and wrong on the whole world. Questionable practices such as bribery will continue in certain countries whether U.S. corporations participate or not. The best that can be hoped is that in the future, international bribery perhaps might be controlled through an international agreement effected through WTO.

The Omnibus Trade and Competitiveness Act of 1988 was passed to limit the scope of the FCPA. The primary change concerned the FCPA's prohibition against payments to third parties by a U.S. firm "knowing or having reason to know" that the third party would use the payment for prohibited purposes. Under the new law, the U.S. firm must have actual knowledge of or willful blindness to the prohibited use of the payment.

The act also clarifies the types of payments that are permissible and would not be considered bribery.[15] For example, under the FCPA as originally enacted, payments to low-level officials who exercise only "ministerial" or "clerical" functions were exempt. Unfortunately, this provision provided little guidance to companies in determining whether a given foreign official exercised discretionary authority: special problems arose in countries in the Middle East and Africa, where foreign officials can be employed part-time. The trade act provides a U.S. business with better guidance by specifying the types of payments that are permissible rather than which individuals can receive them. The act specifies that a payment for a routine government action such as processing papers, stamping visas, or scheduling inspections may be made without criminal liability. These changes to the FCPA make it easier for U.S. companies to do business in foreign countries by removing concerns about inadvertent violations.

■■■■■■■■■■   **International Marketing Highlight 11.3**   ■■■■■■■■■■

A World of Greased Palms

A secret Commerce Department study prepared with the help of U.S. intelligence agencies catalogs scores of incidents of bribery, of aid with strings attached, and other improper inducements by America's trading partners. In the case of strings-attached foreign aid, the deals may violate international trade pacts. And the cost of such practices to the U.S. economy appears enormous. In 1994 alone, U.S. intelligence tracked 100 deals worth a total of $45 billion in which overseas outfits used bribes to undercut U.S. rivals, the study says. The result: foreign companies won 80 percent of the deals. Among the main culprits are some of America's staunchest political allies: France, Germany, and Japan. The corporations involved are not cited by name in the study, but government sources identify premier European high-tech companies—including Germany's Siemens, France's Alcatel Alsthom, and the European airframe consortium Airbus Industrie—as among the major practitioners.

Foreign governments and companies, of course, gripe that the Clinton administration has been doing lots of aggressive advocacy of its own to win deals for U.S. business. "Each time we win a deal, it's because of dirty tricks," says an Airbus official with bitter sarcasm. "Each time Boeing wins, it's because of a better product." Indeed, many officials overseas view the U.S.'s holier-than-thou attitude about shady business practices as naïve and hypocritical.

Source: Business Week, November 6, 1995, p. 36.

Antiboycott Laws

From time to time nations attempt to put pressure on each other through programs of economic boycott. The early 1980s Arab boycott of companies doing business with Israel is an example of such a tactic. Most Arab states did not recognize Israel and hoped that an economic boycott would contribute to Israel's collapse. The oil fortunes of these Arab countries gave them significant economic clout to implement the boycott. Companies that dealt with Israel were blacklisted with the intention of squeezing Israel from all directions and forcing the country into economic isolation.

The U.S. government adopted various measures to prevent U.S. companies from complying with the Arab boycott. For example, the Tax Reform Act of 1976 included a measure that denied foreign income tax benefits to companies that subscribed to the boycott. The law preempts any state or local regulations dealing with boycotts fostered or imposed by foreign countries.[16]

The Arab boycott crumbled toward the end of the 1980s, making it easier for U.S. companies to continue their operations in Israel and at the same time seek out business in Arab states. For example, Coca-Cola Company began making inroads into the Gulf, Lebanon, Jordan, and Saudi Arabia as the boycott became ineffective.[17]

Laws to Protect Domestic Industry

The U.S. government has legislated many laws to protect domestic industry. From time to time, the government sets quotas on imports. For a number of years the sugar import quotas were set so as to preserve about half the market for U.S. producers. Often quotas are split among several countries interested in exporting to the U.S. Such allocation is partly influenced by political considerations. Thus, a certain proportion of a quota may be assigned to a developing country even though its price is higher than that of other exporters. For a few years early in the 1980s, the U.S. government had imposed quotas on Japanese car imports. Recently, a debate has been going on in the federal government about limiting Japanese textile exports to the U.S. by establishing quotas for different categories of textiles.

Quotas, usually provide only temporary relief to domestic industry. In the long run, a domestic industry must stand on its own. If it is inherently inefficient, quotas amount to a support of inefficiency. However, sometimes quotas are appropriately and productively used to buy time so an infant industry can mature and compete effectively.

Laws to Eliminate Tax Loopholes

Many federal laws are designed to eliminate tax loopholes. A prominent example is legislation against *tax havens,* countries that provide out-of-the-ordinary privileges to multinationals in order to attract them to their lands. Tax havens make it more profitable for companies to locate there than in the U.S. There are four types:

1. Countries with no taxes at all, such as the Bahamas, Bermuda, and the Cayman Islands.
2. Countries with taxes at low rates, such as the British Virgin Islands.
3. Countries that tax income from domestic sources but exempt income from foreign sources, such as Hong Kong, and Panama.
4. Countries that allow special privileges, which generally are suitable as tax havens only for limited purposes.

Tax havens offer corporations a legal way to save on taxes. However, a country must offer more than tax benefits to be a good market. Political stability, availability of adequate means of communication and transportation, economic freedom for currency conversion, and availability of professional services are important criteria for evaluating a tax haven.

Tax Treaties

Tax treaties are arrangements between nations that prevent corporate and individual income from being double-taxed. The U.S. has tax treaties with over 56 nations. Thus, foreigners who own securities in U.S. corporations and who are from countries with which there is a tax treaty pay a withholding tax of about 15 percent, while those from non–tax treaty countries pay a 28 percent tax.

The tax treaties are meant to provide a fair deal to individuals and corporations from friendly countries and thus encourage mutually beneficial economic activity. Usually, under a tax treaty, the country where the primary business activity takes place is provided the right to be the principal receiver of tax revenue. A small proportion of the tax may accrue to the other nation. Take, for example, the case of a Pakistani exporter with a business in the U.S. Since there is a tax treaty between the U.S. and Pakistan, the income of the Pakistani businessman, as far as his U.S. operations are concerned, would be taxable under the U.S. IRS rules. However, he would pay only a negligible tax in Pakistan.

Businesses, particularly the MNCs, use tax treaties in various ways to seek maximum benefits. Consider the following situations:

- A tax treaty between the U.S. and England requires a 15 percent withholding tax on dividends.
- A tax treaty between the U.S. and the Netherlands specifies a 5 percent withholding tax.
- A tax treaty between the Netherlands and Great Britain calls for a 5 percent withholding tax. Additionally, dividends from foreign sources are not taxed in the Netherlands.

According to these arrangements, a U.S. company could establish a holding company in the Netherlands that might receive dividend income from a British subsidiary. Moreover, the dividends could be remitted to the parent company in the U.S. The combined tax in the whole process would amount to 10 percent rather than 15 percent.

Tax treaties between the U.S. and different countries are reviewed from time to time. This permits periodic changes in treaty agreements to accommodate changes in the country's monetary and fiscal policies. Usually, a treaty spells out the procedure for consultation and negotiation between officials of the two countries, should disagreements occur.

U.S. Government Support

Nations provide many kinds of support to their companies to enable them to compete successfully for foreign business. Companies belonging to EU countries are often eligible for such government support as low-cost or no-cost bank guarantees, low-cost or no-cost working capital loans, and protection from price escalation.

Traditionally, this type of support has not been available from the U.S. government. In the fall of 1985, however, the U.S. government established a program of bank guarantees similar to those of EU countries.[18] Congress approved the creation of a "war chest" of $300 million to allow the Export-Import Bank to match or beat competitors' subsidies for the benefit of U.S. exporters (see International Marketing Highlight 11.4). In 1992, under pressure from the U.S. during President Bush's trip to Japan, the Japanese automakers promised to increase their purchases of U.S. parts from $9 billion annually to $19 billion in four years and import an estimated 20,000 more U.S. cars per year.[19] For various reasons, this program did not go far.

International Marketing Highlight 11.4

U.S. Subsidizes Big Food Companies in Their Search for Foreign Markets

McDonald's got $465,000 from the U.S. Agriculture Department in 1991 for ads, paper tray liners, and counter displays promoting Chicken McNuggets to customers around the world.

Campbell Soup Co. spent part of the $450,000 it got from the government to remind the people of Japan, Korea, Argentina, and Taiwan to have a V8 juice. Joseph E. Seagram and Sons touted its Four Roses whiskey in Europe and the Far East with $146,000 from the department.

The three companies are among dozens of well-known corporate giants that have collected money under a U.S.D.A. program to find new overseas market for U.S. food, candy, bourbon, wine, ginseng, cotton, mink pelts, and bovine semen. The $200-million-a-year Market Promotion Program is supposed to help U.S. farmers by promoting exports of products that contain at least 50 percent U.S. agricultural commodities. Two-thirds of the grants in 1991 went to industry associations that conduct promotions for products such as strawberries, kiwis, or cling peaches. The remainder went to a long list of companies to advertise their brand-name products. Those brands include Burger King, M&M-Mars, Hershey Foods, Del Monte, Welch's, Ocean Spray Cranberries, Nabisco, and Quaker Oats.

Source: Marketing News, March 2, 1992, p. 7.

Then, in October 1994 the U.S. and the Japanese governments made four new trade deals.[20] Two of these deals made it easier for Americans (and other foreigners) to sell telecom equipment to the Japanese government and to NTT, Japan's biggest telephone firm, which is 65 percent state-owned. The third deal helped foreign firms to seek government's contracts to supply medical equipment. The fourth deal clarified regulations in the Japanese insurance market, permitting companies to change premium and introduce new products without permission from regulators.

International Laws

International law is a huge area of study, impossible to cover here, even perfunctorily. We will focus on certain areas of international law that are of particular relevance to the marketer.

GATT, IMF, and the World Bank were discussed in Chapter 3. Agreements under these institutions compose international laws of sorts that influence business in different ways. The WTO regulations are particularly relevant for marketers since they deal with trade restrictions and barriers that affect market potential.

To give the reader an idea of other areas covered by international law and the agencies that administer these laws, a brief discussion follows of those relating to property protection, UN treaties and conventions, metric transition, UN consumer protection, and regional laws.

Protection of Property

"Property" here refers to patents, trademarks, and the like. In the U.S., businesses seek protection of their property under U.S. laws. For example, a trademark can be registered. In an overseas situation, a multinational enterprise runs the risk of piracy. Stories are told of jeans manufactured in Hong Kong being given the Calvin Klein brand name and sold in Europe at half the usual price. Computer pirates in Taiwan incur the wrath of IBM Corporation. IBM-compatible computers are sold widely in Taiwan by scores of small companies, who manufacture counterfeit machines in violation of IBM's copyrights.[21] The U.S. Patent Trademark Office estimates that intellectual-property losses for U.S. industry, measured in terms of lost licensing opportunities and cost of enforcement, totaled at least $30 billion in 1988 alone[22] (see International Marketing Highlight 11.5).

Companies spend millions of dollars to establish trademarks and brand names. Consider, for example, Coca-Cola, Tide, and Corningware's cornflower pattern. If a foreign firm steals a company's established brand name and uses it on a locally conceived and manufactured product, not only are potential markets lost, but often that company's reputation is hurt if the imitated product is of inferior quality, as it frequently is.

In Ciudad del Este, Paraguay, which borders Argentina and Brazil, counterfeit goods from Asia spill onto the streets, at corners, near bus stops—even in the middle of a four-lane highway. As in the street markets of Mexico City, the shirt with a Nike logo is not a Nike-authorized product. Nor are the Guess watches, the music cassettes, or the video games legitimate.

The Paraguayan border city is just one example of Latin America's informal economy, or *gray market*. Seldom thought of in the context of the logistics chain, this market robs transport companies of cargo to carry, warehousers of freight to store, and insurers of traffic to cover. And, of course, trademark, patent, and copyright violations cost companies in the U.S. and other industrialized countries billions of dollars in lost sales.[23] Yet, many governments in Latin America are willing to close their eyes to the informal economy because it provides needed employment.

U.S. companies are particularly susceptible to piracy because of their lead in many technologies and number of household brand names. In 1992 a federal jury ordered Minolta Camera Co. to pay Honeywell Inc. $96 million for infringing on two Honeywell patents in its autofocus cameras.[24] The intellectual-property protection problem, however, is not limited to U.S. companies. Multinationals from other parts of the world face similar problems. For example, Hitachi Ltd. has accused Korea's Samsung Electronics Co. of using its technology to make dynamic random access memory chips. Hitachi also has sued the U.S.'s Motorola, Inc., charging that its MC88200 chip infringes on a Hitachi patent.[25]

The traditional way of protecting property outside the home country is by obtaining parallel protection in each host country. This process is cumbersome and expensive. It cost one large company almost $2 million to obtain foreign patents. In addition, this process is replete with risks that the patent will not be granted because the standards for patentability in some countries are not compatible with accepted practices in other countries.[26]

There are international conventions and agreements that can make it easier to secure property rights. But overall, international arrangements for property protection are insufficient and inadequate, and brand name/trademark piracy is not actually alleviated. The real problem arises when the question of copyright infringement is not clear-cut. Consider the fight between Lego System (a Danish company), the world's leading maker of children's building blocks, and a U.S. company, Tyco, popularly known for its model trains. Tyco spotted Lego's lack of competition and launched its own high-quality Lego copies called Super Blocks at retail prices 25 percent below Lego's. Thanks in part to its hard-hitting advertising campaign ("If you can't tell the difference, why pay the difference?"), in 1986 Tyco captured more than one-fifth of the $100 million U.S. market for blocks. Lego sued Tyco for copyright infringement in Hong Kong, where Tyco's blocks were made before production was shifted to Taiwan. Following a trial in 1986 that cost each company $2 million, the Hong Kong lower court decided in favor of Lego. However, the appeals court reversed parts of the decision, and both toy makers have appealed to the London Court of Arbitration. In early 1987 the London court upheld the decision of the appeals court.[27]

Interestingly, owing to philosophical differences between code law and common law, sometimes injured parties lose in legal dispute. For example, under common law, the right to property is established by actual use, while under code law the right emerges from legal registration. Thus, if a pirate registered a well-known brand (say, Colgate) in a code-law country (say, Italy), in a legal dispute the actual owner (the Colgate Palmolive Company) may lose to the pirate, at least in Italy. Of course, if the country in question happens to be a friendly country, the U.S. government may be willing to help.

■■■■■■■■■■   **International Marketing Highlight 11.5**   ■■■■■■■■■■

Rounding Up Counterfeiters

Levi Strauss & Co. touts its trousers as "America's original jeans." But these days, so do a lot of others. The famous apparel maker is fighting an unprecedented explosion of counterfeit pants. In 1991 Levi seized 1.3 million pairs of knockoffs, more than five times as many as it usually confiscates in a year. But the new knockoffs, most of which are made in China, differ from the crude copies the company has seen in the past.

Counterfeiters have crossed the threshold. The typical consumer would not be able to detect that they are buying counterfeits. The fakes bear labels saying that they're made in the U.S. and proclaiming that their colored-tab and stitched-pocket design are registered trademarks to help you identify garments made only by Levi Strauss & Co.

Only someone well-versed in the "construction and engineering" of Levis could tell the difference. There are a few identifying marks on the real McCoys, but Levi doesn't want to tell consumers what they are for fear of tipping its hand to counterfeiters. (One difference is that real Levi labels note that they are "made from recycled paper.")

Though the fake Levis look nearly identical, the company contends they may fall apart at the seams. After a few washes, belt loops fall off, rivets rust, and shrinkage control is not what it should be. Levi contends that poor-quality jeans will hurt its reputation.

Counterfeiters are trying to cash in on the huge demand for Levi jeans overseas. Though fakes have been seized in 31 countries, most are destined for the booming European market, where Levis are a status symbol, commanding up to $100 a pair. In 1990 alone, the company's sales in Europe, where Levi sells mostly jeans, rose 55 percent. But Levi can't meet worldwide demand for its best-selling button-fly "501" jeans, most of which are manufactured in the U.S.

Counterfeiters are eager to take up the slack. To combat them, Levi has spent about $2 million on more than 60 investigations, relying on a network of informants in Asia and Europe and trying to build paper trails on the middlemen who drive the market.

Source: The Wall Street Journal, February 19, 1992, p. B1.

Following is a description of the important international conventions for property protection.

International Bureau for the Protection of Industrial Property. This bureau was established by the Paris Convention, to which over 50 nations including the U.S. subscribed. Currently the membership includes some 94 countries. Under this convention, once a company has filed for a patent in one country, it has priority for 12 months in seeking the patent in all other member countries. Further, the convention requires each member country to extend to the nationals of other member countries the same rights it provides to its own nationals.

The Inter-American Convention. Most Latin American countries and the U.S. are parties to this convention. It provides its members protection similar to that of the Paris Convention for inventions, patents, designs, and models.

Madrid Arrangement for International Registration of Trademarks. This forum has 26 members in Europe. The U.S. is not a member of the Madrid Convention. Under the Madrid arrangement, the member countries grant automatic registration in all countries through registration in one of the countries upon payment of the required fee. For example, if a company registers a trademark in Spain, a member country, registration is simultaneously ensured in the other 25 member countries after the appropriate payments are made.

The Trademark Registration Treaty. In the early 1970s, 16 European nations signed a convention to establish a European patent office. Under this convention, the patent office makes one grant for all the member countries under a single European patent law. The European patent office became operational in 1978 in Munich, Germany (see International Marketing Highlight 11.6).

International Marketing Highlight 11.6

Wanted: One Patent for One Market

When it comes to patent applications in Europe, companies have two choices: to take a national route or opt for a "European" solution. The first entails the process of applying for a patent in each member state—a drawn-out, expensive process requiring separate translations, procedures, lawyers, agents, and fees for each state.

On completion, the company will have a number of patents, each of which varies in scope and conditions, and each open to separate interpretations in each national court.

The alternative is to take the "European" route. This involves filing an application at Munich's European Patent Office (EPO). However, the EPO does not grant an EU patent but only a bundle of national patent rights whose terms and conditions will differ according to the respective national laws of the contracting countries—the 15 EU member states plus Switzerland, Liechtenstein, Monaco and six Eastern European states. Once the grant is made, a "national phase" follows that entails a full translation of the filing for each state in which a firm has applied for patent rights. The applicant has to pay for translations, filings and attorney fees.

Source: Crossborder Monitor, September 1998. p.1.

Intellectual-property protection has improved in several problem countries in recent years, particularly Taiwan, Indonesia, and China.[28] This improved protection has largely been the result of political pressure from the U.S. (see International Marketing Highlight

11.7) In the Uruguay Round of GATT negotiations, intellectual-property rights was a new issue deliberated by the nations. The members agreed to a negotiating framework that allowed for conclusion of a comprehensive agreement to govern the *trade-related aspects of intellectual property (TRIPs)*. The Uruguay Round supports the concept of *reciprocity* in the matter of intellectual-property rights (i.e., rights available to nationals are extended to foreigners as well), and applies the concept of "most favored nation" to the area of intellectual-property rights.[29]

Following is a checklist for intellectual-property protection:[30]

- Find out how the country protects intellectual property, if at all.
- Register your copyrights and trademarks in countries in which you do business.
- Clearly spell out dispute-resolution procedures in contracts.
- Explore entering into licensing contracts with likely problem competitors, especially in countries without strong intellectual-property laws.
- Consider distributing only older material overseas, especially in countries where the state of technology is somewhat less advanced.
- Establish relations and cooperate with local customs officials and police.
- Hire a private investigator to gather evidence of piracy and work with local officials.

UN Treaties and Conventions

The United Nations (UN) has established a number of autonomous bodies and agencies to encourage worldwide economic cooperation and prosperity, as follows.

World Health Organization. (WHO): works to improve health conditions. WHO deals with such matters as drug standardization, epidemic control, health delivery systems, and related programs.

International Civil Aviation Organization (ICAO): promotes safe and efficient air travel through regulating flow of air traffic, air-worthiness standards, airport operations, and related communications.

International Marketing Highlight 11.7

Saudi Copyright Law

Saudi Arabia passed a copyright law to curb widespread piracy of such material as videotapes and computer software. The law, approved by King Fahd in December 1989, was in response to pressure from the U.S., where the Motion Picture Association of America has claimed industry losses of about $200 million a year due to piracy of videotapes in Saudi Arabia alone. The new law strictly forbids piracy, but diplomatic sources said much will depend on how the Saudis enforce the law.

Source: The Wall Street Journal, January 18, 1990, p. A16.

International Telecommunications Union (ITU): regulates international communications via radio, telephone, and telegraph. For example, ITU controls and allocates radio frequencies and facilitates intercountry telegraph and telephone communications.

Universal Postal Union (UPU): facilitates postal communication. For example, UPU conducts settlements among nations related to revenue sharing.

International Labor Organization (ILO): protects workers' rights, promotes worker welfare, and enhances the effectiveness of their organizations.

International Telecommunications Satellite Consortium (INTELSAT): deals with matters of telecommunication. INTELSAT's work mainly concerns new satellite communications technology.

International Standards Organization (ISO): another specialized UN agency, ISO is particularly important because its administration bears directly on marketing. ISO promotes standardization of different products and processes. The ultimate purpose is to encourage world trade and business without hindrance from design/style/feature variations among nations.

As an example, the ISO has over 100 committees that are actively engaged in developing uniform international standards in various fields. In 1987 the ISO issued *ISO 9000,* a series of documents that provide guidance on the selection and implementation of an appropriate quality management program for a supplier's operations. The purpose of the program is to document, implement, and demonstrate the quality assurance systems used by companies that supply goods and services internationally.

The impact of these agencies on international business varies. For example, an airframe industry is affected by the ICAO regulations; a WHO agreement might apply to a pharmaceutical company. But the importance of the need for standardization does not vary. A grinding machine still usable in the U.S. might be unsuitable in England for such reasons as differences in electric current and weight measures (in England, power is normally supplied at 220 volts and the metric system is used). Thus, in order to sell a U.S.–made grinding machine, the tolerance measurement may have to be varied to conform to measurements commonly used in Great Britain. Similarly, the electrical wiring may require change for the machine to operate with a different supply power.

Consider the European telecommunications industry: In Spain, the busy signal is three pips a second; in Denmark it is two. Telephone numbers within French cities are seven digits long; in Italy they're almost any length. German phones run on 60 volts of electricity; elsewhere, on 49. Only about 30 percent of the technical specifications involved in phone systems are common from one country to the next.[31]

Needless to say, standardization in the European telecommunications industry is overdue.

Metric Transition

The differences in standards are among the major hindrances to world trade and business development and have led to market opportunity losses for U.S. companies in many nations. International cooperation is overdue in this area. Traditionally, U.S. industry and government have played almost no role in seeking common standards worldwide. This indifference may be attributed to the fact that the overseas business of U.S. firms is proportionately small. In the future, however, U.S. businesses are more likely to participate actively in the standardization effort.

The U.S. Department of Commerce's National Institute of Standards and Technology (NIST), previously known as the National Bureau of Standards (NBS), has been given several new assignments to boost U.S. industry in the world marketplace by seeking standardization. The assignments result from the 1988 Omnibus Trade and Competitiveness Act, which addresses the problem by moving the U.S. closer to the metric system, now used by most of the world's population. The "inch-pound" system of measurement used in the U.S., known as the *customary* or *English* system, was abandoned even by the English when the U.K. switched to the metric system in the early 1970s. Only the U.S. continues to use it.

The 1988 act states that the metric system is "the preferred system of weights and measures for U.S. trade and commerce." It directs the federal government to provide leadership in metric conversion and calls for a preference in government purchasing for metric products. The act requires federal agencies to use the metric system wherever it is practical to do so in procurements, grants, and other business-related activities. The agencies have notified grantees, contractors, and suppliers of the new requirements and of time schedules for meeting the government's deadline.

The act specifies that the federal government has a responsibility to develop procedures and techniques to assist industry, especially small business, as it voluntarily converts to the metric system. Nevertheless, individual groups and industries are still free to decide whether to convert and to determine conversion timetables according to their own needs.

The trade act requires government and industry to use metric units in documentation of exports and imports as prescribed by the International Convention on the Harmonized Commodity Description and Coding System *(Harmonized System)*. This system is designed to standardize international commodity classifications for all major trading nations. The international metric system (SI) is the official measurement system of the Harmonized System.

Congress spelled out in the act the reasons it believes the U.S. would benefit from converting to the metric system:

- World trade is increasingly geared toward the metric system of measurement.
- Industry in the U.S. is often at a competitive disadvantage when dealing in international markets because of its nonstandard measurement system, and is sometimes excluded when it is unable to deliver goods that are measured in metric system.
- The inherent simplicity of the metric system of measurement and standardization of weights and measures has led to major cost savings in certain industries that have converted to that system.
- The metric system of measurement can provide substantial advantages to the federal government in its own operations.[32]

The EU is proceeding aggressively with plans to standardize differing national specifications and testing and certification procedures into a single EU-wide body of uniform standards and regulations. Such standardization can offer real advantages to U.S. businesspeople interested in a large market for their goods. A U.S. product that meets the EU requirements in one member state can be freely marketed throughout the EU.

UN Guidelines on Consumer Protection

After more than six years of work, in April 1985 the UN General Assembly adopted by consensus a set of guidelines on consumer protection. The guidelines cover the following basic consumer principles:[33]

- Insurance of the physical safety of consumers and their protection from potential dangers caused by consumer products.
- Protection of consumers' economic interests.
- Consumers' access to the necessary information to make informed choices according to their individual wishes and needs.
- Availability of effective consumer redress.
- Freedom to form consumer groups or organizations and the opportunity of such organizations to be consulted and to have their views represented.

These guidelines are important because without acceptance of such principles and strong information links on products that have been banned or severely restricted in various countries, sales could continue unabated. In other words, profit motive may override consideration for the harm many products may induce. Implementation of these guidelines by countries currently lacking adequate consumer protection will help make up for that lack.

Regional Laws

Regional laws pertain to specific areas involving a group of countries tied together through some kind of regional economic cooperation. (Chapter 7 examined different forms of regional groupings.) Market groups may legislate laws applicable to MNCs conducting business within the member countries. The most progressive market agreement is represented by the EU. The EU has adopted a variety of directives that deeply affect multinational enterprises. For example, the head offices of MNCs with European-based subsidiaries are required to make disclosures of their global operations to local labor unions twice a year, obliging them to inform and consult with the labor unions on any major decision affecting workers.

Another directive requires MNCs to consolidate the accounts of European subsidiaries. A third directive relates to product-liability standards, effectively eliminating the need for plaintiffs to show negligence to justify injury claims. Under a fourth one, workers would sit on the boards of all public companies. Most radical of all is a directive that makes corporate directors *personally* liable for damages should minority stockholders or creditors, or even employees, of a subsidiary suffer as a result of a corporate headquarters' decision favoring the interests of the parent company and its stockholders.

These kinds of directives are not accepted quickly; the EU lawmaking process is cumbersome. The directives to harmonize the national laws of the 15 members of the EU must first be endorsed by a majority of the 19 European commissioners (two each from Britain, France, Germany, and Italy, one each from the rest, and all appointed for four-year terms by their governments). Draft-stage directives then go to the 520-member European Parliament in Strasbourg, whose main role is to propose amendments for the commissioners' consideration. After receiving the parliament's views, the commission prepares a final draft of the directive and submits it to the Council of Ministers, composed of the appropriate cabinet-level officers from each national government. With the council's consent, a proposal becomes a legally binding EU directive, but even then it does not become law automatically. Enacting legislation to fulfill the intent of EU directives remains a prerogative of national parliaments. For example, in 1985 an EU product-liability directive was adopted by the Council of Ministers after more than eight years of talks. The directive allows consumers to collect damages for injuries from defective products without showing that the manufacturer was at fault. Member nations were directed to pass laws that would comply with the directive within three years, which they did.

Arbitration

Despite their best efforts, U.S. businesspeople working at the international level run into difficulties from time to time with people, companies, or organizations in foreign countries. The conflict may be with the host country government; a native firm, either in the public or private sector; or a multinational firm belonging to a third country. The source of the difficulty may arise from differing interpretations of the contractual terms or because of opposing positions on an ad hoc issue that was not anticipated at the time the contract was made.

There are three ways for an international firm to resolve conflicts. First, the two parties mutually agree to settle the differences. Second, the firm decides to sue the other party. Third, the conflicting parties agree to arbitration. Of the three alternatives, the first one is the best. Usually, however, the conflicting parties cannot realistically be expected to resolve their differences between themselves. Legal action, the second alternative, may not, for a variety of reasons, be in the best long-term interest of the international marketer. Legal action against a native firm would surely affect the reputation of the foreign enterprise, no matter how strong its case. Further, there is no guarantee that the court would make a fair, unbiased decision. Moreover, the legal route can be messy, time-consuming, and expensive.

For example, taking legal action in a trade case can range from an average of $54,700 for a Section 301 violation (an unfair foreign trade practice) to $715,000 or more for a Section 337 case (an infringement or theft of intellectual property rights such as patents, trademarks, and copyrights.) Similarly, legal costs in a dumping case may range from $151,000 to $553,000. An import threat to national security may cost $181,300 to $537,500.[34]

Usually the best recourse of a multinational firm to resolve conflict in a foreign environment is *arbitration,* which can be defined as a process of settling disputes by referring the matter to a disinterested party for a review of the merits of the case and for a judgment. The judgment may or may not be binding on the conflicting parties—hence the term *binding arbitration.* Traditionally, the disputing parties resorted to ad hoc arrangements for arbitration, because prior to 1966 there was no international authority to serve as arbitrator between an international marketer and a host country party. Currently, a number of arrangements are available for arbitration, as follows:

1. The *International Center for Settlement of Investment Disputes (ICSID)* was established in 1966 by the World Bank convention to enable private investors to obtain redress against a foreign state for grievances arising out of an investment dispute. The convention established strict rules for arbitration that may explain in part why it is seldom used:

The Convention provides that, where both parties have consented to arbitration under the auspices of the Center, neither may withdraw its consent unilaterally; and should either party refuse to submit to the jurisdiction of the Center thereafter, an award can nevertheless be entered which will be final, binding, and enforceable without relitigation, in all nations that are members of the Convention. To facilitate the enforcement of awards, each member nation is obliged to designate a domestic court or other authority responsible for enforcement of awards made.

ICSID has not been able to play the role expected by the signatories who created the convention. The problem is that large developing countries, important prospects for direct foreign investment, are not ICSID members. Most of Latin American countries are among the nonsignatories; they subscribe to the *Calvo doctrine* for representation of their position. Named after an Argentine jurist, this doctrine provides that a foreign investor, by virtue of making an investment, implicitly agrees to be treated by the host government as a national and gives up the right to involve any outside agency or home government in the resolution of a dispute. ICSID has received lukewarm support from host countries as an arbitrator of disputes.

2. The *Inter-American Commercial Arbitration Commission* serves to arbitrate disputes for businesses of 21 Western Hemisphere countries, including the U.S.

3. The *International Chamber of Commerce (ICC)* is an association of chambers of commerce worldwide. It has established a court of arbitration that has set rules used in conducting arbitration proceedings. Perhaps of all the arrangements for arbitration, ICC is the most successful. Of the over 200 decisions that the ICC Court of Arbitration made in recent years, only about 24 were questioned by the disputants. Of these 24 decisions, 21 were upheld in the courts when further legal action was pursued.

The ICC arbitration procedure is rather simple. In the first instance, it tries to settle the dispute through mutual conciliation. If that fails, each party is allowed to choose one member of the Court of Arbitration from its current list of distinguished lawyers/ jurists/judges. The third member is appointed by ICC. The Court of Arbitration schedules hearings and, after reviewing the facts presented by the plaintiff and the defendant, makes a decision.

4. The *American Arbitration Association (AAA)* is basically a U.S. tribunal originally established to conduct arbitration among businesses in the U.S. More recently, the AAA extended the scope of its activities beyond the U.S.

5. The *Canadian-American Commercial Arbitration Commission (CACAC)* serves as arbitrator between U.S. and Canadian businesses.

6. The *London Court of Arbitration* has jurisdiction that is restricted to cases that should legally be arbitrated in the U.K. The decisions of this court are legally binding on the parties in dispute under the English law.

A number of other agencies and organizations arbitrate in disputes about foreign direct investment. One of these is the *International Court of Justice (ICJ)*, also sometimes referred to as the *World Court,* a special judicial UN agency. ICJ can be approached for the arbitration of disputes between sovereign nations. Thus, if the U.S. government decides to take up a matter on behalf of a U.S. company that is in a conflict with a government overseas, the dispute can be referred to ICJ for decision. Needless to say, the federal government would pursue the matter only if it involved a national issue. Since ICJ deals only with disputes between nations, and not those between individuals or their companies, and since the government would involve itself only if the matter is of national importance, ICJ has not been extensively used for the settlement of investment disputes.

Another agency is the *Permanent Court of Arbitration (PCA)*. Established by the Hague Conventions of 1899 and 1907, the PCA consists of a small bureau at the Hague and a panel of arbitrators, four from each member country. The arbitrators are chosen from the panel members whenever a case must be examined. PCA has played an insignificant role in connection with international investment disputes. Like the ICJ, use of PCA for arbitration in international investment disputes comes only through the U.S. federal government.

Finally, arbitration may also be conducted by an *International Claims Commission (ICC)*. The ICC is an ad hoc arbitration arrangement. When a substantial number of claims between two countries accumulate, an ICC arbitration tribunal may be established by agreement between the interested nations. ICC's use requires that the U.S. government espouse and raise the MNC's claim against the other nation. To invoke the jurisdiction of any of the last three bodies, the foreign nation in question must consent to arbitration.

Summary

A U.S. corporation involved in international marketing should comply not only with U.S. laws but also with host country laws. Worldwide, different countries follow different sets of laws. An international marketer should be particularly familiar with host country laws pertaining to competition, price setting, distribution arrangements, product liability, patents and trademarks, and advertising.

To fully grasp a country's laws, it is essential to understand the legal philosophy of the country. Countries may follow common law or code law. Common law is based on precedents and practices; England, for example, is a common-law country. Code law is based on detailed rules; Mexico is a code-law country. The legal basis of a country can affect marketing decisions in multifaceted ways.

Another important legal environment aspect is the jurisdiction of laws. The question of which laws will apply in which particular matters must be known. In some instances, those of the country where the agreement was made apply; in others, those of the country where the business was conducted apply. It is desirable to have a jurisdictional clause in agreements. If there is none, when a conflict of interest occurs, it may either be settled through litigation or be referred for arbitration.

In addition to heeding both U.S. and host country laws, international marketers must be aware of treaties and international conventions. By and large, the relevant laws of the host country would be those concerning tariffs, dumping, export/import licensing, foreign investment, foreign investment incentives (provided by the government to attract foreign business), and restrictions on trading activities. The relevant U.S. laws would be those affecting foreign trade, antitrust laws, antiboycott laws, laws to protect domestic industry, laws to prevent loopholes in the existing tax laws (tax haven laws), tax treaties, and laws that pertain to U.S. government support of U.S. business abroad.

Some international treaties and conventions are concerned with the protection of property such as patents, trademarks, models, and the like, in foreign countries. Some international laws have provisions for the encouragement of both worldwide economic cooperation and prosperity and standardization of international products and processes.

If a legal conflict occurs between parties from different countries, one way of resolving it is through arbitration. A number of organizations are available for arbitration of disputes: the International Center for Settlement of Investment Disputes, the Inter-American Commercial Arbitration Commission, the International Chamber of Commerce, the American Arbitration Association, the Canadian-American Commercial Arbitration Commission, and the London Court of Arbitration.

Review Questions

1. Distinguish between code law and common law. Illustrate how the differences between the two may affect marketing decisions.
2. Explain how one might determine which of two different countries' laws would be applicable in the event of a dispute.
3. Define *dumping*. Why do countries pass antidumping laws?
4. Do U.S. antitrust laws apply to U.S. corporations in their international dealings? If so, how does this affect the competitive position of U.S. corporations?
5. What sort of support could the U.S. government provide to help U.S. corporations compete effectively against non–U.S. multinationals?
6. What is arbitration? Discuss the role of the ICC as an arbitration agency.

Creative Questions

1. Internationally adequate protection of intellectual-property rights is important for the U.S. since we as a nation have a higher stake than others in the matter. The WTO agreement provides 20 years of protection for patents, trademarks, and copyrights in the book, software, film, and pharmaceutical industries. Developing countries were given 10 years to phase in patent protection for pharmaceuticals. Is this enough to protect U.S. interests? If not, what additional measures should be adopted?
2. In developing countries, governments have large procurement programs. Often multinational corporations outside the U.S. have high-level government support to

successfully compete for these programs. Should the U.S. provide such help to its companies? What if such help leads to government interference in other business matters?

Endnotes

1. Gillian Rice, " Philosophy and Practice of Islamic Ethics: Implications for Doing Business in Muslims Countries," *Discussion Paper Series*, No. 90–5, The American Graduate School of International Management.

2. Shoshana B. Tancer, " Strategic Management of Legal Issues in the Evolving Transnational Business," *Discussion Paper Series*, No. 99-5, The American Graduate School of International Management.

3. *Advertising Age*, April 2, 1988, p. 34.

4. Ford S. Worthy, "Tightwad Taiwan Starts to Spend," *Fortune*, December 5, 1988, p. 177.

5. "Japanese Rice: The End of An Era," *The Economist*, August 20, 1994, p. 52.

6. Aziz Haniffa, "India Accused of Dumping Steel," *India Abroad*, August 6, 1993, p. 24.

7. Warren J. Keegan, *Multinational Marketing Management*, 3rd ed. (Englewood Cliffs, NJ: Prentice-Hall, 1984), p. 346.

8. *Asia Wall Street Journal Weekly*, February 21, 1994, p. 8.

9. "President Pitchman," *Business Week*, December 6, 1993, p. 42.

10. Doron P. Levin and Thomas F. O'Boyle, "GM's Chairman Runs into Bizarre Problem Under German Law," *The Wall Street Journal*, June 10, 1987, p. 1.

11. A. O. Cao, "Nontariff Barriers to U.S. Manufactured Exports," *Columbia Journal of World Business*, Summer 1980, p. 95.

12. Raymond Vernon, "Antitrust and International Business," *Harvard Business Review*, September–October 1968, p. 86. *Also see* Robert H. Brumley, "How Antitrust Law Affects International Joint Ventures," *Business America*, November 21, 1988, pp. 2–4.

13. "Going for Coke," *The Economist*, August 14, 1999, p. 51.

14. "Coke Said to Face Inquiry Over Sales in Soviet Union," *The Wall Street Journal*, June 12, 1988, p. 22.

15. "Doing Business Abroad with Few Restraints," *The Wall Street Journal*, June 5, 1990, p. B1.

16. Sandra MacRae Huszagh, "Exporter Perceptions of the U.S. Regulatory Environment," *Columbia Journal of World Business*, Fall 1981, pp. 22–31; Samuel Rabino, "An Examination of Barriers to Exporting Encountered by Small Manufacturing Companies," *Management International Review*, No. 1 (1980), pp. 67–74.

17. "A Red Line in the Sand," *The Economist*, October 1, 1994, p. 86.

18. "The New Trade Strategy," *Business Week*, October 7, 1985, p. 90.

19. Allan T. Demaree, "What Now for the U.S. and Japan," *Fortune*, February 10, 1992, p. 80.

20. "U.S.–Japan Trade: Big Deal," *The Economist*, October 8, 1994, p. 76.

21. "IBM Hints for Taiwanese Pirates," *The Wall Street Journal*, October 16, 1984, p. 32. *Also see* Gunter Hauptamn, "Intellectual Property Rights," *International Marketing Review*, Spring 1987, pp. 61–64.

22. *Business International,* May 29, 1989, p. 166.

23. "Gray Market Blues," *Crossborder Monitor*, April 29, 1998, p. 2.

24. "From the Mind of Minolta—Oops, Make that 'Honeywell'," *Business Week*, February 24, 1992, p. 34.

25. "Japanese Reverse Tack on Patent Protection," *The Wall Street Journal*, October 24, 1989, p. B1. *Also see* Thomas J. Maronick, "European Patent Laws and Decisions: Implications for Multinational Marketing Strategy," *International Marketing Review*, Summer 1988, pp. 31–40.

26. See "How U.S. Firm won Patent Suit in China," *Crossborder Monitor*, August 6, 1997, p. 8.

27. Erik Bjerager, "Denmark's Lego Challenges Imitators of Its Famous Toy Blocks Across Globe," *The Wall Street Journal*, August 5, 1987, p. 18.

28. John D. Mittelstaedt and Robert A. Mittelstaedt, "The Protection of Intellectual Property: Issues of Origination and Ownership," *Journal of Public Policy & Marketing*, Spring 1997, pp. 14–25.

29. Subhash C. Jain, "Problems of International Protection of Intellectual Property Rights," *Journal of International Marketing* 4, no. 1 (1996): 9–32.

30. Ibid.

31. Richard L. Hudson, "European Officials Push Idea of Standardizing Telecommunications—But Some Makers Resist," *The Wall Street Journal*, April 10, 1985, p. 32.

32. *Business America*, August 1, 1988, p. 9.

33. "U.N. Rallies to Consumers," *Development Forum*, July–August 1985, p. 14.

34. Virginia M. Citrano, "So, Sue Me," *Northeast International Business*, May 1989, p. 38.

PART 5

International
Marketing
Decisions

CHAPTER 12

Product Policy and Planning

CHAPTER FOCUS _____

After studying this chapter, you should be able to

■ Discuss the perspectives of international product planning.

■ Debate the pros and cons of standardization versus customization of products in overseas markets.

■ Describe various aspects of new-product introduction in international markets.

■ Explain the factors that affect global adoption and diffusion of new products.

■ Compare various branding alternatives for international markets.

■ Describe the role of international product warranties and services.

The product decision is among the first decisions that a marketing manager makes in order to develop a marketing mix. Traditionally, the product decision in international marketing simply has meant exporting products already produced and marketed in the U.S. Now such a simple perspective on product policy will not work. U.S. companies today face strong competition from European and Japanese companies, as well as from newly industrialized countries and emerging nations. At the same time, foreign markets have become more sophisticated, and an American product cannot count on success simply because it is an American product.

Thus, the product decision must be made on the basis of careful analysis and review. The nature, depth, and breadth of the product line; the possibilities of new-product development and innovation; the importance attached to product design (the adaptation and customization of products to suit local conditions vis-à-vis standardization); the decision on foreign R&D; and a planned screening and elimination of unsuccessful products bear heavily on success in foreign markets.

This chapter examines these product-related issues and suggests conceptual approaches for handling them. Also discussed are international packaging and labeling matters, international brand strategy, and warranty and service policies.

Meaning of Product

Products are all around us, and yet it is not always easy to define precisely what a product is. The difficulty lies in the fact that the same product may have a different significance for people in different countries. A refrigerator is a necessity in the U.S. because people tend to depend on a variety of frozen foods and weekly shopping. In Mexico, however, as in other developing countries, food shopping most commonly occurs on a daily basis. A refrigerator there is a luxury for the rich to store either leftovers or perishable foods for a short time.

A definition of *product,* thus, must be comprehensive enough to cover both necessities and luxuries. One way to define it as a bundle of attributes that satisfies a customer demand. It may be offered in the form of a tangible item, a service, or an idea. For example, the attributes of a wine are flavor, taste, consistency, and its quality as a thirst quencher or cool refreshment. Different wines have different attributes, and each brand is intended to meet the demands of a particular set of target customers. The attributes of a corporate jet plane are width of cabin, fuel economy, flight range, speed, and noise level. Businesspersons around the world would prefer different sets of attributes in choosing a plane for their use.

Putting it differently, customers do not simply buy products in the physical sense, they buy *satisfaction,* which is derived from the product's attributes, various features, and characteristics. This fact has important ramifications in defining product objectives.

A company can offer different versions of the same product and thus broaden its product line by catering to the needs of heterogeneous segments of the market. In the U.S., the Coca-Cola Company is a *full-line* soft drink manufacturer producing Classic Coke, Diet Coke, Sprite, Minute Maid, and other soft drinks to cater to the needs of different target groups. Outside the U.S., the company offers just Coca-Cola in most countries. Thus, the Coca-Cola Company is considered a full-line manufacturer at home, but a *limited-line* manufacturer internationally.

International Product Planning

International product planning involves determining which products to introduce into which countries; what modifications to make in the products; what new products to add; what brand names to use; what package designs to adopt; what guarantees and warranties to give; what after-sales services to offer; and finally, when to enter the market. All these are crucial decisions requiring a variety of informational inputs. Chapter 4 on marketing research specifies different ways and sources for gathering appropriate information. Basic to these decisions are three other considerations: (1) product objectives, (2) coordination of product planning activities between headquarters and subsidiary, and (3) foreign collaboration.

The process of product planning in the international context is diagrammed in Exhibit 12.1. A company interested in an international market should first define its business intent based on the objectives of both the corporation and the host country. The product objectives of a company should flow from the definition of its business. Ultimately, the offering should provide satisfaction to the customer, which will be reflected in the realization of the goals of both the corporation and the host country.

Product Objectives

Product objectives emerge from host country and corporate objectives combined via the business definition. The company's goals usually are *stability*, *growth*, *profits*, and *return on investment*. Stated differently, the corporate objectives may be defined in terms of *activities* (the manufacture of a specific product, or export to a particular market), *financial indicators* (to achieve a targeted return on investment), *desired position* (to gain market share and relative market leadership), and all these in combination with each other. Host country objectives vary depending on the country's economic, political, and cultural environment. For example, the typical goals of a less developed country would be to seek faster economic growth, to build a balanced industrial sector, to create employment opportunities, and to earn foreign exchange. On the other hand, the objectives of an oil-rich country might be to provide a modern living standard to its masses in a short time without disrupting the cultural structure of its society and/or to diversify its economy to reduce its dependence on oil over the long term.

Obviously, the objectives of the host country and the company are poles apart. In any market worldwide, however, no company can hope to succeed without aligning itself with the national concerns of the host country. There are no models to use in seeking a description of such an alignment. Conceptually, though, a macroanalysis of a country's socioeconomic perspectives should provide insights into its different concerns and problems. The company can then figure out if its business would help the country in any way, directly or indirectly. The business definition should be developed accordingly.

For example, the shortage of foreign exchange might be a big problem for a country. A multinational marketer's willingness to pursue a major effort of export promotion in the country would amount to an objective in line with the country's need. But a company focused simply on manufacturing and selling such consumer goods as toiletries and canned foods in a nation that is interested in establishing a basic infrastructure for industrial development in the country may not be serving the national interest.

As stated, the definition of product objectives should emerge from the business definition. Product objectives can be defined in physical or marketing terms. "We sell instant coffee" is an example of defining objectives in physical terms. In marketing terms, the objective statement would emphasize the satisfaction of a customer need. The latter method is preferred because it reinforces the marketing concept.

To illustrate the point, assume that Maytag is interested in establishing a plant for manufacturing washing machines and dryers in Egypt. The product objectives may be defined in the following manner:

- *Maytag corporate objective:* Earn a minimum of 25 percent return on investment in any developing country.
- *Egypt's national concerns:* Create employment opportunities and build up faltering foreign exchange balances.

EXHIBIT 12.1   Perspectives of International Product Planning

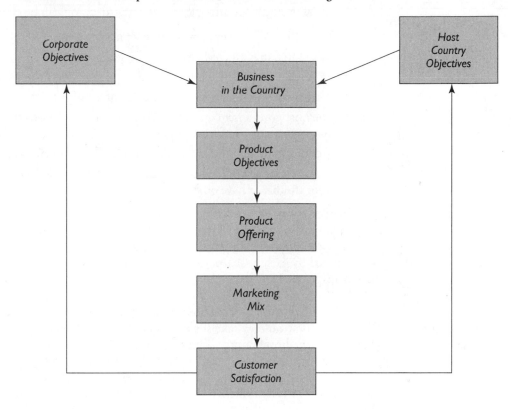

- *Business definition:* Establish a large appliance plant in Egypt to compete effectively in the Middle East.
- *Product definition:* Meet the laundry needs of the masses.

Product Planning   The perspectives of international product planning can be categorized as issues of day-to-day concern on the one hand and strategic issues on the other. The *day-to-day issues* arise in implementing decisions already made. Suppose, in regard to the Maytag example, an issue arises concerning the need for extra precautions to protect working washers and dryers from dust. This issue applies only to the Middle East market, where the climate requires that windows be open all the time, and where the winds carry a lot of dust into the houses. The issue should be handled by local managers. If any specific technological help is needed, it would be sought from the parent corporation on an ad hoc basis.

Strategic issues require major commitments, which must be taken up with the parent corporation. Using the Maytag illustration again, the question might be raised whether motors for the appliances should be imported from Maytag in the U.S. or from a relatively new Japanese subsidiary located in Egypt. Another strategic question could arise with reference to trading with a country that is not on friendly terms with the U.S. Let us assume Egypt does a lot of trade with Libya, but the U.S. has a trade embargo against Libya. Should the Maytag subsidiary in Egypt export the appliances to Libya in view of the U.S. government's trade embargo? Strategic questions cannot be handled by subsidiary management alone; they must be referred to the parent organization.

It is difficult to accumulate an inventory of decisions to label as day-to-day or strategic. It all depends on the individual situation. The subsidiary management must decide if the matter involved is strategic enough to require input from or a decision by the parent. At the risk of overgeneralization, an issue/matter/decision can be considered strategic if:

- The U.S. government comes into the picture.
- Substantial investment needs to be made.
- Previously agreed-upon arrangements would be overturned by a decision.
- Long-term financial interests of the parent are affected.
- The host government appears to be imposing regulations that might affect the long-term survival of the company.
- Technical problems have arisen that cannot be handled locally.
- Certain accusations have been made against the subsidiary that could flare up in labor trouble or have other ramifications.

In addition to ad hoc problems that may be day-to-day or strategic, the parent should require inputs in the form of the subsidiary's plans. Product planning for established product lines and plans for the development and marketing of new product lines would then be prepared by each host country or geographic area and separately submitted to corporate management for approval.

Foreign Collaboration/ Investment

Often international businesses seek foreign collaboration in order to enter world markets. Such collaboration may take shape in a licensing agreement or in a joint venture with a business in the host country. Traditionally, the concept of foreign collaboration has been explained with reference to the *international product life cycle*. As discussed in Chapter 2, essentially this cycle has meant that U.S. exports dominate the world market at first, but then the producers from other developed countries become increasingly competitive—first in their markets, next in third-country markets, and finally in the U.S. market. The cycle may be repeated with successive challenges from producers in developing countries.

In theory, a U.S. corporation should seek foreign collaboration in the third and fourth stages of the international product life cycle, that is, when it is competitively more desirable to produce abroad and compete effectively in foreign markets, as well as in the U.S., through importing from the foreign source. The theory would work if worldwide markets were perfect, which, of course, they are not. Host governments insist on establishing plants even when the plants are not good economic propositions in the international context. For example, a country may opt for a steel mill even though it can import steel from a neighboring country much more economically.

In brief, market imperfections brought about by tariff and nontariff barriers intrude upon the practical application of the theory. In some industries, such as the automobile industry, the theory may fail because investment requirements at the third and fourth stages are tremendous. For this reason, we should not expect auto industries to move from Japan and Europe to emerging developing countries.

An international marketer can also seek foreign collaboration by producing a specialized product in another country in order to take advantage of the peculiar strengths of that country. For example, labor in some nations is cheap, particularly in most developing countries. Other countries have a big pool of scientific talent—India, for example. By collaborating with a foreign company to produce or distribute a product based on an advantage in that company's country, a multinational marketer can gain competitive leverage.

Coca-Cola Company's recent collaboration with Nestlé S.A. of Switzerland illustrates the point. The two companies undertook a multimillion-dollar effort to market canned coffee, either warm or cold in South Korea.[1] The effort was quite successful, leading the Coca-Cola Nestlé Refreshments Co. to roll out Nescafé canned coffee throughout Asia.

Product Design Strategy: Standardization or Customization

An important question that multinational marketers need to answer is whether the product approach successful at home will be equally successful in foreign markets. In other words, a decision must be made about which is the more appropriate of two product design strategies—standardization or customization. *Standardization* means offering a common product on a national, regional, or worldwide basis. *Customization* means adapting a product, that is, making appropriate changes in it, to match local perspectives.

The environmental differences among nations abroad are sometimes great. The degree of difference determines whether product customization, or adaptation, should be chosen over standardization in order to cater to the unique situation in each country. Yet, there are potential gains to consider in product standardization, as will be discussed shortly.[2] International marketers must examine all the criteria in order to decide the extent to which products should vary from country to country.[3]

Decision Criteria   Whether to standardize or to customize is a vexing question with which international marketers have long wrestled. It is simple enough to figure out the rationale for standardization: nothing new needs to be done to make the offering ready for any market, resulting in a significant cost saving. The literature, however, is full of illustrations showing how standardization has led to complete market failure. General Electric Company's debacle in the small-appliance field in Germany and Polaroid's difficulties with the Swinger camera in France are classic examples. At the same time, Volkswagen's success worldwide with the Beetle supports standardization.

Excessive concern with local customization can be troublesome, too. Holland's Philips Company learned the hard lesson that it cannot afford to customize television sets for each European market separately. Standardization became necessary to obtain R&D and manufacturing efficiencies.[4] Because neither strategy—customization or standardization—is superior to the other on its merits, certain criteria should be used to determine which would be desirable in a particular market for a particular product or service and to what extent that strategy should be taken.[5]

Nature of Product   Research on the subject shows that foreign product design strategy varies with the nature of the product. More standardization is feasible in the case of industrial goods than consumer goods. Among consumer goods, nondurables require greater customization than durables, because nondurable consumer goods appeal to tastes, habits, and customs. These traits are unique to each country; therefore, adaptation becomes significant. An alternative to customization, is to limit the target market to a small, identifiable segment.

Market Development   Different national markets for a given product are in different stages of development. A convenient way of explaining this phenomenon is through the product life cycle concept. Products go through several life cycle stages over a period of time, and in each stage different marketing strategies are appropriate. The four stages are usually identified as introduction, growth, maturity, and decline.

If a product's foreign market is in a different stage of market development than its U.S. market, appropriate changes in the product design become desirable in order to make an adequate product/market match. The claim is that Polaroid's Swinger camera failed in

France because the company pursued the same strategy there as in the U.S. at a time when the two markets were in different stages of development. The U.S. market was in the mature stage, while the French market was in the introductory stage.[6]

Even within a country one segment may be ready for a standardized product while others require that the product be adapted. For example, John S. Hill and Richard R. Still found that products targeted to urban markets in less developed countries need only minimal changes from those marketed in developed countries, but the rural markets in LDCs require greater adaptation[7] (see International Marketing Highlight 12.1).

■■■■■■■■■■   **International Marketing Highlight 12.1**   ■■■■■■■■

United Distillers Face Venezuelan Squeeze

With the recent economic decline in Venezuela, overall liquor sales plummeted from 9m cases in 1994 to an estimated 7.3m cases in 1995 and stagnated at that level in 1996. Sales of premium products were hit hardest because of changing demographics as well as falling incomes.

United Distillers, over the past two years, refocused its marketing, advertising, and distribution strategies to counteract the plunge in consumer purchasing power. The goal has been to cut costs, bolster long-term competitiveness and prepare for the economy's turnaround while maintaining brand loyalty and image.

The company took control of its Dewar's White Label, Old Parr, and Black Label brands, which had been licensed out. It shipped its product mix to account for consumers' switch from premium scotches and whiskeys to rum, white spirits, and whiskey-flavored dry spirits. In addition, United Distillers introduced some new products in the value-for-money category, including Gordon's gin and vodka, both of which were made locally. Although these products were cheaper to produce, their correspondingly lower prices cut into profit margins. Despite this drawback, their overall profit potential has been great because the lower prices expand the company's customer base. The key, of course, is to sell high volumes.

New market niches also figure in United Distiller's strategy. A good example is whiskey-flavored dry spirits, such as Country Club, a relatively inexpensive whiskey substitute the company introduced. This market, virtually nonexistent several years ago, now accounts for 500,000 cases per year—roughly equal to Venezuela's whiskey sales.

Source: Crossborder Monitor, February 26, 1997, p. 9.

Cost/Benefit Relationship Product adaptation to match local conditions involves costs. These costs may relate to R&D; physical alteration of the product's design, style, features, or changes in packaging, brand name, performance guarantee, and the like. In contrast, with standardization no R&D is required, since manufacturing technology and quality control procedures have been established, and performance has been tested and improved. Thus, standardization brings certain cost savings. The only big cost that standardization may involve, and it is difficult to quantify, is *opportunity cost*. If a product is customized, presumably it will have greater appeal to the mass market in the host country. The question is, how much greater appeal? Enough to make it worth the cost of customizing? A cost/benefit analysis is necessary to determine what it would cost to customize and what benefits might be expected in the form of market growth. The results of that analysis should then be compared with the same analysis applied to standardization. The net difference indicates the relative desirability of the two strategies.

Legal Requirements Different countries have different laws about product standards, patent laws, and tariffs and taxes. These laws may require product adaptation. For example, in Europe the 220-volt electrical system is used. As a result, European governments set stringent safety standards for such products as irons—cord connections must be stronger, radio interference must be shielded, and so on. Likewise, foreign auto manufacturers must adapt their cars for export to the U.S. because of the U.S. government safety standards and emission control requirements (see International Marketing Highlight 12.2).

Competition In the absence of current or potential competition, a company may continue to do well in a market overseas without ever changing its standard product. But many firms from the newly industrializing countries of Asia are successfully competing against MNCs from the industrialized countries by rapidly adapting their products to changing markets and continually applying more innovative product strategies. In these situations, product customization is essential if a company is to have any chance of maintaining market share.

Traditionally, Kodak could get away by selling a standard film globally because it was so rich, efficient, and powerful. However, with changing competitive conditions, Kodak cannot succeed with parochial attitudes. It is not the only company in the market anymore. Now, for instance, Kodak sells film in Japan with the ruddier flesh tones preferred by the Japanese.[8]

International Marketing Highlight 12.2

Oh, How Life Would Be Easier If We Only Had a Europlug

Those of you who have traveled Europe know of the frustration of electrical plugs, different electrical voltages, and other annoyances of international travel. But consider the cost to consumers and the inefficiency of production for a company that wishes to sell electrical appliances in the European "common" market.

Philips, the electrical appliance manufacturer, has to produce twelve kinds of irons to serve just its European market. The problem is that Europe does not have a universal standard. The ends of irons bristle with different plugs for different countries. Some have three, others two; prongs protrude straight or angled, round or rectangular, fat, thin, and some sheathed. There are circular plug faces, squares, pentagons, and hexagons. Some perforated and some are notched. One French plug has a niche like a keyhole; others carry fuses.

Plugs and sockets are balkanized partly because different countries have different cycles. But the variety of standards also has other causes, such as protective manufacturers. The estimated cost of the lack of universal standards is between $80 billion a year, or nearly 3 percent of the EC's total output of

---

7, 1985, p. 1.

ndards for many products for the entire union and is expected to make further

...m refers to institutions and functions that are neces...
...mand. These include retailers, wholesalers, sal...
...litors and media. The availability, performan...
...ect the product design strategy. For exam...
...where retailers do not have facilities...
...introduce frozen vegtables in developing...
...ies at the retail level (as well as in homes) p...

implementation of the plan. The company therefore developed a line of dehydrated vegetables such as peas, carrots, and beans for countries like India, Pakistan, Kenya, and the Philippines.

Physical Environment The physical conditions of a country (i.e., climate, topography, and resources) may also require product adaptation. For example, air conditioners in a very hot climate, as in the Middle East, require additional features for satisfactory performance. Differences in the size and configuration of homes in some countries affect product design for appliances and home furnishings. European kitchens are usually smaller than U.S. kitchens, and, European homes generally do not have basements. Thus, compactness of design in washers and dryers is a necessity, since they must be accommodated within a crowded area.

Examples, of customized products and marketing include GE's European washing machines, which are designed vertically to conserve water; P&G's Tide detergent and Pantene shampoo, packaged in small, low-priced packets in India, and Whirlpool's Asian International Room Air Conditioner, a lightweight air conditioner.

Market Conditions Cultural differences, economic prosperity, and customer perceptions in the foreign country should also be considered in the deciding whether to adapt a product. Even where tastes are converging, significant national differences will likely persist for many years. In the drinks industry, for example, consumers in heavy beer-drinking countries (the U.K., Germany) are shifting toward wine, and consumers in the heavy wine-drinking countries (France, Italy), toward beer. The trend, but the Germans still consume six times as much beer per capita as the Italians, and much six times as much wine per capita as the British. And these numbers will slowly indeed. [9]

The British prefer a slightly more bitter taste in soup than Americans. difference required the Campbell Soup Company to modify soup ingredi To cater to local taste in Japan, Domino's offers pizza with such toppi teriyaki, apple, rice, and corn. [10]

The masses in many countries cannot afford the variety of produc sumers consider essential. To bring such products as automobiles and the reach of the middle class in developing countries, the products mu modified to cut costs without reducing functional quality.

Foreign products in many cultures are perceived as high-qualit cases, standardization is desirable. On the other hand, if the image of is weak, it is strategically desirable to adapt those products so that the different, rather than typical, of the country. For example, U.S. au ered substandard. Thus, success by American auto manufacturers changed product. [11]

Standardization: A Common Practice

Other things being equal, companies usually opt for standardiz the subject lends support to the high propensity to standardize strategy in foreign markets. For example, an extremely high deg pears to exist in brand names, physical characteristics of produ Hill and Richard R. Still observed,

> More than half the products that MNCs sell in less developed
> companies' home markets. Of the 2,200 products sold by th
> 1,200 had originated in the U.S. or the U.K. [12]

The benefits of standardization are realization of cost savings, development of world wide products, and achievement of better marketing performance. Standardization of products across national borders eliminates duplication of such costs as R&D, product design, and packaging. Further, standardization permits economies of scale.

Standardization also makes it feasible to achieve consistency in dealing with customers and in product design. The consistency in product style—features, design, brand name, packaging—should establish a common image of the product worldwide to help increase overall sales. A person accustomed to a particular brand is likely to buy the same brand overseas if it is available. The global exposure that brands receive these days as a result of extensive world travel and mass media requires the consistency feasible through standardization.

Finally, standardization may be urged on the grounds that a product that has proved successful in one country should do equally well in other countries that present more or less similar markets and similar competitive conditions. For example, Gillette's Sensor razor, launched in 1989 at a cost of $200 million, is the same razor throughout the world, sold with the same advertising[13] (see International Marketing Highlight 12.3).

Rewards of Adaptation

Although standardization offers benefits, too much attachment to standardization can be counterproductive. Marketing environment varies from country to country, so a standard product originally conceived and developed in the U.S. may not really match the conditions in each and every market (see International Marketing Highlight 12.4). In other words, standardization can lead to substantial opportunity loss.

Pond's cold cream, Coca-Cola, and Colgate toothpaste have been cited as evidence that a universal product and marketing strategy for consumer goods can win worldwide success. However, the applicability of a universal approach for consumer goods appears to be limited to products that have certain characteristics, such as universal brand-name recognition (generally earned by huge financial outlays), minimal product knowledge requirements for consumer use, and product advertisements that demand low information content.

Clearly, Coca-Cola, Colgate toothpaste, McDonald's, Levi jeans, and Pond's cold cream display these traits. Thus, whereas a universal strategy can be effective for some consumer products, it is clearly an exception rather than the general rule. Those who argue that consumer products no longer require market tailoring because of the globalization of markets brought about by today's advanced technology are not always correct.

An MNC that intends to launch a new product into a foreign market should consider the nature of its product, its organizational capabilities, and the level of adaptation required to accommodate cultural differences between the home and host country. An MNC should also analyze factors such as market structures, competitors' strategic orientations, and host government demands.[14]

The successful companies realize a simple truth: all consumers are not alike. Take the case of Domino's Pizza delivery. In Britain, customers don't like the idea of Domino's delivery man knocking on their doors—they think it is rude. In Japan, houses aren't numbered sequentially, so finding an address means searching among rows of houses numbered willy-nilly. And in Kuwait, pizza is more likely to be delivered to a waiting limousine than to someone's front door.

Other differences have been noted in making cars, selling soap, and packaging toilet paper. International marketers must understand that just because a product plays in Peoria, it will not necessarily be a hit in Helsinki.

Companies are therefore adapting products to local situations. To satisfy local tastes, products ranging from Heinz ketchup to Cheetos chips are tweaked, reformulated, and reflavored. Fast-food companies such as McDonald's Corp., popular for the "sameness" they offer all over the world, have discovered that to succeed, they also need to offer some local appeal—like selling beer in Germany and adding British Cadbury chocolate sticks to their ice-cream cones in England.

The result is a delicate balancing act for international marketers: how does a company exploit the economies of scale that can be gained by global marketing while at the same time making its products appeal to local tastes? The answer is, "Be flexible," even when it means changing a tried-and-true recipe.

The international marketplace is far more competitive today than in the past, and most likely will remain so. Thus, some sort of adaptation might provide a better match of the product with local conditions for competitive advantage. Sushil Vachani and Louis T. Wells Jr., report that, based on a study of the product decisions of Indian subsidiaries of five multinationals, there remain important consumer segments that have special needs that are not met by global products.[15] Kenichi Ohmae's charges against American companies for not adapting their products to Japanese needs are also revealing:[16] American merchandisers, Ohmae points out, still push such products as oversized cars with left-wheel drive, devices measuring in inches, appliances not adapted to the lower voltage and frequencies necessary in Japan, office equipment without *kanji* capabili-ties, and clothes not cut to smaller Japanese dimensions. Although most Japanese like sweet oranges and tart cherries, the U.S. sends them the opposite. As Japanese consumers compare imported oranges with domestic *mikans* (very sweet tangerines) and cherries with plums (somewhat tangy and sour), they are disappointed in the American offerings.

International Marketing Highlight 12.3

Gillette Tries to Nick Schick in Japan

For Gillette Co., the leading razor maker in most parts of the world, Japan has always been a sore spot. The company, which averages a 65 percent market share in 70 percent of its markets, hobbles along with a 10 percent share of the razor and blade market in Japan.

What has barred the giant Gillette from growing in Japan is not a closed market, unfair Japanese customs, or anything else Japan is accused of. It is rival American Warner-Lambert Co., owner of the Schick brand name. Although Schick trails Gillette in the U.S., it has gained 62 percent of Japan's "wet-shaving" razor and blade market by using the Japanese style of marketing.

Now the battle is heating up as both sides promote new products worldwide. Armed with its popular Sensor brand, Gillette is launching a new strategy. While Schick stresses its Japanese way of marketing, Gillette is emphasizing its "Americanness." It is airing the same ads it runs in the U.S. and selling Sensor in the same packages, with the brand name in bold English letters and a Japanese version of it only in tiny letters in a corner. The company vows to double market share in Japan in the next three to five years. Previously, Gillette had TV ads made just for the Japanese market, although it did use foreign models and sports personalities.

Source: The Wall Street Journal, February 4, 1991, p. B1

International Marketing Highlight 12.4

Taking on Japanese Flavor

Fast-food outlets in Japan are trying to become more Japanese, offering burgers dipped in teriyaki sauce and making buns out of rice. McDonald's Japanese subsidiary, the country's biggest fast-food chain, has added a sandwich of fried chicken soaked in soy sauce to its menu. The company tested the 320-yen ($2.25) item, called Chicken Tatsuta, and found that it sold nearly as well as the Big Mac.

Japanese-style burgers appeal to consumers because they seem more healthful. Moreover, tastes are changing. When U.S. chains first entered Japan two decades ago, what Japanese consumers were looking for in a hamburger was America. But now, consumers say they've gotten the American taste down, and they're asking if we have something else. Wendy's restaurants in Japan offer sandwiches with deep-fried pork cutlets—usually served with a bowl of rice—as well as a version of the teriyaki burger.

Source: The Wall Street Journal, June 19, 1991, p. B1.

There are several patterns and various degrees of differentiation that firms can adopt to do business on an international scale. The most common of these are obligatory and discretionary product adaptation. An *obligatory*, or minimal, product adaptation implies minor changes or modifications in the product design that a manufacturer is forced to introduce for either of two reasons. First, it is mandatory in order to seek entry into particular foreign markets. Second, it is imposed on a firm by external environmental factors, including the special needs of the foreign market. In brief, obligatory adaptation is related to safety regulations, trademark registration, quality standards, and media standards. An obligatory adaptation requires mostly physical changes in the product.

Discretionary, or voluntary, product adaptation reflects a sort of self-imposed discipline and a deliberate move on the part of an exporter to build stable foreign markets through a better alignment of product with market needs or a cultural alignment of the product. An empirical study on the subject showed that product adaptation is most directly influenced by two factors: cultural aspects and legal requirements. Th former is discretionary, and the other is obligatory.

Swiss-based pharmaceutical maker Ciba-Geigy's efforts in adapting its products to local conditions are noteworthy. Basic to the company's adaptation program are its quality circles. These circles include local executives with line responsibilities in packaging, labeling, advertising, and manufacturing. They are responsible for determining if Ciba-Geigy's products (1) are appropriate for the cultures in which they are sold and are meeting the users' needs, (2) are promoted in such a way that they will be used correctly for the purposes intended, and (3) when used properly, will present no unreasonable hazards to human health and safety.[17] (see International Marketing Highlight 12.5).

International Marketing Highlight 12.5

A Car for the Emerging Markets

Suzuki is the car maker to the developing world. The style of the company and its president—a self-described "loan shark" in his early days who married into the Suzuki family and adopted its name—sets them apart from their rivals.

Though Suzuki is a bit player in the U.S., its small, rugged vehicles rule the roads in India and are popular in Eastern Europe and China, markets that U.S. automakers only recently began targeting.

Down-and-dirty vehicles geared to low-tech economies are a Suzuki specialty. In Vietnam, Suzuki engineers observed jerri-built vehicles bouncing through congested Ho Chi Minh City, then cobbled up the Super Carry, $7,000 pint-sized cross between a pickup and a van. The vehicle's backend comes with benches that can seat 12 or tote pigs and rice sacks. Vinyl pull-down shades substitute for glass windows in back.

Suzuki vehicles are fuel-efficient and inexpensive. That is important in nations where annual per capita income is measured in hundreds rather than thousands of dollars and where gasoline costs as much as $4 a gallon. The tiny subcompact Suzuki produced at its Indian joint venture sells for $5,200 and commands 80 percent market share in India. Ford Motor Co.'s new made-in-India Escort costs $17,500. With recession ravaging incomes in once promising markets such as Thailand and Indonesia, Suzuki's leanness is its strength. Suzuki's low-cost plants, simple car models, and frugal operating style enable it to offer rock-bottom prices and still scratch out a profit.

Source: Valerie Reitman, "Frugal Head of Suziki Drives Markets in Asia," *The Wall Street Journal,* February 26, 1998, p. A12.

Developing an International Product Line

Continued success in overseas markets requires the individual designing of a viable product line for each country. To achieve this viability, the composition of the product line may need to be periodically reviewed and changed. Such environmental changes as customer preferences, competitors' tactics, host country legal requirements, and a firm's own perspectives (including its objectives, cost structure, and spillover of demand from one product to another) can all render a product line inadequate. Thus, it may become necessary to add new products or eliminate existing products.

Additions to the product line may take different forms. A firm may simply extend additional domestic products abroad. Alternatively, certain specific products may be sought for a particular foreign country, either locally abroad or in the home country. Finally, new products may be developed for international markets. Also, products may be either eliminated or selectively cut from a line in some countries. There are various ways of obtaining an optimum product line for different international markets.

Extension of Domestic Line

The extension of domestic products to foreign markets follows the logic of the concept of the international product life cycle. Companies develop products for the home market that prove successful and lead to some export orders. As the exports grow, the firm considers setting up a warehouse, a sales branch, or a service center in the foreign locale. Later, the firm finds it more economical to assemble or manufacture the product in the host country.

Relating this process to product-line extension, a firm may initially market a few products overseas. As those markets grow or change, an opportunity may emerge to extend the line by selecting additional products from the domestic line for overseas distribution. A TRW subsidiary in the 1960s, for example, exported fractional horsepower motors to Egypt, Nigeria, India, and a number of other developing countries. In the 1970s many of these countries started manufacturing sophisticated equipment that required large horsepower motors. This change at the customer level made the company's international division choose additional motors for export to these countries.

Another example of product-line extension is provided by the Coca-Cola Company. It began marketing Coca-Cola in Japan in 1958, and as the market developed, it introduced additional beverages: Fanta in 1968, and Sprite in 1970. By 1983 those other products were outselling Coke.[18]

Introducing Additional Products to the International Line

Products may be added to the line for two reasons: (1) to serve an unfulfilled customer need in a particular market overseas or (2) to optimize the existing marketing capacity. For example, a chemical company selling fertilizer and pesticides overseas in developing countries may discover a dire need for good-quality seeds and thus may add such seeds to its line. Alternatively, the same company may feel it has established a good distribution network to serve rural customers but that the network is not being fully utilized. The company may therefore consider products that could be successfully distributed to their rural customers. Such products may or may not be related to the company's business.

For example, in Japan Coca-Cola markets two fruit-drink products, a canned coffee-flavored noncarbonated drink, and a carbonated orange fruit drink that it does not sell in the U.S. Similarly, Coca-Cola markets potato chips in Japan, a business unknown to the company at home.[19] Campbell Soup Company sells gourmet cookies in Europe and Japan but not in the U.S.[20]

Implementation of this strategy alternative can be illustrated with reference to Colgate-Palmolive Company's experience. Colgate distributes internationally a variety of products that belong to other companies. For example, Colgate sold Wilkinson razor blades for their British manufacturer. Colgate did the same for Henkel's (a German company) Pritt Glue Stick.[21]

MNCs often add products differently to their parent country market than to the international market, where product-line strategy alternatives are pursued in response to the needs and opportunities of world markets. The products for addition to the line are determined according to inputs or product specifications received from different markets abroad. Insofar as possible, attempts are made to develop one standardized product to serve customers worldwide.

The decision to add a product to the line is influenced by compatibility considerations regarding marketing, finances, and environment. *Marketing compatibility* involves the match between the new addition and the current and potential marketing compatibilities of the parent company and its foreign subsidiary in matters such as product, price, promotion, and distribution. The closer the proposed product is to current marketing perspectives, the easier it would be to market the product successfully. A low compatibility may affect profitable marketing. Thus, in the earlier example, the chemical company may find adding seeds to its line more compatible than offering leased agricultural machinery.

Sound business judgment requires a full examination of the financial risks and opportunities relative to the product addition under consideration. The common criteria for use in determining the *financial compatibility* of the proposed addition are profitability and cash flow implications.

Environmental compatibility includes concern for the customer, competitive action, and legal or political problems. The inclusion of a product in the line should not pose any problem for either existing or potential customers. At the same time, the competitive reactions to the company's product addition should be projected and evaluated. If the legal or political problems are likely to become a big stumbling block, it might be best to cancel plans to add the product.

Introducing New Products to a Host Country

For the purposes of this discussion, a "new product" is defined as one that is new to the host country but not new to the international market. For example, when Kodak started distributing its pocket camera in Asia in 1982, it was a new product to Sri Lanka, Pakistan, Thailand, and other countries in the region, though not to the U.S., Western Europe, and Japan. Many decisions are required for the introduction of new products in foreign markets. These include decisions about (1) which products to introduce in which different foreign markets, (2) timing and the sequence of introduction, and (3) whether to introduce the product as it is marketed in the U.S., that is, in the standardized form, or to adapt it to the peculiar requirements of the host country.

An empirical study on new-product introductions overseas showed that U.S. corporations frequently introduced new products first to countries culturally similar to the U.S.[22] Thus, Great Britain, Canada, and Australia were the leading recipients of new U.S. international offerings, accounting for almost half of all new-product introductions, and other developed countries accounted for more than one-third. Only one-sixth of new-product introductions were made in developing countries.

New-product introductions to foreign markets also varied by industry. Those in the category of office machines, computers, and instruments were introduced across national boundaries in less than half the cases. On the other hand, textiles, paper, and fabricated metal innovations were entered in foreign markets in 85 percent of the cases.

As far as timing is concerned, U.S. corporations have been introducing new products to overseas markets faster than before. The percentage of foreign introductions within one year of domestic introduction went up from 5.6 percent of all innovations in the period of 1945–1950 to 38.7 percent in 1971–1975. This statistic testifies to the growing importance of new products for successful competition in international markets. Although no empirical evidence is available, in the wake of increasing competition this percentage is probably higher for the 1980s and higher still for the 1990s.

Alternative Ways of Seeking New Products for Foreign Markets A company can develop a new product for a foreign market either internally or by acquisition of another company. Internally, new products are developed through R&D. R&D may be conducted in either the home or the host country. For example, Colgate-Palmolive developed in the U.S. a manual washing device—an all-plastic, hand-powered washer for developing countries. IBM developed IBM 2750 and 3750 electronic private business telephone exchanges within the U.K. For most companies, however, R&D is centralized at home. (A later section will examine the role of foreign R&D in international product policy in detail.)

Many companies add new products through acquisitions. Gillette acquired Braun AG of Germany in order to add electric shavers to its line. Similarly, Gulf Oil acquired Shawinigan Chemical of Canada to enter the field of carbon black. International Telephone and Telegraph (ITT) acquired Rimmel Ltd. of England to enter the cosmetics field.

Rationale for New Products A firm may introduce new products in foreign markets as either a defensive or an offensive measure. Defensively, the new product is expected to help the company compete effectively. For example, a well-established company may be challenged by new competition. In response to this, introduction of a new product may appear to be the most desirable course against the competition. For this reason, with coffee drinking gaining in popularity over tea, the Brooke Bond Tea Company, a British company, decided to introduce its own brand of coffee in a number of Asian countries.

Alternatively, a new product may be introduced to satisfy host government requirements for business related to national development. Thus, Union Carbide, a chemical company, seriously considered adding men's shirts to its portfolio of businesses in India.

A new product may also be developed to evoke local identity. During the 1999 air war against Yugoslavia, McDonald's restaurants, in order to overcome animosity toward a quintessentially American trademark, introduced a domestic pork burger with paprika garnish called McCountry. It was a great success.[23]

New products may also be added because the corporation had earlier licensed its company/brand name to someone else. Union Carbide had to develop a new product/brand for Europe because a German firm had the license for Eveready.

When introduced as an offensive weapon, new products are designed to stimulate growth. Polaroid Corporation sought growth by developing a conventional film because the instant photography market had matured and showed no signs of survival. Branded as Polaroid Super Color, the film was introduced in Spain and Portugal in 1986. In 1988 the company entered it in several other markets.[24] Coca-Cola Company introduces dozens of